1990

Edited by
Bob Staake

Writer's
Digest
Books

Cincinnati, Ohio

*Distributed in Canada by Prentice-Hall of
Canada Ltd., 1870 Birchmount Road,
Scarborough, Ontario M1P 2J7.
Also distributed in Australia by Kirby Books,
Private Bag No. 19, P.O. Alexandria NSW
2015.*

*Managing Editor, Market Books Department:
Constance J. Achabal*

Humor and Cartoon Markets.
*Copyright © 1990 by Writer's Digest Books.
Published by
F&W Publications, 1507 Dana Ave.,
Cincinnati, Ohio 45207. Printed and bound
in the United States of America. All rights
reserved. No part of this book may be repro-
duced in any manner whatsoever without
written permission from the publisher, except
by reviewers who may quote brief passages to
be printed in a magazine or newspaper.*

*International Standard Serial Number
1043-240
International Standard Book Number
0-89879-383-1*

Contents

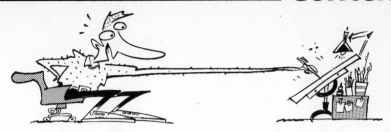

The Markets

Resources

From the Editor

What if my studio went up in flames this afternoon?

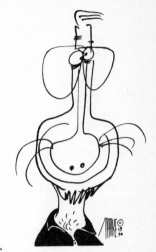

The possibility isn't that farfetched. After all, I have a word processor, fax machine, copier, phone system and TV all plugged into a single outlet. And when I use my electric barbeque starter, the power-sucking gadget zaps every last watt from this side of the house.

Great steaks, but we've got to eat them with a flashlight.

Yet if the sparks *did* fly, if the walls *did* go up in flames like the opening of "Bonanza," I'd grab my books: *The King and Us* by Paul Conrad, Nick Meglin's *The Art of Humorous Illustration*, *Hirshfeld's World*, *Four More Years* by Pat Oliphant. I'd flip all these volumes out my windows like flaming frisbees.

And, of course, I'd toss *Humor and Cartoon Markets* onto my back lawn and hose it down.

When it comes to humor, this book has more information than you can shake a "schtick" at. It's the type of book that I wish *I* had ten years ago. If I did, maybe I wouldn't have had to sell shoes for two particularly ugly weeks in 1979.

There's just too much cool stuff within these pages. Close-up interviews with the top humorists in the country, a Humor Roundtable and copious examples of humorous art. The purpose of all this is to *inspire*—to nudge you on to greatness.

Then, of course, there are the listings. From advertising agencies to book publishers, newspaper syndicates to TV production companies, you'll find over 500 markets for your humor. These are clients who seek funny material, and even funnier yet is the fact that they're willing to *pay* for it!

I suppose the thing that amazed me most about this book was the high level of enthusiastic anticipation which surrounded its publication. I doubt a day went by when I didn't receive a couple letters from cartoonists or phone calls from writers all wondering when the thing would be out.

Well, if you're reading these words, the book is out—happily, the book is *out*!

From the very beginning, my publisher and I agreed that *Humor and Cartoon Markets* would be different from their other market books—not as serious as *Writer's Market*, not as broad as *Artist's Market*. More like *MAD* magazine and *National Lampoon* if they collided in a head-on train wreck. Better yet, the book would appeal to both the amateur *and* professional humorist.

It is indeed a tribute to Writer's Digest Books that I was given a long leash to create this book. I'd like to think that they trusted and believed in my instincts, that they appreciated my insight and knowledge of the humor business. Their confidence was *essential* to the quality of this book. They never once asked me to temper an editorial opinion, sugar-coat information or paint pictures pigmented in various shades of rose.

Certainly, I have to thank my editor, Connie Achabal, for all her work. Connie is a stickler for detail. If I had to write an introduction for the Syndicate section, she gave me 96 lines—not 97. If I had to do a caricature of Jack Davis, it would have to be 1½″ × 2¾″. Don't get me wrong—Connie isn't some sort of weird, psychotic, stormtrooper obsessed by miniscule detail. She's really a terrific, fun lady and when not editing, she tours the upper Midwest as an Elvis impersonator. You talk about *talent*.

My wife, Paulette Fehlig, must be thanked as well. Her duty was to compile all 500 + market listings on to yellow Rolodex cards and she never once called the job "menial." She called it a lot of other things, but *never* menial.

Of course, my six-year-old son, Ryan, was there to tell me if my cartoons were funny. Of all the drawings, Ryan liked my caricature of Paul Conrad best. Play that eerie "Twilight Zone" music, we gave Ryan the middle name of Paul in tribute to "Ol' Con" himself.

But enough of these first person insights. Time to tear into these pages and devour them with kid-like zeal. If you like what you see, let us know. Better yet, if you can think of a way to *improve* next year's edition, simply write, phone or fax. In the meantime, start a fire, pull up a chair, have the dog fetch your slippers—and curl up with a good book.

How to Use Humor and Cartoon Markets

Before you study the listings in this book, take time to read through the explanations for the following sample listing. It will help you to understand and properly use all the information so you can more effectively market your work.

It's important to remember that when you see "SASE" within a listing it refers to a self-addressed, stamped envelope to ensure return of your work. For unsolicited submissions, you should always include a SASE whether or not one is requested in the listing. A "ms" or "mss" refers to "manuscript" or "manuscripts," respectively. See the Glossary at the back of this book for complete explanations of terms.

Listings vary somewhat from section to section since they are designed to incorporate all the requirements for working within a specific market. However, the following listing, from the Magazine section, illustrates well the type of information and details given in all the listings. The numbers in the sample correspond to the numbered explanations that run after the listing.

(1) **CAMPUS LIFE**, 465 Gundersen Drive, Carol Stream IL 60188. (708)260-0114. FAX: (708)260-0114. (2) Estab. 1943. (3) Monthly consumer magazine (10 times a year, combined issues—July-Aug., May-June). (4) Circ. 130,000. (5) Needs humorous writing, gag cartoons, spot cartoons. (6) Accepts previously published humorous articles.

(7) **Gag Cartoons:** (8) Buys 5 gag cartoons/issue; 50/year. (9) Prefers gag cartoons on teen themes that laugh with teens—not at them. Doesn't want gag cartoons on silly puns or worn clichés. For us, the "dream" gag cartoon would be "funny, bizarre, something kids will laugh at and hang up in their lockers." (10) Preferred gag cartoon format is single panel, b&w line art. (11) Submit 5-10 rough drawings/batch to (12) Chris Lutes, Cartoon Editor. (13) Reports back in 5-6 weeks. (14) Returns material if accompanied by SASE. (15) Buys first time rights. (16) Pays $50/b&w on acceptance.

(17) **Tips:** A gag cartoonist should "understand current youth contemporary style; avoid sounding like a parent. Don't send cartoons that look like they were drawn in the 50's."

(18) **Humorous Illustration:** (19) Buys approximately 3 humorous illustrations/issue; 30/year for articles, spots and departments. (20) Works on assignment only. (21) When hiring a freelance humorous illustrator, these abilities are considered: a truly unique drawing style; ability to conceptualize well and clever ideas—good use of metaphors; a clean, graphically pleasing drawing style; effective use of humor; not too much exaggeration or distortion; flexibility, broad potential in drawing style; ability to "fun up" an otherwise "flat" manuscript; businesslike attitude—meets deadlines and responsive to editor's needs; does not need a lot of direction. (22) For first contact, send b&w and color tearsheets, color and b&w promo piece to (23) Jeff Carnehl, Art Director.

(24) **Tips:** "I enjoy trying out new artists and tend to look for more original styles."

(25) **Humorous Writing:** (26) Buys approximately 3-5 humorous pieces/year. (27) Needs humorous nonfiction, humorous teen "slice-of-life," humorous fiction, cartoon stories—*MAD* style. Subject matter includes anything that covers the high-school experience. (28) Length: 500-1,000 words. (29) To query: be

familiar with magazine; make sure article is appropriate; study writer's guidelines. **(30)** Send $2 and SASE for copy of the magazine. **(31)** For first contact send writing sample, query, outline of proposed story, published tearsheets to **(32)** Chris Lutes. **(33)** Reports in 60 days only if interested. **(34)** Samples returned with SASE. **(35)** Buys first time rights. **(36)** Pays $125-300 for 750-2,000 words. **(37) Tips:** "Must be carefully targeted to high school students, should attempt to reflect current humor trends. For style, think the "clean side" of David Letterman; also a Dave Berry style for high school students would work."

(1) Name, address, phone and Fax number.
(2) Date the magazine started publication. Recently formed businesses are often most in need of freelance contributions, however, they have not yet established a track record and there is always a chance they will cease operation.
(3) Type and frequency of publication.
(4) Number of subscribers. This is an indication of the market's size. Publications with large circulations use more work and can pay freelancers better.
(5) Summary of their humor and cartoon needs. A glance at this section of a listing will tell you quickly if the market is looking for your type of work.
(6) Openness of market to buying material that has been published before. This information appears only if it is positive; if a company is *not* interested in seeing previously published work, it will not be mentioned.
(7) Subhead which contains all the details pertaining to the company's request for gag cartoons.
(8) Number of gag cartoons used per issue and per year. This is another sign of the size of the market. You have a better chance of selling your work to a market that uses many gag cartoons every year.
(9) Subject matter of cartoons is indicated. What they don't want to see and their "dream" cartoon are additional indications of what they're looking for. Only submit to a market what they have told you they want.
(10) Format of the work they want submitted.
(11) The number of pieces of work they want to see in one submission.
(12) The contact person (and title). Address your work to this name/title at the address given in **(1)**.
(13) Reporting time indicates how long it will take for you to have a response to your query or submission. Frequently many companies, because of the large number of submissions they receive, cannot respond in the stated amount of time. Wait an additional 2-4 weeks before you inquire about your submission. Also, there are many companies that will respond *only* if they are interested in your work. The listing will give you this information.
(14) Return of your work—or not, if that is their practice. The SASE (self-addressed, stamped enveloped) is always a prerequisite for return of your work.
(15) Rights the company buys. The Glossary defines various types of rights.
(16) Amount and time of payment.
(17) Advice directly from this buyer for the gag cartoonist.
(18) Subhead which contains all the details pertaining to the company's request for humorous illustrations.
(19) Number of humorous illustrations used per issue and per year. This is additional information on the size of the market. You have a better chance of selling your work to a market that uses many humorous illustrations every year.

(20) Work policies, such as this magazine's policy of not buying unsolicited material but assigning projects.

(21) Characteristics/abilities considered before assignments are made. Often this includes the preferred drawing style preferred or openness to many styles.

(22) Materials they want to see included in your submissions package.

(23) The contact person (and title). Address your work to this person/title at the address given in **(1)**.

(24) Advice directly from this buyer for the humorous illustrator.

(25) Subhead which contains all the details pertaining to the company's request for humorous writing.

(26) Number of humorous pieces used per issue and per year. This is another sign of the size of the market. You have a better chance of selling your work to a market that uses many humorous pieces every year.

(27) Type of humorous pieces: fiction or nonfiction, subject matter, style. Only submit to a market what they have told you they want.

(28) Preferred word length of manuscript.

(29) Advice to incorporate into your query letter.

(30) Method of obtaining a copy of the magazine. Knowing what a magazine has already published will help tailor your own submissions to their needs.

(31) Materials they want to see included in your submission package.

(32) The contact person. Address your work to this person at the address given in **(1)** .

(33) Reporting time indicates how long it will take for you to have a response to your query or submission. Frequently many companies, because of the large number of submissions they receive, cannot respond in the stated amount of time. Wait an additional 2-4 weeks before you inquire about your submission. There are some companies that respond only if they are interested in your work. The listing gives you this information also, as in this example.

(34) Return of your work—or not, if that is their practice. The SASE (self-addressed, stamped envelope) is always a prerequisite for return of your work.

(35) Rights the company buys. The Glossary defines various types of rights.

(36) Amount of payment.

(37) Advice directly from this buyer for the humorous writer.

Important Market Listing Information

- *A word about style: This book is edited (except for quoted material) in the masculine gender because we think "he/she," "she/he," "he or she," "him or her" in copy is distracting. We bow to tradition for the sake of readability.*
- *Listings are based on questionnaires, phone calls and verified copy. They are not advertisements nor are markets reported here necessarily endorsed by the editor of this book.*
- *Information in the listings comes directly from the company and is as accurate as possible, but companies and staff come and go, and needs fluctuate between the publication of this directory and the time you use it.*
- **Humor and Cartoon Markets** *reserves the right to exclude any listing that does not meet its requirements.*

Laughing Matters: A Humor Roundtable

Have you ever sat a bunch of funny people at one table?

Neither have we. After all, we've heard the horror stories. Place comedy writers next to cartoonists, comic strip artists beside animators and the "schtick" really hits the fan. Food is thrown, property is destroyed, jokes are hurled at a meteoric pace and the belly aches caused by nonstop laughter push everyone to the brink of swift death.

Hey, we don't have the insurance to cover stuff like *that*. But we *did* want to figuratively get some of the country's top humorists together with the aid of phones, Fax machines, Federal Express and Hank, who rumor has it, is our mailman.

Picture, if you will, this big, fictitious round table. The comedy writers are over here, the humorous illustrators are over there and the cartoonists are over in the bar. The conversation is fast-paced, the laughter deafening. Then the talk turns to the business of humor. Serious, sane insights are given into the subject. Uh oh. We better butt in now—before they start throwing food again.

Humorous Illustration

© Patrick McDonnell

Patrick McDonnell *has specialized in humorous editorial illustration for ten years. Some of his clients are* TIME, Sports Illustrated, Parents Magazine, Parade, Forbes, *Ballantine Books and Johnson and Johnson.*

© Mike Lester

Mike Lester *is a humorous illustrator who has worked primarily in advertising for eight years with such clients as AT&T, Coors, Quaker Oats, Anheuser-Busch and Sumitomo Bank.*

What do you consider the most gratifying part of what you do and what do you consider the worst part?

McDonnell: The best part is what I do. The worst part is you become a hermit doing it.

Lester: The most gratifying part of my job is the act of drawing itself: arranging marks on a page so they become recognizable and entertaining. I also enjoy the people I meet over the phone whose faces I wouldn't recognize if they walked into the room. The down side is some days I'd rather not draw at all.

What are the reasons for your success in this business?

McDonnell: Some talent and the kindness of strangers.

Lester: For some time people have perceived cartoonists as depicting people in a grotesque, unflattering manner: blood-shot eyes, saliva, etc. But that doesn't sell wax paper. I've done a lot of funny stuff that I had to revise because of the constrictions of being an illustrator — not an artist. One's a business. The other's a calling from God. But after a while people begin to call you for what you do best. What I do best is people and dogs in a convertible eating fried chicken.

As a humorous illustrator, you never know what you'll be asked to draw next. Therefore, do you feel that you must be knowledgeable about a wide variety of subject matter?

McDonnell: It doesn't hurt. Although I feel knowing people is the common thread. The human condition is the funny part.

Lester: It doesn't hurt. Techniques that rely on more accurate representations are aided by the use of a morgue or file marked "hands" or "parrots." I tried that in the beginning, but it seemed limiting and unnecessary. Now I usually pull two files: cars and women's apparel (they change weekly). It also helps that I'm not "rendering" a hand or a parrot; I'm trying to make them funny and distorted. Distortion is easier to achieve when you're unincumbered by facts.

When illustrating for an editorial client, are you usually asked to illustrate an idea conceived by the editor/art director or do they supply you with the manuscript and solicit concepts and approaches from you?

McDonnell: I mostly work out my own ideas. That's the challenge and reward.

Lester: Both. It's entirely arbitrary but since I do a small amount of editorial it's insignificant. However, agency art directors are suprisingly more open and flexible than generally thought. But it's important to point out I enjoy collaboration and that's what working with a good art director is. Starting out I gave people pretty much what I saw in a layout but after awhile I realized I was bored and could offer more. That's when I started developing some identity.

Please talk about the importance of individual drawing style. How does one settle on a "style?"

McDonnell: You follow your instincts and heart.

Lester: Robert Weaver said ". . . style is what happens as a result of your most honest labors." I can't do better than that.

A. What do you see as the trends for humorous illustration in the 1990s? B. Does there seem to be more or less call for humorous illustration these days?

McDonnell: A. Noses will get even bigger. B. There will always be a need for a good laugh.

Lester: I'm guardedly pessimistic. It's difficult for me to recommend this line of work to anybody because it's such a preposterous way to make a living. On the other hand, there will always be copy and somebody's got to break it up.

They don't teach you a great deal about the business of art in art school. Most aspiring humorous illustrators think you spend all your time drawing funny little pictures, tell them it isn't so.

McDonnell: You become your own "Mom and Pop" business—secretary, law-yer/agent, accountant, manager, go-fer, cleaning lady and occasionally scribbler of funny little pictures.

Lester: I'm not sure how important it is to know how to run a business compared to knowing how to be a professional. It's true there is grunt work but Frank Sinatra has to brush his own teeth.

Being able to talk on the telephone is an overlooked skill but it helps to know how to express yourself. Being professional in your dealings with anyone goes a long way toward dispelling the image of the dead beat artist. If you don't want to wear a lot of hats, then you don't want to work for yourself.

How does the kid straight out of art school get work?

McDonnell: Don't quit.

Lester: Find a place to screw up. For me that was a newspaper. Nobody remembers yesterday's newspaper. I could experiment with techniques and styles. It also got me published. To a young illustrator being published is paramount. It provides you with credibility in the form of tearsheets. While I'm not advocating anyone work for free, if you draw or paint or write or sing you have to find outlets, and money has little or nothing to do with it.

What is the best single bit of advice you could give to the person who wants to make it as a humorous illustrator?

McDonnell: Be uniquely funny.

Lester: Don't draw feet like Jack Davis. He's already done it and better than you ever will. Find your own personal solutions and ways of redefining your subjects. That's not meant to dismiss the importance of studying great illustration but to be influenced is better than impersonating.

Cartooning

© Bob Thaves

Bob Thaves *has been cartooning professionally for 40 years. His "Frank and Ernest" comic panel is syndicated by NEA (United Media) and appears in 1,200 newspapers.*

© Mark Marek

Mark Marek *'s cartoons and comic strips have appeared in such magazines as* National Lampoon, New York Press, Funnies, PC World *and books like* New Wave Comics, Hercules Amongst the North Americans *and* Patient's Revenge.

What is the most gratifying part of being a cartoonist and what do you consider the worst part?

Thaves: Gratifying: Coming up with a really good gag and drawing. That's exciting! Worst: Deadlines. Having to produce on a schedule, and a very demanding one.

Marek: The most gratifying part: Unedited publication. The worst part: Being labeled a cartoonist.

What are a few reasons for your success in the business?

Thaves: Luck was a major ingredient (seriously). Just having a concept at the right place and time . . . at the time the syndicate was "looking." I think sense of humor has also been a factor.

Marek: Whether or not it's true, I like to think my "success" is due to the combination of individual style and voice.

Do you draw to make yourself laugh or do you draw to make others (editors, syndicates, etc.) laugh?

Thaves: I draw mainly for myself, all other things being equal. It's hard work to draw something I don't really like.

Marek: I draw/write to make myself laugh *and* to make editors laugh (assuming they have a sense of humor). Generally, I'm left to my own devices, being unsyndicated.

Please talk about the importance of individual drawing style and the ability to speak with your own "voice."

Thaves: It is *very* important to me if I am to enjoy and feel rewarded by the work itself. I also feel it's an important ingredient for the success of any feature.

Marek: An individual drawing style is of utmost importance. It creates the venue/environment in which one can display one's own "voice." The only environment, really.

What do you see as trends in comic strips/panels/gags?

Thaves: The current, immediate trend seems to be toward "family" strips/panels — Mother, Father, son, daughter, dog and cat. I believe it is temporary and will change. I hope so.

Marek: I really wouldn't know about trends. I'd like to see less middle-of-the-road safe humor, the kind normally seen in daily papers/refrigerator doors.

When you were a kid, you probably thought it would be great to be a cartoonist because all they do is sit around and draw and get paid for it. Then you became a cartoonist and you realized how wrong you were. What should aspiring cartoonists understand about cartooning other than the simple material of physically drawing?

Thaves: The vision wasn't entirely "wrong." But what I underestimated is how extensive the nondrawing part is. The correspondence load is heavy, as is the "business" part: recordkeeping, contracts, etc.

Marek: Self motivation and (again) developing a unique style peculiar to your point of view are very important. Since a cartoonist works for the most part on a self-employed (freelance) status, motivation is essential to getting and keeping the work and jobs flowing.

How does the aspiring cartoonist with talent get into this business?

Thaves: New/unique material plus perseverance plus *luck*. There is an enormous amount of competition; lots of really talented people are out there.

Marek: a) Develop a personal style; b) Persevere until you find that style, and persevere until someone publishes your style.

What is the best single bit of advice you could give the aspiring cartoonist?

Thaves: Create something that is uniquely *yours*. Don't mimic or go for what seems to be "in" and trendy at the moment. If you're successful, you'll have to live with your characters a long time; make sure you genuinely like them.

Marek: Write a lot and draw a lot.

What else would you like to discuss with aspiring cartoonists?

Thaves: Don't get caught up in your self-image as an "artist." The syndicated comic exists to sell newspapers; the paper doesn't exist just so you have a place to show your work. This is a business, and remember what your role is — if you are not willing to be a *commercial* artist, you should do something else.

Marek: I *don't* advise studying popular strips or really comics at all. That doesn't mean to suggest not to read those strips, just don't "study" them.

If you could do it all over again, what would you do differently?

Thaves: Not much except a) start even earlier (sooner); b) insist on retaining the legal rights to the characters I created.

Marek: Professionally, nothing. Personally, I wish (back in high school) I had not run that red light (accidentally) while waving to my civics teacher in the next car.

Bob Thaves' "Frank and Ernest" has been a syndicated comic panel for 18 years. Thaves answers the following specific questions on syndication.

How many strips/panels did you create and submit to the syndicates before selling your current strip/panel:

None — "Frank and Ernest" was the first one. I was very lucky.

When it comes to strips/panels, what do you think the syndicates are looking for?

Like TV, they seem to look for whatever is "hot" or trendy at the moment. Probably because that's what the newspaper editors want. Newspapers are conservative and basically conformists. They try to appeal to the mass segment of their audience and do not try to develop the variegated, smaller segments. They fear controversy and don't want to "make waves" in their comics pages.

What encouragement can you offer regarding the syndication business?

What can I say? If I can make it, anybody can (really). New features appear every year. . . . trust yourself.

Mark Marek has been cartooning professionally for seven years. He answers the following questions on non-syndicated cartooning.

Do you draw a regular cartoon feature for a specific publication? If so, what and for whom?

"Two-Fisted Management" for *PC World* magazine.

What is it you try to accomplish with the cartoon?

I try to set up a series of panels that sustain a fairly even level of humor throughout. A punchline is only important in as much as editorial demands request it. I prefer to avoid proselytizing but I do like to leave a sly imprint of opinion.

Editorial Cartoons

Mike Peters *is the Pulitzer-prize winning editorial cartoonist for the* Dayton Daily News *and is syndicated in 280 papers by United Media.*

Brian Basset *has been the editorial cartoonist for* The Seattle Times *for eleven years.*

When did you begin doing editorial cartoons and when did you realize that this was the profession for you?

Peters: In high school; I was about 15 years old.

Basset: I began during my sophomore year of high school, after a summer internship at the *Kentucky Post*. Between my junior and senior years I decided to pursue it professionally.

What is your philosophy regarding editorial cartooning?

Peters: You've got to *feel* something about what you're drawing. If I did ten cartoons on say gun control (which I feel very strongly about) maybe four or five of them would be successful. If I did four cartoons about the budget deficit, which I feel nothing about, I'd be surprised if *any* were good. I can feel mad about a subject or I could feel funny about it, but the most important thing is to feel.

Basset: My cartoons are a reflection of my personality. I'm *not* an assassin with a pen and don't try to be. I try to offer strong and solid opinions just like any other editorialist.

What skills do you consider your best/worst (caricature, writing, use of humor, drawing style, etc.)?

Peters: I enjoy all of the skills that you refer to. Sometimes the drawing is the most fun, sometimes it's the idea. I feel if the process is not *fun*, then something is wrong. Often I see cartoons that look agonizing and I know it must have been as painful to draw as it is to see.

Basset: Probably my best would be my drawing style. It comes rather easy and is fun for me. Writing is still the hardest part.

There are only so many newspapers able to hire their own editorial cartoonists. How competitive is editorial cartooning?

Peters: I hang around with about six or seven other cartoonists; we *never* talk about how many papers one another is in.

Basset: I think it's very competitive, but I also feel that the ones who work hard at all aspects of their craft will land a job other than at K-Mart.

How does one succeed in editorial cartooning? How does one get to the point where they're seen in 700+ newspapers? Do you feel the most widely syndicated editorial cartoonists are necessarily the best?

Peters: I don't know. I never did know why people pick or choose certain cartoonists. It may be their editorial viewpoint. It may be their attitude or their batting average, I don't know.

Basset: Just 'cause McDonalds sells the most hamburgers doesn't mean they make the best. A successful cartoonist should stand his or her town on end, become part of the community.

Since becoming syndicated do you find yourself drawing a different editorial cartoon? How have the realities of syndication affected you and your work?

Peters: No, I never did a cartoon thinking if it would *sell*. I try to do cartoons that please me. If I think it's strong or if I think it's a good hit on someone, that's my only litmus test.

What kind of schooling do you think an editorial cartoonist should have?

Peters: History, English and then art.

Basset: Preferably a liberal arts background with emphasis in the social sciences and fine art.

Talk about the importance of "exposure," the importance of just getting your work published (in high school/college papers, local newspapers or weeklies, etc.).

Peters: Extremely. I did cartoons for local papers when I was a junior in high school, plus radio stations, high school, local magazines—anything that would go in a portfolio.

Basset: Very important. I call it the Fear of Embarrassment. To do your very best—putting yourself out in front of people—without saying something stupid. Great motivation for me.

Assuming that someone just graduated from school is going to have to bide his time until there's an opening for an editorial cartoonist, how should he spend that time (i.e. drawing on local politics for the local newspaper, submitting to the syndicates, seeking out a professional, staffed editorial cartoonist who is privy to job openings, etc.)?

Peters: All the above. Try to get a job behind a drawing board.

Basset: Drawing on local politics is a good way to sharpen one's skills. Even if there's no place to get published I'd say do *one* good cartoon a week for the experience and portfolio.

Now there's an opening and our new graduate (along with 75 other guys) submits his stuff for consideration. How can he distinguish himself from the rest of the pack?

Peters: Actually believe the paper's editorial policy or your life will be hell. Only show them your best stuff—and don't give up!!!

Basset: His work should be original, understandable and opinionated.

What important piece of advice can you pass along to the aspiring editorial cartoonist? What do you wish a professional editorial cartoonist had told you to do?

Peters: Get experience and READ.

Basset: My advice: Know your subjects. You're a commentator, not a court jester. That doesn't mean you can't use humor—you obviously can and should.

Editorial cartooning has gone through quite an evolution. In the 70s we saw an increased use of humor and satire. Now that it's 1990, what do you see as the future for editorial cartooning?

Peters: I hope it's in a process of change. Art is change; you can only grow if you change. In editorial cartooning though, you've got to have that "fire in the belly" or else our profession dissolves into illustration.

Basset: I'm afraid there are still too many humorists in the profession. Eventually I see a return to stronger graphic images.

Animation

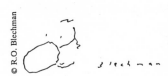

© R.O. Blechman

R.O. Blechman *is associated with The Ink Tank where he directs, produces and sometimes styles animated films. Recent projects are commercials for Pepsico, Hershey's and American Express; station I.D.s and spots for MTV, Elektra Records and Showtime.*

© Shamus Culhane

Shamus Culhane *has been in animation since 1930, working on the characters of Betty Boop, Koko the Clown, Woody Woodpecker, Snow White and Pluto and also writing/editing. He currently confines himself to writing and is the author of* Talking Animals and Other People *and* Animation from Script to Screen.

Before getting to where you are today, please explain the types of jobs you had in the animation field. Is it a necessity for aspiring animators to "pay their dues?"

Blechman: I myself did storyboards before I became a director/producer. This isn't necessarily the route to take—or any other for that matter. There is no one route to anywhere.

Culhane: I started out at J.R. Bray working for Walter Lantz as an errand boy, then painter and inker. At Fleischer's I became an inbetweener, then animator, later animating/director and writer. I worked at Disney's from 1935 to 1939 ending up as a Pluto specialist. But from there on I jumped from director to animator, writer, layout-man, designer, story-board artist, story-editor and producer as the occasion required.

This hop-scotch career enables me as a director to be very aware of the problems in every film I work on. It's good to have done them, if for nothing else than the fact that sometimes one wants to make an entire film independently.

What type of animation do you principally produce?

Blechman: Advertising. However, I have produced some shorts, two full hour television programs and hope and expect to do my first animated feature.

Culhane: It may come as a surprise to many people who think they know details of my career. My main feat was not marching the dwarfs home in "Snow White," it was writing or story-editing and producing 104 five-minute films about the Revolutionary War for television.

What do you consider the most gratifying part of your job? What is the worst part of your job?

Blechman: I really enjoy doing a good spot almost as much as a good hour program. Almost. Obviously a more demanding project well done is more satisfying than a small spot. The worst part of my job? Dealing with agency block-heads.

Culhane: I have great reverence for the phenomenon of talent in any form. So whenever I exercise mine, I am grateful that I detect no loss of ability in my drawing and even an improvement in my writing skills. I would never dream of retiring. At 81 I work every day.

The worst section of my career was when I produced TV spots. I soon became known as an enfant terrible, just because I refused to let incompetent Madison Avenue types tell me how to do my films. I met some very wonderful people in the ad business, but I also met some of the worst psychopaths and sociopaths.

What are a few reasons for your success in this business?

Blechman: That's a hard one to answer. In honesty, everything adds up to one's success—all sorts of things, some good (one's talent) and some not so good (one's recognizability, "Hey, let's get a Blechman!").

Culhane: I am one of the most disciplined people in the field. At 12 I was playing the violin two hours everyday, doing homework, then drawing for several hours. When I was learning etching, I etched and printed until 5 a.m. and did this for months until I learned the techniques. I approached animation with the same intensity, going to Dan Graham's art class [in the Disney Studio] five nights a week for over a year.

What distinguishes a great, innovative animator or animation studio from another? What is the key to excellence?

Blechman: A great, innovative animator draws well, thinks well and feels his situations out deeply. He is, to a great extent, a filmmaker. A great studio hires these animators, and finds artists and creates material for them.

Culhane: There are only a very few innovators in each profession. The distinguishing factor is a reluctance to use habits, disdain for specialists, curiosity, willingness to discard habits or old principles (even if painfully achieved) and try something just because it is new. Since not everybody can be an innovator, there is nothing wrong with being a damn good follower.

Perhaps more so than any other art form, animation is in a constant state of evolution; today's trend is yesterday's cliche. What do you see as the future for animation in the 1990s? Will there be an increasing demand for animation?

Blechman: My hope—but not necessarily my expectation—is that the revolution in comic strips will find its counterpart in animation. Is there an increasing demand for the stuff? I don't know.

Culhane: I look forward to more independent filmmaking as the computer gets cheaper and more facile. I believe that pictures made by large groups are never as meaningful as films made by one person with perhaps a few assistants in the noncreative areas.

Interest in animation is increasing among the young, in spite of a poor labor market, so it must be that the art form itself is appealing to the modern mind. It should, because the computer is making other media look primitive.

How has computerized animation affected traditional cel-by-cel animation in this country?

Blechman: Computerized animation has enhanced our creative possibilities when we transfer material from film to tape.

Culhane: Right now there are too many people making titles for TV who have nothing better to offer than floating rectangles and sparkles—for the most part they are engineers with a smattering of artistic talent and no imagination or creativity.

The amount of graphic garbage the TV-viewing public has to endure is dreadful. The artists have to take over, and the agency art directors will have to be zapped before computer animation can be used artistically for television.

The audience is about as alert to these optical insults as a drunken sow, so I guess there will be no pressure to improve from that quarter. I think it's going to be a case of "talent will win eventually." In the interim we suffer.

What didn't they teach you in art/animation school that you feel should have been taught?

Blechman: I never went to art school. If I had I probably would have been kicked out as a rebel—at least from any art school of my generation.

Culhane: I never went to an art school, except for Don Graham's class in the Disney Studio. He was a superb teacher so I have no complaints. I studied techniques of painting and etching, perspective and anatomy from books at home. I think that most teachers really want the students to follow what they themselves learned.

In school, students should be urged to be adventurous, I think that's the most important quality. Next is the need to set a very high standard for one's self and stick to that grimly, despite businessmen who will want to lower your standards. Schools do not mention the pitfalls of the outside world at all. I would fill the students' ears with horror stories and send them into the world with a working knowledge of the artist's role in this country. It's not a pretty picture. Right now students enter the labor market like lambs led to slaughter.

Aspiring animators want to get into animation because it looks fun. They think it's all drawing. But, if they knew the truth, they'd realize that animators also have to:

Blechman: I'll re-write that sentence to read "Aspiring animators want to get into animation because they're crazy about making films." If they think it's merely fun, it may not be the wrong business for them (there are plenty of studios that are right for them) but we are the wrong studio for them.

Culhane: ... be educated persons. An animator should be interested in fine art, feature films, music and literature, all of his/her life. One must learn to see, not look, and store impressions automatically, keenly aware of the life going on around you.

How does the kid straight out of art/animation school get started?

Blechman: Self-produce shorts. I know it's the hard way, but I don't know of any better way other than going to a good film school.

Culhane: The new kid should probably enter a going animation studio, one with a good reputation, that is producing computer and cel animation. Take any job that is offered in order to get in. Money at this point is no object. Avoid the schlog houses like a plague.

No animation school can give you real life experience, because it's a different atmosphere than the outside world.

The main object at this time is to acquire experience in working with top animation people. Not only animators, but directors, layout and background people. Damn near starve if you must, but get on the staff and learn.

What is the single best piece of advice you could give to the person wanting to make it as an animator?

Blechman: Go to a film school like Cal Arts and make films. As Jerry Rubin said in the Sixties, "Do it."

Culhane: The best advice would be to guard your talent. It is fragile as a flower, and your most precious asset, spiritually as well as socially. In the commercial world you will have to wage an ongoing battle against attempts to prostitute your talent. Once you are willing to subvert your talent, it will never recover. Remember that.

I guess the main thing is the need to be a fine draftsman. Your entire life should be one long time of improving your drawing. There is no way to replace or substitute fine draftsmanship. Even if you want to be a director, your drawing can inspire the whole staff.

Humor Writing

Al Batt *is a humor writer whose work has been published in* The New Yorker, Playboy, National Enquirer, Good Housekeeping *and* Cosmopolitan. *He has also written for comic strips and panels, advertising and comedians.*

Nick Meglin *is primarily known for his writing in* MAD *magazine (one of "The Usual Gang of Idiots") but he also writes humorous books, magazine fiction and TV scripts. He is the author of* The Art of Humorous Illustration.

Frank Hughes *has written for syndicated panel/comic strip cartoonists and freelance magazine cartoonists; has sold quips, anecdotes and jokes to* Reader's Digest *and* Family Weekly; *sold one-liners to radio comedy services as well as monologues and jokes to nightclub and TV comedians. He has also taught a course in humor writing at Temple University.*

What are the reasons for your success in this business?

Batt: Hard work and family encouragement. Love of reading.

Meglin: As is with most "success stories" being in the right place at the right time with the right can of beans is essential.

Hughes: A modicum of talent . . . and a maximum of perseverance. Many cartoon ideas of mine have been sold 20 or more years after the cartoonist originally "held" those gags. It isn't lack of talent that causes most writers to fail to become humor writers but too many give up in one year because they haven't become a success. Whoever told writers that becoming successful was easy?

What is your personal philosophy about humor?

Batt: Chekhov said, "A man is what he believes." To write humor, you must know that you can. It is a pleasant thought realizing that my mind produces material that unifies people in laughter.

Meglin: *MAD* is satirical and has no philosophy. We write for ourselves and hope our readers go along for the ride. We try to be funny within the context of a valid premise.

Hughes: Write not what you alone think is funny but what the majority of people think is funny. I personally prefer subtle satire but it doesn't sell . . . .I don't write to please my own preferences but to please market preferences.

Do you prefer writing humor as the solitary author or do you prefer being a member of a larger, collaborative team? What are the advantages and disadvantages of both?

Batt: I have only worked independently. I've worked with many via phone or mail, but the actual writing I've always done all alone.

Meglin: Solitary on personal work (it's *personal* work); teamwork on all *MAD* magazine work (*MAD* is *not* a personal vehicle).

Hughes: I prefer writing alone and feel strongly that Shakespeare's works could never have been written by a committee. Too often group writing results in compromise to make certain that all member efforts are incorporated into the final product. They get average results and average is the "best of the worst" and "the worst of the best." I worked only one time with another writer and there was too much nit-picking of each other's work. Some people can work together as a writing team, but I cannot.

How do you find work?

Batt: Referrals.

Hughes: I buy almost every market list that is published. I find that one sale resulting from the information pays for the price of the list many times over. I also send out my resume with clippings of my published humor and humorous advertisements to local advertising and public relations companies. Members of the Professional Writers Conference Group often recommend me to clients.

If you write for a cartoonist/performer, do you write specifically for that individual or do you write generic material and then submit the appropriate material to the appropriate individual?

Batt: Both.

Hughes: Yes and no. Yes, when I am writing for a stand-up comic: I study his/her style, pacing, phrasing, timing, etc. and write accordingly. It is foolish to try to send material rejected by Comedian "A" to Comedian "B" without rewriting it in "B's" style.

When writing for daily syndicated cartoonists I study the strip, story-line, type of gags, characterization, and write specifically for that comic strip.

For freelance magazine cartoonists I write "generic" material that if rejected by cartoonist "A" often is accepted by Cartoonist "B" without re-write.

What are the advantages/disadvantages of writing for a "client" (i.e., ad agency, etc.)? What are the advantages/disadvantages of writing for yourself (a humorous magazine piece, humor trade book, etc.)?

Batt: For the client, you have a definite market, target and payment. For yourself, you write what you enjoy and think is funny — then hope to see it published along with your name.

Hughes: Better pay, usually, and the maximum use of your writing time, when you write for a specific client. In addition, once you get your foot into the editorial door more assignments usually come your way. Not so when you write on speculation.

Besides the ability to write funny and well, what other skills must the humor writer possess?

Batt: Self-motivation and persistence are most important. Must have marketing skills and the ability to run a business. Optimism, as in everything, is also a necessity.

Hughes: Almost as important as the creative aspects of humor writing is a sound knowledge of business practices. I was lucky in that I was an "Efficiency Expert" and many of the methods I developed for companies I also used in controlling my creative output and recordkeeping. I have written more than a half-million cartoon ideas on 3×5 slips of paper and merely recording on the slip the cartoonist to whom I sent it was a chore. So I coded each cartoonist with a letter-number code. (For example Bo Brown was A-1, Glenn Bernhardt was A-2, etc.) I had a printer print 3×5 slips with the preprinted codes on the slip. I then typed the carbon on the reverse of those slips and when I sent a batch of cartoon ideas to Bo Brown, I merely used a conductor's punch and punched through the control number A-1 rather than writing his name on each of the carbon gag-slips.

What are the "harsh realities" of humor writing?

Batt: It's hard work. It's not always fun to be funny. It's a business if you're going to do it right.

Meglin: Knowing someone in the field doesn't mean a thing. We buy what we like/need from *anyone*! And that's true with everyone I've been associated with in publishing and TV.

Hughes: One harsh reality of humor writing is that it is ephemeral, like smoke that quickly fades away. If you don't believe this read an anthology of humor writers of 50 years ago. What was then thought funny is no longer funny because the "frame of reference," the butt of humor has changed.

Comedy is big—bigger than ever. How has this increased and broadened opportunities for the aspiring humor writer?

Batt: More and more markets—specialized magazines, TV, radio disc-jockeys, humor books, many more comedians, mass merchandising, t-shirts, mugs, greeting cards.

Meglin: With most comics writing their own material and more writers competing for fewer jobs in the sitcom field, I believe it's getting more difficult for new writers. The print showcase is about the same.

Hughes: With more and more cable TV comedy networks, the market for comedy material in the 1990s is going to be insatiable. There will be more opportunities for the humor writer in the next decade than there has been in the past 40 years.

Another trend is the move away from mass circulation "general interest" magazines and more emphasis on "special interest" magazines. Study these new magazines. Write humor to their specific needs. All of the editors don't realize it yet, but in time the readers of those "special interest" magazines will want to see humor related to their interests.

What do you see as trends for humor/comedy writing in the 1990s?

Batt: More and more comedians, more TV specials with comedians—more and more material needed.

Meglin: I doubt it, but I hope the trend towards outrageous as opposed to funny is thwarted. Too many practitioners believe shock is humor—it can be, but it's not inherent in itself.

Hughes: More "off-the-wall" type of humor similar to Larson's "The Far Side." *MAD* magazine pioneered that new wave of humor about three decades ago and it finally is being adopted by our mass culture.

How does the humor writer get started?

Batt: He writes, writes and writes some more. Show it to people; send it to people. Write for the local newspaper, local radio, local comedians, local advertising agency, etc.

Meglin: Like everyone else: *Professional* submissions, good work accompanied by a self-addressed, stamped envelope!

Hughes: By not being the "Life of the Party" but by *studying* how the life of the party makes people laugh.

Second, begin at the bottom. This is heresy for most beginning writers; they want to start at the top and THEN learn their craft. Learn your craft first in the minor leagues—your local church newspaper, local weekly newspaper and small circulation magazines. Bombeck started by writing a humor column for her local neighborhood newspaper; a Dayton, Ohio newspaper picked it up, then a syndicate picked it up.

What is the single best piece of advice you could give the aspiring humor writer?

Batt: Read, write and work at it every day.

Meglin: Don't sacrifice the important things in life—friends, family, art and love for your "profession." Living beats achievement by a mile.

Hughes: Read and study humor. If you want to write like Bombeck study ten of her columns. HOWEVER, DON'T TRY TO DUPLICATE BOMBECK . . . develop your own style. Also: a) develop more perseverance; b) type faster; c) don't give up on a good idea—and more importantly, don't give up on yourself.

Feel free to discuss any other topics that would be of interest to these aspiring humor writers.

Batt: Not everyone laughs at my best work. This isn't what I strive for. I want my work to be laughed at by the best people.

Meglin: Once you realize the absurdity of life—it's neither logical, rational, fair or simple—you're ready to write satire and strike familiar chords in readers.

Hughes: I wish everyone who reads (and studies) this book becomes a far better humor writer than he is now. Why? Isn't that statement encouragement to increase my own competition? Yes, it is, but established humor writers *want* more competition . . . the better the competition, the *better* their own writing must become. Another tip: Read every book that deals with humor writing. The more you learn about humor writing the better you will become. My own personal preference: Steve Allen. Get any book related to humor he has written. They are chock full of information, and as Steve once observed "All writers need lots of chocks."

If you could do it all over again, what would you do differently?

Batt: I would have changed my college major to English or journalism. Also I would have done some stand-up comedy—maybe really given it a shot.

Meglin: I'd have taken more chances, run more risks, and—unlike Blanche Du Bois ("Streetcar")—*not* trusted in the kindness of strangers!

Hughes: I would have started earlier. It wasn't until I entered high school and edited the school humor paper that I became interested in writing humor. Second thing, I would have been more critical of my writing efforts and wouldn't have sent out most of the humor pieces I did.

TV Comedy

Madelyn Davis *has been writing professional humor/comedy for 41 years. Her credits include "I Love Lucy," "Here's Lucy," "Lucy," "Lucy-Desi Hours," "Alice" and "Private Benjamin." She is currently working on pilots for cable TV.*

Andrew Nicholls *and* **Darrell Vickers** *are head writers for "The Tonight Show" (for which they've received 3 Emmy nominations) and have also worked with Bob Thaves ("Frank & Ernest"), Mickey Rooney, George Carlin, Alan Thicke, Joan Rivers and others. Originally from Canada, they have been a comedy writing team for 20 years.*

What are the reasons for your success in this business?

Davis: Lucille Ball and a lot of luck.

Nicholls: It's an enormous help to be completely untalented in every other field of endeavor. In our case, also, we took every writing job we could find. We took jobs for $2. We sent jokes to ventriloquists, jokes to cartoonists at inhouse electrical contracting magazines, anything.

Vickers: Eventually we started getting some breaks and we were ready to take advantage of them.

Nicholls: We picked up our first U.S. sale through *Writer's Market* where Bob Thaves was advertising for cartoon gag writers. For a few years we pestered everyone we could find with special material.

Vickers: Nowadays we have an agent who pesters them for us. If we're approaching someone new, we send sample jokes or scripts and a resume.

Do you prefer writing humor/comedy as the solitary author or do you prefer being a member of a larger, collaborative team? What are the advantages/disadvantages to both of those situations?

Davis: Write with a partner if you can find one. Pick out the funniest person you know. I did and was lucky enough to get Bob Carroll.

Vickers: Andrew and I have been writing together for 20 years, so obviously we have no problem collaborating with each other. Well, maybe the occasional problem.

Nicholls: Basically, we feel that "large collaborative teams" are what have ruined most of today's television. The problem with a collaborative effort is that somebody in the room ultimately has to decide what goes on the page. Unless you're that person, it can be very frustrating.

Vickers: When you write for yourself, you get to say what you want. You just don't always get to eat what you want.

What do you see as the trends for humor/comedy writing in the 1990s?

Davis: Humor seems to be based more on reality today, especially in TV. Instead of burning the roast when the boss is coming for dinner, the plots seem to be about unmarried women in their late 30s who want to have a child before it's too late with a man who won't have to get involved once the baby is born. But funny is funny no matter what year it is.

Vickers: There'll be more comedy and it won't be as—good.

Comedy is big—bigger today than ever. Has this increased and broadened the opportunities for the aspiring humor/comedy writer?

Davis: This makes for more markets but unfortunately there seem to be more comedy writers.

Nicholls: In TV anyway it's broadened the opportunities for the marginally talented. Producers are diving further into the shallow end of the talent pool to come up with staffs. For the talented, as always, there's just a bigger crowd of carpetbaggers to push through to get to the front.

Please talk about what you learned about humor/comedy writing outside of the classroom. How does life itself teach the humor/comedy writer?

Davis: Everything that happens to you or to people around you has a funny side. We used a lot of ordinary things that happened to us as a basis for some of the "Lucy" scripts. If your script is based on real life, the audience will relate to it.

Would you recommend any specialized schooling for a humor/comedy writer? How important is it to study other sitcoms/programs to understand and appreciate the current state of humor/comedy?

Davis: Some of the best classes I know are at UCLA Extension. They are taught by professional TV writers and are most helpful. Study every comedy show there is, even the bad ones. Especially study a show if you hope to write for it.

What is the best single bit of advice you could give to the aspiring humor/comedy writer?

Davis: Someone once asked the first Tarzan what advice he would give to the next actor who played the role and he said "Don't let go of the vine."

Nicholls: Cultivate the ability to conceal contempt.

Vickers: A bubbly, winning personality can be a goldmine. Unfortunately, most of the best writers seem to be depressed little wretches, but the people in charge of hiring never seem to grasp this simple concept.

How does the kid, straight out of college find work? How does he work his way up the professional ladder?

Davis: Worm your way in as close as possible to where they produce the TV comedy shows, as a secretary or an usher or a go-fer. Once you are on the inside you can push your scripts under the producer's door.

Nicholls: Don't get started. Go back, it's a trap. It's nothing but endless grovelling degradation. If you stupidly ignore this advice, you're on your way.

Vickers: In TV, you have to be near your market. Unless you're writing for a funny weatherman, that means moving to Los Angeles or New York.

Nicholls: Cartoonists don't care so much, but producers like to be able to attach a face to the person they're rejecting.

What are the "harsh realities" of humor/comedy writing?

Davis: Terrible hours and it's awfully hard on your stomach.

Nicholls: One of the harshest realities in television comedy is, you're going to spend your life doing a very difficult thing, trying to persuade fairly impenetrable people that they need your jokes more than they need their money.

Vickers: The thing with a script, a sitcom, a screenplay, is that you can love it; they can love it; you can sell it; and when it finally shows up on the air or the screen there's not one word you wrote.

If you could do it all over again, what would you do differently?

Davis: If I could do it all over again, I'd do it all over again.

Vickers: We'd become much richer a lot quicker with far less work.

Nicholls: The Bay of Pigs. It was a bad idea and I regret it unreservedly.

Do you want to talk about any other topics that would be of interest to aspiring humor/comedy writers?

Davis: Be sure you really have a good sense of humor. But don't be afraid to try it. Look at all the other people who made it—why shouldn't you?

Vickers: We've pretty well always written specifically for the person to whom we were trying to sell the stuff. We have a friend who wasn't sure early in his career whether he wanted to write for Carson or Letterman. So he aimed somewhere in the middle, and ended up writing for neither. Things didn't take off for him until he began tailoring his jokes for a specific person.

Nicholls: You can get lazy, too, writing generic stuff and thinking "Oh, I'll find someone who just adores this later."

Vickers: Be Steven Bochco's favorite nephew. You'll never regret it.

Nicholls: If that doesn't work for you, try this: Find some humorist you admire enormously, alive or dead, and write as if he was reading over your shoulder.

The Business of Humor

by Bob Staake

Lest you think humor is all fun and games and rim shots, read on. Contrary to popular opinion, humor is a very serious business. Take our advice—*please.*

The freelance humorist: Mercenary of mirth

A writer, cartoonist or illustrator makes a big decision when choosing to freelance. He decides that a regular, steady paycheck is unimportant, but the freedom to sleep in until 10:30 a.m. *is*. But since freelancing has a lousy retirement program, you've got to get your perks where and when you can.

It takes a very special person to freelance. All jokes aside, the freelancer *must* discipline himself much more rigidly than the doodler or writer who punches an employer's time clock from 9 to 5. Since the freelancer works with clients on an as-needed basis, he doesn't have the client physically breathing hot air down his collar as he bangs out his copy or inks in his drawing. Rather, the client gives him a deadline and it becomes the freelancer's responsibility to *meet* that deadline.

Because of the demanding nature of the business, the attrition rate for freelancers is *extremely* high. Having tested the freelance waters, many cartoonists, illustrators and writers disconnect the phones and go looking for *regular* paying stints.

But for those who accept the roller coaster nature of freelancing, the rewards can be high. The key to success is a combination of things—talent is fine, but you must *nurture* that talent. Mailing out samples of your work is terrific, but you must do it *professionally*. Self-promotion is essential, but you must do it *effectively*. There are many extremely talented cartoonists, writers and illustrators out there—but to increase your odds of success, it is important to understand there's much more to humor than the physical drawing or writing of it.

Professionalism: Are we sophomoric yet?

When one takes into account what a competitive business freelancing is, it is puzzling that freelancers don't project a more professional image.

One hundred dollars can't buy you much professionalism these days, but it *can* get you started. Here's what you get: 500 8½×11 sheets of imprinted letterhead, 500 imprinted #10 envelopes, 500 business cards, 500 imprinted labels for oversized envelopes and, of course, the limited typesetting needed for these items. And for a nickel, you've got a crisp, high-quality photocopy of a sample article, cartoon or illustration.

However unfair, a client *does* make a snap judgment about you by the initial image you project. When you mail a package of material to him, the package becomes your "silent salesperson." Since you are essentially asking this client for work, it stands to reason that you want to put your best foot forward. Really, it's no different than an in-person job interview. You wouldn't meet a potential employer in a tank top and a beanie cap. Likewise, you shouldn't shove a bunch of dog-eared cartoons, illustrations or articles in an envelope and slip it in the corner mailbox.

And while most writers have no problem when it comes to drafting professional cover letters, many cartoonists and illustrators do. Bad grammar, poor sentence structure and sloppy syntax is just plain *unprofessional*. After all, you want potential clients laughing at your cartoons — not your sophomoric writing ability.

Self-Promotion: Effectively blowing your own horn

In most professions, self-promotion is considered tacky at best. But when it comes to freelancing, it is the accepted norm — a key to your very survival.

Self-promotion "collateral" can be just about anything — from a printed color sheet of your humorous illustration to a black and white brochure listing clients for whom you have written. Some freelancers go crazy with self-promotion. Cartoonists have mailed out 3-D glasses and posters of their work; animators have distributed flip books; and writers have sent bricks silk-screened with their name, address and phone numbers to prospective clients (would *you* throw away a two pound brick?).

In addition to keeping your work in front of decision-making eyes, self-promotion provides you with an opportunity to promote your originality, creativity, cleverness and communication skills.

Approaching a market: Is anybody home?

The great thing about *Humor and Cartoon Markets* is that you aren't blindly sending material to markets which wouldn't be receptive to it. The purpose of each listing is to provide you with a comprehensive profile of the markets so that you can better determine on whom to spend postage.

Once you have decided that Dootenheimer, Inc. publishes humorous greeting cards in sync with your wacky sense of humor, you'll want to send them an introductory package of your material. While there are some standard items which should be included in this package (cover letter, client list and/or resume, general samples of work, business card), you may want to include a sample or two which is specifically suited to their needs.

Then, if the market is receptive to your material, you'll be able to get a more complete idea of their company. At that point, your vision becomes 20/20 and a follow-up package can be assembled with ideally suited samples.

Phone follow-up: Can we talk?

While nobody wants to ring up a four digit phone bill, a few well-placed, Ma Bell-aided words can work wonders.

One or two weeks after sending your introductory package, give the recipient a quick phone call. No speeches, no long harangues, just a quick call to touch base, to make sure the person received your materials and had a chance to look at them.

At this point you can quickly determine their receptiveness or lack of it.

Assuming that they've fallen head over heels for your material, ask them to keep it on file and not to hesitate calling when your services are needed.

Certainly, the encouraging reaction from a potential client is a wonderful opportunity for you to further promote your professionalism. Drop the client a note thanking him for taking the time to talk with you on the phone, reaffirm your desire to work with him on a project and toss in a *new* sample. It is important to keep a record of what you sent him in your introductory package so that you don't re-send any of those materials. Sending the same thing twice leaves the appearance that you aren't doing much new work.

Mailing list: I'm still alive!

Over time, you will be able to compile a mailing list of clients with whom you've worked and those who offer strong potential.

It is therefore important to court these clients with periodic, self-promotional mailings. The frequency of these mailings can vary—some cartoonists send quarterly promotions to 500 select clients, some humorous illustrators mail 3,000 color promo pages twice a year, while some humor writers occasionally pepper 150 editors with samples of their work.

Since such lists must be updated when art directors, editors or creative directors change jobs, storing such a list in a word processor or computer makes the job much easier.

Planned properly, a mailing to 500 potential clients will reward you with enough work to pay for the mailing itself, and then some—at least that's what you should aim for. You also never really know when assignments are being made. A magazine art director may be looking for a humorous illustrator when all of a sudden your mailing arrives—tah dah! This happens more often than you might believe.

Advertising: "The home of crazy low prices"

You're no different than a blender. After all, you too have to be sold. And while direct mail self-promotions tend to work best for a humorist, you may also want to back up such marketing with advertising.

Although writers have few forums for their ads and seem limited to classifieds in select publications, humorous illustrators and cartoonists can promote their work in established illustration directories like *Creative Black Book*, *American Showcase* and other regional resources. However, ads in these forums are expensive propositions—a color page can cost you between $4,000 and $10,000. Nonetheless, these directories afford the illustrator a high profile and get his work in front of thousands of decision-making buyers.

Negotiating: Bucks for yucks

Once your promotions have worked; your phone calls have proved fruitful; and your professionalism duly impresses your clients, you'll get work.

This is where a business sense, not sense of humor, is of paramount importance. Payment for work varies and is generally determined by usage. For example, a client will pay much more for a color cartoon which will be used in a consumer magazine advertising campaign than he will for a black and white ad which will be used one time in a trade journal. Fees for writing are determined by similar considerations.

The Graphic Artists Guild publishes suggested pricing guidelines for visual artists and *Writer's Market* prints an incredible, alphabetized list of suggested rates for writing services called How Much Should I Charge?

However, leaving the negotiation of prices up to a literary or illustration agent frees you up to *create* humor—not price it.

The last laugh

It's a funny biz, this humor thing. While nurturing your cartooning, animation, humorous illustration and writing talent should be your primary concern, don't neglect to develop good business practices. Not surprisingly, the successful freelancer spends almost as much time administering to business concerns as he does drawing or writing funny things. In the end, you'll find yourself laughing—all the way to the bank.

Continuing education: On and on

There's so much to learn about the business of humor. We've compiled this nifty list of reading material which will enable you to keep on top of this wacky biz (and hey—subscriptions are tax-deductible!).

Magazines

Advertising Age, 740 Rush St., Chicago, IL 60611

ADWEEK, A/S/M/ Publications, 49 E. 21st St., New York, NY 10010

Airbrush Action, 317 Cross St., Lakewood, NJ 08701

Animation Magazine, P.O. Box 25547, Los Angeles, CA 90025

Art Direction, 6th Floor, 10 E. 39th St., New York, NY 10016-0199

The Artist's Magazine, 1507 Dana Ave., Cincinnati, OH 45207

Bullseye, P.O. Box 36, Lynbrook, NY 11563

Cartoonist Profiles, 281 Bayberry Ln., Westport, CT 06880

Comedy USA Newswire, 915 Broadway, New York, NY 10010

Comics Career, 601 Clinkscales, Columbia, MO 65203

Communications Arts, 410 Sherman Ave., Box 10300, Palo Alto, CA 94303

Editor and Publisher, 11 W. 19th St., New York, NY 10011

Factsheet Five, 6 Arizona Ave., Rensselaer, NY 12144-4502

Gag Recap Publications, Box 86, East Meadow, NY 11554

Get Animated!, P.O. Box 1458, Burbank, CA 91507

Greetings Magazine, MacKay Publishing, 309 Fifth Ave., New York, NY 10016

HOW Magazine, 1507 Dana Ave., Cincinnati, OH 45207

Modern Cartooning and Gagwriting, P.O. Box 1142, Novato, CA 94947

Political Pix, Box 804C, Norwich, VT 05055

Print, 9th Floor, 104 Fifth Ave., New York, NY 10017

Publisher's Weekly, 205 W. 42nd St., New York, NY 10017

Publishing News, Hanson Publishing Group, Box 4049, Stamford, CT 06907-0949

Step-By-Step Graphics, 6000 N. Forest Park Dr., Peoria, IL 61614-3597

Witty World, Box 1458, North Wales, PA 19454

Writer's Digest, 1507 Dana Ave., Cincinnati, OH 45207

Illustration directories

ADWEEK Portfolios, A/S/M Communications, 49 E. 21st St., New York, NY 10010

American Showcase, 724 Fifth Ave., New York, NY 10019

Chicago Creative Directory, 333 N. Michigan Ave., Chicago, IL 60601

Creative Black Book, Friendly Press, 401 Park Ave. S., New York, NY 10016

The Creative Illustration Book, 115 Fifth Ave., New York, NY 10003

Madison Avenue Handbook, Peter Glenn Publication, 17 E. 48th St., New York, NY 10017

RSVP, Box 314, Brooklyn, NY 11205

The Work Book, Scott and Daughters Publishing, #204 1545 Wilcox Ave., Los Angeles, CA 90028

Books

Animation: From Script to Screen, by Shamus Culhane, St. Martin's Press, 175 Fifth Ave., New York, NY 10010

The Animator's Workbook, by Tony White, Watson-Guptill Publications, P.O. Box 2013, Lakewood, NJ 08701

Art Director's Annual, 250 Park Ave. S., New York, NY 10003

The Art of Humorous Illustration, by Nick Meglin, Watson-Guptill Publications, P.O. Box 2013, Lakewood, NJ 08701

Artist's Market, Writer's Digest Books, 1507 Dana Ave., Cincinnati, OH 45207

Best Editorial Cartoons of the Year (annual), edited by Charles Brooks, Pelican Publishing, Box 189, 1101 Monroe St., Gretna, LA 70053

Comedy Writing Secrets, by Melvin Helitzer, Writer's Digest Books, 1507 Dana Ave., Cincinnati, OH 45207

The Craft of Comedy Writing, by Sol Saks, Writer's Digest Books, 1507 Dana Ave., Cincinnati, OH 45207

Gale Directory of Publications, Penobscot Bldg., Detroit MI 48226

Graphic Artist's Guild Handbook: Pricing and Ethical Guidelines, F&W Publications, 1507 Dana Ave., Cincinnati, OH 45207

A Guide to Greeting Card Writing, edited by Larry Sandman, Writer's Digest Books, 1507 Dana Ave., Cincinnati, OH 45207

Handbook of Magazine Article Writing, by Lisa Collier Cool, Writer's Digest Books, 1507 Dana Ave., Cincinnati, OH 45207

How to Draw and Sell Cartoons, Ross Thompson and Bill Hewison, North Light Books, 1507 Dana Ave., Cincinnati, OH 45207

How to Draw and Sell Comic Strips, by Alan McKenzie, North Light Books, 1507 Dana Ave., Cincinnati, OH 45207

Humor, edited by The Society of Illustrators, Madison Square Press, Suite 510, 10 E. 23rd St., New York, NY 10010

Literary Market Place, R.R. Bowker Company, 245 W. 17th St., New York, NY 10011

Standard Directory of Advertising Agencies, National Register Publishing, 3004 Glenview Rd., Wilmette, IL 60091

Working Press of the Nation, National Research Bureau, Suite 1150, 310 S. Michigan Ave., Chicago, IL 60604

Writer's Market, Writer's Digest Books, 1507 Dana Ave., Cincinnati, OH 45207

Bob Staake is a freelance cartoonist who has drawn for such clients as Paramount Pictures, MGM, Anheuser-Busch, Mattel, The Los Angeles Times, USA Today, *King Features Syndicate,* Parents, *Ralston Purina and AT&T. Staake is the illustrator of Jay Leno's best selling book,* Headlines (Warner Books) *and is currently writing a book on the art of caricature for North Light Books. For a cheap laugh, he once sneaked onto the grounds of Richard Nixon's San Clemente estate and walked around until he was unceremoniously escorted out by the Secret Service. He's that kind of guy. Born in Los Angeles, Staake now makes his home in St. Louis, Missouri.*

The Markets

Advertising/ Public Relations

Advertising. A world where hyperbolic copy can make a household cleanser a household name, where the winners of wars are colas and where men in lifeboats cruise your toilet.

An odd, dream-like world where *anything* can happen and, for the right price, usually does. Copywriters are paid $3,000 to write about the virtues of lanolin and illustrators are paid ten grand to render Scruffy blissfully crunching on a mint-flavored dog biscuit.

Few in the industry would deny that money, big money, attracts people to the profession—from creative directors to account executives, media buyers to art directors and, of course, writers and illustrators.

The illustrator

A highly-polished, savvy humorous illustrator who understands how to market his work can make a yearly six figure in advertising. Read my lips (so sayeth the President) as I stress the word "savvy."

Those humorous illustrators successful in this field are the ones who understand the importance of advertising their work: promoting it, employing agents or representatives to sell it, securing high-profile projects and, of course, nurturing and developing a sophisticated illustration style that the market is receptive to in the first place.

If you're starting fresh, if you want to get your feet wet in advertising's finger bowl, the direct mail approach should be your first step. In assembling a package of work for an agency art director, it is advisable to only send material which he can hang on to. The *last* thing you want is to have it returned. Send a color self-promotional page (2,500 9×12 color pages of your work can be printed for less than $700), a black and white self-promo page, a client list, business card, resume and succinct cover letter.

However, don't think that just because you've sent out 500 direct mail promotions that the phone is going to be ringing off the hook. At best you'll get a job, even two, and cover the cost of the direct mail promotion. Your goal is to get the art director to hang on to your work. Then when a project surfaces which is suited to your brand of humorous illustration, your phone may jingle.

Depending on your success, you may want to plan your own advertising campaign by taking out full page ads in one or two of the illustration directories. Get out your checkbook—a color page in *American Showcase* is about $5,000, a similar page in *Creative Black Book* will set you back by about $8,000. You've heard the saying, "It takes money to make money." ?

The most common misconception among humorous illustrators is that if they do a considerable amount of work for magazines, they'll be welcomed with open arms into advertising. Wrong. With few exceptions, humorous illustrators who successfully draw for editorial clients aren't always able to succeed in advertising.

The writer

The writer will also be pleased to learn that when it comes to copy, advertising has a healthy sense of humor. While a humorous illustrator's specialized, graphic style may pigeonhole him and limit the work he can do for a particular agency, writers seem more able to *nurture* ongoing relationships with agencies since they are better able to flex and bend from account to account.

If possible, put together a package of your work which shows a broad range of writing ability and various applications. Keep your presentation clean, professional and provide the potential buyer (usually the Creative Director) with tearsheets (or copies of them), client list, resume, business card and, of course, a succinct cover letter.

Rights

Rights and usages negotiated for advertising work are extremely varied. This is where an agent or representative becomes important. One time rights, all rights (for which a Work for Hire contract must be signed to assign copyright), per usage fees and, in the case of humorous illustration, the sale of the original artwork, are terms that must be specified at the inception of the project.

Thanks to technology, it is now much easier for the freelance humorous illustrator or writer in Marion, Ohio to work with the ad agency in Santa Monica, California. You can thank the Fax machine for that. In fact, agencies now *expect* to do business with freelancers who have Fax machines in their offices — or at least have access to one.

THE AD WORKS, INC., Four Gorham Ave., Westport CT 06880. (203)454-2388. FAX: (same, call first). Estab. 1984. Advertising agency that provides print ads, brochures and promotional pieces for hotels, restaurants, retail stores and professionals. Needs humorous illustration, humorous copywriting, caricature and cartoons. Uses humorous material for print and radio. 20% of freelance humorous illustration is for print ads. Prefers to work with freelancers with fax capabilities.
Humorous Illustration: Works with approximately 6 freelance humorous illustrators/ month or 60/year. Looking for freelance humorous illustrators who are flexible and not "prima donnas." For first contact send cover letter and b&w tearsheets (or photocopies) to Dick Commer, President. Reports back within 1 week. Returns materials if accompanied by a SASE. Keeps materials on file. Negotiates rights purchased. Pays $30-85 by the hour or $100-500 by the project. Payment is based on complexity of project, ability of illustrator to work well under our art direction, client's budget, possibility of a long term agency/illustrator relationship, skill of illustrator and schedule of illustrator.
Humor Writing: Works with approximately 2 humor oriented writers/month or 10/year. Looking for freelance humorous writers who are "light" in approach. For first contact send cover letter, client list, tearsheets, writing samples and audio tape to Dick Commer. Reports back within 1 week. Returns materials if accompanied by a SASE. Negotiates rights purchased. Pays $40-60/hour, $200-400/day and by the project depending on time considerations. Payment is based on complexity of project, skill of writer, turnaround, ability of writer to work well under our creative team, business manner and professionalism of writer, client's budget, schedule of writer, usage and possibility of a long term agency/writer relationship. Tips: "Cartoonists have excellent possibilities for advertising work. The problem is knowing who is available."

ADVANCE ADVERTISING AGENCY & ART STUDIO, 606 E. Belmont #202, Fresno CA 93701. (209)445-0383. Estab. 1951. Advertising agency and art/design studio that provides direct mail, newsletters, mailing pieces, illustrations, flyers, folders, TV production, vocal talent, photography, logo design, cartoons, copywriting, radio shows, commercials and business specialties for retail stores, musical societies, service businesses, clubs, independent merchants, jazz bands, etc. Current clients include Howard Leach Auctions, Fresno Dixieland Society, High Sierra Jazz Club, Mr. G's Carpets, Windshield Repair Service and Club Casino. Needs humorous illustration, cartoons and music related humorous items. Uses humorous material for print. 100% of freelance humorous illustration is for print ads.
Humorous Illustration: Works with approximately 12 freelance humorous illustrators/ year. Looking for freelance humorous illustrators who are "priced for our market and clients." For first contact send appropriate samples of versatility to Marty Nissen, Production Manager. Reports back only if interested. Returns materials if accompanied by a SASE or keeps materials on file. Negotiates rights purchased. Pays $30 minimum/ hour. Payment is based on turnaround, ability of illustrator to work well under our art direction, client's budget, skill of illustrator and usage.
Humor Writing: Looking for freelance humorous writers who fit the needs of particular client or campaign. For first contact send ½″ demo cassette to Marty Nissen. Reports back only if interested and if accompanied by a SASE. Pays $30/hour minimum according to skill of writer, turnaround and client's budget. Tips: "Important to keep in mind that markets vary greatly in sophistication, pay scale, usage, etc. What might be considered a 'good buy' in San Francisco may be out of the question in our market. Local union situations may also be a factor."

AM/PM ADVERTISING, 196 Clinton Ave., Newark NJ 07108. (201)824-8600. FAX: (201)824-6631. Estab. 1962. Advertising agency that provides marketing; advertising; national ads, TV commercials and sales promotion for consumer package goods companies, in food, health and beauty aids. Current clients include J & J, Nabisco, Revlon, P & G, American Cyanamid, Carter Wallace, Bristol Myers and Lever Brothers. Needs humorous illustration, animation, humor oriented comprehensives, humorous copywriting, caricature, animatics, cartoons and storyboards. Uses humorous material for print, video tape, TV, radio and audiovisual. 50% of freelance humorous illustration is for print ads.

Humorous Illustration: Works with approximately 10 freelance humorous illustrators/year. Looking for freelance humorous illustrators who have the talent to fit the project. For first contact send resume to Robert Saks, President. Reports back within weeks only if interested. Returns materials if accompanied by a SASE. Keeps materials on file. Buys one time rights. Pays $50-150 by the hour. Payment is based on ability of illustrator to work well under our art direction, client's budget and possibility of a long term agency/illustrator relationship.

Humor Writing: Works with approximately 6 humor oriented writers/month. Looking for freelance humorous writers "who have the talent to fit the project." For first contact send resume to Robert Saks. Reports back within weeks. Returns materials if accompanied by a SASE. Buys first time rights. Pays $50-150 by the hour. Payment is based on business manner and professionalism of writer, client's budget and possibility of a long term agency/writer relationship. Tips: "Creative ability is *solving* the problem successfully, *within budget/time restraints*, and following professional instructions/directions."

LEWIS BENEDICT BEDECARRÉ, 2924 Clayton Rd., Concord CA 94519. (415)825-5555. FAX: (415)686-2365. Estab. 1971. Full service advertising agency for hotel, entertainment and home building clients. Needs humorous illustration, animation, humorous copywriting, caricature and greeting cards. Uses material for print and radio. 75% of freelance humorous illustration is for print ads.

Humorous Illustration: Works with 2-4 freelance humorous illustrators per year. For first contact send cover letter, resume, client list, b&w and color tearsheets, b&w and color promo pieces and slides to Jay Bedecarré, President. Reports back only if interested. Returns materials if requested and accompanied by a SASE. Pays $10-35/hour; $100 minimum/project. Payment is based on complexity of project, skill of illustrator, turnaround, ability of illustrator to work well under our art direction, client's budget, usage and possibility of a long term agency/illustrator relationship.

Humor Writing: Works with 1-2 humor oriented writers per year. For first contact, freelancer should send cover letter, resume, client list, tearsheets, writing samples, ½" demo tape and audio tape to Jay Bedecarré, President. Reports back on submissions only if interested. Returns materials if interested and accompanied by a SASE. Buys first time rights, one time only rights, all rights, reprint rights or negotiates rights purchased. Pays $10-25/hour, $100 minimum/project. When establishing payment, considers complexity of project, skill of writer, turnaround, ability of writer to work under creative team, client's budget, usage and possibility of a future agency/writer relationship.

JOHN BERGDOLL ASSOCIATES, 99 Francis St., Waltham MA 02154. (617)894-7172. FAX: (617)899-0312. Estab. 1988. Advertising agency that provides brochures, posters and general advertising for industrial corporations, schools and hotels. Needs humorous illustration, humorous copywriting and storyboards. Uses humorous material for print, video tape, radio and audiovisual. 5% of freelance humorous illustration is for print ads. Prefers to work with freelancers with fax capabilities.

Humorous Illustration: Works with approximately 4 freelance humorous illustrators/year. For first contact send cover letter, resume, color tearsheets, b&w promo piece and color promo piece. "Photocopies are fine for my files." Send to John Bergdoll, Creative Director. Reports back only if interested. Keeps materials on file. Buys all rights or negotiates rights purchased. Payment is based on turnaround and client's budget.

Humor Writing: Currently does not work with humor oriented writers. For first contact send cover letter, resume, tearsheets and writing samples to John Bergdoll. Reports back only if interested. Keeps materials on file. Negotiates rights purchased. When establishing payment considers turnaround and client's budget.

CAHNERS EXPOSITION GROUP, 221 Columbus Ave., Boston MA 02117. (617)536-8252. FAX: (617)536-8719. Trade and public exposition producer that provides trade and public shows worldwide annually for auto, computer, travel, home/real estate, electronics and other industries. Needs humorous illustration, animation and cartoons. Uses humorous material for print, video tape, TV, radio and audiovisual. 30% of freelance humorous illustration is for print ads. Prefers to work with freelancers with fax access.

Humorous Illustration: Works with approximately 4-8 freelance humor illustrators/year. For first contact send cover letter, resume, client list, b&w promo piece and color promo piece to Sheldon Lesser, VP Marketing Communications. Reports back only if interested. Returns materials only if requested. Keeps materials on file. Buys reprint rights or negotiates rights purchased. Payment is based on complexity of project, turnaround and skill of illustrator.

Humor Writing: Works with approximately 2-4 humor oriented writers/year. For first contact send cover letter, resume, client list and writing samples to Sheldon Lesser. Reports back only if interested. Keeps materials on file. Buys reprint rights or negotiates rights purchased. Negotiates payment by project. Tips: "Pricing really depends on the job itself and how the freelancer works. We use humor in some of our videos. Most of our copywriting is done in-house."

CHEVALIER/SCHAKENBACH ADVERTISING, Two Westborough Business Park, Westborough MA 01581. (508)366-1476. FAX: (508)366-1480. Estab. 1981. Advertising agency that provides full service advertising services, strategy, creativity and media placement to high technology corporations, (lasers, fiberoptics, micro-electronics) and high end retail (leisure boats, imported car dealers). Current clients include Electronic Designs, Inc., Sumitomo Fiberoptics, Laser Engineering and Matec Corporation. Needs humorous illustration, caricature and cartoons. Uses humorous material for print. 50% of freelance humorous illustration is for print ads. Prefers to work with freelancers with fax capabilities.

Humorous Illustration: For first contact send b&w promo piece and color promo piece to James D. Schakenbach, V.P./Creative Services. Reports back only if interested. Does not return materials. Negotiates rights purchased. Pays $75 minimum by the project. Payment is based on complexity of project, client's budget, skill of illustrator and usage. Tips: "I'm finding it difficult to identify possible freelancers without spending a lot of time looking through portfolios. I need a source of samples so I can begin qualifying people before I ever talk to them."

COMMUNICATION ASSOCIATES, Suite Two, 5810 Jameson Court, Carmichael CA 95608. (916)487-3000. FAX: (916)483-4637. Estab. 1979. Advertising agency and art/design studio that provides graphic design art to hospitals, art galleries, political firms and law firms, small business and corporations. Current clients include Ramos Oil Company, Marshall Hospital, New Blends, Inc., TEXTEK, Inc., Gallery of the American West and Governor George Deukmajian. Needs humorous illustration, humorous copywriting and caricature. Uses humorous material for print. 75% of freelance humorous illustration is for print ads.

Humorous Illustration: Works with approximately 1 freelance humorous illustrator/month. Looking for freelance humorous illustrators who have additional communication/design skills. For first contact send cover letter, b&w tearsheets and b&w promo piece to Tana Leigh Gabriel, Art Director. Reports back within 2 weeks. Returns materials if accompanied by a SASE. Keeps materials on file. Negotiates rights purchashed. Pays $10 minimum by the hour or $250 minimum by the project. Payment is based on complexity of project, turnaround, ability of illustrator to work well under our art direction, client's budget and skill of illustrator.

Humor Writing: Works with approximately 7 humor oriented writers/year. Looking for freelance humorous writers who are funny without the use of sexual or ethnic material. For first contact send cover letter and writing samples to Tana Leigh Gabriel. Reports back within 2 weeks. Returns materials if accompanied by a SASE. Keeps materials on file. Negotiates rights purchased. Pays $200 minimum by the project according to complexity of project, skill of writer, turnaround, ability of writer to work well under our creative team and client's budget.

CREATIVE DIMENSIONS, 2369 Park Ave., Cincinnati OH 45206. (513)961-4400. FAX: (513)961-5400. Estab. 1971. Advertising agency that provides full service radio, TV, direct mail, print, collateral, P.O.P. outdoor, etc. for financial institutions, auto dealers, Anderson Windows, furniture companies and cabinet companies. Needs humorous illustration and copywriting. Uses humorous material for print, TV and radio. 10% of freelance humorous illustration is for print ads.

Humorous Illustration: Works with 1-8 freelance humorous illustrators/year. For first contact send b&w tearsheets and color tearsheets to Sam McClausland, Art Director. Reports back within a few days. Returns materials if requested. Buys all rights. Pays by project with no set maximum or minimum. Payment is based on client's budget, possibility of a long term agency/illustrator relationship and usage.

Humor Writing: "To date, everything has been in-house, but we are changing this. Looking for freelance humorous writers who can write material for a long-running campaign we presently have. Also, if they can come up with campaign ideas of their own." For first contact send writing samples, demo tape if possible and audio tape to Arnold R. Barnett, CEO. Reports back within days. Returns materials if requested. Buys all rights. Pays varied amounts by the project according to client's budget, usage and possibility of a long term agency/writer relationship. Tips: "We are primarily interested in humorous radio campaigns. We are the largest radio agency in this area. Many of our campaigns are humorous. Because of the number of spots we are responsible for creating each month, we are increasing our dependence on freelancers."

CREATIVE MARK/COMM, 8504 Ridgewood Rd., Rock Island IL 61201. (309)787-2322. Estab. 1984. Advertising agency that provides all aspects of marketing and advertising to new business start-ups, corporations, development groups, not-for-profit organizations and tourism entities. Current clients include Alter Co., Quad City Development Group, Davenport (IA) Museum of Art and Quad City Industrial Center. Needs humorous illustration, layouts and keyliners. Uses humorous material for print, video tape and TV. 90% of freelance humorous illustration is for print ads.

Humorous Illustration: Works with approximately 1 freelance humorous illustrator/month. Looking for freelance humorous illustrators who are within a 60 mile radius. For first contact send cover letter, resume, b&w tearsheets, color tearsheets and b&w promo piece to Jodie S. Kavensky, President. Reports back only if interested. Returns materials if requested. Keeps materials on file. Negotiates rights purchased. Pays $40 minimum by the hour and $200 minimum by the project. Payment is based on complexity of project, turnaround, client's budget and usage.

Humor Writing: Works with approximately 1 humor oriented writer/month; 12/year. Looking for freelance humorous writers who are within a 60 mile radius. For first contact send cover letter, resume, tearsheets and writing samples to Jodie S. Kavensky. Reports back only if interested. Returns materials if requested. Keeps materials on file. Negotiates rights purchased. Pays $30 minimum by the hour or $200 minimum by the project according to complexity of project, client's budget, turnaround and usage.

CROSS KEYS ADVERTISING, INC., 329 S. Main St., Doylestown PA 18901-4814 . Estab. 1981. Advertising agency that provides full service advertising dealing in all forms of media for automotive, retail stores, banks, developers and industries. Current clients include Porsche Motorsport North America, The Thompson Organization (automotive dealerships) and Penns Grant Corporation (commercial and industrial developers). Needs humorous illustration, animation and humorous copywriting. Uses humorous material for print, video tape and radio. 60% of freelance humorous illustration is for print ads. Prefers to work with freelancers with fax capabilities.
Humorous Illustration: Works with approximately 4 freelance humorous illustrators/year. For first contact send cover letter, b&w tearsheets and b&w promo piece to Laura Thompson, President. Returns materials only if requested. Keeps materials on file. Negotiates rights purchased. Payment is based on complexity of project, turnaround, business manner and professionalism of illustrator, ability of illustrator to work well under our art direction, client's budget and skill of illustrator.
Humor Writing: Works with approximately 4 humor oriented writers/year. For first contact send cover letter, writing samples and audio tape to Laura Thompson. When establishing payment considers complexity of project, skill of writer, turnaround, ability of writer to work well under our creative team, business manner and professionalism of writer and client's budget.

JOHN CROWE ADVERTISING AGENCY, 1104 South 2nd St., Springfield IL 62704. (217)528-1076. Estab. 1954. Advertising agency that provides full service media, printing, promotion, production, direct mail, design and full graphics service, art work (commercial and fine art), photo retouching and illustration art to industrial, commercial, retail, banking, publishers, aviation, architects, city, state, federal, medical and displays. Needs humorous illustration, humorous copywriting, caricature, animatics and cartoons. Uses humorous material for print, video tape, TV and radio. 10% of freelance humorous illustration is for print ads.
Humorous Illustration: Works with approximately 3 freelance humorous illustrators/year. Looking for freelance humorous illustrators who are requested by clients. For first contact send cover letter, resume, client list and b&w tearsheets to Bryan J. Crowe, Art Director. Reports back within 10 days if interested. Keeps materials on file. Negotiates rights purchased. Pays $25 maximum by the hour. Payment is based on complexity of project, client's budget and skill of illustrator.
Humor Writing: Works with approximately 3 humor oriented writers/year. For first contact send cover letter, resume, client list, tearsheets and writing samples to Bryan J. Crowe. Reports back within 10 days. Keeps materials on file. Negotiates rights purchased. Pays $25 maximum by the hour according to complexity of project, skill of writer and client's budget.

R.I. DAVID & COMPANY, 3601 W. Devon Avenue, Chicago IL 60659. (312)478-7483. FAX: (312)478-7482. Estab. 1950. Advertising agency that provides advertising and sales materials in foreign languages to all markets. Needs humorous copywriting. Uses humorous material for print, video tape, TV, radio and audiovisual. 75% of freelance humorous illustration is for print ads. Prefers to work with freelancers with fax access.

Humor Writing: Looking for freelance humorous writers who are native born with foreign language capacity. For first contact send resume, client list and tearsheets to Alicia Adams, Vice President. Reports back only if interested. Does not return materials. Keeps materials on file. Buys all rights. Pays 10¢ minimum by the word. When establishing payment considers complexity of project, skill of writer, turnaround and client's budget.

DGS & D ADVERTISING, 10293 N. Meridian, Indianapolis IN 46290. (317)575-9910. Estab. 1985. Advertising agency that provides full service to restaurants, banks, carpet companies, service companies, manufacturers, business-to-business and corporate. Current clients include Long John Silvers, Rent-A-Center, USA Funds and Lilly. Needs humorous illustration, animation, humorous copywriting, animatics, storyboards and slide shows. Uses humorous material for print, video tape, TV and radio. 50% of freelance humorous illustration is for print ads. Prefers to work with freelancers with fax capabilities.

Humorous Illustration: Works with approximately 2 freelance humorous illustrators/month; 25/year. For first contact send cover letter, client list, b&w tearsheets, color tearsheets and b&w promo piece to Roger C. Dobrovodsky, VP Creative. Reports back only if interested. Returns materials only if requested. Keeps materials on file. Negotiates rights purchased. Payment is based on complexity of project, client's budget, skill of illustrator and usage.

Humor Writing: Works with approximately 4 humor oriented writers/month; 40/year. For first contact send cover letter, tearsheets, writing samples, audio tape and ½" demo tape to Roger E. Dobrovodsky. Reports back only if interested. Returns materials only if interested. Keeps materials on file. Negotiates rights purchased. Pays $100 minimum by the project according to complexity of project, skill of writer, ability of writer to work well under our creative team and client's budget.

DIEGNAN & ASSOCIATES, P.O. Box 298, Oldwick NJ 08858. (201)823-7951. FAX: (201)832-9650. Estab. 1977. PR firm that provides services for corporations. Current clients include Cerberus Pyrotronics, Reeco, Liquiflo and UC Industries. Needs humorous illustration, animation, humor oriented comprehensives, humorous copywriting, caricature, animatics and cartoons. Uses humorous material for print, video tape and TV. 100% of freelance humorous illustration is for print ads.

Humorous Illustration: Works with approximately 6 freelance humorous illustrators/year. For first contact send b&w tearsheets to N. Diegnan, President. Reports back within 1 week. Keeps materials on file. Negotiates rights purchased. Pays $50 minimum by the hour. Payment is based on complexity of project.

Humor Writing: Works with approximately 6 humor oriented writers/year. For first contact send writing samples to N. Diegnan. Reports back within 1 week. Keeps materials on file. Negotiates rights purchased. Pays $50 minimum by the hour according to complexity of the project.

CHARLES EDELSTEIN ADV., INC., 92 Austin Drive, Holland PA 18966. Estab. 1971. Advertising agency that provides annual reports, collateral and print ads to corporations, banks and stores. Needs humorous illustration, humor oriented comprehensives, humorous copywriting, caricatures, cartoons and storyboards. Uses humorous material for print, video tape, radio and audiovisual. 75% of freelance humorous illustration is for print ads.

Humorous Illustration: Works with approximately 6 freelance humorous illustrators/year. For first contact send b&w tearsheets and b&w promo piece to Charles Edelstein, President. Does not return materials. Keeps materials on file. Negotiates rights purchased. Pays $15-30 by the hour or $75-200 by the project. Payment is based on complexity of project, turnaround, business manner and professionalism of illustrator, ability of

Close-up

Jack Davis
Cartoonist

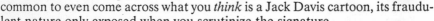
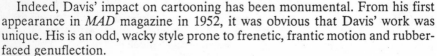

Jack Davis has more followers than The Pied Piper. But unlike The Pied Piper, who beguiled the throngs with a cacophony of melodies, it is Davis' cartooning that mesmerizes his devotees.

Aspiring cartoonists (and even professionals) shamelessly mimic Davis' style, copy his characters and take hero worship to its extreme. It is not uncommon to even come across what you *think* is a Jack Davis cartoon, its fraudulent nature only exposed when you scrutinize the signature.

Indeed, Davis' impact on cartooning has been monumental. From his first appearance in *MAD* magazine in 1952, it was obvious that Davis' work was unique. His is an odd, wacky style prone to frenetic, frantic motion and rubber-faced genuflection.

"My drawing style appealed to a lot of people who had no taste," says Davis in his typically humble manner. "I even look back to the stuff I drew at EC Comics, and compared to Johnny Craig, Wally Wood, George Evans, Harvey Kurtzman, Willy Elder, all these beautiful artists, my work looked pretty grotesque—but it was different."

Influenced by the films of Walt Disney, Davis studied the master's animated cartoons and learned how to effectively stage, plot and block his cartoons. "The Disney films," recalls Davis, "were frightening, well animated and you couldn't get actors to play those roles—I was just awestruck by those movies."

Yet Davis credits radio with his ability to imagine. "We didn't have TV," Davis points out, "but we did have radio. You would imagine what you were listening to and your mind would wander. I developed an ability to think up something instead of seeing it already done."

Raised on the comics of the 1930s, Davis appreciated the lush, detailed drawings of cartoonists like Hal Foster and Alex Raymond. "It was mind-boggling how they drew," Davis says. "Today's comic strips have become little, cute, sarcastic things instead of the beautiful artwork—that's kind of sad."

Yet Davis does appreciate certain comic strips. " 'Calvin and Hobbes' is wonderful because it's so different—it's almost like *Winnie the Pooh*," says Davis. "And Gary Larson draws so bad that he's great—his stuff knocks me out even before I read the punchline! But there are many cartoonists who do things somebody else has already done or they draw like somebody else."

Davis' high profile as a *MAD* magazine cartoonist results in a steady workload of editorial and advertising assignments. Although his work has appeared in *TIME*, *Newsweek*, *TV Guide*, *Playboy* and *LIFE*, Davis prefers advertising to editorial projects.

"Advertising," says Davis, "has always paid better so I've pursued it more than editorial. In the beginning, however, agencies wouldn't use me, saying I looked 'too much like *MAD*.' But in 1965 I did an ad series for NBC and other agencies saw that it worked. From that point on, agencies sort of opened the doors for me."

Presently, about 75% of Davis' work is for advertising and he prides himself on his ability to draw at almost breakneck speed. "Depending on the detail," says Davis, "on the average I'll get a layout over the Fax and pencil out my drawing in about an hour. I Fax the drawing to the client and they Fax the approval back and I can render the final ad drawing in a day."

He sees advertising as a pendulum. "Things swing back and forth in this business," Davis explains. "When I came along, people in advertising couldn't appreciate cartoons and then all of a sudden they did—and now things are on the down swing again and you don't see too many cartoons."

When it comes to cartooning for advertising, Davis in many ways invented the wheel. "When I came along," reminds Davis, "there was no competition. I kind of set the trend in many ways—I was a breakthrough. But now there is a lot more competition, so a young person has to hang in there. You have to be really good, enjoy and love your work and believe in yourself."

His advice to the aspiring cartoonist is wise—recognizing the importance of short term sacrifice for long term gain. "The greatest thing you must do at a young age," Davis asserts, "is gain exposure—even forego the money—just get your stuff seen. There are so many talented people who want to be cartoonists—and there just isn't enough room for everybody."

—Bob Staake

Let's Do Lunch*: Davis portrays the lengths that some illustration representatives will go to clinch a gig. In fact, Davis' own representatives, Gerald and Cullen Rapp, sent out this black and white postcard to promote the cartoonist's "wacky style prone to frenetic, frantic motion and rubber-faced genuflection."*

© 1990 Jack Davis

illustrator to work well under our art direction and client's budget.

Humor Writing: Works with approximately 6 humor oriented writers/year. For first contact send resume and tearsheets to Charles Edelstein. Does not return materials. Keeps materials on file. Negotiates rights purchased. Pays $15-30 by the hour or $120-240 by the day according to complexity of project, skill of writer, turnaround, ability of writer to work well under our creative team, business manner and professionalism of writer and client's budget.

EGD—EDWARD G. DORN & ASSOCIATES, INC., 1801 H Hicks Rd., Rolling Meadows IL 60008. (312)991-1270. FAX: (312)991-1519. Estab. 1971. Advertising agency and art/design studio that provides full service advertising, marketing, sales promotion, PR, graphics and printing to business-to-business, consumer, industrial and service companies. Current clients include Goulding, Jeycom, Airphone and Bostic/Emhart. Needs humorous illustration, caricature, cartoons, storyboards and slide shows. Uses humorous material for print and audiovisual. 50% of freelance humorous illustration is for print ads. Prefers to work with freelancers with fax capabilities.

Humorous Illustration: Works with approximately 1 freelance humorous illustrator/month. Looking for freelance humorous illustrators who have fresh ideas and top drawing ability. For first contact send cover letter, resume, client list, b&w tearsheets and color tearsheets to Kathleen Dorn, VP Personnel. Reports back within 1 week if interested. Returns materials if requested; otherwise keeps materials. Buys all rights. Pays by the project. Payment is based on complexity of project, client's budget, possibility of a long term agency/illustrator relationship and skill of illustrator.

Humor Writing: Works with approximately 2 humor oriented writers/year. Looking for freelance humorous writers who can also illustrate. For first contact send cover letter, resume, client list and writing samples.

FERRARI, INC., 95 Madison Ave., New York NY 10016. (212)532-3220. FAX: (212)685-9205. Estab. 1974. Advertising agency that provides full service marketing, media, print ads, broadcast, radio, brochures and annual reports to cable networks, entertainment companies, television syndicates and financial institutes. Current clients include Financial News Network, Spelling Entertainment, Worldvision Enterprises and Federal Home Loan Bank. Needs animation, humorous copywriting and caricature. Uses humorous material for print and radio. 5% of freelance humorous illustration is for print ads. Prefers to work with freelancers with fax capabilities.

Humorous Illustration: Works with approximately 2 freelance humorous illustrators/year. For first contact send cover letter and b&w tearsheets to Robert Weissberg, Creative Director. Reports back within 4 days only if interested. Returns materials only if requested. Keeps materials on file. Negotiates rights purchased. Pays $20-50 by the hour and $150-1,500 by the project. Payment is based on complexity of project, turnaround, ability of illustrator to work well under our art direction, client's budget, possibility of a long term agency/illustrator relationship and skill of illustrator.

Humor Writing: Works with approximately 2 humor oriented writers/year. Looking for freelance humorous writers who have proven flexibility, "can take direction without a battle and understands various businesses." For first contact send cover letter and writing samples to Nick Constantino, Copywriter. Reports back within 3 weeks only if interested. Returns materials only if interested. Keeps materials on file. Negotiates rights purchased. Pays $15-40 by the hour, $50-125 by the day and $100-1,000 by the project. Payment based on complexity of project, skill of writer, ability of writer to work well under our creative team, client's budget and possibility of a long term agency/writer relationship.

THE GUARAMELLA FITZGERALD AGENCY, Turquoise Square Productions, 8226 Sunset Boulevard, Los Angeles CA 90046. (213)650-8321 or 650-6911. FAX: (213)650-8287. Estab. 1983. Advertising agency that provides advertising, print collateral and broadcast to lifestyle/leisure products, companies and services. Current clients include Daily Grill, Varitel Video, Genesis Entertainment, King World, Panavision Hollywood, IDC Services, Broadcast Design and Northrop. Needs humorous illustration, animation, humor oriented comprehensives, humorous copywriting, caricature, animatics and storyboards. Uses humorous material for print, video tape, TV and radio. 70% of freelance humorous illustration is for print ads.

Humorous Illustration: Works with approximately 3 freelance humorous illustrators/year. For first contact send b&w promo piece, color promo piece and portfolio to Paul Gross, Creative Director or John Beach, Sr., Art Director. Reports back within 3 days. Returns materials only if requested and accompanied by a SASE. Keeps materials on file. Negotiaties rights purchased. Payment is based on client's budget.

Humor Writing: Works with approximately 10 humor oriented writers/year. For first contact send writing samples to Dan Bockman, Co-Creative Director. Reports back only if interested. Returns materials if accompanied by a SASE. Keeps materials on file. Negotiates rights purchased. When establishing payment considers client's budget.

FITZSIMONS ADVERTISING & PUBLIC RELATIONS, 750 Midland Building, Cleveland OH 44115. (216)241-5656. FAX: (216)241-5658. Advertising agency that provides full service advertising and public relations to investment, industrial and retail. Needs humorous illustration and humorous copywriting. Uses humorous material for print and video tape. 75% of freelance humorous illustration is for print ads. Prefers to work with freelancers with fax capabilities.

Humorous Illustration: Works with approximately 2 freelance humorous illustrators/year. Looking for freelance humorous illustrators who can work within a budget. For first contact send b&w tearsheets to Joy Woodward, Art Director. Negotiates rights purchased. Payment is based on complexity of project, turnaround, client's budget and skill of illustrator.

Humor Writing: For first contact send writing samples and 3/4" demo tape to Joy Woodward. When establishing payment considers complexity of project, ability of writer to work well under our creative team and client's budget.

GREGORY M. FLEJTUCH, 351 Bahia Lane, San Rafael CA 94901. (415)453-9037. Estab. 1987. Art/design studio that provides collateral, print ads and P.O.P. to fast food chains, art galleries, photography studios and ad agencies. Current clients include Taco Bell, Pepsi (Tracy-Locke Advertising), Pizza Hut, California Grapes (BBDO Advertising) and Erika Meyerovich Gallery. Needs humorous illustration and humorous copywriting. Uses humorous material for print. 10% of freelance humorous illustration is for print ads. Prefers to work with freelancers with fax capabilities.

Humorous Illustration: Works with approximately 2-3 freelance humorous illustrators/year. Looking for freelance humorous illustrators who can work under tight deadlines, within our budget. For first contact send b&w tearsheets, color tearsheets, b&w promo piece and color promo piece to Gregory M. Flejtuch, Art Director/Designer. Reports back within days only if interested. Returns materials if accompanied by a SASE. Keeps materials on file. Negotiates rights purchased. Pays $350-1,500 by the project. Payment is based on complexity of project, client's budget and style or styles of illustrator.

Humor Writing: Looking for freelance humorous writers "who are available when we need them and can work within our budget." For first contact send resume, tearsheets, writing samples and "anything that can be kept on file" to Gregory M. Flejtuch. Reports back within days only if interested. Returns materials if accompanied by a SASE. Keeps materials on file. Negotiates rights purchased. Pays $350-1,500 by the project according to complexity of project, skill of writer, client's budget and usage.

THE HITCHINS COMPANY, 22756 Hartland St., Canoga Park CA 91307. (818)715-0510. Estab. 1984. Advertising agency that provides full service advertising to various clients. Needs humorous illustration, humorous copywriting, caricature and cartoons. Uses humorous material for print. 100% of freelance humorous illustration is for print ads. Prefers to work with freelancers with fax capabilities.

Humorous Illustration: Works with irregular numbers of freelance humorous illustrators/month. For first contact send cover letter, resume and b&w tearsheets (if available) to W. E. Hitchins, President. Reports back only if interested. Does not return materials. Keeps materials on file. Negotiates rights. Pay depends on job and client and is based on client's budget.

Humor Writing: Works with irregular numbers of humor oriented writers/month. For first contact send cover letter, resume and writing samples if available to W. E. Hitchins. Reports back only if interested. Returns materials only if interested. Keeps materials on file. Negotiates rights purchased. Pays according to project and client. When establishing payment considers client's budget.

BERNARD HODES ADVERTISING, 1101 Embarcadero Rd., Palo Alto CA 94303. (415)856-1000. Estab. 1970. Advertising agency that provides recruitment advertising and employee communications for high tech, finance, health care, retailers, apparel manufacturers and aerospace. Current clients include Sun Micro Systems, Ford Aerospace, National Semiconductor, American Savings, Wells Fargo Bank, Seagate Technologies, Community Hospitals of Central California, S. Agnes Med Center, Levi Straus and Clorox. Needs humorous illustration and humorous copywriting. Uses humorous material for print. 100% of freelance humorous illustration is for print ads. Prefers to work with freelancers with fax capabilities.

Humorous Illustration: Works with approximately 2 freelance humorous illustrators/ year. For first contact send cover letter, resume, client list, b&w tearsheets and color tearsheets to Casey Mallough, Production Manager. Reports back only if interested. Does not return materials. Keeps materials on file. Buys all rights or negotiates rights purchased. Pays $150-2,000 by the project. Payment is based on client's budget, possibility of a long term agency/illustrator relationship and usage.

Humor Writing: Works with approximately 6 humor oriented writers/year. Looking for freelance humorous writers who have prior advertising copywriting experienced with a major ad agency. For first contact send cover letter to Mike Doyle, Senior Copywriter. Reports back only if interested. Does not return materials. Does not file materials. Buys all rights. Pays $15-50 by the hour and $250-2,000 by the project according to client's budget, usage and possibility of a long term agency/writer relationship.

JH MEDIA DIRECTIONS, P.O. Box 6091, Evanston IL 60204. (312)675-6555. Estab. 1972. Advertising agency that provides annual reports, print advertising, general distribution for syndicated political and humor cartoons for publications and guidebooks for corporations, retail stores, publications, food and mail order companies. Current clients include Heinemann's Bakeries, Clear Choice Swimwear, SuperBody, Mustard's Restaurants, Antique Emporium and Carousel Connection. Needs humorous illustration, humor oriented comprehensives, caricature and cartoons. Uses humorous material for print, video tape and TV. 80% of freelance humorous illustration is for print ads.

Humorous Illustration: Works with approximately 8 freelance humorous illustrators/ month; 85/year. Looking for freelance humorous illustrators who can do humor with a sharp edge and "can really, really draw detailed work." For first contact send photocopies and tearsheets of printed and new material to Dennis Dorner, President. Reports back only if interested. Returns materials only if accompanied by a SASE. Negotiates rights purchased. Pays $25-200 by the hour and $25-500 by the project. Payment is based on turnaround, ability of illustrator to work well under our art direction, client's budget and skill of illustrator.

Humor Writing: Works with approximately 3 humor oriented writers/month; 40/year. For first contact send resume and writing samples to Dennis Dorner. Reports back only if interested. Returns materials only if accompanied by a SASE. Negotiates rights purchased. Pays $25-2,500 or more by the project according to skill of writer, ability of writer to work well under our creative team and client's budget. Tips: "Illustrations must be done fast and excellent. Black & white illustration in detailed and shadowy styles of those such as Wil Elder and Jim Pierce. Writers must give us potential ideas ahead of established writers we use. They must *create* projects in order for us to use them."

JERRYEND COMMUNICATIONS, INC., RD #2 Box 356H, Birdsboro PA 19508-9328. (215)689-9118. FAX: (215)689-5297. Estab. 1980. Advertising agency that provides annual reports, collateral, soft shoe dancing, hard sock dancing, audiovisual, public relations, newsletters, public speaking, speechwriting and "you-need-it-we-got-it" for financial, industrial, nonprofit, community services, etc. Current clients include CTCE Federal Credit Union, RCA Lancaster Credit Union, CT&T (telephone co.), Berkshire Associates and Goodwill Industries of Mid-Eastern Pennsylvania. Needs humorous illustration, humor oriented comprehensives, humorous copywriting and slide shows. Uses humorous material for print, radio and audiovisual.

Humorous Illustration: Works with approximately 4-5 freelance humorous illustrators/year. Looking for illustrators "who can develop art to meet our client's special needs—we will attempt to prepare from descriptions or stick sketches." For first contact send resume and b&w tearsheets to Gerard E. End, Jr., VP/Creative Director. Reports back only if interested. Returns materials if accompanied by a SASE. Keeps materials on file. Buys all rights. Pays $50-100 by the hour and $250-500 by the project. Payment is based on ability of illustrator to work well under our art direction and skill of illustrator.

Humor Writing: Works with approximately 3-4 humor oriented writers/year. "Looking for freelance humorous writers who are able to write on a given situation and writes better than me." For first contact send client list, tearsheets and writing samples to Gerard E. End, Jr. Reports back only if interested. Returns materials if accompanied by a SASE or keeps materials on file. Buys all rights. Pays $25-50 by the hour, $200-400 by the day and $50-400 by the project according to skill of writer, turnaround and ability of writer to work well under our creative team. Tips: "Our clients range from ultra conservative to fun-loving. They enjoy and appreciate subtle as well as broad humor. I hate to have to explain a story, but I love puns."

HOWARD KAHN & ASSOCIATES, INC., 301 East 79th St., #25B, New York, NY 10021. (212)734-8265. FAX: (212)535-4609. Estab. 1984. Advertising agency that specializes in amusements and attractions and pet stores/pet products. Needs humorous illustration, animation, humorous copywriting and storyboards. Uses humorous material for print, video tape, TV and radio. 5% of freelance humorous illustration is for print ads. Prefers to work with freelancers with fax capabilities.

Humorous Illustration: Works with a few freelance humorous illustrators/year. "Looking for freelance humorous illustrators who have information on file with us." For first contact send cover letter, resume, client list, b&w tearsheets, color tearsheets, b&w promo piece and color promo peice to Howard Kahn, President. Reports back only if interested. Keeps materials on file. Buys all rights. Illustrator should quote payment. Payment is based on complexity of project, turnaround, professionalism of illustrator, ability of illustrator to work well under our art direction, client's budget, possibility of a long term agency/illustrator relationship, skill of illustrator, schedule of illustrator and usage.

Humor Writing: Works with a few humor oriented writers/month. Looking for free-lance humorous writers who have information on file with us. For first contact send cover letter, resume, client list, tearsheets, writing samples, ½" or ¾" demo tape and audio tape to Howard Kahn. Reports back only if interested. Keeps materials on file. Writer should quote payment. When establishing payment considers complexity of project, skill of writer, turnaround, ability of writer to work well under our creative team, professionalism of writer, client's budget, schedule of writer, usage and possibility of a long term agency/writer relationship. Tips: "We are a new, small, developing agency. All material on file is helpful."

KARALIAS ADVERTISING, 9 South Main St., Ipswich MA 01938. (508)356-9665. Estab. 1986. Advertising agency and art/design studio that provides ads, packaging, direct mail pieces, computer graphics for games (Nintendo, Sega, PC) posters, brochures, logos and miscellaneous design for all typs of clients. Current clients include Microsmiths, Parker Brothers, Pierce Furniture, Nynex, Charles River Apparel, First National Bank and Mass Eye & Ear. Needs humorous illustration, animation, humor oriented compre-hensives, humorous copywriting, caricature, animatics and cartoons. Uses humorous material for print, video tape and radio. 50% of freelance humorous illustration is for print ads.
Humorous Illustration: Works with approximately 4 freelance humorous illustrators/year. For first contact send resume and client list to George Karalias, Creative Director. Reports back only if interested. Keeps materials on file. Negotiates rights purchased. Pays $20 minimum by the hour and $100 minimum by the project. Payment is based on complexity of project, turnaround, client's budget and possibility of a long term agency/illustrator relationship.
Humor Writing: Works with approximately 2-3 humor oriented writers/year. For first contact send cover letter, resume and client list to George Karalias. Reports back only if interested. Keeps materials on file. Negotiates rights purchased. Pays $20 minimum by the hour, $80 by the day and $250 by the project according to complexity of project, turnaround and client's budget.

LARSEN COLBY KORALEK, 4727 Wilshire #600, Los Angeles CA 90010. (213)931-0009. Estab. 1984. Advertising agency that provides ads, print, TV, outdoor and radio to high tech, financial, auto and public service agencies. Current clients include VLSI, Vitesse, Subaru Dealers, Green Peace and Financial. Needs humorous illustration, humorous copywriting and storyboards. Uses humorous material for print and radio. 99% of free-lance humorous illustration is for print ads. Prefers to work with freelancers with fax capabilities.
Humorous Illustration: For first contact send b&w promo piece and color promo piece to Bill Snituer, Associate CD. Returns materials if accompanied by a SASE. Negotiates rights purchased. Pays $150-8,000 by the project. Payment is based on com-plexity of project, turnaround and client's budget.
Humor Writing: For first contact send ½" or 3/4" demo tape and audio tape to Rick Colby, VP-CD or Judy Haruki, Producer. Does not return materials. Keeps materials on file. When establishing payment considers complexity of project, turnaround and client's budget.

LAVIN ASSOCIATES, 12 Promontory Drive, Cheshire CT 06410. (203)272-9121. Estab. 1947. Advertising agency that provides direct mail to industrial corporations. Needs humorous illustration, humor oriented comprehensives, humorous copywriting and car-toons. Uses humorous material for print and audiovisual. 10% of freelance humorous illustration is for print ads.

Humorous Illustration: Works with approximately 1 freelance humorous illustrator/ year. Looking for freelance humorous illustrator who is locally based. For first contact send cover letter and b&w tearsheets to Dr. Henry Lavin, Senior Associate. Reports back only if interested. Keeps materials on file. Buys reprint rights. Payment is negotiable. Payment is based on client's budget.

Humor Writing: Works with approximately 1 humor oriented writer/year. For first contact send cover letter and writing samples to Dr. Henry Lavin. Reports back only if interested. Keeps materials on file. Buys reprint rights. Payment is negotiated according to client's budget.

EDWARD LOZZI & ASSOCIATES, Suite 101, 9348 Civic Center Dr., Beverly Hills CA 90210. (818)995-8036. FAX: (818)783-8000. Estab. 1979. Communications, PR firm and news media consultants that provide video and electronic media specialties, medical and legal law suit promotions and publications for corporations, personalities, restaurants, authors, surgeons, medical centers, hospitals, motion pictures and TV productions. Current clients include Oxygenetics Inc., Dr. Christian Bernard, Tina Louise, Applause Magazine, Jon Voight, Estate of Rudy Vallee and George Barris Productions. Needs humorous illustration, animation and cartoons. Uses humorous material for print, video tape, TV and audiovisual. 24% of freelance humorous illustration is for print ads. Prefers to work with freelancers with fax capabilities.

Humorous Illustration: Works with approximately 1 freelance humorous illustrator/ month; 10-12/year. For first contact send cover letter and b&w tearsheets to Edward Lozzi, President. Reports back only if interested. Returns materials if accompanied by a SASE. Keeps materials on file. Negotiates rights purchased. Pays $50-100 by the hour, negotiates by the project. Payment is based on complexity of project, client's budget and possibility of a long term agency/illustrator relationship.

Humor Writing: Works with approximately 1 humor oriented writer/year. For first contact send cover letter and writing samples to Edward Lozzi. Reports back only if interested. Returns materials if accompanied by a SASE. Keeps materials on file. Negotiates rights purchased. Pays $50-100 by the hour according to complexity of project, client's budget and possibility of a long term agency/writer relationship.

T. J. LOWENHAUPT, INC., Box 1027 Jackson Heights, New York NY 11372. (718)639-4222. Estab. 1981. Advertising agency and communications company. "We design and develop materials for distribution on diskette: electronic brochures, catalogs and annual reports." The firm serves insurance companies, banks, online services and publishers. Current clients include Citicorp and NYNEX. Needs humorous illustration, animation and cartoons. Uses humorous material for online diskette. Prefers to work with freelancers with fax capabilities.

Humorous Illustration: Works with approximately 2 freelance humorous illustrators/ year. For first contact send b&w promo piece to M. Cohen, Creative Director. Reports back only if interested. Returns materials if accompanied by a SASE. Negotiates rights purchased. Pays by the project, with a $500 minimum. Payment is based on client's budget, complexity of project and skill of illustrator.

MANN BUKVIC ASSOCIATES, 405 W. 4th St., Cincinnati OH 45202. (513)241-4444. Advertising agency that provides TV, radio, print, collateral, annual reports, but mostly ads. Current clients include Cincinnati Zoo, Tri-County Mall, Hudephol-Schoenling and Ryland Homes. Needs humorous illustration and animation. Uses humorous material for print, possible TV, newspaper and collateral. 100% of freelance humorous illustration is for print ads. Prefers to work with freelancers with fax capabilities.

Humorous Illustration: Works with approximately 1 freelance humorous illustrator/ year. "Looking for freelance humorous illustrator who has printed pieces we can have for our files for reference." For first contact send b&w tearsheets, color tearsheets,

A Picture for Paramount: *When Mary Trainor, an Art Director for Los Angeles-based B.D. Fox & Friends Advertising needed "comic booky" art, she turned to Carol Lay. Lay, a successful comic book artist, was asked to draw the poster for the Paramount Pictures release "The Blue Iguana" and was instructed to load her drawing with "madcap action, South American ambiance and black humor." "I gave them two sketches," Lay recalls, "one was executed in an action-adventure style, and the other (which they ultimately used) was more cartoony and loaded with gags from the storyline." When it comes to marketing her work, Lay "has no strategy—it's mostly word of mouth."*

b&w promo piece and color promo piece to Teresa Newberry, Executive Art Director. Reports back within 3 days. Returns materials only if requested. Keeps materials on file. Negotiates rights purchased. Payment is based on complexity of project, business manner and professionalism of illustrator, ability of illustrator to work well under our art direction, client's budget and skill of illustrator. Tips: "I don't think we would use a humorous writer at this point. We have used humorous illustrators though—but not that often. Maybe once a year. That could increase though."

MCKEE ADVERTISING, 1375 Higgins Rd., Elk Grove Village IL 60007. (312)956-8188. FAX: (312)956-0181. Advertising agency, PR firm and promotional company that provides ads, collateral, sill sheets, PR and promotional material to business-to-business. Current clients include Graber, Wasco, Ace Hardware and Novi American. Needs humorous illustration, cartoons and storyboards. Uses humorous material for print and audiovisual. 90% of freelance humorous illustration is for print ads. Prefers to work with freelancers with fax capabilities.
Humorous Illustration: Works with approximately 5-10 freelance humorous illustrators/year. For first contact send cover letter, resume, b&w tearsheets, color tearsheets, b&w promo piece and color promo piece to Theresa Mronka, Sr. Art Director. Reports back only if interested or keeps on file. Returns materials only if requested and accompanied by a SASE. Buys all rights or negotiates rights purchased. Pays $20-100 by the hour or $20-500 by the project. Payment is based on complexity of project, turnaround, ability of illustrator to work well under our art direction, client's budget and possibility of a long term agency/illustrator relationship.

MCNALL & BLACKSTOCK ADVERTISING AND DESIGN, Suite 200, 739 East Walnut St., Pasadena CA 91101. (818)796-0495. FAX: (818)796-0428. Estab. 1978. Advertising agency that provides print, trade show exhibit, collateral and catalogs to financial, industrial, computer and food companies. Needs humorous illustration, humorous copywriting, caricature, cartoons, storyboards and slide shows. Uses humorous material for print, video tape and audiovisual. 50% of freelance humorous illustration is for print ads. Prefers to work with freelancers with fax capabilities.

Humorous Illustration: Works with approximately 1 freelance humorous illustrator/ month. For first contact send b&w tearsheets and b&w promo piece to John Blackstock, Creative Director. Does not return materials. Buys all rights. Pays $75-1,000 by the project. Payment is based on complexity of project, turnaround, business manner and professionalism of illustrator, ability of illustrator to work well under our art direction, client's budget, possibility of a long term agency/illustrator relationship, skill of illustrator and schedule of illustrator.

THE MARKET CONNECTIONS, 4020 Birch St. #203, Newport Beach CA 92660. (714)731-6273. FAX: (714)852-1819. Estab. 1986. PR firm that provides public relations/ marketing services, works with packaged goods manufacturers, professional services, retailers and business-to-business. Current clients include All American Gourmet Company, Home Delivery Services, Inc., Active Sales, Chef America, Advanced Business Software and Baxter Edwards. Needs humorous illustration, animation, caricature, cartoons and storyboards. Uses humorous material for print, video tape and radio. 5% of freelance humorous illustration is for print ads.
Humorous Illustration: Works with approximately 1-2 freelance humorous illustrators/month. For first contact send portfolio to Janie Roach, President. Reports back within 5 days. Does not return materials. Buys all rights. Pays $500-2500. Payment is based on complexity of project. Query for humor writing.

NEWMARK'S ADVERTISING AGENCY, INC., 253 West 26th St., New York NY 10001. (212)620-7600. FAX: (212)620-7605. Advertising agency that provides annual reports, collateral and print ads to banks, business-to-business, real estate and recruitment agencies. Current clients include Jack Parker Corp., Perforated Pattern Corp. and Kinney Shoes. Needs humorous illustration. Uses humorous material for print and audiovisual. 20% of freelance humorous illustration is for print ads.
Humorous Illustration: Works with approximately 1 freelance humorous illustrator/ year. Looking for freelance humorous illustrators who are talented and reliable. For first contact send b&w tearsheets or color tearsheets to Al Wasserman, Creative Director. Reports back only if interested. Keeps materials on file. Buys all rights. Pays $100-1,000 by the project. Payment is based on complexity of project and client's budget.
Humor Writing: Looking for freelance humorous writers who have written for radio or TV. For first contact send writing samples to Al Wasserman. Reports back only if interested. Keeps materials on file. Buys all rights. Pays $150-700 by the project according to complexity of project and client's budget.

PACE MARKETING COMMUNICATIONS, 1021 Village Walk, Guilford CT 06437. (203)453-9191. Estab. 1970. Advertising agency, PR firm, communications and marketing company that provides full-service, all media, all collateral, plus interior design, signage, etc. for development industries, corporations, banks, professionals, real estate agencies, residential and commercial developers, health care and education. Current clients include Empire State Land Co., The Forsthoffer Group, Weinstein & Anastasip CPA, The Wilton Bank and Cushman & Wakefield. Needs humorous illustration, animation, humor oriented comprehensives, humorous copywriting, cartoons and storyboards. Uses humorous material for print, TV, radio and collateral. 10% of freelance humorous illustration is for print ads, "but we have done more in the past." Prefers to work with freelancers with fax capabilities.
Humorous Illustration: Works with approximately 3-5 freelance humorous illustrators/year. Work must be "readable" and visually distinctive and related to upscale markets. For first contact send client list, one b&w tearsheet, one color tearsheet, slides or a printed reproduction of several pieces to Richard Fortunato, Art Director. "Reports back within 2-10 days on specific jobs we have assigned." Returns materials. Buys first time rights, all rights or negotiates rights purchased. Pays $20-100 by the hour or $100-

1,500 by the project. Payment is based on complexity of project, turnaround, ability of illustrator to work well under our art direction, client's budget, skill of illustrator, usage and quality issues.

Humor Writing: All previous work done internally. Looking for freelance humorous writers "when we don't have internal capability." For first contact send client list, writing samples, audio tape and demo tape to Patricia Greco, Senior Copywriter. "Reports back within 2-10 days on specific jobs we have assigned." Returns materials. Buys all rights or negotiates rights purchased. Pays $10-100 by the hour, $50-500 by the day, $100-1,000 by the project. When establishing payment considers complexity of project, skill of writer, turnaround, ability of writer to work well under our creative team, client's budget, usage and quality issues.

PEARTREE ADVERTISING, 231 E. 51st, New York City NY 10022. (212)751-2588. FAX: (212)753-8896. Estab. 1979. Advertising agency that provides print ads, brochures, fashion and fabric specialties to manufacturers. Current clients include Ideas, Botany and Superba. Needs humorous illustration and humorous copywriting. Uses humorous material for print. 10% of freelance humorous illustration is for print ads. Prefers to work with freelancers with fax capabilities.

Humorous Illustration: Works with approximately 2 freelance humorous illustrators/ year. Looking for freelance humorous illustrators who are easy to work with. For first contact send b&w promo piece to Joyce Silverman, Creative Director. Does not return materials. Negotiates rights purchased. Payment is based on complexity of project, client's budget and usage.

Humor Writing: Works with approximately 2 humor oriented writers/year. Looking for freelance humorous writers who have an excellent book, resume, does revisions and listens. For first contact send client list, tearsheets and writing samples to Joyce Silverman. Does not return materials. Negotiates rights purchased. When establishing payment considers complexity of project, client's budget and usage.

PIERSON & FLYNN, 405 N. Wabash, Chicago IL 60611. (312)644-6090. FAX: (312)644-3521. Estab. 1982. Advertising agency that provides TV and print ads to corporations, department stores and restaurants. Current clients include Ace Hardware, Salad Singles and Western Salad Dressing. Uses humorous illustration, animation, humor oriented comprehensives, humorous copywriting and storyboards for print, TV and radio. 30% of freelance humorous illustration is for print ads. Prefers to work with freelancers with fax capabilities.

Humor Writing: Send all writing materials to Art Pierson, Creative Director. Returns materials only if interested. Buys all rights or negotiates rights purchased. Pay varies. When establishing payment considers complexity of project, skill of writer, turnaround, ability of writer to work well under our creative team, business manner and professionalism of writer, client's budget and usage.

PIHAS, SCHMIDT, WESTERDAHL, 319 SW Washington, Portland OR 97204. (503)279-4076. FAX: (503)279-4066. Estab. 1972. Advertising agency that provides services to corporations, power companies, hotels, resorts and banks. Current clients include Pacific Power & Light, U.S. Bank and Plaid Pantry Convenience Stores. Prefers to work with freelancers with fax capabilities. For first contact send cover letter, resume, b&w promo piece and color promo piece to Rachael Golden, Creative Assistant. Reports back only if interested. Returns materials only if requested. Keeps materials on file. Negotiates rights purchased. Payment is based on turnaround, client's budget and skill of illustrator.

Humor Writing: For first contact send cover letter, resume, writing samples, audio tape and ½" demo tape to Rachael Golden. Reports back only if interested. Keeps materials on file. Negotiates rights purchased. When establishing payment considers complexity of project, skill of writer and client's budget.

PHILLIP ROSLER ASSOCIATES, INC., P.O. Box 2565, North Babylon NY 11703. (516)321-6273. Estab. 1981. Advertising agency and PR firm that provides full service. Needs cartoons and storyboards. Uses humorous material for print. 85% of freelance humorous illustration is for print ads.

RZA ADVERTISING/PR, 122 Mill Pond Rd., Park Ridge NJ 07656. (201)391-8500. FAX: (201)391-2679. Estab. 1970. Advertising agency and PR firm that provides all-around service. Current clients include Delta Dental, Empire Transports, Car Accounts and Titan Tool. Needs humorous illustration, animation, humor oriented comprehensives, humorous copywriting, caricature, animatics, cartoons and storyboards. Uses humorous material for print, video tape, TV and radio. 90% of freelance humorous illustration is for print ads. Prefers to work with freelancers with fax capabilities.
Humorous Illustration: Works with approximately 4 freelance humorous illustrators/month; 50/year. For first contact send color promo piece, slides and portfolio to Charlene Laver, Art Director. Keeps materials on file. Buys reprint rights or all rights. Payment is based on complexity of project, turnaround, client's budget, possibility of a long term agency/illustrator relationship, skill of illustrator and usage.

SCHENKIEN INC., Suite 1400, 1125 17th, Denver CO 80202. (313)292-6655. FAX: (313)292-3569. Estab. 1975. Advertising agency that provides full service to corporations, banks, department stores, restaurants and resorts. Current clients include Vail Valley, Partek and Contel. Needs humorous illustration, humor oriented comprehensives, humorous copywriting, animatics, cartoons and storyboards. Uses humorous material for print, TV and radio. 40% of freelance humorous illustration is for print ads. Prefers to work with freelancers with fax capabilities.
Humorous Illustration: For first contact send cover letter and b&w tearsheets to Creative Director. Returns materials only if requested and accompanied by a SASE. Negotiates rights purchased. Pays $50-1,000 by the project. Payment is based on ability of illustrator to work well under our art direction, client's budget, possibility of a long term agency/illustrator relationship and skill of illustrator.
Humor Writing: Works with approximately 2 humor oriented writers/month. For first contact send cover letter, writing samples and demo tape to Creative Director. Returns materials only if interested and accompanied by a SASE. Negotiates rights purchased. Pays $50-1,000 by the project. When establishing payment considers skill of writer, ability of writer to work well under our creative team, client's budget and possibility of a long term agency/writer relationship.

SHARK COMMUNICATIONS, 182 Battery St., Burlington VT 05401. (802)658-5440. FAX: (802)658-0113. Estab. 1986. Advertising agency that provides annual reports, collateral and print ads to corporations, banks and restaurants. Current clients include Mount Snow/Killington Ski Resorts and the University of Vermont. Needs humorous illustration and humorous copywriting. Uses humorous material for print, video tape, TV and radio. 80% of freelance humorous illustration is for print ads.
Humorous Illustration: Works with approximately 10 freelance humorous illustrators/year. For first contact send cover letter and b&w promo piece to Peter Jacobs, Creative Director. Reports back only if interested. Returns materials if accompanied by a SASE. Keeps materials on file. Negotiates rights purchased.
Humor Writing: For first contact send cover letter and writing samples to Peter Jacobs.

SPENCER VISUALS, 134 Kings Hwy. E, Haddonfield NJ 08033. (609)354-6222. FAX: (609)354-6223. Advertising agency that provides advertising, marketing, graphic design and full service to business-to-business, consumer products, health care, retail and high technology companies. Current clients include Hella, Inc., USA-Video, Laser Track, Met Life and Ingram & Picker. Needs humorous illustration, humorous copywriting, caricature and cartoons. Uses humorous material for print. 70% of freelance humorous illustration is for print ads. Prefers to work with freelancers with fax capabilities.

TNT MARKETING, 3030 Roanoke, Kansas City MO 64108. (816)561-7785. Estab. 1986. Promotional marketing for packaging, premiums and promotional programs. Current clients include Wendy's, Burger King and McDonalds. Needs animation and cartoons. Uses humorous material for presentation and product. 5% of freelance humorous illustration is for print ads. Prefers to work with freelancers with fax capabilities.
Humorous Illustration: For first contact send cover letter, color tearsheets and color promo piece to Tony Hoffman, President. Reports back only if interested. Returns materials only if requested. Keeps materials on file. Buys new designs only. Pays $25 minimum by the hour and $1,000 minimum by the project. Payment is based on complexity of project, ability of illustrator to work well under our art direction and ability of illustration/designer.
Humor Writing: Works with approximately 2 humor oriented writers/month. Looking for freelance humorous writers who can write for the children's market, age 3-12. For first contact send cover letter and writing samples to Tony Hoffman. Reports back only if interested. Keeps materials on file. Pays $25 minimum by the hour and $200 minimum by the project. When establishing payment considers complexity of project, ability of writer to work well under our creative team and ability of writer.

TRACY-LOCKE, P.O. Box 50129, Dallas TX 75250. (214)969-9000. FAX: (214)855-2480. Estab. 1914. Advertising agency that provides full service. Serving soft drink companies, banks, oil and gas, department stores and snack foods clients. Current clients include Pepsi, Phillips Petroleum, Ben Hogan Co., Borden, Dillards, Frito-Lay and Texas Commerce Bank. Needs humorous illustration, animation, animatics and storyboards. Uses humorous material for print. 99% of freelance humorous illustration is for print ads. Prefers to work with freelancers who have fax capabilities.
Humorous Illustration: Works with approximately 3 freelancer humorous illustrators/month; 50 jobs/year. For first contact send cover letter, b&w tearsheets, color tearsheets or b&w promo piece or color promo piece to Jennifer Fountain, Art Buyer. Reports back only if interested ("or if I have a job for them"). Returns materials only if requested; keeps materials. Negotiates rights purchased. Pay "absolutely depends on the job." Payment is based on complexity of project, turnaround, client's budget, skill of illustrator and usage.

WILSON & WILSON ADVERTISING AND PUBLIC RELATIONS, INC., Suite 109, 3880 S. Bascom Ave., San Jose CA 95124. (408)371-8331. FAX: 377-5273. Estab. 1985. Advertising agency that provides services for business to business, trade publication ads, collateral and printed materials. Current clients include Mini Micro Supply Co., Inc., Ellenburg Capital Corporation, Anthem Electronics, Casey-Johnson Sales Inc. Needs humorous illustration, humorous copywriting, slide shows. Uses humorous material for print, radio, audiovisual. 60% of freelance humorous illustration work is for print ads. Prefers to work with freelancers who have fax capabilities.
Humorous Illustration: Works with approximately 2-3 freelance humorous illustrators/year. Looking for freelance humorous illustrators who are familiar with Macintosh systems. For first contact send cover letter, b&w tearsheets, b&w promo piece, color promo piece to Erica Wilson, Art Director. Reports back. Returns materials only if requested and if accompanied by a SASE; otherwise keeps materials. Buys all rights or

negotiates rights purchased. Pays by the hour $35-120; by the project $100-350. Payment is based on complexity of project, turnaround, business manner and professionalism of illustrator, ability of illuustrator to work well under our art direction, client's budget, possibility of a long term agency/illustrator relationship and skill of illustrator.

Humor Writing: Works with approximately 4-5 humor oriented writers/year. Looking for freelance humorous writers who have Macintosh/modem capability. For first contact send cover letter, writing samples, audio tape, resume, client list, tearsheets to Rick Wilson, Creative Director. Reports back or returns material only if interested. Keeps materials on file. Buys all rights or negotiates rights purchased. Pays by the hour: $35-100; by the project: $100 or according to complexity of project, ability of writer to work well under our creative team, manner and professionalism of writer, client's budget, possibility of a long term agency/writer relationship, skill of writer and turnaround.

WINFIELD ADVERTISING AGENCY, 120 S. Central, St. Louis MO 63017. (315)863-4524. Advertising agency that serves industrial and retail business and banks. Needs humorous illustration and cartoons for print and TV. 90% of humorous illustration work is for print ads.

Humorous Illustration: Works with 2-3 freelance humorous illustrators per year. "We are more apt to hire a freelance humorous illustrator is he is flexible, versatile; and can also write copy to go along with illustration/cartoon." For first contact, freelancer should send b&w and color tearsheets, b&w and color promo pieces or whatever seems appropriate to Greg Holtzman, VP Creative. Reports back only if interested. Returns materials if accompanied by a SASE. Keeps materials on file. Negotiates rights purchased. Payment is based on complexity of project, skill of illustrator, turnaround, business manner and professionalism of illustrator, ability of illustrator to work well under art direction, client's budget and possibility of future agency/illustrator relationship.

Humor Writing: Works with 1 humor oriented writer per year. For first contact freelancer should send resume and writing samples to Gary Holt, VP Account Service. Reports back only if interested. Keeps materials on file. Negotiates rights purchased. Considers complexity of project, skill of writer, turnaround, ability of writer to work well under our creative team, business manner and professionalism of writer and client's budget when establishing payment.

KATHY WYATT & ASSOCIATES, 14 Smull Avenue, Caldwell NJ 07006. (201)226-3376. FAX: (201)226-6986. Estab. 1975. Advertising agency that provides small technical and industrial support to high tech and scientific clients. Current clients include Instruments SA and Rudolph Research. Needs humorous illustration, humorous copywriting and cartoons. Uses humorous material for print. 100% of freelance humorous illustration is for print ads.

Humorous Illustration: Works with approximately 2 freelance humorous illustrators/year. "Looking for freelance humorous illustrators who have the style we are looking for." For first contact send cover letter and b&w tearsheets to Kathy Wyatt, President. Reports back only if interested. Returns materials only if requested. Negotiates rights purchased. Pays $25-100 by the hour. Payment is based on ability of illustrator to work well under our art direction and usage.

Humor Writing: Works with approximately 2 humor oriented writers/year. For first contact send cover letter and writing samples to Kathy Wyatt. Reports back only if interested. Returns materials only if interested. Negotiates rights purchased. Pays $15-100 by the hour according to ability of writer to work well under our creative team, client's budget and usage.

When it comes to animation, patience is not only a virtue, it's a necessity.

Next time you watch an animated commercial on television, think about this: Every one second of filmed animation requires approximately 12 drawings. That's 360 drawings for a 30 second spot, 720 for a one minute tag and, as long as we have the calculator out, 64,800 doodles for a standard hour and a half feature.

Animation has gone through a renaissance of sorts. Thanks in part to a bunny with a speech impediment (yes, the rabbit in question is Roger), the public has a renewed interest in the art form. And animation film festivals, once the cultural diet of college students, art snobs and punks, are being attended by broader theater audiences than ever before.

Computer animation has also heightened this appreciation. We're *inundated* with the stuff—and most of us don't even know it. In an average night of television, it's almost impossible to distinguish the live action from the computer generated imagery, and clients pay spectacular sums for these spectacular graphics.

While animation options for the humor writer are somewhat limited (most scripts are handled by a client's advertising agency), there are terrific opportunities for the humorous illustrator and independent animator.

One example

Olive Jar is a small, Boston-based animation studio. They produce a wide variety of animation primarily for television commercials. From cel to clay, stop motion to cut outs—Olive Jar steers clear of the computer, preferring instead to produce animation by more traditional means.

"I'm always looking for new, wild styles of animation," says Bill Jarcho, Olive Jar's Creative Director. "I look for animation ability, but more importantly,

I'm looking for *versatility*. That's very important in this business."

While a resume tells an animation studio about your history, most are more interested in your demo tape (either ½″ or ¾″). "A resume is fine," says Jarcho, "but we want to see what really matters—your *animation*! I don't care if your stuff is wild or inventive, funny or bizarre—it can be as graphically strange as possible—as long as it's *good*."

Happily, there is a growing trend among animation studios to employ outside humorous illustrators to design characters and to give a new twist or look to various animation projects. "Any illustration style is applicable to animation," says Jarcho, "and humorous illustration sells—particularly in this country."

However, Jarcho is quick to mention one drawback of working with freelancers. "There are a lot of freelancers who have terrific talent," he says, "but they also have a tendency not to be able to work too well with other people—as a part of the collaborative effort. Most of them are used to working alone, so when you put them into a different environment, they can have problems. It would be wonderful if some of these freelancers were a bit more *professional*—and that doesn't mean putting on a coat and a tie."

Payment

Every animation studio approaches payment differently, and most projects are handled on a case by case basis. A freelance animator can be paid an hourly wage or can be assigned a budget for the delivery of the entire project. In the latter case, the studio may advance the animator half of the contracted fee and half upon completion of the project, or a third of the fee advanced, a third midstream, a third upon completion.

In any case, it is highly recommended that the freelance animator negotiate and hammer out a written contract with the studio. It doesn't happen often, but projects *have* been completed by a freelance animator where upon the studio has had no money left to pay his salary.

The freelancer will also want to determine if he will be allowed to use work created for an animation studio or client in his own demo tape or self-promotions. Often this is a stipulation overlooked not only by the freelance animator, but by the animation studio and even the client as well.

For those with gypsy blood, freelance animation opportunities exist at studios around the country. But Jarcho cautions the freelancer to understand the nature of the business. "This is a *commercial* studio," he says. "We all love and respect animation independently produced, but a studio creates animation for a *client*. For the freelance animator to work with us, he has to keep his ego at home."

ACME ANIMATION & DESIGN, 342 Newbury St., Boston MA 02115. (617)267-5200. FAX: (617)437-9582. Estab. 1988. Animation studio that provides traditional cel and cutting-edge computer animation for ad agencies and corporations. Some top clients are McDonald's, Digital, PBS, NFPA (National Fire Protection Association), Hills and Apollo Computers. Produces cel animation, special effects and computer animation. Uses freelancers for cel animation.
Humorous Illustration: 10% of work is done by freelance illustrators. For first contact send cover letter, resume and tearsheets to Bob Palmer, President. Materials are filed. Reports back only if interested. Negotiates rights purchased. Payment depends on the

density of the animation artwork. Tips: "Our clients seem to be wanting animation that is more character oriented. Even if the character is on the screen for only ten seconds, his/her design and motion should indicate that this character has a life history. Clients like instant 'Tony the Tigers.' "

AMBIVISION, INC., One Kinderkamack Rd., Oradell NJ 07649. (201)262-2624. FAX: (201)599-2922. Estab. 1985. Video programming. "Content must be on the conservative side to serve a general audience, but the technology can be avante garde, cutting edge, etc. We serve medical market waiting areas." Uses freelancers for animation, storyboarding and live action.
Humorous Illustration: For first contact send demo tape (VHS on ¾") to Susan Samuels, Vice President Program Acquisitions. Materials are filed. Returned if accompanied by a SASE. Reports back within 2 weeks. Buys reprint rights. Pays $2,100 minimum per project for animation and specialized animation work.

ANIMART FX., 812 S. Weber St., Colorado Springs CO 80903. (719)630-7818. FAX: (719)473-2478. Estab. 1981. "We do cel and computer animation film and video, full inhouse design, scripts, storyboards and promotion. We specialize in cel animation and special effects." Clients are advertising agencies, PR firms and corporations, including State of Colorado, Hanna-Barbera, Warner Bros., Disney and Filmotion. Produces cel animation, clay animation, stop motion, 3-D, special effects, computer animation, video graphics and live action. Uses freelancers for assistant animators.
Humorous Illustration: 20% of work is done by freelance illustrators. Also subcontracts. "I mention this only because our future needs may expand well beyond our now minimal freelance requirements." For first contact send resume. "We'll ask if more is needed." Send to Bob or Linn Trochim, Producers/Directors. Materials are filed, returned if accompanied by a SASE. Reports back only if interested. Negotiates rights purchased. Pay is all negotiable by contract. Tips: "If you're a qualified animator—go to L.A. or New York for money. Otherwise it doesn't matter. It's a tough business."
Humor Writing: "May need freelancers to help us with humor writing in the future." For first contact send resume to Bob or Linn Trochim, Producers. Materials are returned only if requested. Reports back only if interested. Negotiates rights purchased. Pay is negotiable by contract.

ANIMATION COTTAGE, 4789 Vineland, #204, N. Hollywood CA 91602. (818)763-0077. Estab. 1970. Animation studio that provides artistic rendering of traditional movement as well as avant garde animation. A top client is ABC Network. Produces cel animation, special effects, video graphics and animation directly on cel with grease pencil. Uses freelancers for full animation, storyboarding, character development and layout. Prefers to work with freelancers who have fax capabilities.
Humorous Illustration: Submission materials are filed and not returned. Pays $500-4,000 by the project and $12-50 by the foot for animation. Tips: "Know your craft and don't try to bluff—it doesn't pay!"
Humor Writing: 100% of work is done by freelance writers for series and specials. For first contact send cover letter, resume, writing samples and client list to Marija Miletic Dail, President. Materials are filed; returned if requested. Buys all rights or negotiates rights purchased. Pays $1,000-5,000 by the project. Tips: "We have a real need for animation writers who write visually rather than verbally."

ANIVISION, 981 Walnut St., Pittsburgh PA 15234. (412)563-2221. Animation studio. Produces cel and clay animation and stop motion. "If large project, we use in-betweeners and styling people" for animation, character development and pencil testing.

Humorous Illustration: 10% of work is done by freelance illustrators, mostly for ink and paint work. Send to Rick Catizone, Director.
Humor Writing: 10% of work is done by freelance writers. Needs freelance writers for large projects and input on script writing. Send to Rick Catizone.

ANNI-MATION VIDEO SPECIAL EFFECTS, 179 John St., 8th Fl., Toronto M5T 1X4 Canada. Computer animation for TV commercials. Produces special effects, computer animation and video graphics. Uses freelancers for character animation and storyboarding.
Humorous Illustration: 10% of work is done by freelance illustrators. Send to: Bob Allward, Producer.

AVAILABLE LIGHT LTD., 3110 W. Burbank Blvd., Burbank CA 91505. (818)842-2109. Estab. 1983. Animation studio with cutting edge style working in motion picture, special effect animation and live action. Some top clients are ILM, Paramount and Disney. Produces 3-D, motion control and special effects. Uses freelancers for special effect animation.
Humorous Illustration: 70% of work is done by freelance illustrators. Also subcontracts. For first contact send VHS demo tape to J. Van Vliet. Materials are returned if accompanied by a SASE. Reports back only if interested. Pays $16 hour minimum for special effects animation. Tips: "Hang in there!"

BALL & CHAIN ANIMATION, 164 Fairfield Ave., Stamford CT 06902. (203)324-0018. Animation studio and production house. Produces cel animation, some stop motion, 3-D, special effects, computer animation, motion control and live action. Uses freelancers for model building, camera operatics, cel animation, storyboarding, character development, live action, comprehensives and pencil testing.
Humorous Illustration: Approximately 50% of work is done by freelance illustrators. For first contact please send all animation submissions to: Chuck Jepsen, Executive Producer.
Humor Writing: 90% of work is done by freelance writers. Needs freelance writers for scripts for TV programs. For first contact send all writing submissions to: Chuck Jepsen.

BIGMAN PICTURES CORP., 133 W. 19th St., New York NY 10011. (212)242-1411. Estab. 1983. Animation and special effects production house that provides avant garde, traditional and cutting-edge style to advertising agencies, PR firms and corporations. Produces cel animation, clay animation, stop motion, special effects, motion control, live action and time lapse. Uses freelancers for cel and montage animation, storyboarding, character development, live action, pencil testing, inbetweening, ink and paint.
Humor Writing: 25% of work is done by freelance writers. Needs freelance writers for promotional material, commercial spots, speculative projects. For first contact send cover letter, resume and demo tape (VHS on ¾") to John Donnelly, President. Materials are filed and returned if requested. Negotiates rights purchased. Pays $200-5,000 by the project.

BROADCAST ARTS, 632 Broadway, New York NY 10012. (212)254-5400. FAX (212)529-5506. Special effects production house. Produces cel animation, clay animation, stop motion, 3-D, special effects, video graphics, motion control and live action. Uses freelancers for cel animation, storyboarding, character development, live action and pencil testing. "We have our own directors but like to work with new directors."

Humorous Illustration: Approximately 80-90% of work is done by freelance illustrators. Please send all animation submissions to: Adele Solomon, Talent Cordinator.
Humor Writing: 100% of work is done by freelance writers. "We deal mostly with an agency." Needs freelance writers for commercial spots, developing ideas for corporate ID's, writing for shows, original programing. Please send all writing submissions to Adele Solomon.
Tips: "We are also interested in working with interns (young minds) and people who are interested in sales and marketing, art, etc."

BUZZCO ASSOCIATES INC., 110 W. 40th St., New York NY 10010. (212)840-0411. Animation studio and production house. Produces cel animation, stop motion and live action. Uses freelancers for character development, live action and comprehensives.
Humorous Illustration: Approximately 10% percent of work is done by freelance illustrators. Please send all animation submissions to Candy Kugel, Director/Producer.
Humor Writing: Approximately 10% of work is done by freelance writers.

CELLULOID STUDIOS INC., 1422 Delgany St., Denver CO 80202. (303)595-3153. FAX: (303)595-4908. Produces animatic and live action TV commercials. Produces cel animation, stop motion, special effects, motion control, live action. Uses freelancers for cel animation, animation storyboarding, character development and live action.
Humorous Illustration: Approximately 25% of work is done by freelance illustrators. Please send all animation submissions to Nancy Maginn, Production Manager.

COLOSSAL PICTURES, 2800 3rd St., San Francisco CA 94107. (415)550-8772. FAX: (415)824-0389. Film and design production house. Produces cel animation, clay animation, stop motion, 3-D, special effects, computer animation, motion control, live action. "We use freelancers for everything from live action to animation production."
Humorous Illustration: Approximately 3% of work is done by freelance illustrators. Send all animation submissions to Jeff Kahan, Manager of Animation Production.

DANLEYQUEST, P.O. Box 53900, Indianapolis IN 46253. (317)453-4895. Estab. 1988. Production house and animation studio. "Our style is traditional." Produces cel animation and special effects. Use freelancers for animation, storyboarding and character development.
Humorous Illustration: 50% of work is done by freelance illustrators. Also subcontracts. For first contact send storyboard samples, sample drawing or writing to Michael Danley, President. Materials are filed; returned only if requested. Reports back within 2 weeks. Buys all rights. Pays for storyboarding/comp work, $13.50-37.50 an hour. For animation work, $13.50-37.50 an hour.
Humor Writing: 50% of work is done by freelance writers. Needs freelancers for storyboarding. For first contact send writing samples to Michael Danley. Materials are filed; returned only if requested. Reports back within 2 weeks. Buys all rights. Pays $13.50-37.50 an hour. Tips: "When it comes to freelance writing, we have a real need for scripts."

DUCK SOUP, 1026 Montana Ave., Santa Monica CA 90403. (213)451-0771. Produces TV commercial animatics. Produces cel animation. Uses freelancers for animation — Fruit Loop commercial as example. Some commercials seen on Saturday morning TV.
Humorous Illustration: Moderate amount of work is done by freelance illustrators. Please send all animation submissions to Mark Medernech, Producer.

J. DYER, INC., Suite 900, 3340 Peachtree Rd., Atlanta GA 30326. (404)266-8022. Estab. 1984. Animation studio that provides multi-design, traditional and mixed media cel animation, computer motion control, 3-D models and video compositing of film elements for advertising agencies, live action production companies, and sometimes corporate or retail clients. Some top clients are McDonald's, Ford, Hardee's, Brach's Candy Company, CNN, WTBS, regional banks, hospitals, local card dealers and Delta Airlines. Produces cel animation, 3-D Logo treatments, special effects, motion control, live action, rotoscope and mixed media film graphics composited on tape. Uses freelancers for animation key and in-between drawing, storyboarding, character development, live action, pencil testing, stat camera operations, inkings, paintings, camera operators, matte prep, rotoscope art and model construction. "Prefer to work with freelancers who are willing to work in my studio."

Humorous Illustration: 20% of work is done by freelance illustrators, mostly background art for animation. For first contact send demo tape on ¾″ to Illene Dyer, Studio Manager. "Normally, freelance animators don't have substantial demo reels or many copies. They usually make an appointment and come and show us a portfolio of art that may or may not relate to animation." Materials are filed and returned only if requested. Reports back only if interested. "If the work shows merit, we'll put you on the list and call as jobs come up." Buys all rights. "All part time labor is paid a flat hour wage and waves ownership of art under 'Georgia Work for Hire' laws." Pays $12-20 by the hour for storyboarding; painters start at $6.50/hour; $12/hour for in-between, stat camera, paste up, rotoscope, matte cutting, key animation; $12/hour for specialized animation. Tips: "Our clients seem to be wanting more animation that shows them the style, technique, character's etc. on a demo reel that relates to the immediate project they are thinking about. This gives them a secure feeling that they're not having to create anything that seems risky or original. They're all scared. We just try to keep a diverse, contemporary reel that we constantly update. It's an ever-changing animation menu. Be flexible."

Humor Writing: Very little work is done by freelance writers. Usually the agency supplies copy. Needs freelance writers for commercial spots. There are cases, however, when agencies are extremely weak in the copy writing department and they ask for our help. For first contact send demo tape ¾″, but call first. Materials are returned only if requested. Reports back only if interested. Buys all rights "work for hire." Negotiates fees. Tips: "When it comes to freelance writing, we have a real need for humor and someone who can write copy for animation action."

FLYING FOTO FACTORY INC., P.O. Box 1166, 107 Church St., Durham NC 27702. (919)682-3411. Animation studio and production house. Produces cel animation, stop motion, special effects and motion control. Uses freelancers for animation (traditional character animation).

Humorous Illustration: Percentage of work done by freelance illustrators depends on project at hand. Please send all animation submissions to Casey Herbert, Owner/President.

GALLERY IN MOTION, 2928 Wisconsin, St. Louis MO 63118. (314)772-0820. FAX: (314)776-6505. Estab. 1989. Animation gallery. "We offer all forms of animation art, including production cels, pre-production drawings, model sheets, storyboards and backgrounds. We also will search for particular characters and scenes. Clients are collectors of animation-oriented art. Offers cel animation. "We would be interested in seeing the artwork of new animators."

HANNA-BARBERA PRODUCTIONS, 3400 Cauhuenga Blvd. W., Hollywood CA 90068. (213)851-5000. FAX (213)969-1200. Animation studio. Produces cel animation, 3-D (in the future), computer animation and live action. Uses freelancers for animation, storyboarding, character development, live action, comprehensives and pencil testing.

Close-up

Bill Plympton
Animator

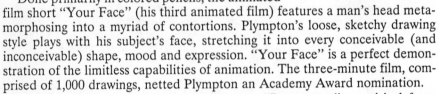

People were laughing out loud at Bill Plympton's cartoons.

After years of drawing comic book characters, editorial cartoons and humorous illustrations for appreciative but silent readers, Plympton had finally arrived at his childhood dream — animation.

Done primarily in colored pencils, the animated film short "Your Face" (his third animated film) features a man's head metamorphosing into a myriad of contortions. Plympton's loose, sketchy drawing style plays with his subject's face, stretching it into every conceivable (and inconceivable) shape, mood and expression. "Your Face" is a perfect demonstration of the limitless capabilities of animation. The three-minute film, comprised of 1,000 drawings, netted Plympton an Academy Award nomination.

Plympton's first major animated film was "Boomtown," a satirical farce about the absurdity of the arms race, developed from a radio script by Jules Feiffer. Completed in 1985 as a nonprofit venture, "Boomtown" was a critical, if not financial, success. The 1,000 drawings required for the film took six months to render.

"Drawing Lesson Number Two," his second animated short, was completed in 1987 and "Your Face" followed shortly after.

Encouraged by his increasing success after only three animation projects, Plympton decided to look into some of the cartoon book projects he had tried to sell earlier. He translated them into animated films and many were well received by international film festivals and various distributors, garnering Plympton a number of awards and financial gain. Among these successful book-to-film conversions were: "How to Kiss" (1988), "One of Those Days" (1988) and "25 Ways to Quit Smoking" (1989).

Unlike most cartoonists, his major childhood influence was not *MAD* magazine, but rather the animation of Walt Disney, Warner Brothers and Tex Avery.

He dabbled a bit in animation in college at Portland (Oregon) State University, but lack of technical knowledge and lack of money led him nowhere. He also did not feel there was much of a market at that time for animation.

But that has all changed, says Plympton, who now lives in New York City. One big reason is the recent success of the feature film "Who Framed Roger Rabbit?" " 'Roger Rabbit' helped make animation a viable, mainstream vehicle," says Plympton.

Plympton's current project is his own first animated feature film. "Smasheroo" will be a bizarre, surrealistic comedy to run approximately 70 minutes, requiring some 500,000 drawings. "In animation," Plympton points out, "you really appreciate how long a second is—about 6 or 7 drawings."

To aspiring animators, Plympton offers the following advice: "Go to a good art school (Cal Arts in Los Angeles, for one, which is funded by Disney). Or start at an animation house. Hanna-Barbera is one of the big studios in Los Angeles, and New York has several smaller ones. Consider the commercial studios too. Most of them also produce music videos.

"Or do like I did—do your own films and send them to film festivals where all the distributors can see them. They may buy yours!"

Plympton learned a painful lesson regarding film rights at the beginning of his animation career when he signed away rights to "Your Face." "Be wary of signing a contract too soon," he cautions. "Don't get rushed into anything and try not to sign away exclusive rights."

The biggest obstacle to sustaining a career in animation, says Plympton, is money. "To be an animator, one must be very resourceful." Plympton suggests methods to sustain oneself along the way: "Sell your original drawings; seek out film festivals with cash awards; and try to arrange paid lectures and tours showing your films."

Plympton uses money from past projects to finance new ones. His income is primarily from foreign markets, theatrical, nontheatrical and television distributors and film festivals.

For Bill Plympton, the real satisfaction of animation isn't in the money, the awards or peer approval. "It's seeing it with an audience. When you're there and you know these people are enjoying your work, it's the biggest thrill there is. It's a total high."

—Paulette Fehlig

"25 Ways to Quit Smoking"   ©1989 BILL PLYMPTON

Humorous Illustration: Please send all animation submissions to David Kirschner, President (CEO).

Humor Writing: Need freelancers mostly for storyboarding. Please send all writing submissions to Paul Sabella, Director of Creative Projects. Tips: "We are going through some changes. A new company, Bed Rock Productions, will handle live action projects."

THE INK TANK, 2 W. 47th St., New York NY 10036. (212)869-1630. FAX: (212)764-4169. Animation and graphic design studio. Produces cel animation, stop motion, special effects, computer animation and live action. Uses freelancers for ink and paint artists (fills in colors) and opaquers, animation, storyboarding, live action and pencil testing.

Humorous Illustration: Approximately 50% of work is done by freelance illustrators. Please send all animation submissions to J.J. Sedelmaier, Executive Producer.

KCMP PRODUCTIONS, INC., 9 E. 37th St., New York NY 10016. (212)679-8400. FAX: 679-1091. Estab. 1981. Animation studio and production house. "We do traditional cel animation and specialize in Roro scope, live and animated." Clients are advertising agencies. Some top clients are McCann-Erickson and Grey. Produces cel animation, special effects and live action. Uses freelancers for animation (animators, storyboarding, character development and live action.) Prefers to work with freelancers who have fax capabilities.

Humorous Illustration: 35% of work is done by freelance illustrators. "We also use freelance animators, assistant animators, designers, layout people, etc." For first contact send resume to Phil Kimhelman, Director of Animation. Materials are filed; returned only if requested. Pays per job as *budgeted*. Tips: "Our clients seem to be wanting more animation that is *Roger Rabbit* styled, although their budgets do not permit it. We are using more shadows and creative lighting, with more dimension."

KOLIBA FILM STUDIOS—BRATISLAVA CZECHOSLOVAKIA, %IFEX, 201 W. 52 St., New York NY 10019. (212)582-4318. FAX: (212)956-2257. Estab. 1953. Animation studio and production house. Clients are film producers, advertising agencies and television stations. Some top clients are Beta Films—Munich, International Film Exchange Ltd—New York, Today Home Entertainment—Los Angeles. Produces cel animation, claymation, stop motion, special effects and live action. Uses freelancers for character development and live action.

Humorous Illustration: Approximately 5% of work is done by freelance illustrators. Subcontracts animators to help with overflow. For first contact send cover letter, resume and demo tape (on VHS on ¾") to Gerald Rappoport. Materials are returned only if requested. Reports back within 2 months. Buys first time rights, all rights or negotiates rights purchased.

Humor Writing: Approximately 25% of work is done by freelance writers. Needs freelance writers for storyboarding for animated cartoon subjects. For first contact send cover letter, writing samples and ideas to Gerald Rappoport. Materials are returned. Reports back within 2 months. Buys first time rights, all rights or negotiates rights purchased. Tips: "When it comes to freelance writing, we have a real need for good stories for 1 minute to 10 minute subjects animation."

KROYER FILMS, 1612 W. Olive, Burbank CA 91506. (818)842-9948. FAX: (818)842-6362. Estab. 1985. Animation Studio. "We use many cartoon styles from Tex Avery to Disney. We do have a computer system for 3-D effects." Clients are agencies, big film studios and corporations. Some top clients are Warner Bros., Epcot, Disney Studio and Leo Burnett Advertising. Produces cel animation, 3-D, special effects, computer animation and live action. Uses freelancers for animation (all types), storyboarding and character development. Prefers to work with freelancers who have fax capabilities.

Humorous Illustration: 40% of work is done by freelance illustrators. Also subcontracts. For first contact send resume to Bill Kroyer, President. Materials are filed; returned if accompanied by a SASE. Reports back only if interested. Negotiates rights purchased. "We pay union scale or more." Tips: "Our clients seem to be wanting more animation that is funny! Do good work, be on time. Take direction well."

Humor Writing: 20% of work is done by freelance writers. For first contact send cover letter and writing samples to Bill Kroyer. Materials filed; returned if accompanied by a SASE. Reports back only if interested.

OLIVE JAR ANIMATION, 44 White Pl., Brookline MA 02146. (617)566-6699. FAX: (617)566-0689. Estab. 1984. Animation studio that provides humor and attention grabbers for advertising agencies, PR firms, broadcast clients and corporations. Some top clients are Eastman Kodak, Miller Brewing, Procter & Gamble, HJ Heinz and Busch Gardens. Produces cel animation, clay animation, stop motion, special effects and live action. Uses freelancers for animation, storyboarding, character development, live action, cell animation, clay animation, stop motion and special effects.

Humorous Illustration: 95% of work is done by freelance illustrators. Also uses freelance illustrators for live action and animation spots. For first contact send cover letter, resume, b&w print samples, storyboard samples and client list to Bill Jarcho, Principal/Creative Director. Materials are filed. Reports back in weeks. Negotiates rights purchased. Sorry, policy is *not* to list pay scales. Tips: "Show creative and imaginative artwork. Concepts are just as important as execution."

Humor Writing: 50% of work is done by freelance writers. Needs freelance writers for commercial spots. For first contact send cover letter, resume, writing samples and client list to Bill Jarcho. Materials are filed. Reports back in weeks. Negotiates rights purchased.

UNIVERSAL IMAGES, 26011 Evergreen, Southfield MI 48076. (313)357-4160. Estab. 1983. Computer animation that provides leading edge for agencies, production companies, automotive and broadcast. Some top clients are Gall & Rice, Sandy Corp., Maritz Communications and Creative Universal. Produces cel animation, 3-D, computer animation, video graphics and live action. Uses freelancers for storyboarding and character development. Tips: "Be available at all hours, be optimistic, show individualism, be receptive to outside ideas and take criticism constructively."

Humor Writing: 100% of work is done by freelance writers. Needs freelance writers for corporate material. For first contact send cover letter, resume and demo tape, either VHS or ¾". Materials are filed or returned only if requested. Reports back in days.

MARK ZANDER PRODUCTIONS, 8th Fl. 118 E. 25th St., New York NY 10010. (212)477-3900. FAX: (212)529-5236. Estab. 1978. Animation Studio/Production House. "We do traditional cel animation with emphasis on Disney and line animation styles, metamorphic animation on paper, stop motion, computer animation and live action/animation." Clients are advertising agencies. Some top clients are Grey, J. Walter Thompson, Saatchi and Young and Rubicam Advertising. Produces cel animation, claymation, stop motion, 3-D, special effects, computer animation, motion control and live action. Uses freelancers for cel animation.

Humorous Illustration: Subcontracts. For first contact send cover letter, ¾" demo tape and client list to Christopher Zander, Producer/Sales. Materials are filed. Reports back within 1 week. Tips: "Our clients seem to be wanting more rotoscope. Your reel is the most important element for getting work. If your reel isn't strong enough, do some animation on spec."

Art/Design Studios

While you may draw the line and ink the illustration or brainstorm the copy and crunch it out on your word processor, an art/design studio may take the credit for it.

Sound odd? Not really. After all, the art/design studio would have commissioned you *directly* to create the contracted art or writing for one of *their* clients.

They secure the job, work directly with the client in the development of the concept and, in most cases, produce the entire project—from art to copywriting, typesetting to printing—with the help of a diverse and talented pool of freelance illustrators, artists, designers and writers.

Advertising agencies, public relations firms, corporations and businesses all call on art/design studios to handle their creative needs. They're contracted to create a myriad of communicative materials in this wild and wooly age of information.

Advertisements (primarily print), posters, point-of-purchase (p-o-p) displays, collateral, package design, signage, corporate identity, direct mail and other eclectic odds and ends—they all have to come from somewhere, and more often than not they're the products of art/design studios.

The good design studios are the ones that have meticulously cultivated a certain image and are known for their particular "design attitude"—the general, overall "look" of their projects. Yet the successful art/design studio must be versatile and able to bounce all over the drawing board creating a conservative, corporate look for this account, giving a chaotic, new wave feel to the next.

A case in point

Manhattan Design is an art/design studio well known for creating cutting edge imagery for clients like HBO, Warner Brothers Records and MTV. In fact, Manhattan Design created MTV's instantly recognizable, revolutionary logo—a logo dubbed by *TIME* magazine as one of the "Designs of the (1980s) Decade."

"The MTV logo was revolutionary," says Frank Olinsky, partner of Manhattan Design, "because it was designed to be constantly changing. There *are* no corporate colors to it. Every time the logo is illustrated, animated or filmed, it appears different. That in itself is very unprecedented."

While almost all of the material which Manhattan Design creates has a certain degree of humor, Olinsky would like there to be more. "Everything we do," he says, "has a light quality. Maybe 100% of what we do utilizes humorous copy, 60% uses humorous illustration. But we'd love to use humor 100% across the board."

If a client wants the best out of Manhattan Design, they give the studio latitude. "We like to have creative freedom," says Olinsky, "if we don't have a long leash, we don't work very well. In turn, we try and give the illustrators, writers and photographers with whom we work the same amount of freedom."

Art/design studios cull their creative services from many sources. Naturally, they refer to creative resources like *Creative Black Book* and *American Showcase* and exhibit bloodhound-like detective ability when they have to track down the perfect illustrator for that special account.

But a well-prepared, professional direct mail presentation from an illustrator or writer can effectively pique the interest of an appropriate buyer—and timing is important.

A week after sending your material, follow up with a quick phone call—just to touch base. If the individual expresses interest in your work, terrific—put them on your permanent mailing list and update them with new samples of your work on a periodic basis. But if they respond unenthusiastically, politely request that they keep your material on file.

In the end, be yourself. Submit work truly representative of what you do. "Sometimes," says Olinsky, "an illustrator or writer submits what he *thinks* we want to see—they try to second guess us. When it comes to illustrators, we like to feel confident about what kind of work they do and then give them the ball and let them run with it."

ALLEN & ASSOCIATES, 9605 Sepulveda #5, Sepulveda CA 91343. (818)894-9123. FAX: (818)894-9525. Estab. 1981. Art/design studio. Serves real estate, museums, advertising agencies. Some top clients are CBS, Buena Vista Television, Museum of Modern Art, MOCA. Needs humorous illustration and humorous copywriting for brochures, print ads, P.O.P., packaging, direct mail, posters, magazine illustration, annual reports, promotions and premiums. 10% of work done by freelance humorous illustrators is for print ads. Prefers to work with freelancers who have fax capabilities.
Humorous Illustration: Is interested in nurturing an ongoing relationship with a humorous illustrator. For first contact send cover letter, resume, client list, b&w tearsheets, color tearsheets, b&w promo piece and color promo piece to Mark Allen, Creative Director. Reports back only if interested. Keeps materials on file. Buys all rights. Pays by the project: $100-2,500. Considers complexity of project, skill of illustrator,

ability of illustrator to work well under art direction, turnaround, business manner and professionalism of illustrator, client's budget, usage, possibility of long term agency/ illustrator relationship when establishing payment.

Humor Writing: Works with 3 freelance writers/year. For first contact send cover letter, resume, client list and tearsheets to Mark Allen. Reports back only if interested. Keeps materials on file. Buys all rights. Pays by the project, $100 minimum. Considers complexity of project, skill of writer, ability to work well under direction of creative team, turnaround, business manner and professionalism of writer, client's budget, usage, possibility of long term agency/writer relationship when establishing payment.

APARTMENT 3-D, 1009 S. Berry Rd., Saint Louis MO 63122. (314)961-2303. FAX: (314)961-6771. Estab. 1983. 3-D Studio. "Apartment 3-D is a full-service design studio specializing in the creation of 3-D imagery for advertising agencies, design groups, corporations and marketing clients. Publishes 3-D self-promotional posters for illustrators, manufactures custom 3-D glasses and produces 3-D television programming." Some top clients are Ralston Purina, *Adweek*, Turner Broadcasting, Bazooka Bubble Gum, Anheuser-Busch, Jim Henson Productions, Rockwell International. Needs line art for conversion into 3-D for packaging, collateral, promotions, TV commercials, direct mail, premiums and posters. 70% of work done by freelance humorous illustrators is for print. Prefers to work with freelancers who have fax capabilities.

Humorous Illustration: Works with 2 freelance illustrators/month, 10 per year. When hiring freelance illustrators, looks for one who understands how to "design" for 3-D— able to grasp what works and what doesn't. For first contact send cover letter, resume, client list, b&w tearsheets and b&w promo piece to Bob Staake, President. Reports back within 4 weeks only if interested. Returns material if accompanied by a SASE. Keeps material on file if interested. Negotiates rights purchased. Pays by the project: $100-10,000. Considers complexity of project, ability to work well under art direction and client's budget. Apartment 3-D also publishes 3-D self-promotional posters for illustrator, manufactures custom 3-D glasses and produces 3-D TV programming.

JOHN BARNARD, 48 West 21 St. 3rd Fl., New York NY 10010. (212)627-1147. Estab. 1973. Ad agency that provides print advertising, product collateral, corporate I.D. to manufacturers and importers. Contracts home furnishing businesses. Needs ad headlines. Prefers to work with freelancers who have fax capabilities. Uses freelance humorous illustrators on a one-time-only basis. For first contact send b&w tearsheets to John Barnard, President. Reports back only if interested. Returns materials if accompanied by a SASE. Buys all rights. Considers complexity of project, client's budget and usage when establishing payment.

Humor Writing: Works with 1 freelance writer/year. For first contact send tearsheets to John Barnard. Reports back only if interested. Returns materials if accompanied by a SASE. Buys all rights. Considers complexity of project, client's budget and usage when establishing payment.

JUDY BARNETT, 5755 Riverwood Dr. NW, Atlanta GA 30328. (404)843-9235. FAX: (404)255-7239. Estab. 1976. Art/design studio that provides P.O.P., annual reports, collateral, print advertising, brand identity, packaging, comps and illustration for corporation. Some top clients are Curtis 1000, Kimberly Clark and Pacific Dunlop. Needs cartoons and humorous copywriting for brochures, direct mail and radio spots (humor writing). 20% of work done by freelance humorous illustrators is for print ads. Prefers to work with freelancers who have fax capabilities.

Humorous Illustration: Works with 2 freelance illustrators/month or 24/year. When hiring freelance illustrators, "looks for someone who charges competitively, delivers on deadline and is terrific." Uses freelance humorous illustrators on a one-time-only basis. For first contact send b&w promo piece to Judy Barnett, Art Director. Reports back within 2 weeks only if interested. Returns materials only if requested. Buys all rights or negotiates rights purchased. Pays by the hour: $20-65. Considers complexity of project, skill of illustrator, ability of illustrator to work well under art direction, turnaround, business manner and professionalism of illustrator, client's budget, usage and schedule of illustrator when establishing payment.

Humor Writing: Works with 5 freelance writers/year. When hiring freelance writers, looks for someone who is good and delivers on time. For first contact send photocopied writing samples to Judy Barnett, Director. Reports back within 2 weeks. Returns materials only if requested. Negotiates rights purchased. Pays by the hour: $30-75. Considers complexity of project, skill of writer, ability of writer to work well under direction of creative team, turnaround, business manner and professionalism of writer, client's budget, usage, schedule of writer, and the possibility of long term agency/writer relationship when establishing payment.

BEHR-LEMONS CREATIVE, 701 4th Ave. So., Minneapolis MN 55415. (612)333-0324. FAX: 333-8584. Estab. 1980. Art/design studio. "We do P.O.P., print advertising and video for T.V." Serves ad agencies, business to business, retailing. Some top clients are Reader's Digest Publications, General Mills and Cole-Sewell Manufacturing. Needs humorous copywriting for brochures, annual reports, print ads, collateral, promotions, TV commercials, direct mail and P.O.P. 30% of work done by freelance humorous illustrators for print ads.

Humorous Illustration: Works with 2 freelance illustrators/year. Is interested in nurturing an ongoing relationship with a humorous illustrator. For first contact send b&w tearsheets, color tearsheets, b&w promo piece and color promo piece to Rick Lemons, Creative Director. Reports back only if interested. Returns materials only if requested. Keeps material on file. Buys first time rights or negotiates rights purchased. Pays by the hour: $40-70; by the project: $250-1,500. Considers complexity of project, skill of illustrator, ability of illustrator to work well under art direction and client's budget when establishing payment.

Humor Writing: Works with 1 freelance writer/month. For first contact send photocopied writing sample to Rick Lemons, Creative Director. Reports back only if interested. Returns material only if requested. Keeps materials on file. Negotiates rights purchased. Pays by the project: $250-800. Considers complexity of project, skill, client's budget and possibility of long term agency/writer relationship when establishing payment.

BERSON, DEAN, STEVENS, Suite 112, 22048 Sherman Way, Canoga Park CA 91303. (818)713-0134. FAX: (818)713-0417. Estab. 1981. Art/design studio that provides P.O.P., annual reports, collateral, print advertising, radio advertising and packaging for corporations, manufacturers and retailers. Some top clients are Pepsi-Cola, Siemens and 3M National. Needs cartoons and humorous copywriting for brochures, print ads, collateral, direct mail, posters, magazine illustration, promotions and premiums. 20% of work done by freelance humorous illustrators is for print ads. Prefers to work with freelancers who have fax capabilities.

Humorous Illustration: Works with 1-2 freelance illustrators/month or 6-8/year. Is interested in nurturing an ongoing relationship with a humorous illustrator. For first contact send cover letter, resume, client list b&w tearsheets, color tearsheets to Lori Berson, Creative Director. Reports back only if interested. Returns materials only if requested. Keeps materials on file. Negotiates rights purchased. Pays by the hour: $40-80; by the project: $50-2,000. Considers complexity of project; skill of illustrator; ability of illustrator to work well under art direction; turnaround; business manner and professionalism of illustrator; client's budget; usage; possibility of long term agency/illustrator relationship when establishing payment.

Humor Writing: Works with 1-2 freelance writers/month. For first contact send cover letter, resume, client list, tearsheets and photocopied writing samples to Lori Berson. Reports back only if interested. Returns materials only if requested. Keeps materials on file. Buys one time rights. Pays by the hour: $40-80; by the project: $100-1,000. Considers complexity of project; skill; ability to work well under direction of creative team; turnaround; business manner and professionalism of writer; client's budget; usage; possibility of long term agency/writer relationship when establishing payment.

BIG CITY GRAPHICS, 8270 SW 116 Terrace, Miami FL 33156. (305)235-4700. Estab. 1976. Art/design studio that provides graphic design, corporate graphics, print advertising, direct mail and publication design to ad agencies, corporations, hospitals, resorts and industries. Some top clients are FPL, Radisson Hotel, Joe Robbie Stadium/Miami Dolphins, South Miami Hospital and Merchandise Mart. Needs humorous illustration, cartoons and humor oriented comprehensives for brochures, print ads, collateral, direct mail, posters, magazine illustration, slide shows and promotions. 30% of work done by freelance humorous illustrators is for print ads.
Humorous Illustration: When hiring freelance illustrators, looks for a definite style to fit the assignment and ability to work with art director. Is interested in nurturing an ongoing relationship with a humorous illustrator. For first contact send cover letter, b&w tearsheets and color tearsheets to Joe Rodriguez, owner. Reports back within 2 weeks only if interested. Keeps materials on file. Negotiates rights purchased. Considers complexity of project; skill of illustrator; ability of illustrator to work well under art direction; turnaround; client's budget; usage; possibility of long term agency/illustrator relationship when establishing payment.
Humor Writing: Works with 4-5 freelance writers/year. When hiring freelance writers, looks for strong ability to identify assignment's needs, ability to work well with creative staff and willingness to make changes if needed. For first contact send cover letter, tearsheets and photocopied writing samples to Joe Rodriguez. Reports back within 2 weeks only if interested. Returns materials only if requested. Keeps materials on file. Negotiates rights purchased. Considers complexity of project; ability of writer to work well under direction of creative team; turnaround; client's budget; usage; possibility of long term agency/writer relationship when establishing payment.

LEONARD BRUCE DESIGNS, P.O. Box 2767 #226, Jackson TN 38302. (901)668-1205. Estab. 1984. Art/design studio and syndicate that provides syndicate cartoons, strips, pushes cartoons to be syndicated and provides help for gag writers and cartoonists. Some top clients are United States Space Education Association, Starlog and United Cartoonists Syndicate. Needs humorous illustration, caricature and cartoons for posters, magazine illustration, catalogs and industrial film. 10% of work done by freelance humorous illustrators is for print ads.
Humorous Illustration: Works with 3 freelance illustrators/month. When hiring freelance illustrators, looks for someone "off the wall" who dares to be different and is a good illustrator. Uses freelance humorous illustrators on a one-time-only basis. Is interested in nurturing an ongoing relationship with a humorous illustrator. For first contact send cover letter, resume, client list and b&w tearsheets to Leonard Bruce, Syndicator Cartoonist. Reports back within 3 weeks. Returns materials if accompanied by a SASE. Does not keep materials on file. Buys first time rights. Pays by the project: $15-30. Considers complexity of project; skill; business manner and professionalism; possibility of long term agency/illustrator relationship when establishing payment.
Humor Writing: Works with 2 freelance writers/month; 12/year. "When hiring freelance writers, looks for someone who works well with my style of cartoons." For first contact send cover letter, resume, client list, tearsheets and photocopied writing samples to Leonard Bruce. Reports back within 2 weeks. Returns materials if accompanied by a SASE. Does not keep materials on file. Buys one time rights. Pays by the project: $10-

25. Considers complexity of project; skill of writer; turnaround; business manner and professionalism of writer; usage; schedule of writer; possibility of long term agency/ writer relationship when establishing payment.

CHEVAL ELECTRONIC DESIGN STUDIO, 432 E. Pales Feny, Atlanta GA 30305. (404)240-0188. FAX: (404)262-3722. Estab. 1988. Art/design studio and computer design/access that provides computer design studio set up for access to local agencies/ designers and in house design for P.O.P. and collateral for agencies and corporations. Some top clients are Coca-Cola, Georgia Pacific, John Portman & Associates and Bacardi. Needs humorous illustration and cartoons for brochures, P.O.P., collateral and direct mail. Prefers to work with freelancers who have fax capabilities.
Humorous Illustration: Works with 6 freelance illustrators/year. Is interested in nurturing an ongoing relationship with a humorous illustrator. For first contact send cover letter, client list, b&w promo piece and color promo piece to Terri Cooper. Reports back only if interested. Returns materials only if requested. Keeps materials on file. Buys all rights. Payment varies by the project. Considers complexity of project, skill of illustrator, ability of illustrator to work well under art direction, turnaround and client's budget when establishing payment.
Humor Writing: Works with 2 freelance writers/year.

ROBERT COONEY GRAPHIC DESIGN, P.O. Box 684, Point Reyes Station CA 94956. (415)663-8230. Estab. 1977. Art/design studio. "We are a freelance design studio specializing in publications, magazines, newsletters, corporate identity and collateral." Serves small businesses, nonprofit institutions, political and humanitarian groups, publishers and individuals. Some top clients are Strawberry Press, Feather River Co., Amnesty International, Marin Agricultural Land Trust, Medical Self Care. Needs humorous illustration, caricature and cartoons for brochures, magazine illustration, collateral and direct mail. 10% of work done by freelance humorous illustrators is for print ads.
Humorous Illustration: Works with 1 humorous illustrator/month; 6-10/year. When hiring freelance illustrators, looks for one who shares an irreverent and independent point of view and is funny and competent. Uses freelance humorous illustrators on one-time-only basis. Is interested in nurturing an ongoing relationship with a humorous illustrator. For first contact send cover letter, b&w tearsheets, b&w promo piece and examples to Robert Cooney. Reports back within 2 weeks only if interested. Returns materials only if requested and accompanied by a SASE. Keeps material on file. Negotiates rights purchased. Pays by the project or b&w work: $25-250. Considers complexity of project, skill of illustrator, client's budget, usage and the artist's rates when establishing payment.
Tips: "The kind of cartoons and humor I would be interested in seeing is that coming from an anti-war perspective, promoting equality, social justice and nonviolence, or generally a more peaceful and honest world. Editorial cartoons are a good example."

DAWSON DESIGN, 7250 Beverly Blvd. #101, Los Angeles CA 90036. (213)937-5867. Estab. 1974. Art/design studio and ad agency that provides annual reports, collateral, print advertising and packaging to corporations and banking institutions. Some top clients are Powell Corp., MCA, Abbutt, Xerox, Security Pacific Bank, Quest Records, Capital Records, Los Angeles Zoo and DPIC Capsules. Needs caricature, cartoons, storyboards, humor oriented comprehensives and humorous copywriting for brochures, print ads, P.O.P., packaging, collateral, direct mail, posters, slide shows, catalogs and annual reports. 60% of work done by freelance humorous illustrators is for print ads.
Humorous Illustration: Works with 6 freelance illustrators/year. Uses freelance humorous illustrators on a one-time-only basis. For first contact send cover letter, resume, client list, b&w tearsheets and color tearsheets to Cris Dawson, Creative Director. Reports back only if interested. Returns materials if accompanied by a SASE. Keeps

materials on file. Negotiates rights purchased. Considers complexity of project; skill of illustrator; ability of illustrator to work well under art direction; turnaround; business manner and professionalism of illustrator; client's budget; and schedule of illustrator when establishing payment.

Humor Writing: Works with 6 freelance writers/year. For first contact send cover letter, resume, client list and tearsheets to Chris Dawson. Reports back only if interested. Returns materials only if requested and accompanied by a SASE. Keeps materials on file. Considers complexity of project; skill of writer; ability of writer to work well under direction of creative team; turnaround; business manner and professionalism of writer; client's budget; usage; and possibility of long term agency/writer relationship when establishing payment.

ERIC GLUCKMAN COMMUNICATION INC., 60 East 42nd St., New York NY 10165. (212)697-3670. FAX: (212)286-9205. Estab. 1973. Art/design studio that provides graphic design, brochures, magazines and corporate ads for mostly small to medium size firms and magazines. Needs humorous illustration, caricature and cartoons for print ads, collateral, direct mail, posters, magazine illustration, catalogs, annual reports and promotions. 30% of work done by freelance humorous illustrators is for print ads.

Humorous Illustration: Works with 10 freelance illustrators/year. When hiring freelance illustrators, looks for "someone who will work on concept development with us." Uses freelance humorous illustrators on a one-time-only basis. Is interested in nurturing an ongoing relationship with a humorous illustrator. For first contact send b&w tearsheets, color tearsheets, b&w promo piece and color promo piece to Eric Gluckman, President. Reports back only if interested. Keeps materials on file. Negotiates rights purchased. Pays by the project: $50-3,500. Considers complexity of project, skill of illustrator and turnaround when establishing payment.

GRAPHIC ART RESOURCE ASSOCIATES, 257 West 10th Street, New York NY 10001. (212)929-0017. Estab. 1969. Ad agency. Uses humorous material for "whatever project seems appropriate for such an approach."

Humorous Illustration: Works with 1 freelance illustrator every 5 years. When hiring freelance illustrators, looks for likable style. Uses freelance humorous illustrators on a one-time-only basis. For first contact send b&w promo piece and color promo piece to Robert Lassen, Owner. Does not report back but will call if services are desired. Does not return materials. Keeps materials on file. Buys all rights. Pays by the project: $150 minimum (negotiated). Considers complexity of project; skill of illustrator; ability of illustrator to work well under art direction; turnaround; business manner and professionalism of illustrator; client's budget; possibility of long term agency/illustrator relationship and ability to fulfill requirements of project when establishing payment.

Humor Writing: Works with 1 freelance writer every 10 years. For first contact send photocopied writing samples and business card to Robert Lassen. Does not report back. Does not return materials. Keeps materials on file. Buys all rights. Pays by the project: $150 minimum negotiated. Considers complexity of project; skill of writer; ability of writer to work well under direction of creative team; turnaround; business manner and professionalism of writer; client's budget; and ability to fill requirements of project when establishing payment.

IMAGE PRODUCTIONS, 115 W. Church, Libertyville IL 60048. (312)680-7100. Estab. 1978. Art/design studio. Business-to-business marketing communications including promotion, packaging, collateral, editorial, P.O.P. Clients include advertising agencies, corporations, health care industry and not-for-profit institutions. Needs caricature and cartoons for magazine illustration and slide shows. Prefers working with freelancers with fax capabilities.

Humorous Illustration: Works with 2 humorous illustrators per year. For first contact send cover letter, client list, b&w tearsheets and b&w promo piece to Beth Engel, Partner. Reports back only if interested. Returns materials if accompanied by SASE. Keeps materials on file. Pays $50 minimum per project. Considers complexity of project, ability of illustrator to work well under art direction, turnaround and client's budget when establishing payment.

ALAN LEITSTEIN GRAPHICS, 1500 NW 92 Ave., Plantation FL 33322. (305)475-7108. Estab. 1974. Art/design studio that provides P.O.P., annual reports, brochures, ads, package design, newsletters and posters to advertising agencies, corporations, banking institutions and manufacturing companies. Needs humorous illustration, storyboards and humorous copywriting for brochures, print ads, direct mail, posters and promotions. 30% of work done by freelance humorous illustrators is for print ads.
Humor Writing: For first contact send cover letter, resume and samples of styles to Alan Leitstein, President. Reports back within 2 weeks only if interested. Does not return materials. Keeps materials on file. Buys all rights. Pays by the hour: $40-75. Considers complexity of project, skill of writer, ability of writer to work well under direction of creative team and client's budget when establishing payment.

MANHATTAN DESIGN, 47 W. 13th St., New York NY 10011. (212)620-0506. FAX: (212)757-1852. Estab. 1980. Art/design studio. Design services primarily but not exclusively for the music and entertainment industry. Clients include MTV, Elektra Records, Warner Bros. Records, 10,000 Maniacs, B-52s and R.E.M. Needs humorous illustration and humorous copywriting for brochures and print ads. Prefer to work with freelancers who have fax capabilities.
Humorous Illustration: Uses 3 humorous illustrators/year. Interested in nurturing an ongoing relationship with a humorous illustrator. For first contact, send b&w tearsheets, color tearsheets and b&w promo piece to Manhattan Design. Reports back only if interested. Returns material if accompanied by SASE. Keeps materials on file. Negotiates rights purchased. Payment "depends on job." Considers these factors when establishing payment: client's budget; usage.
Humor Writing: Works with 1-2 humor writers/year. For first contact send photocopied writing samples to Manhattan Design. Returns material if accompanied by SASE. Negotiates rights purchased. Considers these factors when establishing payment: complexity of project; ability of writer to work well under direction of creative team; turnaround; client's budget; usage.

MARKETING COMMUNICATIONS SERVICES, 5217 Oliva Ave., Lakewood CA 90712. (213)630-8439. Marketing/advertising company that provides print ads, collateral, promotional pieces, government agency proposals, publicity releases and feature articles, sales letters and A-V presentations for small agencies, design shops, entrepreneurs and small business firms in manufacturing (medical electronic, industrial electronics). Some top clients are Hughes Aircraft, TRW, Verite Technology Group Inc., Panel Concepts and General Pneumatics. Needs humorous illustration for brochures and print ads. 80% of work done by freelance humorous illustrators is for print ads. Prefers to work with freelancers who have fax capabilities.
Humorous Illustration: When hiring freelance illustrators, looks for someone who can contribute to a creative concept. Uses freelance humorous illustrators on a one-time-only basis. For first contact send resume, client list, b&w tearsheets and color tearsheets to Bill Ormsby, President. Reports back within days if interested. Returns materials if accompanied by a SASE. Buys one time rights. Pays by the hour: $35-50 minimum; by the day $500 maximum; by the project: $2,000 maximum. Considers complexity of project, skill of illustrator, ability of illustrator to work well under art direction, turnaround and client's budget when establishing payment.

MARGARET PATTERSON CO., 234 Clarendon St., Boston MA 02116. Estab. 1981. Art/design studio that provides annual reports, collateral, print advertising and corporate identity to financial, medical and nonprofit organizations. Needs humorous illustration and humorous copywriting for brochures, print ads and newsletters. 10% of work done by freelance humorous illustrators is for print ads. Prefers to work with freelancers who have fax capabilities.

Humorous Illustration: Works with 4-8 freelance illustrators/year. When hiring freelance illustrators, looks for someone "who does a lot of roughs." Is interested in nurturing an ongoing relationship with a humorous illustrator. For first contact send b&w tearsheets to Margaret Patterson, owner. Reports back only if interested. Does not return materials. Keeps materials on file. Buys one time rights or negotiates rights purchased. Pays by the hour: $50-75. Considers complexity of project; skill of illustrator; ability of illustrator to work well under art direction; turnaround; business manner and professionalism of illustrator; client's budget; usage; schedule of illustrator; possibility of long term agency/illustrator relationship when establishing payment.

Humor Writing: Works with 5 freelance writers/year. When hiring freelance writers, looks for someone who has good marketing sense and meets deadlines. For first contact send photocopied writing samples to Margaret Patterson. Reports back only if interested. Does not return materials. Keeps materials on file. Buys one time rights. Pays by the hour: $50-75. Considers complexity of project; skill of writer; ability of writer to work well under direction of creative team; turnaround; business manner and professionalism of writer; client's budget; usage; schedule of writer; possibility of long term agency/writer relationship when establishing payment.

PRINTING TODAY, 202-212 South 3rd St., Coopersburg PA 12036. (215)282-4561. FAX: (215)282-4561. Estab. 1980. Provides complete layout and full-service printing. Needs humorous illustration, caricature, cartoons and humorous copywriting for brochures, print ads, packaging, direct mail, posters, magazine illustration, catalogs, annual reports, promotions and premiums. Prefers to work with freelancers who have fax capabilities.

Humorous Illustration: Works with 1 freelance illustrators/month. Is interested in nurturing an ongoing relationship with a humorous illustrator. For first contact send cover letter and b&w promo piece; fax to Mike Zweifer, Owner. Reports back only if interested. Returns materials only if requested and accompanied by a SASE. Negotiates rights purchased. Pays by the hour: $5-100; by the day: $50-500; by the project: $5 minimum; by b&w work: $10 minimum; by color work: $25 minimum. Considers complexity of project, ability of illustrator to work well under art direction, turnaround, client's budget, usage and schedule of illustrator when establishing payment.

Humor Writing: Works with 1 freelance writer/month. For first contact send cover letter and photocopied writing samples to Mike Zweifer. Reports back only if interested. Returns materials if requested and accompanied by SASE. Negotiates rights purchased. Pays by the hour: $5-100; by the day: $50-500; by the project: $10 minimum. Considers complexity of project, turnaround and client's budget when establishing payment.

PATRICK REDMOND DESIGN, The Security Building, Suite 300E, 757 Raymond Ave., St. Paul MN 55114. (612)224-7155. FAX: (612)224-7155. Estab. 1966. Art/design studio. Logo and trademark design; publication design—books, magazines, newsletters; packaging; posters; brochures for retail, financial, food, arts, education, publishing, computer, manufacturing, ad agencies, government, nonprofit and community organizations. Clients include Dayton Hudson Department Stores, Peavey Company, Norwest Corporation and Dos Tejedoras Fiber Arts Publications (over 90 clients have used graphic design and/or illustration by Patrick Redmond). Needs humorous illustration, caricature and humorous copywriting for brochures, print ads, collateral, direct mail, posters, magazine illustration and promotions. 10% of freelance humorous illustration is for print ads. Prefers freelancers with FAX capabilities.

Humorous Illustration: Works with 4 humorous illustrators/year. More apt to hire a humorous illustrator who is fast, uses fax, has demonstrated track record—consistent quality and a look you can count on. Is interested in nurturing an ongoing relationship with a humorous illustrator. For first contact send cover letter, resume, client list, b&w tearsheets and b&w promo piece to Patrick Redmond, President. Reports back on submissions in 2 weeks if interested. Does not return materials. Keeps materials on file. Negotiates rights purchased. Pays: $70-400 for b&w work, $250 minimum for color work. Considers complexity of project, skill of illustrator, ability of illustrator to work well under art direction, turnaround, business manner and professionalism of illustrator, client's budget, usage, schedule of illustrator and possibility of long tern agency/illustrator relationship when establishing payment.

Humor Writing: Is more apt to hire a freelance humor writer who has demonstrated ability to deliver what is needed. For first contact freelancer should send cover letter, resume, client list, tearsheets and photocopied writing samples to Patrick Redmond, Design/Owner/President. Reports in 2 weeks only if interested. Does not return materials. Keeps materials on file. Negotiates rights purchased. Pays: $300 minimum/project. Considers complexity of project, skill of writer, ability of writer to work well under direction of creative team, turnaround, business manner and professionalism of writer, client's budget, usage, schedule of writer and possibility of long term agency/writer relationship when establishing payment.

VISUAL IDENTITY, Suite L-5 & L-6, 6250 Mountain Vista, Henderson NV 89014. (702)454-7773. FAX: (702)454-6293. Estab. 1986. Art/design studio that provides P.O.P., annual reports, collateral, print advertising, brand identity and packaging to advertising agencies, corporations and the hotel and gaming industry. Some top clients are Circus Circus, Colorado Belle, Edgewater, U.S. Mint, Geisha Lighting, various location movies and TV series. Needs humorous illustration, caricature, cartoons, storyboards and humorous copywriting for brochures, print ads, TV commercials, P.O.P., packaging, collateral, direct mail, posters, magazine illustration, catalogs, industrial films and radio spots (humor writing). 20% of work done by freelance humorous illustrators is for print ads. Prefers to work with freelancers who have fax capabilities.

Humorous Illustration: Works with 10 freelance illustrators/month or 100/year. When hiring freelance illustrators, looks for someone who "meets our needs." Uses freelance humorous illustrators on a one-time-only basis. For first contact send cover letter, resume, client list, b&w tearsheets, color tearsheets, b&w promo piece and color promo piece to William Garbacz, Creative Designer. Reports back within 2 weeks. Returns materials only if requested. Keeps materials on file. Buys all rights. Pays by the hour: $25-100. Considers complexity of project, skill, ability of illustrator to work well under art direction, turnaround, client's budget and usage when establishing payment.

Humor Writing: Works with 3 freelance writers/month. For first contact send cover letter, resume, client list, tearsheets and photocopied writing samples to William Garbacz. Reports back within 2 weeks. Returns materials only if requested. Keeps materials on file. Buys all rights. Pays by the hour: $25-100. Considers complexity of project, skill of writer, ability of writer to work well under direction of creative team, turnaround; client's budget and usage when establishing payment.

WALKER & COMPANY MARKETING COMMUNICATION, Suite #101, 2001 E. Campbell, Phoenix AZ 85016. (602)955-1496. FAX: (602)955-1867. Estab. 1985. Ad agency and marketing firm that provides marketing, public relations, media placement and advertising design to hospitals, liquor stores, doctors, lawyers, pet stores and developers. Some top clients are Petsmart/Petfood Warehouse, Newman's Liquour Barn, Commercial Blueprint and Framer's Wholesale. Needs humorous illustration, cartoons and humorous copywriting for brochures, print ads, P.O.P., collateral, direct mail, posters, magazine illustration and catalogs. 90% of work done by freelance humorous illustrators is for print ads. Prefers to work with freelancers who have fax capabilities.

Humorous Illustration: Works with 5 freelance illustrators/year. When hiring freelance illustrators, looks for copywriters and someone who works well with other people and clients. Is interested in nurturing an ongoing relationship with a humorous illustrator. For first contact send cover letter, resume, client list, b&w tearsheets, color tearsheets, b&w promo piece and color promo piece to Ginger Gillilland, Art Director. Reports back only if interested. Returns materials only if requested. Keeps materials on file. Buys one time rights or negotiates rights purchased. Pays by the hour: $100 maximum; by the day: $500 maximum; by the project: negotiable. Considers complexity of project; skill of illustrator; ability of illustrator to work well under art direction; turnaround; business manner and professionalism of illustrator; and client's budget when establishing payment.

Humor Writing: Works with 3 freelance writers/month. When hiring freelance writers, looks for someone who can work within client's budget. For first contact send cover letter, resume, client list, tearsheets and photocopied writing samples to Ginger Gillilland, Art Director or Lesle Walker, President. Reports back only if interested. Returns materials only if requested. Keeps materials on file. Negotiates rights purchased. Pays by the hour: $100 maximum; by the day: $500 maximum; by the project: $2,000 maximum. Considers complexity of project, ability of writer to work well under direction of creative team, turnaround, client's budget and usage when establishing payment.

MOSER WHITE, 7120 Windsor Lake Pkwy., Rockford IL 61111. (815)877-7760. FAX: (815)877-8184. Estab. 1984. Art/design studio. "We are an advertising design firm (9 people) with a wide variety of projects, such as package design, sales literature, display design, catalogs and annual reports." Serves industrial manufacturing in camping, beverage and food industries, publishing, medical, restaurants and retail. Some top clients are Mobil Oil, Dean Foods, Duplex Products, Sundstrand Corp., Precision Twist Drill, Century Tool and Manucturing Co., Sears, Winnebago Camping Equipment, Random House, Kabel News Co., ABC Publishing and Harvestore. Needs humorous illustration, caricature, humor oriented comprehensives and humorous copywriting for brochures, print ads, direct mail, P.O.P., direct mail, posters and promotions. 75% of work done by freelance humorous illustrators is for print ads. Prefers to work with freelancers who have fax capabilities.

Humorous Illustration: Works with 6 freelance illustrators/month. When hiring freelance illustrators, looks for one who has a portfolio he can leave or show a client. Uses freelance humorous illustrators on a one-time-only basis. For first contact send b&w tearsheets, b&w promo piece, color promo piece and portfolio to Carl White, Creative Director. Reports back within 3 days. Returns materials if accompanied by a SASE. Keeps materials on file. Buys all rights. Pays by the project: $100-1,100. Considers ability of illustrator to work well under art direction, business manner and professionalism of illustrator, client's budget, schedule of illustrator and possibility of long term agency/ illustrator relationship.

Humor Writing: Works with 3 freelance writers/year. For first contact send tearsheets and photocopied writing samples to Rick Moser, Creative Director. Reports back within 2 days. Returns material if accompanied by a SASE or keeps materials on file. Buys all rights. Pays by the hour: $25-100. Considers ability of writer to work well under direction of creative team, client's budget, schedule of writer and possibility of long term agency/ writer relationship.

If you doubt the popularity of humor, go into a bookstore.

Hear that? The chuckling, the snickering, the snorting sound of a stifled laugh honking through a pair of nostrils. No, those noises aren't coming from the Self-Help section or from behind the Biography shelf — they're coming from the Humor section.

Imagine that. An entire section devoted to funny things. Collections of re-printed comic strips, original cartoon books, hilarious fiction and even agglom-erations of gross jokes sick enough to cause most normal tummies to bubble.

Take a look at *The New York Times* Best Seller List. Happily, the top ten positions are no longer solely occupied by Jackie Collins, Sidney Sheldon and James Michener. Rather, names like Gary Larson, Berke Breathed and Bill Watterson appear regularly on the list and testify to the public's appetite for humor.

"Humor is very strong today," says Pat Redding, associate editor of Topper Books. "The public seems more open to it, but there have always been success-ful humor books (in years past, reprints of *Peanuts*, *The Wizard of ID*, etc). But books like that had mass appeal and were merchandised that way. Today, hu-mor books are packaged a little differently."

One indication of Topper's dedication to humor is their plan to publish more original material. "Topper *used* to publish nothing but collected reprints of comic strips," says Redding, "but in 1991, about 60% of our humor trade paperbacks will be comic strip reprints, about 40% will be original humor titles. Then in 1992, we hope to totally reverse those figures (60% original, 40% reprints)."

Culling through the countless submissions which cross her desk, Redding looks for material which is "original, very funny, very good and surprises me. Really good humor will work on all levels — it has sophisticated *and* general

appeal." But Redding doesn't care too much for material which relies on a trend or fad as a crutch. "By the time you recognize a trend," she says, "it's probably peaked.

"Looking for talent is hard work," says Redding. "Weeding through the submissions, you see a lot of bad stuff, a lot of mediocre stuff, and a little good stuff. There are a lot of *really* funny people out there, so why don't they send me *really* funny stuff?"

Yet when she does recognize talent, Redding makes every effort to support it. "If I see potential in a cartoonist, illustrator or writer's work," says Redding, "I try to encourage them without making any big promises. There is, after all, a fine line between a rejection letter and a rejection letter that includes a word or two of encouragement."

Manuscripts

Individual book publishers have individual needs. However, if you have written a humorous opus, most editors would prefer that you query them with a written outline of your book, a SASE, a resume or bio and a sample chapter. The latter can serve *you* extremely well — particularly if your chapter is extremely good. The best thing you can give an editor is a taste — which leaves them salivating for your *complete* manuscript.

You may, however, want to explore the possibility of having your manuscript represented by a literary agent. An agent "legitimizes" you and the good ones are fully immersed in the intricacies of the publishing industry. They know which publishers would have an interest in your manuscript, but more importantly, they know individual editors at individual publishing houses ("doing lunch" *does* pay off). Agents are not only known for being able to get their feet in the door, they're known for wearing steel-capped shoes.

Artwork

Similarly, an original cartoon book can be submitted by the cartoonist or via an agent. If you have a cartoon book in mind which would require a total of 120 individual cartoons, draw up 15 to 20 as samples. If you submit the material directly, include a written outline explaining the book's premise, a succinct cover letter, perhaps a self-promotional page showing black and white examples of your finished cartoon work and, of course, a SASE.

A humorous illustrator or cartoonist who is interested in the *illustration* of books should send self-promotional material to the appropriate individual, usually an art director, although more and more editors are making art assignments. Color and black and white samples would be essential ingredients in such a mailing, and a cover letter, resume, client list and business card should be mandatory. Again, provide material which the publisher can hang on to — if it has to snooze, let it snooze in *their* files, rather than yours.

Industry pricing varies drastically. Publishers pay author royalties anywhere from 3-25% of the wholesale, retail or net price. Publishers can offer healthy advances, set you up with anemic stipends or offer no up-front money at all. This is why an agent, if you can secure one, is so important. Drawing up a detailed profile of each publisher can be a daunting task at best, but an agent has the inside track.

Fortunately, humor is alive and well-stocked by your better booksellers. And as long as funny keeps selling, publishers will keep publishing it; people will keep buying it; and *The New York Times* will keep listing it.

BEAUXARTS, P.O. Box 2210, San Francisco CA 94126. (415)986-3030. FAX: (415)543-2681. Estab. 1969. Publishes trade paperback originals. Humor line includes satire. Recently published *Jerry Brown*, a collection of devastating caricatures.
Humorous Illustration: Works with approximately 3 freelance humorous illustrators/year. Needs humorous illustration for nonfiction titles, caricature, illustrators for syndication of offensive humor. Will supply ideas to artists with talent. Uses freelance humorous illustrators primarily for X-rated imagery. When hiring a freelance humorous illustrator, considers skill of artist, willingness to depict the unthinkable. Buys all rights. For first contact send cover letter, b&w tearsheets, color tearsheets to Duke Mantee, Project Manager. Reports back in weeks only if interested. Returns materials if accompanied by a SASE. Pays $100 color cover; $50 b&w inside illustration; $75 color inside illustration.

BEHRMAN HOUSE, 235 Watchung Ave., West Orange, NJ 07052. (201)669-0447. FAX: (201)669-9769. Estab. 1921. Publishes Jewish books for children and adults. Humor line includes children's books. Recently published *The Amazing Adventures of the J People, My People,* and *The Ten Commandments.* Prefers working with freelancers who have fax capabilities.
Humorous Illustration: Works with approximately 4 freelance humorous illustrators/year. Needs humorous illustration for fiction and nonfiction titles, cartoons, caricature. Uses freelance humorous illustrators primarily for illustrating texts. When hiring a freelance humorous illustrator, considers skill, drawing style, ability to take art direction well, compatibility of drawing style with text, professionalism, businesslike attitude. Buys reprint rights. For first contact send cover letter, resume, client list, b&w tearsheets, portfolio to Adam Siegel, Editor. Reports back in weeks. Keeps materials on file. Pays $200 b&w book cover; $400 color cover; $25 b&w inside illustration; $15 color inside illustration.
Humor Writing: Published 2 humor titles last year. Works with approximately 2 freelance humorous nonfiction writers/year. Uses freelance humor writers primarily for children's books. Needs humorous nonfiction writing. Fiction mss needed on family, religion, people, anything related to Judaism. Nonfiction mss needed on Judaism. Buys reprint rights. Send cover letter, resume, writing sample, sample chapter, outline of manuscript. Send all humor fiction and nonfiction to Adam Siegel, Editor. Returns materials "if we don't use them." Pays per project and pays on a royalty basis 2% (min) on retail price or makes outright purchase of $500 minimum. Average advance $200.

BEST EDITORIAL CARTOONS, Pelican Publishing Company, P.O. Box 189, Gretna LA 70054. (504)368-1175. FAX: (504)368-1195. Estab. 1926. Publishes Best Editorial Cartoons of the Year series. "Cartoons must have appeared in printed form in magazines or newspapers."
Humorous Illustrations: Needs editorial cartoons only. "There is no cash payment for cartoons used. Each cartoonist receives 2 copies of the edition he/she is in. Cartoonists send in what they consider their top 5 cartoons. These are sent to Chuck Brooks, who puts them into categories and then chooses the best of each category. The categories are determined by what has happened in the previous year." Cartoonists interested in being included should send a letter to Pelican requesting to be put on mailing list for next edition. Letters with information of where to send cartoons go out in November.

COMPUTER TECHNOLOGY RESOURCE GUIDE, Crumb Elbow Publisher, P.O. Box 294, Rhodendron OR 97049. (503)622-4798. Estab. 1983. Publishes mass market books. Humor lines include original cartoons, written humor.

Humorous Illustration: Needs humorous illustration for fiction and nonfiction titles, cartoons and caricature. When hiring a freelance humorous illustrator, considers skill, drawing style, ability to take art direction well, compatability of drawing style with text, professionalism, businesslike attitude and patience. "We get very busy and he or she may think that we've forgotten about them, but we won't." Buys first time rights. For first contact send cover letter, resume, client list, b&w tearsheets and slides to Michael P. Jones, Editor. Reports on submissions within 2 months ("or sooner depending upon how busy we are.") Pays in published copies.

Humor Writing: Published 4 humor titles last year through Crumb Elbow Publishing. "We're just starting to use humor-oriented computer books from freelancers." Needs humorous fiction and nonfiction writing. Fiction mss needed only on computers. Nonfiction humor mss needed on computers and human interaction, problems with computers controlling our lives, computers fouling up our lives. Buys first time rights. Send query to Michael P. Jones, Editor. Reports on submission within 2 months ("or a lot sooner, depending upon how busy we are.") Returns materials if accompanied by a SASE. Pays in published copies.

CROSSING PRESS, P.O. Box 259, Bala Cynwyd PA 19004. "For an anthology of women's humor. I am looking for prose, poetry, essays, art, cartoons, photography, letters, sketches, you-name-it." No length or subject matter limitations. Previously published and simultaneous submissions OK. Payment is a small stipend ($20 tops) plus a copy. Send to Rosalind Warren by April 1, 1990.

DENLINGER PUBLISHERS LTD, P.O. Box 76, Fairfax VA 22020. (703)830-4646. FAX: (203)830-5303. Estab. 1926. Publishes hardcovers, trade paperback originals.

Humorous Illustration: Needs humorous illustration for fiction and nonfiction titles. When hiring a freelance humorous illustrator, considers skill, drawing style, ability to take art direction well, professionalism, businesslike attitude. Buys all rights. For first contact send cover letter, resume, b&w promo piece to W.W. Denlinger, Publisher. Reports back within 7 days. Returns materials if requested and accompanied by SASE. Pays $100-500 b&w and color book cover; $10-30 b&w and color inside illustration.

Humor Writing: Uses freelance humor writers primarily for specialty books. Fiction mss needed on self help. Nonfiction mss needed on dogs. Buys all rights. For first contact send cover letter, resume, query to W.W. Denlinger. Reports back within 2 months. Returns materials if accompanied by SASE. Pays 10% royalty. Outright purchase $100-5,000. Also flat fee per copy royalty. Advance negotiable, but usually never.

EDUCATIONAL INSIGHTS, 19560 S. Rancho Way, Dominguez Hills CA 90220. (213)637-2131. Estab. 1962. Publishes textbooks, teaching material and produces educational toys and games. Humor line includes children's stories. Recently published *Brainboosters*, *Cliffhangers* and *Tuff Stuff Stories*.

Humorous Illustration: Works with 25 freelance humorous illustrators/year. Needs humorous illustration for fiction and nonfiction titles, cartoons and caricature. Uses freelance humorous illustrators primarily (80%). Send excellent samples and cover letter. When hiring a freelance humorous illustrator, considers skill, ability to take art direction, compatability of style with text, professionalism, businesslike attitude and drawing style. Buys all rights. For first contact, send cover letter, color promo piece, color tearsheets, slides and client list. Send to C.J. Bentz-Conner, Art Director. Reports back in 10 days. Returns materials only if requested and if accompanied by SASE. Keeps materials on file. Pays b&w cover $50-350; color cover $200-1,000; b&w inside illustration $25-100; and color inside illustration $50-600.

Humor Writing: Inhouse staff published 20 humor titles last year.

FIVE STAR PUBLICATIONS, P.O. Box 3142, Scottsdale AZ 85271-3142. (602)941-0770. Estab. 1985. Publishes hardcovers, paperback and trade paperback originals and textbooks. Humor line includes children's books, cookbooks, how-to books, parenting, child and senior care—"Humorous drawings are needed for most books we publish." Recently published *Nannies, Maids & More: The Complete Guide for Hiring Household Help* and *Shakespeare for Children: The Story of Romeo & Juliet.*
Humorous Illustration: Works with approximately 3 freelance humorous illustrators/year. Needs humorous illustration for fiction and nonfiction titles. "We prefer realism versus abstract drawings." Send sample drawings, resume and salary requirements. When hiring a freelance humorous illustrator, considers skill, drawing style, ability to take art direction, professionalism, businesslike attitude and ability to work within a time frame. "We buy all rights." For first contact should send cover letter, resume client list and b&w promo piece. Send to Linda Foster Radke, Publisher. Reports back only if interested. Returns materials if accompanied by SASE. Keeps materials on file. Pays b&w book cover $50 on up; color cover $50 on up; b&w inside illustration $10 on up; color inside illustration $25 on up.
Humor Writing: Works with approximately 3 freelance humorous nonfiction writers/year. 2 freelance humorous fiction writers/year.

GOLDEN WEST PUBLISHERS, 4113 N. Longview Ave., Phoenix AZ 85014. (602)265-4392. Estab. 1972. Publishes paperback and trade paperback originals. Humor line includes original cartoon books and illustrated nonfiction books with Western theme. Recently published *Cowboy Slang, Cowboy Country Cartoons* and *Conflict at the Border.*
Humorous Illustration: Works with approximately 2 freelance humorous illustrators/year. Needs cartoon books and humorous illustration for nonfiction titles. Cartoon books should have Western or Southwestern theme. When hiring a freelance humorous illustrator, considers compatibility of drawing style with text. Buys all rights. For first contact send cover letter, b&w tearsheets to Hal Mitchell, Editor. Reports back within 2 weeks. Returns materials if accompanied by SASE. Pays royalties; semi-annual payments.
Humor Writing: Published 2 humor titles last year. Works with approximately 2 freelance humorous nonfiction writers/year. Uses freelance humor writers primarily for books with Western theme. Needs humorous nonfiction writing. Nonfiction mss needed on cooking, gardening, driving, traveling, sightseeing, etc., all with Western slant. Buys all rights. Send query to Hal Mitchell. Does not accept dot matrix submissions. Reports back within 2 weeks if accompanied by SASE. Pays royalty of 6-10% on retail price. No advance.

GRAPEVINE PUBLICATIONS, INC., P.O. Box 118, Corvallis OR 97339. (503)754-0583. Estab. 1983. Publishes trade paperback originals, "how-to"and instructional softcover books.
Humorous Illustration: Works with approximately 4 freelance humorous illustrators/year. Needs humorous illustration for nonfiction titles. Uses freelance humorous illustrators primarily for illustrating instructional materials. When hiring a freelance humorous illustrator, considers skill, ability to take art direction well, compatibility of drawing style with text, professionalism and businesslike attitude. Buys all rights. For first contact send cover letter, resume, b&w tearsheets to Mr. Chris Coffin, Editor-in-Chief. Reports back within 1 month if accompanied by SASE.

HARVEST HOUSE PUBLISHERS, 1075 Arrowsmith, Eugene OR 97402. (503)343-0123. Publishes hardcovers, trade paperback originals, mass market paperbacks. Humor line includes written humor, joke books, trivia, puzzles/games—all with evangelical Christian theme. Recently published *World's Greatest Collection of Clean Jokes* and *Proverbs for People.*

Humorous Illustration: Works with approximately 2 freelance humorous illustrators/ year. Needs humorous illustration for fiction titles. Send samples and query with SASE. When hiring a freelance humorous illustrator, considers skill, ability to take art direction well, compatibility of drawing style with text. For first contact send cover letter, resume to Fred Renich, Production Manager. Reports back within 2 months if accompanied by a SASE.

Humor Writing: Published 4 humor titles last year. Fiction and nonfiction mss needed with an evangelical Christian theme. For first contact, send cover letter, resume, query, writing sample, sample chapter, outline of manuscript for fiction and nonfiction to LaRae Weikert, Manuscript Coordinator. Reports back within 2 months. Returns materials if accompanied by SASE.

HORIZON PUBLISHERS AND DISTRIBUTORS, INC., 50 South 500 West, P.O. Box 490, Bountiful UT 84011. (801)295-9451. Estab. 1972. Publishes hardcovers, paperback originals, textbooks. Humor line includes original cartoon books and stationery. Recently published *Quick & Easy Cooking, Celestial Symbols,* and *Golden Harvest in Ghana.*

Humorous Illustration: Send all humorous illustration submissions to Norma Dalton, Editorial Assistant. Reports back within 3-4 months if accompanied by a SASE. Pays royalty of 5-12% on wholesale price. Send a query letter first. "We will request a synopsis and sample chapter if interested." Send all humor fiction or nonfiction to Suzanne Hill. Reports back within 3-4 months. Returns materials if accompanied by a SASE. Pays royalty. No advance.

INNER TRADITIONS INTERNATIONAL, Imprints: Destiny Books, Park Street Press, One Park Street, Rochester VT 05767. (802)767-3174. FAX: (802)767-3726. Estab. 1976. Publishes humor trade, hardcovers, trade paperback originals, textbooks. Recently published *Driving Your Own Kurma* by Swami Beyondananda, *In Search of the New Age* by Chris Kilhim. Prefers working with freelancers who have fax capabilities.

Humorous Illustration: Works with approximately 2 freelance humorous illustrators/ year. Needs humorous illustration for nonfiction titles. Uses freelance humorous illustrators primarily for humor books. When hiring a freelance humorous illustrator, considers skill, drawing style, compatibility of drawing style with text. Buys all rights. For first contact send cover letter, resume, b&w tearsheets, portfolio to Estella Arias, Art Director. Reports back within 2 weeks if requested and accompanied by a SASE. Pays $200-800 color cover; $40-60 b&w inside illustration; $50-80 color inside illustration.

Humor Writing: Published 1 humor title last year. Works with approximately 1 freelance humorous nonfiction writer/year. Uses freelance humor writers primarily "for one book if it comes up." Needs humorous fiction and nonfiction writing. Fiction mss needed on new age topics, self-help. Nonfiction mss needed on religion, yuppies, new age gurus, men's new roles, natural medicine, etc. Send a short letter with synopsis, table of contents and sample chapter. Buys all rights. For first contact, send query to Leslie Colket, Managing Editor. Accepts submissions via disk with hard copy. Reports back within 2 months if interested. Returns materials if accompanied by SASE. Pays per project, $1,000 for 30,000 words; royalty of 6% on retail price. Average advance of $2,000.

Tips: "Look at other books. Is your subject topical? Does it add a new slant to the topic? Does your book make fun of new age ideas, people, lifestyle, etc? Not interested in straight humor. We publish very little humor but are interested in books, ideas, proposals that poke fun at new age phenomena. This can be anything from dimestore gurus to macro-neurotics, to whole foods (like do-nuts) etc."

INTERVARSITY PRESS, P.O. Box 1400, Downers Grove IL 60515. (708)964-5700. FAX: (708)964-1251. Estab. 1940. Publishes hardcovers, trade paperback originals. Humor line includes cartoon books. Recently published *Way Off the Church Wall.*

Humor Writing: Send all humor fiction to Andrew T. LePeau, Managing Editor. Accepts submissions submitted via fax. Reports back within 10 weeks. Returns materials if accompanied by a SASE. Pays royalty of 5-15% on retail price or makes outright purchase $600-2,500. Average advance of $3,000.

MCN PRESS, Box 702073, Tulsa OK 74170. Estab. 1962. Publishes hardcovers, trade paperback originals. Humor line includes original cartoon books and military subjects. **Humorous Illustration:** Works with approximately 2-3 freelance humorous illustrators/year. Needs cartoons, humorous illustration for nonfiction titles. When hiring a freelance humorous illustrator, considers skill, ability of to take art direction well. Buys all rights. For first contact send cover letter and original art to Jack Britton, Publisher. Reports back within 2 weeks. Returns materials if requested and accompanied by SASE. Pays $5-50 b&w book cover; $10-100 color cover; $1-5 b&w inside illustration; $10-100 color inside illustration.
Humor Writing: Works with approximately 2-3 freelance humorous nonfiction writers/year. Needs cartoons.

MEADOWBROOK PRESS, 18318 Minnetonka Blvd., Deephaven MN 55391. (612)473-5400. FAX: (612)475-0736. Estab. 1975. Publishes hardcovers, trade and paperback originals and humor trade. Humor line includes original cartoon books and written humor. Recently published *Grandma Knows Best, But No One Ever Listens, Italian Without Words.*
Humorous Illustration: Works with approximately 5 freelance humorous illustrators a year. Needs cartoons and humorous illustration for nonfiction titles. When hiring a freelance humorous illustrator, considers skill, drawing style, ability to take art direction well, compatibility of drawing style with text, professionalism and businesslike attitude. Buys all rights. For first contact send cover letter and resume to Kevin Bowen, Art Director. Reports back on submissions within 6 weeks. Returns materials if accompanied by a SASE. Keeps materials on file. Pays color cover $100-500; b&w inside illustration $25-100; color inside illustration $25-100.
Humor Writing: Published 9 humor titles in last year. Works with approximately 5-10 freelance humorous nonfiction writers/year. Needs humorous fiction and nonfiction writing. Fiction mss needed on babies, dads, moms, grandparents, weddings, marriage, retirement, graduation and other gift-giving occasions. To sell fiction, send an outline and sample chapters. To sell nonfiction, send sample chapters and a proposal. Buys all rights. Send cover letter, query, sample chapter and outline of ms to Lisa Schwimmer, Submissions Editor. Accepts dot matrix and fax submissions. Reports back in 6 weeks. Returns materials if accompanied by a SASE. Keeps materials on file. Pays $1,000-5,000 per project, royalty basis 5-7.5%. Offers an average advance of $2,500. Ignore what most "How to Write" books say and start with a strong concept — for us, something pertaining to a gift occasion such as new baby, graduation, retirement, engagement, weddings, etc.

NELSON-HALL PUBLISHERS, 111 N. Canal St., Chicago IL 60606. (312)930-9446. Estab. 1909. Publishes hardcovers, trade paperback originals, textbooks. Humor line includes scholarly and educational books.
Humorous Illustration: When hiring a freelance humorous illustrator, considers skill, compatibility of drawing style with text. Buys one time rights. For first contact send cover letter, b&w tearsheets, b&w promo piece to Richard O. Meade, General Manager. Reports back within 1 month if interested. Returns materials if requested and accompanied by SASE, or keeps materials on file. Pays $50-100 b&w inside illustration.
Humor Writing: Rights purchased depends on author contract. Does not accept dot matrix submissions.

NEW VICTORIA PUBLISHERS, P.O. Box 27, Norwich VT 05055. (802)649-5297. Estab. 1976. Publishes paperback originals and trade paperback originals. Humor line includes original cartoon books, written humor, mystery, romance and feminist titles. Recently published *Gray Magic, Found Goddesses,* and *As the Road Curves.*

Humorous Illustration: Works with approximately 1 freelance humorous illustrator/ year. Needs humorous illustration for fiction titles and cartoons. Uses freelance humorous illustrators primarily for covers and cartoons. Send samples. When hiring a freelance humorous illustrator, considers skill, drawing style, compatibility of drawing style with text. Buys all rights; pays royalties on cartoon collections. For first contact send cover letter, b&w tearsheets to Claudia Lamperti, Editor. Reports back within 2 weeks. Returns materials if accompanied by a SASE. Pays $100 b&w book cover; $25 b&w inside illustration.

Humor Writing: Published 2 humor titles last year. Works with approximately 2 freelance humorous fiction and nonfiction writers/year. Uses freelance humor writers primarily for fiction. Needs humorous fiction writing. Fiction mss needed on lesbian-feminist issues, mysteries, cartoons, etc. Nonfiction mss needed on history of feminism. Buys all rights, negotiated. For first contact, send writing sample, outline of manuscript to Claudia Lamperti. Accepts submissions via disk. Reports back within 2 weeks. Returns materials if accompanied by a SASE. Pays 10% royalty on wholesale price or in copies. No advance.

NORTH LIGHT BOOKS, 1507 Dana Ave., Cincinnati OH 45207. (513)531-2222. FAX: (513)531-4744. Imprint of F&W Publications. Publishes trade paperback originals. Recently published *Clutter's Last Stand, Make Your House do the Housework.* Prefers working with freelancers who have fax capabilities.

Humorous Illustration: Works with approximately 3 freelance humorous illustrators/ year. Needs cartoons, humorous illustration for nonfiction titles. Uses freelance humorous illustrators primarily for books. Send non-returnable samples for file. When hiring a freelance humorous illustrator, considers drawing style of artist. Buys one time rights. For first contact send b&w tearsheets to Carol Buchanan, Art Director. Reports back only if interested. Returns materials if accompanied by a SASE. Pays $50-200 b&w for color book cover; $15-75 b&w inside illustration; $50-150 color inside illustration.

PACIFIC PRESS PUBLISHING ASSOCIATION, 1350 North Kings Rd., Nampa ID 83687. (208)456-2500. FAX: (208)465-2531. Estab. 1874. Publishes hardcovers, trade paperback originals, paperback originals, textbooks, youth magazine, Christian lifestyle magazines. Humorous illustrations are used to illustrate nonfictional magazines and books. Recently published *Jumping off the Retirement Shelf, Too Much Salt and Pepper, A Tippy Canoe and Canada Too.* Prefers working with freelancers who have fax capabilities (or access to a fax machine in their town).

Humorous Illustration: Works with approximately 40 freelance humorous illustrators/ year. Needs cartoons, humorous illustration for nonfiction titles, caricature. Uses freelance humorous illustrators primarily for magazines. "Send slides or printed samples we can keep as reference of the artist's style." When hiring a freelance humorous illustrator, considers skill, drawing style, ability to take art directions well, compatibility of drawing style with text, professionalism, businesslike attitude and ability to meet deadlines. Buys one time rights, first time rights, sometimes second use rights at a later date. Send cover letter, b&w tearsheets, color tearsheets, or slides to Art Department. ("We have 7 art directors who buy illustrations on a regular basis.") Reports back only if interested. Returns materials if requested or keeps materials on file. Pays $550-1,000 ($700, normally) for color cover; $50-$300 b&w inside illustration; $100-$500 ($300-400, typically) color inside illustration.

PADRE PRODUCTIONS, P.O. Box 840, Arroyo Grande CA 93421-0840. (805)473-1947. Estab. 1974. Independent book producer/packager. Publishes hardcovers and trade paperback originals. Humor line includes original cartoon books.

Humorous Illustrations: Works with approximately 10 freelance humorous illustrators/year. Needs humorous illustration for nonfiction titles, cartoons and cartoon books. Uses freelance humorous illustrators primarily for nonfiction illustration. Send photocopies or tearsheets illustrating various styles; submit theme-oriented book proposal. When hiring a freelance humorous illustrator, considers skill and drawing style of artist and topic ideas. Buys all rights. For first contact send cover letter, resume, b&w tearsheets, color tearsheets and b&w promo piece. Send to: Lachlan P. MacDonald, Publisher. Reports back only if interested. Returns materials if accompanied by SASE. Keeps materials on file. Payment varies.

Humor Writing: Mss are needed on the publishing industry.

Tips: "We are interested in seeing book manuscripts or proposals for small cartoon books, 64 pages or more, devoted to such subjects as book publishing, freelance writing, underwater diving and photography, California lifestyle, professional outdoor photography, raising or being raised by cats, same for dogs, other single-subject themes."

PLAYERS PRESS INC., P.O. Box 1132, Studio City CA 91614. (818)789-4980. Estab. 1965. Publishes hardcovers, trade paperback originals, mass market paperbacks, paperback originals, textbooks, hard cover reprints. Humor line includes written humor, theater specialty. Recently published *Late 4th Partner, A Matter of Degree, Humorous Monologues for Actors.*

Humorous Illustration: Works with approximately 1-3 freelance humorous illustrators/year. Needs humorous illustration for nonfiction titles. Uses freelance humorous illustrators primarily for covers/plates. When hiring a freelance humorous illustrator, considers skill of artist, drawing style, ability to take art direction well, compatibility of drawing style with text, professionalism and businesslike attitude. Buys all rights. For first contact send cover letter, resume and b&w tearsheets to Marjorie E. Clapper, Associate Editor. Reports back only if interested. Returns materials if requested; keeps material on file. Pays $10-100 b&w book cover; $25-500 color cover; $5-50 b&w inside illustration.

Humor Writing: Published 3 humor titles last year. Works with approximately 1-10 freelance humorous nonfiction writers/year. Uses freelance humor writers primarily for plays, monologues and scenes. Needs humorous fiction and nonfiction writing, dramatic writing for theater material. Fiction mss needed on all subjects in theater format. Nonfiction mss needed on performing arts, theater, film, television. Buys all rights. For first contact, send query to Robert W. Gordon, Vice President, Editorial. Accepts agented submissions only. Does not accept dot matrix submissions. Reports back within 4 months if interested. Returns materials if accompanied by a SASE. Pays per project $50-250 for 1,000-10,000 words; royalty of 8-10% on wholesale price; outright purchase $50-5,000 for publishable work. Average advance varies depending on material.

Tips: "We are interested only in theatrical works."

POMEGRANATE PRESS, LTD., 3236 Bennett Drive, Los Angeles CA 90068. (213)850-6719. FAX: (213)876-5696. Estab. 1986. Independent book producer/packager. Publishes hardcovers, trade paperback originals, humor trade. Humor line includes illustrated humor, written humor. Recently published *The Logical Lexicon of Useless English, Word of Mouth.*

Humorous Illustration: Works with approximately 2-3 freelance humorous illustrators/year. Needs cartoons, humorous illustration for nonfiction titles, caricature. When hiring a freelance humorous illustrator, considers skill, drawing style, compatibility of drawing style with text, professionalism, businesslike attitude. For first contact send cover letter, resume, b&w tearsheets to Ben Martin, Creative Director. Reports back only if interested. Returns materials if accompanied by a SASE; keeps materials on file. Pays $500-1,000 color cover.

Humor Writing: Published 1 humor title last year. Negotiates rights purchased. For first contact, send cover letter, resume, query to K.L. Scott, Publisher. Accepts submissions via disk "if asked for." Does not report back. Returns materials if accompanied by a SASE. Pays royalties of 10% on retail price. Average advance $1,000.

PRICE STERN SLOAN, 360 N. La Cienega Blvd., Los Angeles CA 90048. (213)657-6100. FAX: (213)855-8993. Estab. 1964. Publishes mass market paperbacks, humor trade, hardcovers, paperback originals and trade paperback originals. Humor line includes written humor, original cartoon books/humor books. Recently published *Murphy's Law Books*, *How to be a Jewish Mother*, *How to be an Italian*, *How to be a Celebrity*, and *Cheapskates Handbook*.

Humorous Illustration: Works with approximately 3 freelance humorous illustrators/year. Needs humorous illustration for fiction titles, cartoons. Uses freelance humorous illustrators primarily for humor books. Submit query letter and sample illustrations (no original artwork). When hiring a freelance humorous illustrator, considers skill, drawing style, ability to take art direction well, compatibility of drawing style with text, professionalism, businesslike attitude. Buys all rights. For first contact send cover letter, color or b&w promo piece to Jill Weisman, Editorial Assistant. Reports back within 6 weeks only if interested. Returns materials if accompanied by a SASE or keeps materials on file.

Humor Writing: Published 4-6 humor titles last year. Works with approximately 4-6 freelance humorous fiction writers/year. Uses freelance humor writers primarily for humor books. Needs humorous fiction writing. Mss needed on society, people, business world, family, government, self-help, etc. Buys all rights. For first contact, send query, cover letter and outline of manuscript for fiction and nonfiction to Jill Weisman. Reports back within 6 weeks. Returns materials if accompanied by a SASE; does not file materials.

Tips: "Writers should keep on top of trends by visiting bookstores, screening bestseller lists, etc."

ROSE PUBLISHING CO., INC., Suite 208, 2723 Foxcraft Rd., Little Rock AR 72207. (501)227-8104. Estab. 1973. Publishes humor trade. Humor line includes Southern and regional expressions; "it's not fattening if—"; editorial cartoons. Recently published *Southern Legislative Dictionary I & II*, *How to Talk Dirty Like Grandad*, *How to Talk Funny Like Grandma*.

Humorous Illustration: Works with approximately 3 freelance humorous illustrators/year. Needs local illustrators and editorial cartoonists only. When hiring a freelance humorous illustrator, considers compatibility of drawing style with text. Negotiates rights purchased. For first contact send b&w tearsheets to Gale Stewart, Managing Editor. Reports back only if interested. Returns materials if accompanied by a SASE.

Humor Writing: Published 3-4 humor titles last year. Works with approximately 3-4 freelance humorous nonfiction writers/year. Needs humorous nonfiction writing, regional expressions, jokes and stories. Nonfiction mss needed on regional expressions, stories, jokes. Send a summary and sample chapter. Negotiates rights purchased. For first contact, send cover letter, writing sample, sample chapter, outline of manuscript to Gale Stewart. Accepts submissions via disk if accompanied by printout. Reports back only if interested. Returns materials if accompanied by a SASE. Pays royalty of 10% on retail price. No advance.

Tips: "We publish short humor books only, 65-70 pages."

RUTGERS UNIVERSITY PRESS, 109 Church St., New Brunswick NJ 08901. (201)932-8174. Estab. 1937. Publishes hardcovers, trade paperback originals, hardcover reprints, trade paperback reprints. Humor line includes collection of Sidney Harris Science cartoons, comic novels, humorous essays. Recently published *Einstein Simplified*, by Sidney Harris (cartoons); *Tales of a Low Rent Birdie*, by Pete Dunne (essays); *The Cruz Chronicles* (humorous novel). "Harris book may have been a one-shot deal. His name recognition among scientists was crucial."

Humorous Illustration: When hiring a freelance humorous illustrator, considers skill, drawing style, ability to take art direction well, compatibility of drawing style with text, professionalism, businesslike attitude. Buys one time rights and reprint rights. Send all humorous illustrations to Barbara Kopel, Production Manager.

Humor Writing: Uses freelance humor writers primarily for novels. Fiction mss needed on science, medicine, nature, women's studies. Nonfiction mss needed on science, medicine, natural history. Send proposal or mss to the attention of Kenneth Arnold, Director. Negotiates rights. For first contact, send cover letter, resume, query, writing sample, published tearsheet, entire manuscript, sample chapter, "as much as possible" for fiction and nonfiction to Kenneth Arnold. Reports back within 3-4 weeks. Returns materials if requested and accompanied by a SASE. Pay is subject to negotiation.

Tips: "We prefer gender-free, bias-free language and illustrations. Avoid generic 'he' for example. Avoid making all scientists male, all assistants female, all figures obviously white. We do not regularly publish humor, but obviously are open to it. Well-crafted comic novels have the best chance."

SHAPOLSKY PUBLISHERS, INC., 136 West 22nd St., New York NY 10011. (212)633-2022. FAX: (212)633-2123. Estab. 1986. Independent book producer/packager. Publishes hardcover reprints, humor trade, hardcover originals, paperback originals, trade paperback originals. Humor line includes "whatever has the potential to sell well." Recently published *The Joy of Depression, Guide to Being a Man in a Woman's World: How to be Macho without Offending Anyone.*

Humorous Illustration: Works with approximately 3 freelance humorous illustrators/year. Needs humorous illustration for fiction titles, nonfiction titles, cartoons and caricature. Send a few photocopies of best material for consideration. When hiring a freelance humorous illustrator, considers skill, drawing style. Buys all rights or reprint rights. For first contact send cover letter, b&w promo piece. "Black and white photocopies are best as they are least problematic to return." Send submissions to Ian Shapolsky, Publisher. Reports back within 1 month. Returns materials if requested and accompanied by a SASE. Pays $100-500 for b&w and color book cover; $20-250 for b&w and color inside illustration.

Humor Writing: Published 4 humor titles last year. Works with approximately 3 freelance humorous fiction and nonfiction writers/year. Uses freelance humor writers primarily for new book projects. Needs humorous fiction and nonfiction writing. Fiction mss needed on relationships, parodies, self-help and spoofs. Interested in seeing nonfiction mss on relationships, cooking and religion. Buys first time rights, reprint rights, all rights or negotiates rights purchased. Send cover letter and query to Ian Shapolsky. Accepts agented submissions only. Reports back within 1 month only if interested. Returns materials if requested and accompanied by a SASE. Pays $250-5,000 per project, royalty of 6-15% on retail price, outright purchase $350-7,000. Average advance $3,000.

Tips: "Humor buyers are tough cookies, so try to be on the cutting edge of a new, unusual concept or genre of humor. Be different so we can awe the bookstore buyer with your book."

THE SPEECH BIN, INC.P.O. Box 218, 231 Clarksville Rd., Princeton Junction NJ 08550-0218. (609)799-3935. FAX: (609)799-9530. Estab. 1984. Publishes textbooks and books for speech-language pathology, audiology, and special education markets.
Humorous Illustration: Works with approximately 5-6 freelance humorous illustrators/year. Needs humorous illustration for nonfiction titles. Uses humorous/cartoon art for children's books, texts, diagnostic tests. When hiring a freelance humorous illustrator, considers skill and drawing style, ability to take art direction, compatability of drawing style with text, professionalism, businesslike attitude of artist. Buys all rights "but will negotiate rights purchased." For first contact freelancer should send cover letter, resume, client list and b&w tearsheets to Jan J. Binney, Senior Editor. Reports back in 3 months. Returns materials only if requested and accompanied by SASE. Keeps materials on file. Pays $5-50 b&w inside illustration
Humor Writing: Submit query. "This is a specialized market. We generally consider art only, but are interested in looking at books and treatment materials for children with communication disorders and other handicaps. Send all humor nonfiction to Jan J. Binney. Accepts FAX submissions. Reports back in 3 months. Returns materials only if requested and accompanied by SASE. Pays royalty of 8% minimum.

STERLING PUBLISHING CO., INC., 387 Park Ave. S., New York NY 10016. (212)532-7160. FAX: (212)213-2495. Estab. 1949. Publishes hardcovers, trade paperback originals and trade paperback reprints. Humor line includes children's humor collections, humorous monologues and plays. Recently published *696 Silly School Jokes* and *Comedy Writer's Workbook*.
Humorous Illustration: Works with approximately 5 freelance humorous illustrators/year. Needs humorous illustration for nonfiction titles. Uses freelance humorous illustrators primarily for book illustration. "Send Xerox samples we can keep in our files." When hiring a freelance humorous illustrator, considers skill and drawing style. Buys all rights. For first contact send cover letter, resume if available, b&w tearsheets, color tearsheets to Sheila Anne Barry, Juvenile Editor. Reports back only if interested. Returns materials if requested and accompanied by a SASE, keeps materials on file. Pays $400 color cover; $15-20 b&w inside illustration "or inside illustration on royalty basis where they are a major part of the book."
Humor Writing: Published 6 humor titles last year. Works with approximately 10 freelance humorous nonfiction writers/year. Uses freelance humor writers primarily for children's books (humor collections). Needs humorous nonfiction writing for children only. Nonfiction mss needed of riddles, jokes, fun activities. "Query us first, by phone or letter." Buys all rights to work on royalty basis. For first contact, send cover letter, resume if available, query to Sheila Anne Barry. Reports back within 2 months only if interested, unless SASE is enclosed. Returns materials if accompanied by SASE. Pays royalty of 5-10%. Advance "depends on material."

TAYLOR PUBLISHING COMPANY, 1550 W. Mockingbird Lane, Dallas TX 75235. (214)637-2800 ext. 220. Estab. 1980. Publishes hardcovers, trade paperback originals, paperback originals, humor trade. Humor line includes written humor. Recently published *What Sign is Your Pet?*, *Waspleg and Other Mnemonics*.
Humor Writing: Published 2 humor titles last year. Works with approximately 2 freelance humorous nonfiction writers/year. Needs humorous nonfiction writing. Negotiates rights purchased. For first contact, send cover letter, sample chapter to Jim Donovan, Senior Editor. Accepts modem, fax and disk submissions. Reports back within 1 month. Returns materials if requested, does not file materials. Pays royalties of 7-10% on retail price. Average advance $5,000.
Tips: "Humor, of course, is highly subjective and thus, hard to pin down. But an attempted definition of the kind of humor we're looking for would include the following adjectives: fresh, topical, intelligent, original, and most importantly, funny."

TOPPER BOOKS, 200 Park Ave., New York NY 10166. (212)692-3700. Estab. 1985. Imprint of Pharos Books. Publishes trade paperback originals, humor trade. Humor line includes reprint collections, original cartoon books. Recently published *When Do the Good Things Start, U.S. Acres, Mother Goose & Grimm*.
Tips: "We would like to see humor manuscripts focused on trends. Advances are in the range of $2,000-7,000."

TRILLIUM PRESS, 217 High St., Monroe NY 10950. (914)783-2999. Estab. 1978. Publishes trade paperback originals, paperback originals, textbooks.
Humorous Illustration: Needs humorous illustration for fiction and nonfiction titles, cartoons, caricature. Buys all rights. For first contact send cover letter, b&w tearsheets to Pam Leavens, Art Director. Reports back only if interested. Keeps material on file.
Humor Writing: Published 20 humor titles last year.
Tips: "We are interested in illustrators and cartoonists, but not generally in manuscripts."

WORD PUBLISHING, (Div. of Word, Inc.), Suite 1000, 5221 North O'Connor, Irving TX 75039. Estab. 1951. Publishes hardcovers, trade paperback originals, mass market paperback originals. Recently published *Life Everlaughter* (many serious topics written with a light touch), *Scuff Marks on the Ceiling* (a book on parenting).
Humorous Illustration: Works with approximately 2 freelance humorous illustrators/year. Needs cartoons, humorous illustration for nonfiction titles. Uses freelance humorous illustrators primarily for book illustration. When hiring a freelance humorous illustrator, considers skill, drawing style, ability to take art direction well, compatibility of drawing style with text, professionalism, businesslike attitude. Buys all rights. For first contact send cover letter, b&w tearsheets, color tearsheets to Tom Williams, Design Director. Reports back only if interested. Returns materials if accompanied by a SASE, keeps material on file. Pays $250 b&w book cover; $600 color cover; $75-150 b&w inside illustration.

WYRICK & COMPANY, P.O. Box 89, Charleston SC 29402. (803)722-0881. Estab. 1986. Publishes hardcovers, trade paperback originals. Humor line includes written humor; cartoon books. Recently published *Anguished English*, *Get Thee to a Punnery* and *Animal Crackers*.
Humorous Illustration: Works with approximately 3 freelance humorous illustrators/year. Needs humorous illustration for fiction and nonfiction titles. Uses freelance humorous illustrators primarily for book illustration and covers. When hiring a freelance humorous illustrator, considers skill, drawing style, ability to take art direction well, compatibility of drawing style with text, professionalism, businesslike attitude. Negotiates rights purchased. For first contact send cover letter, resume, client list, b&w tearsheets, color tearsheets to Charles L. Wyrick, Jr., Editor-in-Chief. Reports back within 2 months. Returns materials if accompanied by a SASE. Pays $150-650 b&w book cover; $250-850 color cover; $10-150 b&w inside illustration; $25-200 color inside illustration.
Humor Writing: Published 2 humor titles last year. Works with approximately 3 freelance humorous nonfiction writers/year and 2 freelance humorous fiction writers/year. Needs humorous fiction and nonfiction writing. Fiction mss needed on language, the arts, history, regional (esp. the South), business, government. Nonfiction mss needed on language, the arts, history, politics. Negotiates rights purchased. For first contact, send cover letter, writing sample, entire manuscript or sample chapter to Charles L. Wyrick, Jr. Reports back within 3 months. Returns materials if accompanied by a SASE. Pays royalties of 6-12% on retail price. Average advance $500.

Wham! Bam! Kapow! Zonk! Kappoey! Blam! Zap!

Considered yet unused names for The Seven Dwarfs? Afraid not. In the world of comic books, these expressive words are as commonly used as toothy newsprint.

Comic books are a whole world unto themselves. All the rules, conventions and practices normally associated with other markets are essentially cast to the wind in comic book publishing.

First, a "comic book publisher" can be almost anybody. From a corporate, mega-hero purveyor like Marvel to a guy clad in Batman underwear publishing a 12-part science fiction epic from his Manhattan, Kansas basement. Business sense, marketing plans and long term strategies need not necessarily be the comic book publisher's chief concerns — on the contrary, a fanatical love of the genre is the soup that keeps these folks publishing.

Still over-saturated with science fiction, adventure and laser-equipped mutant themes, many comic book publishers express the desire to get away from such hackneyed, formula genre and into humor-oriented art and writing.

While pay fluctuates incredibly (from $20 to perhaps $250 per page for cartooning and generally less for writing), the profession can be lucrative. "I gotta assume," says Kathe Todd, editor of Rip Off Press, "that if you have a big selling book, if you sell 250,000 copies per title, you can make as much as a lawyer."

But the business, Todd admits, isn't exactly run by corporate types. "We're really all grownups doing kid stuff," she says. "Comic book publishing has always had a little bit of a child-like sense to it — and sometimes that comes off as 'unprofessional.' "

Flooded with unsolicited submissions, Todd "loves to receive a package of material that makes me stop everything I'm doing. I'll get a crisp manila envelope addressed in wonderful lettering. Inside will be 10 photocopies of finished comic art that show drawing or storytelling ability and an understanding of reproduction techniques. If available, there's a copy of a published comic book and a cover letter that says who the submission is from, and what his or her immediate aspirations are."

If Todd likes what she sees, she contacts the artist or writer. "I jump on people who have talent," she says. "There is quite a degree of competition in this business for the really good people — that's because there aren't that many of them out there."

But if there are few truly good cartoonists around, Todd says there is no shortage of unprofessional ones. "A lot of these cartoonists have never grown up," she says. "They're marching to a different drummer, but they do so with a certain lack of professionalism. They're wonderful people; they do terrific stuff, but they don't make deadlines. It's almost like they avoid getting their stuff in on time as another form of rebellion. All they really want to do is draw funny pictures and then hope their check comes in the mail on time."

And while our intent is not to impugn or malign the comic book industry as a whole, we would be remiss if we did not touch on the issue of payment. Many cartoonists, writers and artists have complained about the sluggish payment policies of certain publishers. Although you should negotiate payment terms (net 30, 60 or 90 days, upon publication, royalty schedule, etc.), it is almost impossible to enforce terms even with a 350 lb. henchman named "Vito." Suffice to say, the most professional publishers will honestly abide by the terms negotiated. It simply takes time, experience and word of mouth to determine who's naughty and who's nice.

ACME PRESS LTD, 391 Coldharbour Ln., London, SW9 8LQ England. (01)274-7478. FAX: (01)274-4615. Estab. 1986. Audience is comprised of US and UK comic shops and general public. Circ. up to 100,000 internationally. Titles: *James Bond 007, Point Blank, Speakeasy, Lea, Maxwell the Magic Cat.*
Subject Needs: Would like to find projects that will appeal to general book readers as well as comic book fans. Artwise, looking for material of a high quality that could appeal to European publishers. Doesn't want to see typical comics genre fiction.
How to Contact: Humorous writers and cartoonists/humorous illustrators should send samples, published tearsheets and business card to Dick Hansom, Editorial Director. Also interested in seeing samples from pencil artists and inking artists. No dot matrix submissions. Prefers to work with freelancers with fax capabilities. To query with ideas for a new humorous comic book title send photocopied art and story outline. Reports back on unsolicited submissions/queries via letter in 3 months. Returns samples with SASE.
Terms: Payment negotiable

BLACKBIRD COMICS, P.O. Box 3211, Austin TX 78764. (512)445-5087. Estab. 1985. Audience is comprised of 18-35 year olds. Circ. 10,000 nationally/internationally.
Subject Needs: "Would like to find at least one good humor title aimed at 18-35 year olds, not too ridiculous — possibly based on life experiences, but not necessarily. Maybe a romantic comedy?" Doesn't want to see degrading humor; sleazy humor, sleazy anything; unfunny animals.
How to Contact: Humorous writers and cartoonists/humorous illustrators should send samples to John Nordland II, Editor/Publisher. For artist/writer guidelines, send #10 SASE. To query with ideas for a new humorous comic book title send photocopied art

and story outline. Reports back on unsolicited submissions/queries via letter in 2 weeks. Returns material if requested.

Terms: Payment for writing is on a royalty basis, 50% of net or $25-35/page; for cartooning, on royalty basis, 50% of net or $25-50 per b&w page upon invoice (net 30).

Tips: "Following trends makes a writer/artist just that, a follower. A writer should write honestly, without looking to see what the 'market' is up to. That's the only way to stay 'fresh.' " The dream for any publisher would be "a writer/artist or team with a full grasp of their medium—be it humor or horror, or whatever, and the ability to produce some consistency." The key to the success of a cartoonist is "flexibility, diversification and the ability to work unattended (self discipline, the desire to produce work regardless of being contracted to do so, just for the sake of 'doing it'). Should have a love of the medium, the ability to accept criticism, a good grip of 'body language' and a 'clarity' of work." A writer should have "diversity, ability to accept criticism, have a good sense of dialogue and clear plot and write for the love of writing. He should write to be read, not to impress."

BLUE COMET PRESS/AND TAMI COMICS, 1708 Magnolia Ave., Manhattan Beach CA 90266. (213)545-6887. Estab. 1986. Audience is comprised of mostly adventure and fantasy with some super-heroes, but most sword and sorcery. Circ. 5,000. Titles: *Varmints, Special Done Irregular, Funny-Animal Book, Regular Titles—Bladesmen, Rough Raiders, Zorann: Star-Warrier.* Approximately 20% of art and writing titles are humor oriented.

Subject Needs: "We need talented sword & sorcery artists that want exposure and are willing to work for little until we build our sales and find a more secure place to sell our books than the 'direct market.' We are looking into new markets. Don't want to see any beginners, we want professional quality artists looking for exposure that want to help build a company and secure a future for themselves."

How to Contact: Humorous writers should send writing samples to C.A. Stormon, President/owner. Cartoonist/humorous illustrators should send art samples, business card and a cover letter explaining credits/background to C.A. Stormon. Also interested in seeing samples from pencil artists, layout artists, inking artists, letterers and painters. For artist/writer guidelines or sample copy, send $2.50 and #10 SASE. To query with ideas for a new humorous comic book title send photocopied art and story outline. Reports back on unsolicited material only if interested. Returns material if requested.

Terms: Payment for writing is $30 for 10-page story. No royalties at this time; cartooning, b&w per page $10-40; b&w cover $50-200; 4-color cover $100-200. Sales for b&w comics are at an all time low. "We may have to change our dates and pay on a percentage of profit basis. If we make no money, no payment to anyone, only exposure and free copies." Pays upon publication.

Tips: "In today's comic book market, if you are not one of the big 4-5 publishers and you are doing B&W comics, you cannot have a successful book. Even if you have the most popular subject matter, top quality art and big name professional talent drawing it. The retailers cut our titles first when they have too much Batman product that month. Even though the retailers know they have customers for our books, and when our books even sell-out they will just cut our order instead of cutting back on one or two titles that don't sell well from the big 2. We have to find new markets or there will be no small independent publishers at all! A good example of a 'Dream comic book' is *Teenage Mutant Ninja Turtles.* Started with 3000 copies now has a cartoon show, cereal, color and b&w comics that all sell well regardless of market swings. My dream comic would be a comic that retailers could not ignore, and that would sell enough comics to make a living off of. I don't think there is a 'key to success' in comics. I have seen very very talented people show their art and never get hired! But I think what you want to hear is 'You must love to draw. If you don't love drawing more than sex or anything, then forget it. You have to draw and practice, day in and day out, every day! Until you lose all your friends, and you become a hermit, and you have to draw and practice from life not comic books, but just never quit and practice!' To be a success in writing comics, you have to find a small company like mine that likes your work, then you have to write for years on end for nothing to get the experience to know what must be done to get into the bigger publishers. You must start in the small independent market to learn the craft before you'll get better jobs."

C & T GRAPHICS/NEW VOICE PRODUCTIONS, RD #1, Box 80-C, Houghton NY 14744. Estab. 1981. Audience is comprised of comic book readers, fans and collectors. Circ. 5,000 nationally. Titles: *The Highly Unlikely Adventures of Mighty Guy.* Approximately 60% of art and writing titles are humor oriented. Approximately 50% of artwork and writing titles are by freelancers.

Subject Needs: Would like to find humor and satire comic strips and stories 6-12 pages in length. Also original art proportional to 5½ × 8½ (inquire about longer features), b&w art only. "Humor material is urgently needed." Doesn't want to see graphic adult material, preachy religious material.

How to Contact: Humorous writers should send a complete manuscript, a cover letter and sample photocopy pages with SASE to New Voice Productions, Editor. Cartoonist/ humorous illustrators should send art sample copies and a cover letter to New Voice Productions. Also interested in seeing samples from pencil artists, inking artists and letterers. No dot matrix submissions. For artist/writer guidelines, send $.50 and a business size SASE. To query with ideas for a new humorous comic book title send penciled pages and entire manuscript. Reports back on unsolicited submissions/queries via letter in 6 weeks. Returns samples with SASE.

Terms: Payment for writing is on a royalty basis, 2.5% gross of cover price times number of copies sold; for cartooning, on royalty basis, 3.5% of gross of cover price times numbers of copies sold. Pays on publication.

Tips: "Trying to cash in on a current comic book trend will avail the artist/writer nothing. Trends come and go. In the six months it usually takes to put a pilot book together, the current trend will have changed anyway. Strive for originality. Forget what everyone else is doing—even if it is successful." The dream comic book for any publisher would be "one that breaks new ground in art and storytelling and still captures the public's imagination." The key to success of a cartoonist is they "must know people. It's not enough to be a brilliant illustrator, or even riotously funny. You must have some insight into human nature." Writers should have "the same. They should know people not as a 'market', but as human beings. Reach out to your audience as individual people, and the 'market' will fall into place."

COMICOZ, P.O. Box 549, Redcliffe, Queensland Australia 4020. (07)203-4071. FAX: (07)283-1871. Estab. 1988. Audience is comprised of male, 14 years and older. Circ. 10,000. Titles: *John Dixon's Air Hawk Magazine.* Approximately 20% of art or writing titles are humor oriented. 100% of artwork or writing titles are by freelancers.

Subject Needs: Would like to find approximately 5 page stories, self-contained that are really funny. Doesn't want to see items from artists/cartoonists whose work is unprofessional, pornographic or of no commercial value.

How to Contact: Humorous writers should send published tearsheets, cover letter and business card to Nat Karmichael, Editor. Cartoonist/humorous illustrators should send art samples, published tearsheets, business card and ideas to Nat Karmichael. Also interested in seeing samples from layout artists. For artist/writer guidelines, send $2 and SASE. To query with ideas for a new humorous comic book title send photocopied art and story outline. Reports back on unsolicited submissions/queries in 2 months due to mail delays. Returns material if requested.

Terms: Payment for writing is on royalty basis, 5% wholesale price times print run of magazine; for cartooning, on royalty basis, 5% wholesale price times print run of magazine or $100-250 per b&w page, $200-350 four-color upon publication.

COMICS CAREER, 601 Clinkscales, Columbia MO 65203. (314)445-0083. Estab. 1988. A magazine aimed at amateur and aspiring comics creators. Circ. 150-300 nationally.
Subject Needs: "I need magazine-style articles and interviews on comics writing and art. I also need cartoons especially having to do with cartooning/writing. I don't need very basic 'How to Make a Submission' articles."
How to Contact: Humorous writers should send a short query to Kirk Chritton, Writer. Send cartooning submissions to Kirk Chritton, Editor. For artist/writer guidelines, send #10 SASE. Reports back on unsolicited submissions/queries via letter in 1 month. Returns samples with SASE.
Terms: Contributor's copy is sent.
Tips: The key to the success of a cartoonist in this market is "being able to balance the traditional comics storytelling style with a new dynamic twist."

DARK HORSE COMICS, 2008 SE Monroe, Milwahie OR 97222. (503)652-8815. Estab. 1986. 3rd biggest direct sales comics publisher biggest in the country. Books targeted for a 18-25 year old market. Circ. 15,000 nationally. *Aliens, Predator, Aliens Vs. Predator* and *Flaming Carrot.* Approximately 20% of artwork and writing titles are humor oriented. 100% of artwork and writing titles are by freelancers.
Subjects Needs: Most of the humor material shows up in 8 page stories in *Dark Horse Presents.* "At this point we don't want to see book-length stories or proposals for new series."
How to Contact: Cartoonist/humorous illustrators should send published tearsheets, art samples and a cover letter explaining credits/background. to Cris Warner. Also interested in seeing samples from pencil artists, letterers, layout artists and inking artists. For artist/writer guidelines, send #10 SASE. To query with ideas for a new humorous comic book title send photocopied art and story outline. Reports back on unsolicited submissions/queries via letter in 2 months (at the most—quicker if interested). Returns samples with SASE.
Terms: Pay depends on art quality, etc. Terms for payment are 30 days net upon invoice.

ECLIPSE, P.O. Box 1099, Forestville CA 95436. (707)337-1521. Estab. 1978. Audience is comprised of adults and young adults for graphic albums and young adults and older adolescents for our periodical comic books. Circ. up to 400,000. Titles: *The Hobbit, James Bond, Miracleman, Appleseed, Tapping the Vein, Zot!* Approximately 8% of art or writing titles are humor oriented. 100% of artwork or writing titles are by freelancers.
How to Contact: "Humorous writers/cartoonist/humorous illustrators should send for our guidelines (SASE with request) and we'll tell you how to submit a portfolio to Submissions Editor." Also interested in seeing samples from pencil artists, inking artists and realistic renderers; humorous caricaturists who can *paint* their art. No dot matrix submissions. For artist/writer guidelines, send #10 size SASE. To query with ideas for a new humorous comic book title send photocopied art or story outline. Reports back on unsolicited submissions/queries via letter in 3 months but only if SASE is included.
Terms: Payment for writing is $35-50 per page against an 8% royalty split; artist and writer pay $100-150 per page against a total of 8% royalties split between writer and artist upon invoice (net 30). Pays full payment as per contract kill fee for writing/cartooning.
Tips: "Better color technologies (laser scanning) has led to development of fully painted, slick 'art' comics. The trend now is toward fine art, realistic rendering and high quality printings." The dream comic book for any publisher would be "one produced *on time* by a great artist, with good sales potential and fully painted in a style halfway

between 'academic' and 'ad art'. Like, say a comic book by Norman Rockwell, N.C. Wyeth or Maxfield Parrish about the heroic adventures of a young woman who becomes a DEA agent, carries a gun and falls in love with the man she's been sent to set up for a drug bust by her crooked DEA boss who is actually in the pay of the medallion Cartel. And I want it next week! (The guy turns out to be okay, because he's a secret agent, so iuthey blow away the crooked DEA guy and the whole thing ends with a nice clinch against a background of sunset — no, make that dawn — in the mountains). "Cartoonists and writers should "know 3 things: 1) how to draw; 2) how to meet a deadline; 3) how to interact with fellow humans in a pleasant way."

FANTACO ENTERPRISES INC., 21 Central Ave., Albany NY 12210. (518)463-1400. FAX: (518)463-0090. Estab. 1978. "We publish horror, suspense and science fiction comics." Target audience is age 16-50; international distribution. Circ. 40,000. Titles: *Alien Encounters, Hembeck, Shriek, Smilin' Ed* and *Gore Shriek*. Approximately 10% of art and 30% of writing titles are humor oriented. 100% of artwork and writing titles are by freelancers.
Subject Needs: Abstract, surrealism photo-realism, dream imagery. Good humor material with horror or suspense setting. Doesn't want to see super heroes of *any* kind, "good girl" art, pre-pubescent sex fantasies, sex/violence stories, macho tales or x-rated material.
How to Contact: Cartoonist/humorous illustrators should send published tearsheets, business card, art samples and a cover letter explaining credits/background to Tom McKinnon, Editor. Also interested in seeing samples from letterers. To query with ideas for a new humorous comic book title send photocopied art. Returns samples with SASE.
Terms: Payment for cartooning: b&w per page, $35-110; b&w cover, $125-200; 4 color cover, $200-500. Pays on publication. Pays full payment kill fee if material does not run.
Tips: "The super hero market is bloated and sorely in need of a major fall from grace. Develop a unique concept, supply attractive art and be honest with your audience." A "dream" comic book would include "visually stunning art, completely inked and lettered; and intriguing story and a knockout painted and fully separated cover." The key to the success of a cartoonist or writer in this market is to "keep your ego in check; retain a sense of humor; remember you are in a highly competitive marketplace; remember that in the big scheme of things that noe of this really matters."

FANTAGRAPHICS BOOKS, 7563 Lake City Way NE, Seattle WA 98115. (206)524-1967. FAX: (206)524-2104. Estab. 1976. Audience is normal intelligent human beings who enjoy reading, among other things, comics. Circ. up to 25,000. Titles: *Love and Rockets, Eightball, Usagi Yojimbo, Peter Bagge's Hate, Eye of Mongombo, Yahoo, Unsupervised Existence*. Approximately 50% of writing titles and 50% of art are humor oriented. 100% of humor oriented titles are by freelancers.
Subject Needs: "We don't have 'needs' per se; we publish what we like. No superheroes, no parodies of super-heroes or genre crap; we don't dislike panels and short strips, but don't really have a lot of places to publish them."
How to Contact: Humorous writer should send published tearsheets and writing samples (but, "frankly, we tend to discourage writers; we're not set up to match up writers and artists at this point.") to Robert Boyd, Submissions Editor. Cartoonist/humorous illustrator should send published tearsheets and art samples to Robert Boyd, Submissions Editor. For artist/writer guidelines, send #10 SASE. To query with ideas for a new humorous comic book title send photocopied art and story outline. Reports back on unsolicited material via letter in 2 months. Returns samples with SASE.
Terms: For writing pays percentage of gross. For cartooning pays 6-8% of gross or $15 minimum per b&w page. "Our terms for payment are contractually negotiated advance upon delivery, royalties 45 days after publication."

Close-up

Kim Thompson
Publisher
Fantagraphics Books

"Blam!" isn't a part of Kim Thompson's vocabulary. Neither is "Zap!", "Pow!" or even "Kaboom!"

While Thompson and co-partner Gary Groth publish comic books, they steer clear of the traditional sci-fi, super hero, adventure and fantasy genre as if they caused life-threatening skin rashes.

Rather, their Fantagraphics Books publishes cutting edge humorous material—the kind of stuff that a Marvel or DC would toss in the dumpster; the type of stuff that the hip, sharp and discerning comic book fanatic sucks up with a straw.

After all, it is Fantagraphics that publishes such eclectic offerings as *Love and Rockets, Dog Boy, Itchy Planet, Christmas with Supeswine, Lust of the Nazi Weasel Women.* Odd stuff to be sure, and just plain, old-fashioned weird funny. Perhaps the weirdest thing is that Fantagraphics not only survives, but thrives.

"Basically," says Thompson, "Gary and I publish stories told in words and pictures that we would like to see. If we like something, we publish it. If we don't like it, we don't publish it. Whatever the Fantagraphics line looks like is very directly the result of our personal taste, convictions and prejudices, which is usually not the case with other publishers in the field."

To a great degree, Fantagraphics owes its success to its isolationism. "This is the classic, arrogant statement," warns Thompson, "but we really don't have any competition. That's because the type of material we're doing is of no interest to the other publishers. They become interested if we take it. An awful lot of the books we publish, that people go absolutely ape over, are books that nobody else wanted to touch. *Love and Rockets*, for example—nobody understood what we saw in it and seven years later it remains one of the big comic book phenomenons of the 1980s."

Each week, Thompson's Seattle-based office is inundated with submissions, though few are what he is looking for. "We're tired of seeing stupid super hero and stupid fantasy stuff—you know, a guy who goes to another galaxy, gets himself a sword and fights the evil forearm monsters. Basically, those people have no imagination and no ability to think beyond what they have seen or read in the last couple years. Imagination is really at a premium these days."

When the mail comes, Thompson is like a flea market browser. Ripping open the envelopes, he doesn't know what he's looking for, but he'll know it when he sees it. "Can you imagine," he asks, "before *Love and Rockets* was presented to us to say we were looking for that? There are more options in comics today—there is increasing stylistic diversity. The electric thing about comics is what happens between the words and images."

While having a proclivity for breaking the rules, Thompson believes strongly in one artistic tradition—the ability to draw. "The persistent conviction I hear from young cartoonists is the belief that you don't have to learn how to draw to learn how to cartoon. If you look at 'The Wizard of Id' or 'B.C.' which are just lines and squiggles, you think 'Aha!—I'll just draw lines and squiggles!' But you can't do those lines and squiggles unless you know the basics of drawing, how the human body is put together. Obviously, a lot of young cartoonists are reluctant to go through the hassle of actually learning how to draw—but you need that infrastructure.

"For instance," Thompson continues, "Sergio Aragones who does 'GROO' for Marvel is a better artist and better draftsman than anybody else working at Marvel. He has a far better understanding of anatomy, gesture, perspective, of analyzing space—yet his is the most 'cartoony' stuff at Marvel."

For the writer, Thompson encourages truth and discourages the analyzing of comic book writing trends. Thompson asks, "Is a writer going to write for a market or is he going to write for himself? Are you going to show the editor what you think he wants to see, or are you going to show him something you feel like expressing—something that you want to put down on paper regardless of whether or not you're going to sell it?"

But in the long run, is this idealism *realism*? Sure, this "art for art's sake" attitude sounds noble, sounds good on paper, but is it practical? "Obviously," Thompson asserts, "there are all sorts of levels of compromise. Obviously, there are very few people who draw or write exactly what they want. I mean, Robert Crumb would be one example of somebody who does 100% what he wants to, but at some point you slip into the gray area of the genre or within the restrictions that the publisher gives to you. Fantagraphics has even reached the point where we realize that there is material so unsaleable that we have to be cautious about it."

Still, alternative publishers like Fantagraphics afford cartoonists and writers a freedom virtually nonexistent at the big publishing houses. The joke about working for one of the mega-publishers is that you get a big paycheck—and an even bigger ball and chain.

"If you're working on a 'Spiderman' issue," says Thompson, "and you draw the web a certain way and your editor asks you to change it, you do it because that's part of the deal and you're paid an enormous amount of money. If you think you're going to be able to go off and do whatever you please, you aren't."

Happily, life at Fantagraphics doesn't resemble The Gulag Archipelago. Whip cracking is almost nonexistent; the water torture has subsided and Thompson and Groth continue to cultivate an environment conducive to creative originality. Unlike other publishers in this imitative, rather than innovative, field, Fantagraphics not only has a sense of humor, but a line to prove it. And so far, nobody seems to be missing the "Blam!" or "Pow!"

—*Bob Staake*

Tips: "Market trends are too depressing to go into at the moment. There may be an upsurge in the 1990s, but humor is pretty well dead in the direct-sales comic-book market. (The fact that we publish 50% humor material can be attributed to utter mulishness on our part.) For just about any other publisher in the current marketplace, a dream comic book is a semi-pornographic, ultra-violent, full-color super-hero mutant ninja movie tie-in. For us, a dream comic book is a deeply personal work by a cartoonist completely in command of his craft, regardless of format or subject matter. The key to financial success is a willingness to pander. Artistic success? Do what you wanna do (not guaranteed, but it sure helps)."

Are You Sure This Is How We Play Billiards? *When Fantagraphics Books assigned 28 pages of comic stories to Chicago-based cartoonist Dan Clowes, their only instructions were "do something brilliant." Three months later, Clowes had sunk* Eightball *in the corner pocket. On each copy sold, Clowes is given a royalty by Fantagraphics. Describing his cartoon style as "expressionistic, surreal, sardonic, grimly naturalistic and wacky," Clowes wanted to design a cover which "would visually imply the many levels of satire included in this particular* Eightball *comic—also, naked girls sell magazines!"*

© Dan Clowes

FIRST PUBLISHING, 435 N. LaSalle St., Chicago IL 60610. (312)670-6770. FAX: (312)670-6793. Estab. 1982. Audience is predominantly male, 2 years of college, 22 years old. Circ. 500,000. Titles: *Classics Illustrated*, *Lone Wolf and Cub*, *Teenage Mutant Ninja Turtles* and *Beauty and the Beast*. Approximately 10% of writing titles are humor oriented. 100% of writing titles are by freelancers.

Subject Needs: "We are looking for action-adventure series in all genres. We are also looking for writers who are familiar with cartoon and daily comic strip's characters. We are open to any submission geared to a 17-year-old and older audience."

How to Contact: Humorous writers should send a complete manuscript, business card, writing samples and a cover letter detailing credits/background to Robert Garcia, Senior Editor. For artist/writer guidelines, send #10 SASE. To query with ideas for a new humorous comic book title send photocopied art, entire manuscript and story outline. Reports back on unsolicited submissions/queries only if interested. Returns samples with SASE.

Terms: Payment for writing is negotiable per page, $25-60. Pays upon approval. Pays ⅓ kill fee for writing.

Tips: "Be aware that the comic book market is more demanding than ever. The characters you present have to be well-rounded and the situations well-examined. The audience is more sophisticated, and that means selling a new series to them is more difficult."

People want to be entertained, and a new series needs to have a good balance between seriousness and comic relief. Overbalance it in either direction, and you will have a successful book. Commercially, the "dream comic book" would be a top-flight creator matched with a widely-known property that suits his/her talents and sensibilities (i.e. Wendy Pini and our *Beauty and the Beast* series). An entertaining, well-balanced comic series presented by an artist/writer team who complement and ehhance each other's work is the strongest "dream comic book." You have to be well-read inside of comics to avoid clichéd storylines, and well-read outside of comics, especially in the areas that your series covers. If you are writing a contemporary thriller, you must instill that comic with verisimilitude. You must also study people and their idiosyncracies, a good series character is multi-dimensional, and should have unconscious mannerisms that add depth to his/her character, as well as a strong sense of self. People follow series characters who know who they are in an uncertain world."

4WINDS PUBLISHING GROUP, INC., P.O. Box 5208, Lancaster PA 17601. Estab. 1988. Audience is comprised of American direct sales comic book stores and historical museum/gift shop markets. Circ. 14,000. Titles: *Moving Fortress, Attu, the Time Prisoner* (graphic novel series) *Wilderness—the True Story of Simon Girth, the Renegade* (graphic novel).
Subject Needs: Would like to find serious adventure, science fiction and especially accurate historical graphic novels. Doesn't want to see any comic book freelance scriptors. "We have a reliable stable of scriptors that we can call on."
How to Contact: Cartoonist/humorous illustrators should send photo copies of art samples and business card with SASE to Timothy Truman and Charles Dixon, publishers. Also interested in seeing samples from pencil artists and inking artists. No dot matrix submissions. To query with ideas for a new humorous comic book title send photocopied art, pencils and/or inks. Reports back on unsolicited submissions/queries only if interested. Returns samples with SASE.
Terms: Payment for cartooning is on royalty basis, 60% of net or $50-150/page; $100-200 b&w color; $150-300 four color upon arrival (net 30). Pays ½ kill fee for writing/cartooning.
Tips: "We don't like to set limitations. I know several cartoonists/illustrators who've made their mark by going *against* trends and proving that good work with guts will overshadow anything 'trendy'. We're still looking for the dream comic book. As long as the artist or writer shows *power and heart*, that's what we go for!" The key to the success of a cartoonist is "to be *on time!* To have original-looking work—not work that looks 'just like' the artists' favorite illustrator. To present work that's clean and reproducible. To have looked at art other than cartoons or comic books!" Writers should "be confident, but not pushy; to be on time! They should have read something other than comic books! Have a knowledge of film pacing and dialogue."

GREEN ISLAND, 5700 El Dorado Apt. A, El Cerrito CA 94530. (415)528-8615. Estab. 1988. Audience is comprised of mostly 15-35 year old readers. Circ. 300. Titles: *Strange Air*. Approximately 15% of art titles are humor oriented and 50% of writing titles. 100% of artwork or writing titles are by freelancers.
Subject Needs: Would like to find small press artist with talents in mature and intelligent storytelling and design (the subject matter is of no importance). Must also have the ability to meet deadlines. Doesn't want to see one-panel gags and multi-panel strips (unless they are of a professional nature).
How to Contact: Humorous writers should send a complete manuscript to Dylan Williams. Cartoonist/humorous illustrators should send art samples which must be penciled and inked to Dylan Williams, Editor. Also interested in seeing samples from pencil artists and letterers. No dot matrix submissions. For artist/writer guidelines, send a legal size SASE. To query with ideas for a new humorous comic book title send photocopied

art and story outline. Reports back on unsolicited submissions/queries via letter within 1-2 weeks. Returns material if requested.

Tips: "An artist/writer must be unique in art or story. The dream for any publisher would be anything that meets the deadline. The key to success of a cartoonist or writer is patience, persistence and perseverance. We are a small press company and therefore we cannot pay artists. Instead, we work on the following system. The artist can order copies for publishing cost and then take them to stores and sell them on commission or sell them to friends and such for cover (50¢ higher than publishing). We are also NOT looking for artists published by major companies; they have already had a break. We need 'small pressers' who are aiming to become professional comic artists. Copies of *Strange Air* and our other magazines are sent to comic magazines for review, larger companies for inspection and shown to 'major' artists for criticism."

INNOVATION PUBLISHING, 3622 Jacob St., Wheeling WV 26003. (304)232-7701. FAX: (304)232-4010. Estab. 1988. Audience is comprised of anybody who buys comic books. Circ. 30,000. Titles: *The Vampire Lestat, Cyberpunk, Hero Alliance, Justice Machine, The Maze Agency*. Approximately 10% of art and writing titles are humor oriented. 100% of artwork and writing titles are by freelancers.

Subject Needs: "Anything fresh and innovative—comics that are marketable concepts, but which you wouldn't expect to see from one of the larger companies." Doesn't want to see anything that resembles mainstream super hero titles.

How to Contact: Humorous writers should send writing samples, a cover letter detailing credits/background and comic book scripts to Scott Rockwell, Submissions Editor. Cartoonis/humorous illustrators should send art samples and a cover letter explaining credits/background to Scott Rockwell. Never send originals. Also interested in seeing samples from pencil artists, inking artists, letterers, colorists and painters. For artist/writer guidelines, send #10 SASE. To query with ideas for a new humorous comic book title send penciled pages, inked pages, photocopied art and story outline. Reports back on unsolicited submissions/queries via letter in 4 weeks with proper SASE only.

Terms: Payment for writing varies per book; for cartooning varies per book. Pays 10% kill fee for writing and 10% for cartooning.

Tips: "This is one of the craziest, most unpredictable markets in human history. We just try to publish well-written, well-drawn comic books and cross our fingers. Licensed projects are currently doing very well, as in our project *The Vampire Lestat* and several others. If a publisher can get a movie or novel that will be a big hig, a comic book adaptation of same will almost certainly be a big seller as well. The key to the success of a cartoonist is MEETING DEADLINES! Also, a slick and consistent style derived from a close observation of real life. Originality and spontaneity in characterization, dialogue and situations within a commercial framework are essential for a writer."

JABBERWOCKY GRAPHIX, P.O. Box 166255, Irving TX 75016. Estab. 1975. Audience is comprised of a wide range, no specific single markets. Circ. 10,000. Titles: *Adventures of Olivia, Fever Pitch, Goodies, Stuff* and *Amused to No End*. Approximately 75% of art and writing titles are humor oriented. Approximately 50% of artwork and writing titles are by freelancers.

Subject Needs: Sexually-oriented adult material, humorous stories but also serious. Artwork must be of attractive people, either cartoon or realistic styles. "We are presently well-stocked on our non-sexual titles." Doesn't want to see violent themes, rape, bondage, etc.

How to Contact: Humorous writers should send writing samples of a sexual/erotic nature, a cover letter detailing credits/background to Jabberwock Graphix. Cartoonist/humorous illustrators should send art samples of a sexual/erotic nature, a cover letter explaining credits/background to Jabberwocky Graphix. Also interested in seeing samples from pencil artists and inking artists. For artists/writers guidelines send $1.25 and request copy of latest full catalog and legal size SASE. To query with ideas for a new humorous comic book title send photocopied art, entire manuscript and story outline. Reports back on unsolicited submissions/queries via letter in 2-6 weeks. Must include a SASE.

Terms: Payment for writing and cartooning varies.

Tips: "If all you are interested in doing is something to cash in on market trends, we're not interested. If you have a project you are personally interested in doing, you'll do better work on it. Following market trends is about the most *anti*-creative thing you could do. The key to the success of a cartoonist or writer in this market is a combination of talent, perseverance and good luck."

KNOCKABOUT COMICS, 10 Acklam Road, London England W10 5QZ. (01)969-2945. FAX: (01)960-6865. Estab. 1975. Audience is comprised of teenage and adult readers. Circ. 15,000. Titles: *Jazz Funnies, Lady Chatterley's Lover, Calculus Cat* by Hunt Emerson, *Trombone* anthology title, *Freak Brothers* (under license for the U.K.). 100% of art or writing titles are humor oriented. 100% of artwork or writing titles are by freelancers.

Subject Needs: Would like to find adult material (of an 'underground' style). "We want the most unusual strips, but only of professional quality. We don't want to see science fiction, super heroes, fantasy or toilet jokes."

How to Contact: Humorous writers should send writing samples, published tearsheets and a cover letter detailing credits/background to Carol Bennett, Editor. Send all cartooning submissions to Hunt Emerson, Editor. To query with ideas for a new humorous comic book title send penciled pages, photocopied art and story outline. Reports back on unsolicited submissions/queries only if interested. Returns samples with SASE if requested.

Terms: Payment for writing is $37-55/page. For cartooning $50-80 per b&w page; pays $100-300 advance upon publication. Pays $100 kill fee for writing/cartooning.

MAD, 485 MADison Ave., New York NY 10022. (212)752-7685. Estab. 1952. Audience is comprised of everyone over six who likes to laugh. Circ. 1,000,000.

Subject Needs: "Funny stuff! Especially prized are articles on current hot trends. We'll take a look at anything you think is funny. Send a paragraph or two explaining your premise and three or four examples of how you plan to carry it through, describing visual content. Rough sketches are welcomed but not necessary." Doesn't want to see straight text pieces. No poetry, song parodies, movie or TV satires (unless they're entirely different in format or approach from what we're currently doing), cartoon "characters" or rewritten MAD-like stuff.

How to Contact: Send all writing submissions to Nick Meling/John Ficarra, Editors. Send all cartooning submissions to Leonard Brenner, Art Director.

Terms: Payment for writing, $350 for outright purchase of manuscript; b&w per MAD page, $350. Pays upon approval.

Tips: "MAKE US LAUGH!"

MALIBU GRAPHICS INC, publishing as Eternity Comics, Adventure Comics, Aircel Comics, 1355 Lawrence #212, Newbury Park CA 91320. (805)499-3015. FAX: (805)498-4244. Estab. 1986. Audience is comprised of 18-30 year old males. Circ. 50,000. Titles: *Robotech: Sentinels, Trouble with Girls, Ninja High School, Capt. Harlock, Leather & Lace* and *Scimidar*. Approximately 10% of art and writing titles are humor oriented. 100% of artwork and writing titles are by freelancers.

Subject Needs: "Action titles with humorous elements work best for us. We like to add four-to-six titles a year in this direction." Doesn't want to see Archie Harvey or animation style unless Japanese animation style.

How to Contact: Humorous writers should send proposal (no longer than 5 pages) to Chris Ulm, Editor-in-Chief. Cartoonist/humorous illustrators should send published tearsheets and multi-panel page samples to Chris Ulm, Editor-in-Chief. Also interested in seeing samples from pencil artists, inking artists, letterers, any and all. For artist/writer guidelines, send #10 SASE. To query with ideas for a new humorous comic book title send penciled pages, inked pages and story line. Reports back on unsolicited submissions/queries via letter in 3 months.

Terms: Payment for writing: royalty basis, 5-7% of net; for cartooning: 9-13% of net. Pays $100-500 advance paid 15 days after acceptance additional percentage paid 45 days after publication. Pays 10% of advance kill fee for writing and cartooning.

Tips: "To have a successful comic book title, the artist/writer must be aware that the industry is crowded with talent and that a good portion of the buying public are collectors—not necessarily readers. Also, the average comic book buyer is now more than 20 years old. The "dream comic book" for any publisher would be a brand new concept that would be able to generate both high per copy sales, but also various licensing possibilities . . . games, posters, T-shirts, etc. The key to the success of a cartoonist in this market is completing work at the same quality level as their samples on or prior to deadline."

MANUSCRIPT PRESS, INC., Box 336, Mountain Home TN 37684. (615)926-7495. Estab. 1976. Audience is general. Circ. 4,000. Titles: *Comics Revue, Prince Valiant.* Approximately 50% of art/writing titles are humor oriented. No artwork or writing titles are by freelancers.

Subject Needs: "We do reprints of syndicated comic strips only, e.g. Bloom County, Steve Canyon. We are not looking for submissions at this time. No dot matrix submissions."

Terms: Payment for cartooning is $10 per b&w page upon publication.

MISCELLANIA UNLIMITED PRESS, 4731 Roosevelt Way NE, Seattle WA 98105. (206)633-4003. Estab. 1989. Comic books and children's books; all ages and mature readers. Circ. 20,000. Titles: *Snap* (humor anthology), *Billy Nguyen, The Desert Peach, Funny Business.*

Subjects Needs: *Snap* is general (think of the early *MAD*), *Funny Business* is funny animal-oriented for all ages. Also looking at proposals for ongoing titles. Doesn't want to see Rambo-types, splatter, super heroes, satire or parody. Our humor needs are mainly directed toward complete ongoing books where the humor arises from the situation and characterization, not relying on preknowledge of other comic books, movies, etc.

How to Contact: Humorous writers should send a complete manuscript and published tearsheets. Note: Mainly interested in complete projects. Send to Dennis Weber, Editor. Cartoonist/humorous illustrators should send published tearsheets and art samples. Primarily intereted in complete projects. Send to Cindy Murata, Art Director. Also interested in seeing samples from letterers. For artist/writer guidelines, send a #10 SASE. To query with ideas for a new humorous comic book title send complete proposal if ongoing title; or full story to anthology editor. Reports back on unsolicited submissions/queries in 4-6 weeks.

Terms: Payment for writing and cartooning is on a royalty basis of 4% net over 8,000 copies sold (or combination thereof). Pays 50% upon approval balance upon publication plus 45 days. Pays 5% kill fee for writing/cartooning, only if canceled by publisher for cause other than lateness or nondelivery.

Tips: "This is the kind of thinking that has the *Jungle Book* characters becoming WWI flying aces under Disney. I believe a comics creator who has some skill, but is totally dedicated to his/her vision will create a book with *at least* a cult following. The "dream comic book" for any publisher would be one that sells a billion copies . . . but seriously, what I look for is one that makes *me* want to see what happens next, a page turner. The key to the success of a cartoonist or writer in this market is dedication."

NBM PUBLISHING CO., 35-53 70th St., Jackson Heights NY 11372. (718)458-3199. FAX: (718)458-3228. Audience is comprised of well-educated 18-32 year olds. Titles: *Treasury of Victorian Murder, Penguins Behind Bars.* Approximately 20% of art or writing titles are humor oriented. 100% of artwork or writing titles are by freelancers.
Subject Needs: Would like to find humor graphic albums—satire especially sought. Doesn't want to see bad taste, sophomoric humor.
How to Contact: Humorous writers should send writing samples and a cover letter detailing credits/background to Terry Nantier, publisher. Cartoonist/humorous illustrators should send art samples and a cover letter explaining credits/background to Terry Nantier. Also interested in seeing samples from: letterers and layout artists. To query with ideas for a new humorous comic book title send photocopied art and story outline. Reports back on unsolicited submissions/queries via letter in 4 weeks. Returns samples with SASE.
Terms: Payment for writing is on royalty basis, 2% of gross, for cartooning on royalty basis, 8% of gross; pays negotiated in advance.

NEW ENGLAND COMICS, Box 1424, Brockton MA 02403. (508)583-8046. FAX: (508)584-7387. Estab. 1983. Circ. 400,000. Audience is age 15-25. Titles: *X-men, Spiderman, MAD, The Tiek and Batman.* 100% of art or writing titles are humor oriented. 100% of artwork or writing titles are by freelancers.
Subject Needs: Would like to find horror, super-hero and science fiction. Doesn't want to see x-rated material, graphic violence and obscene language.
How to Contact: Humorous writers should send a complete manuscript, writing samples, published tearsheets, a cover letter detailing credits/background, business card and complete story art to Bob Polio, Art Director or George Suarez, Editor. Cartoonist/humorous illustrators should send original art samples, art samples, published tearsheets, a cover letter explaining credits/background, business card and complete story to Bob Polio or George Suarez. Send all cartooning submissions to Bob Polio or George Suarez. Also interested in seeing samples from pencil artists, layout artists, inking artists, letters and others. No dot matrix submissions. To query with ideas for a new humorous comic book title send penciled pages, inked pages, original art, photocopied art, entire manuscript or story outline. Reports back on unsolicited submissions/queries via letter in 3 weeks. Returns samples with SASE if requested.
Terms: Payment for writing is negotiated.

NOW COMICS, A DIVISION OF CAPUTO PUBLISHING, INC., Suite 1750 322 S. Michigan, Chicago IL 60604. (312)786-9013. Estab. 1985. Audience is comprised of both younger and adult readers. Circ. 750,000. Titles: *The Green Hornet, Ralph Snart Adventures, The Real Ghostbusters, Fright Night, Speed Racer.* Approximately 20% of art titles are humor oriented. 30% of writing titles are humor oriented. 100% of artwork titles are by freelancers. Approximately 80% of writing titles are by freelancers.
Subject Needs: "We will consider any idea that's original and unusual. We will be putting out a fair number of in-house titles next year, so we'll be pretty busy, but an off-the-wall idea will always get a look." Doesn't want to see "caped crusaders with umpteen super-powers or 'adults only' material."
How to Contact: Humorous writers should send writing sample and a cover letter detailing credits/background to Tony Caputo, President/Editor-in-Chief. Cartoonist/humorous illustrators should send art samples, a cover letter explaining credits/background. No originals, please; good-quality copies. SASE to Michele Mach, Art Director. Also interested in seeing samples from pencil artists, layout artists, inking artists and letterers. Dot matrix submissions acceptable. To query with ideas for a new humorous

comic book title send photocopied art, story outline and sample script pages. Reports back on unsolicited submissions in 4 weeks. Returns samples with SASE. Returns material if requested.

Terms: Payment for writing and cartooning, varies. Pays upon invoice (net 30/60/90).

Tips: "The Big Two (Marvel & DC) have a pretty good lock on the superhero market. The trend for independent publishers is to publish books about more human-sized heroes, or to go for subversive-type humor. There is an untapped readership for anti-hero stories, or heroes who walk the edge. The 'dream comic book' for any publisher would be a book whose artists/writers understand the concept of a deadline! Preferably one with complex stories and well-defined, vivid characters who are capable of being more than one dimensional in their actions and motivations. The key to the success of a cartoonist in this market is originality of style, and good execution. Whatever style you use, do it well—no slopping or fudging. Pay attention to background detail—little, throwaway visual bits can add depth and humor. Success for a writer again is originality. For the writer, the trick is to find the balance between too many words (talk balloons have limited space) and simplistic, Dick-and-Jane dialogue. Make each word do something, and choose the ones that express as much as possible. Throwaway gaglines are wonderful, if there's room for them."

ONE HORSE LEAD WORKS, 4-207 Harbord St., Toronto, Ontario M5S 2R2 Canada. (416)537-0005. Estab. 1988. Audience is comprised of more mature people interested in the exploration of the medium of sequential art; the alternative buyer. Circ. 500. Titles: *Playground, Headcheese.* Approximately 60% of art or writing titles are humor oriented. 100% of artwork or writing titles are by freelancers.

Subject Needs: Would like to find self-contained stories, 1-10 pages in length, finished work. Shades of the high 50's and classic American jazz. Work which is fully expressed in the comic format only. No work which gains its impact from merely being offensive, adolescent heroic fantasy, the grammatically incorrect and uninspired.

How to Contact: Humorous writers should send a complete manuscript, a cover letter detailing credits/background and compatible examples or names which would portray your work accurately to Kathryn Kuder, Editor. Cartoonist/humorous illustrators should send art samples and a cover letter explaining credits/background to Stuart Immonen, Art Director. Also interested in seeing samples from pencil artists and inking artists. No dot matrix submissions. For artist/writer guidelines, send legal size SASE. To query with ideas for a new humorous comic book title send penciled pages, inked pages, photocopied art, entire manuscript and story outline. Reports back on unsolicited submissions/queries via letter within 3 weeks. Returns samples with SASE.

Terms: Payment for writing is $5-15 per page. For cartooning, $10-50 per b&w page, $50-75 per b&w cover, $50-75 per 4 color cover upon publication.

Tips: "The key to the success of a cartoonist is talent and original vision in a market saturated with titles which overstayed their welcome."

SHELDON OPPENBERG ASSOCIATES, Box 321, Hartsdale NY 10530. (212)829-1328. Estab. 1986. Audience is comprised of adults. Circ. 15,000. Titles: *Celebration Funnies.* "We publish only one magazine at this time." Approximately 75% of art or writing titles are humor oriented. 100% of artwork or writing titles are by freelancers.

Subject needs: 75% humor oriented, good b&w drawing, pantomine (sight gags).

How to Contact: Humorous writers should send published tearsheets, business card and a cover letter detailing credits/background to Sheldon Oppenberg, Editor/Art Director. Cartoonist/humorous illustrators should send cartooning submissions to Sheldon Oppenberg, Art Director. Also interest in seeing samples from layout artists, inking artists and letterers. No dot matrix submissions. For artist/writer guidelines send #10 SASE. To query with ideas for a new humorious comic book title send photocopied art and story outline. Reports back on unsolicited material in 2 weeks. Returns material if requested. Do not send originals unless requested.

Terms: Payment for writing is $50. For cartooning, b&w per page, $25-35; b&w cover, $100-175.

Tips: "The artist/writer must create something the fan can relate to, something in vogue. The 'dream comic book' would be great art and copy and a magazine that sells well, too. The key to the success of a cartoonist/writer in this market is being able to convey a message to the reader."

PASTIME PRODUCTIONS, 7715 SW 35th, Portland OR 97219. (503)293-1577. Audience is comprised of collectors and traditional style comic lovers everywhere. Titles: *Portland Underground Comik* (1983-84) and *Shocking Fear* (83-84).

Subject Needs: American satire, satirizing television, celebrities, politics, religion and people in general. Doesn't want to see fantasy, amateur stuff or serious super-hero.

How to Contact: Humorous writers should send writing samples and a cover letter detailing credits/background to Marcus Reed, Publisher/Owner. Cartoonist/humorous illustrators should send SASE, original arti samples, art samples and a cover letter explaining credits/background to Marcus Reed. Also interested in seeing samples from letterers. Dat matrix submissions acceptable. For artist/writer guidelines, send #10 size SASE. To query with ideas for a new humorous comic book title send photocopied art and story outline. Reports back on unsolicited submissions/queries via letter in 3 weeks, usually sooner. Returns samples with SASE.

Terms: Payment for writing is $10; for cartooning, b&w per page $10-75 (negotiable), 4 color cover $50-100 (negotiable). Pays upon publication.

Tips: "The market tends to get bogged down by repetition of character styles, book themes, etc. The artist/writer must break new ground to keep things interesting. The 'dream comic book' for any publisher would be *MAD* — almost perfect. It's completely original — its supported almost entirely by circulation, which means reader interest and it fun material. The key to the success of a cartoonist in this market is originality of style within given guidelines. You have to look at the values of your potential readers and communicate to them visually in a style that they can relate to. I feel that the freelance writer in this business has a rough time. If I was going to make it on writing alone, I would develop working relationships with artists and sell as a team."

PURE IMAGINATION, 88 Lexington Ave. 96, New York City NY 10016. (212)682-0025. Estab. 1974. Audience is comprised of pop culture publications for 12-40 year olds. Circ. varies internationally. Titles: *Betty Pages, Pure Images.* Approximately 5% of art and 10% of writing titles are humor oriented. Approximately 75% of artwork or writing titles are by freelancers.

Subject Needs: Would like to find people with new ideas; art ability is really secondary. No long proposals, comic book pages with more than two close-ups per page.

How to Contact: Humorous writers should send a cover letter detailing credits/background to Pure Imagination. Cartoonist/humorous illustrators should send a cover letter explaining credits/background and photocopies to Pure Imagination. Also interested in seeing samples from pencil artists, layout artists, inking artists and letterers. To query with ideas for a new humorous comic book title send photocopied art. Reports back on unsolicited submissions/queries only if interested.

Terms: Payment for writing is 5¢ per word F.N.A. only. For cartooning, depends on job upon invoice (net 30). Pays ⅓ kill fee for writing/cartooning.

Tips: "We don't presume that market trends are valuable. Just the opposite. *Dark Night, Watchmen* and *Swamp Thing* all *set* trends, but nothing that followed the trends succeeded. Our suggestion is to come up with a unique approach and create your own trend. Produce the thing that *you* know, and it will always ring true. The dream comic book for any publisher would be a package produced by someone who is drawing the pictures that have never been done before, coming up with the ideas not previously conceived and asking the unasked questions. For it to be a true 'dream book' the creators would have to have the work ethic to not miss a deadline. The key to success of a cartoonist is having the ability to work with an editor and the ability to make all of his deadlines. The artist must not only want to draw well, but *must* want to tell a story. They must understand how movies are directed and apply the same techniques to their work. The best artists have always worked beyond their own fields, and returned with their own versions of what they saw. Writers should have the ability to write visual stories. Comics are a visual medium, so the writer must also understand cinematic technique. Understanding how to convey personality in small chunks of dialogue. The successful writer must be able to write short stories well, but most important they must be original. New ideas must be a way of life."

RIP OFF PRESS, INC., P.O. Box 4686, Auburn CA 95604. (916)885-8183. FAX: (916)885-8219. Estab. 1969. Audience is comprised of 18-35 and older, ex-hippies, college educated iconoclastic types. Circ. 30,000 internationally. Titles: *Fabulous Furry Freak Brothers, Miami Mice, Doll.* Approximately 75% of art titles are humor oriented. 100% of artwork titles are by freelancers.
Subject Needs: Would like to find new comic creators with an offbeat, adult sense of humor and a sure hand with a pen. Doesn't want to see full length books from previously unpublished cartoonists, crude pencil sketches, children's comics, text stories, super hero/sword and sorcery.
How to Contact: Cartoonist/humorous illustrators should send letter size xeroxes of finished comic book pages to Kathe Todd, Editor. Also interested in seeing samples from letterers. No dot matrix submissions. For artist/writer guidelines, send #10 SASE. To query with ideas for a new humorous comic book title send photocopied art or story outline. Reports back on unsolicited submissions/queries only if interested. Returns samples with SASE if requested.
Terms: Payment for cartooning is $25-75 per b&w page, $50-150 per 4-color upon publication. "We don't kill."
Tips: "Unquestionably the classic comic book genre represented by the publications of Marvel and DC is still the most popular. There is a trend for more adult-oriented plots, detailed characterizations and other concessions to the advancing average age of comic fans, however. In the non-mass market, mostly black and white comics published by Rip Off Press, the trend is for hardcore sex combined with humor and/or soap-opera-like plot lines to be the best selling type of material. The dream comic book for any publisher would be one such as *Freak Brothers #1*, which has continued to sell steadily in the many tens of thousands of copies over the entire 18 years since it was first published. For a cartoonist wishing to achieve success with his or her own creations (as opposed to becoming a cog in the comics machine at one of the Big Two companies), a fertile imagination and a captivating, original approach plus a professional, sharp-looking drawing style. In the market of newspaper strips, the drawing style isn't nearly as important as the ideas behind it. It is also important for a cartoonist to be enough on top of business matters that he or she does not enter into unfavorable contracts or find his or her work stolen by publishers that do not pay."

ROLLER PUBLICATIONS, P.O. Box 221295, Sacramento CA 95822. (916)429-8522. Estab. 1986. Circ. 300. Audience is white males age 14-40. Titles: *Fine Art Comics* and *Comic Update.* Approximately 30% of art and writing titles are humor oriented. Approximately 20% of artwork titles are by freelancers; 50% of writing titles are by freelancers.

Subject Needs: Single panel gag to multi-panel strips. Multi-page strips amounting to no more than three pages. No restrictions.

How to Contact: Humorous writers should send a complete manuscript to Andrew L. Roller, Editor. Cartoonist/humorous illustrators should send original art samples to Andrew L. Roller. No dot matrix submissions. For artist/writers guidelines, send any size SASE. To query with ideas for a new humorous comic book title send inked pages, camera ready art and entire manuscript. Reports back on unsolicited submissions/queries in 2 weeks. Returns material if requested.

Terms: Payment for writing or cartooning is a contributor copy on publication.

Tips: "We don't worry about market trends here. We pride ourselves on individual creativity. The 'dream comic book' for any publisher would be A)one that sells like hot cakes, B)one that doesn't sell at all, but is ultimately regarded as having lasting value. Do what you love, the money will follow. Concentrate on setting and meeting your own standards and you will invariably produce something of quality. Concentrate on gratifying others, and you will simply join the legions of schlock mongers."

TRIDENT COMICS, Unit 3, 28 Canal St., South Wigston Leicester England LE8 2PL. (0533)477-661. FAX: (0533)477-668. Estab. 1989. Audience is comprised of 18-30 year olds with above average intelligence. Circ. 10,000. Titles: *Trident* (anthology), *Saviour, Man Elf, Shadowmen, Leir.*

Subject Needs: Would like to find very diverse, humorous, funny animal, satirical, adult or whatever. All submissions read with interest. Doesn't want to see very mainstream, super-action-adventure stories which are solely for children.

How to Contact: Humorous writers should send writing samples and a cover letter detailing credits/background to Martin Skidmore, Editor. Also interested in seeing samples from pencil artists, inking artists, letterers and color artists. To query with ideas for a new humorous comic book title send photocopied art or story outline. Reports back on unsolicited submissions/queries in 3 months. Returns samples with SASE.

Terms: Payment for writing is $15 minimum/page. For cartooning, $30 minimum for b&w page, $100 minimum for b&w cover, $150 minimum for color cover, upon publication. Pays 50% kill fee for writing/cartooning.

UNDERGROUND SURREALIST MAGAZINE, P.O. Box 2565, Cambridge MA 02238. (617)891-9569. Estab. 1986. Audience is comprised of cartoons—people of all ages, educated. Circ. 400 internationally. Titles: *Underground Surrealist Magazine #4* and *"Going to the Dogs."* Approximately 90% of art and writing titles are humor oriented. 100% of artwork and writing titles are by freelancers.

Subject Needs: Comic panels, strips and stories. Doesn't want to see pornography, pointless stories.

How to Contact: Humorous writers should send cartoons to Mick Cusimano, Editor. Cartoonist/humorous illustrators should send art samples to Mick Cusimano. Also interested in seeing samples from pencil artists and inking artists. For sample copy send $3 and 8½ × 11 size SASE. To query with ideas for a new humorous comic book title send photocopied art. Reports back on unsolicited submissions/queries in 2 weeks. Returns material if requested.

Terms: Pays in contributors copies.

Tips: "Humor, satire on any subject. Figures in action, even slapstick as opposed to two heads just talking to each other. Animals are O.K. Don't try to be another Gary Larson. There's already one of him. The "dream comic book" for any publisher would be cartoonists from many countries with a variety of styles, that look good next to the great cartoonists—Hogarth, Daumier, Gilram Cruickshank. The key to the success of a cartoonist is zany, funny, lively stories with well defined characters, good drawing."

Gags/ Entertainers

People are amazed by so many things.

We're amazed that when you add vinegar to baking soda, it bubbles. We're amazed you can fax a drawing from Los Angeles to New York in less than 15 seconds. And, of course, we're amazed George Burns is still walking around.

And when it comes to cartoonists and comedians, we're amazed that many of them use the services of outside writers. We have an easier time accepting traces of mercury in our drinking water than accepting the fact that our favorite stand-up comedian buys jokes from a guy in Des Moines. We simply assume if the joke came out of the comedian's mouth, it originated in his brain. And if the cartoon is signed by Joe Blow, then he not only inked the art, but wrote the idea as well. Appearances (and monologues) can be so deceiving.

Actually, the practice is quite common, but you won't find comedians going out of their way to *advertise* their need for gags, jokes or one-liners and rarely do you come across a cartoonist talking about the advantages of creative collaboration.

To be sure, gag writing is an "inside" business. Talking with gag writers, networking with these funny folks, you soon learn which comedians seek one-liners about their in-laws, which gag cartoonists need man-shipwrecked-on-deserted-island ideas and which comic strip artists are looking for balloon banter so they can get in an extra 18 holes.

How to submit

The best way to approach gag writing is with a 25¢ stamp. Is there a comic strip that you have a symbiotic relationship with? How about a comedian who makes you wonder if you were Siamese twins separated at birth? Then go ahead — introduce yourself.

Put together a succinct, business-like letter and inquire whether or not they are receptive to unsolicited writing submissions. Comic strip cartoonists can be reached through their syndicates which forward their mail. Gag cartoonists can be contacted through magazines in which their work appears. And you can get a hold of comedians by writing to their agents or managers (Comedy USA publishes the definitive sourcebook of comedians and their representatives.)

Then, of course, there's this nifty chapter, over 50 funny people who are hoping that you're just a little bit funnier than they are. They're looking for everything — from cartoon ideas about lawyers to one-liners about relationships, from jokes on politics to gags on motherhood.

Generally speaking, gag writers submit individual jokes, gags, one-liners or ideas on 3 × 5 index cards, although some comedians and cartoonists prefer that the material be typed on 8½ × 11 paper. No matter how the material is submitted, it should be accompanied by a SASE if you hope it ever sees the interior paint job of your mailbox.

Payment and terms

You'll find that payment doesn't vary too much and that most gag writers don't gargle with champagne. Many comedians pay rates more laughable than their acts ($50 for a joke is big time). Comic strip artists might pay $20, $40 even $100 for a strip idea, but gag cartoonists generally chop up their fee by retaining 75% and giving 25% to the gag writer.

Terms jump all over the place (like my five year old after a bowl of Sugar Frosted Flakes). Most comedians pay upon acceptance (after you have signed an agreement relinquishing all rights to the material). Comic strip cartoonists generally pay within 30 days of the date on which your idea is published, and gag cartoonists pay on publication — once they are paid by the magazine, they cut a check for you.

If a gag cartoonist elects to draw up your idea, prepare yourself for the long haul as they submit it to publication upon publication. The submission process can be an excruciating one taking months (years?) until the drawing finds a home or unceremoniously ascends to cartoon Heaven.

Ideally, you establish an ongoing, collaborative relationship with the comedian or cartoonist and are even called upon to "brainstorm" ideas or to add a new twist to their material. But chemistry, needless to say, is the critical ingredient for such a partnership — oil and water may not mix, but put a couple of terrifically funny people in a blender and you've got, well, a big mess.

GEORGE B. ABBOTT, 9120 SW 17 Terrace, Miami FL 33165. (305)223-6506. Began selling cartoons in 1983. 60% of cartoons are written by gag/joke writers or outside sources. Cartoons have recently appeared in *National Enquirer, McCall's, Woman's World, American Legion*, Cartoon Features Syndicate and King Features.
How to Contact: Submit sample gags, any number on 3 × 5 cards or paper. "Would consider any gag, any time." Reports in 2-3 weeks. Returns material only if provided with SASE. Pays writers 25% of total fee paid for cartoon.

Tips: "The single best tip to an aspiring cartoonist or gag writer is hang in there! Only sure way to fail is to give up."

Just for Laughs: "The funniest cartoon ever published is a skier with ski tracks around a tree, by Charles Addams. The single best use for a rejection slip is to increase resolve to draw and sell more cartoons."

JEAN ADAMS, 6337 Droxford St., Lakewood CA 90713. (213)867-2954. Began publishing cartoons in 1987. Cartoons have recently appeared in non-profit organization/school newspapers.

How to Contact: Submit sample gags; 10 gags/jokes per batch on 8½ × 11 paper. Looking for gags on following subjects: radio station, popular and older records, gym/exercise and library. Reports in 1 month. Returns material only if provided with SASE. Pays writers 33% of total fee paid for cartoon.

Tips: The secret to a great gag/joke is that the gag must be set up for the viewer to expect a certain reaction and then you surprise him with a twist to his expectation. The single best tip to an aspiring cartoonist or gag writer is keep at it, don't give up. Look for the humor in all situations and express that humor in your drawings.

Just for Laughs: "The funniest cartoon ever published is a man is in hospital bed and family gathered around—his grandson informs him that Uncle Harry and Uncle Bob have been arguing over who gets the piano. The single best use for a rejection slip is lining the bottom of a bird cage."

EDOUARD BLAIS, 2704 Parkview Blvd., Robbinsdale MN 55422. (612)588-5249. Estab. 1982. 50% of cartoons are written by gag/joke writers or outside sources. Cartoons have recently appeared in *Gallery, Sun, Letters, Saturday Evening Post, Woman's World* and *Globe*.

How to Contact: Submit 12-15 gags/jokes per batch on 3 × 5 cards (slips). Looking for gags on following subjects: general, farm, rural, children's and adult humor. Doesn't want to see gags on computers and science. Reports in 1 week. Returns material only if provided with SASE. Pays writers 25% of total fee paid for cartoon.

Tips: "Be persistent. Stay away from the obvious humor, or humor that requires a very specialized knowledge."

Just for Laughs: The funniest cartoon ever published is "Two dinosaurs talking, one to the other: 'Wow, nice of you to notice. I've been on a diet for a month and have already lost five tons.' "

ASHLEIGH BRILLIANT, 117 W. Valerio St., Santa Barbara CA 93101. (805)682-0531. Name of features: Pot-shots, Brilliant Thoughts. Began selling cartoons in 1967. Number of cartoons written by gag/joke writers or outside sources varies. Cartoons have recently appeared in *Reader's Digest, Youth Beat, Rocky Mountain News*.

How to Contact: "My work is so unconventional that freelancers will only be wasting their time unless they first study it carefully. A catalog and samples are available for $2 and a SASE." Submit on 3½ × 5½ ready-to-print word and picture. Reports in 3 weeks. Returns material only if provided with SASE. Pays $40 minimum outright purchase of gag/joke.

FRANCIS H. BRUMMER, 601 Arnold Ave., Council Bluffs IA 51503. Name of feature: Rum. Began selling cartoons in 1954. 98% of cartoons are written by gag/joke writers or outside sources. Cartoons have recently appeared in *Good Housekeeping, VGW, American Machinist.*

How to Contact: Submit on 3 × 5 cards only. Looking for gags on following subjects: working women, machine shop, insurance sales, teenage, topical such as Valentine Day, Easter, Thanksgiving and Christmas (apply them to office, shops and sales, etc.). Doesn't want to see vulgar material. Reports in 2 weeks. Returns material only if provided with SASE. Pays "25% top writers; 30% that furnish me with the type of gags I need."

JOE BURESCH, 6142 Carlton Ave., Sarasota FL 34231. (813)922-8833. Dinah Mite; (weekly). Began selling cartoons in 1936. 10% of cartoons are written by gag/joke writers or outside sources. Cartoons have recently appeared in *King Features, Good Housekeeping* and *National Enquirer.*
Tips: "A great gag/joke should have good expressions and a very short caption. An aspiring cartoonist should lock the door and chain himself to the drawing table."
Just for Laughs: The funniest cartoon ever published: A very small man sits behind a huge steering wheel of car. The salesman says: "Notice the feeling of power." "If you get a rejection slip toss it in the wastebasket and go on to the next batch of cartoons."

FORD BUTTON, 3398 Chili Ave., Rochester NY 14624. (716)889-3045. Began selling cartoons in 1958. 10% of cartoons are written by gag/joke writers or outside sources. Cartoons have recently appeared in *National Lampoon, National Enquirer, Good Housekeeping, Phi Delta Kappan* and many trade, technical and fraternal publications.
How to Contact: Submit cover letter and sample gags; 12-15 gags/jokes per batch on 3×5 cards or paper. Looking for gags on following subjects: education—classroom, school boards and college level; family situations—home, school, etc.; captionless gags on the above plus off-beat scenes. "Doesn't want to see anything sexy or the girlie type gag. Especially anything that *Hustler* might buy!" Reports in days. Pays writers 30% of total fee paid for cartoon.
Tips: "The secret to a great gag/joke is that unique balance between the picture and short caption, if needed. The single best tip to an aspiring cartoonist or gag writer is draw and think at the same time! *Never quit* but draw, draw and think daily. This will tune you up to being a creative humorist. It will also rid you of all the cliches that have been worked to death."
Just for Laughs: "The funniest cartoon ever published is anything Johnny Hart or Brant Parker creates! They're funny! If I weren't a cartoonist, I'd probably be a jazz musician. The single best use for a rejection slip is starting charcoal fires in the grill during the summer and starting fires in the fireplace during the winter months."

WILLIAM CANTY, Box 1053, S. Wellfleet MA 02663. (508)349-7549. Name of strip: All About Town. Began selling cartoons in 1952. 10% of cartoons are written by gag/joke writers or outside sources. Cartoons have recently appeared in *Good Housekeeping* and *Saturday Evening Post.*
How to Contact: Submit cover letter, sample gags, resume, tearsheets; 10 gags/jokes per batch on 3×5 cards. Looking for gags on general subjects. Doesn't want to see adult material. Reports in 7 days. Returns material only if provided with SASE. Pays writers 30% of total fee paid for cartoon.
Tips: "The secret to a great gag/joke is that it must be *funny*. The single best tip to an aspiring cartoonist or gag writer is be persistent and have a stomach for rejection."
Just for Laughs: "The funniest cartoon ever published is George Booth's cartoon of a teenage boy sitting on porch as a pretty girl walks by—mom says 'whistle you dumb bastard.' If I weren't a cartoonist, I'd probably be a monk. The single best use for a rejection slip is nothing, because the paper they're written on is too rough."

FRAN CAPO, 85-20 167th St., Jamaica NY 11432. (718)657-8055. Agent/management: Ken Franklin. Fran Capo has been in the business for 6 years and has performed on "The Late Show," "Mid-day Live" and several cable shows. Act is primarily stand-up. Uses gag/joke writers for TV appearances and live act/routine on subjects which include relationships, parents, animals, what if's, baby material. Doesn't want to see foul material. Buys 2 gags/joke/one-liners per year.

How to Contact: Submit 10-12 gags/jokes per batch on 8½ × 11 paper. For first contact send cover letter, resume, sample material/jokes/gags and audio tape. Reports back within 2 weeks only if interested. Returns materials if accompanied by SASE. Keeps material on file. Buys all rights. Pays $10.

Tips: The benefits of working with gag/joke writers are "when pressed for time, [you] can always use fresh material; it's another brain source."

DAVE CARPENTER, Box 520, Emmetsburg, IA 50536. (712)852-3725. Began selling cartoons in 1976. 40% of cartoons are written by gag/joke writers or outside sources. Cartoons have recently appeared in *National Enquirer, Better Homes & Gardens, Good Housekeeping, Wall Street Journal, Saturday Evening Post, Boys Life.*

How to Contact: Submit sample gags. 20 gags/jokes per batch, no more than one batch/week from a writer, on 3 × 5 cards or paper. Looking for gags on the following subjects: office situations, general and family. Doesn't want to see x-rated material. Reports in 1 week. Returns material only if provided with SASE. Pays writer 30% of total fee paid for cartoon.

Tips: The secret to a great gag/joke is a gag that takes a different and funny look at *everyday life.* "The best tip is PERSISTENCE!!! Be very critical of your work — make sure that your gags are crisp! And funny — not tired old jokes."

MICHAEL CARRINGTON, Suite #29, 370 Court St., Brooklyn NY 11231. (212)724-2800. Michael Carrington has been in the business for 7 years. Former host of Nickelodeon's game show "Think Fast;" has performed at "The Comic Strip," Catch a Rising Star and Dangerfield's. Act is stand-up. Uses gag/joke writers for live act/routine, public appearances. Uses everything from acupuncture to x-rated movies (i.e. television, city life, childhood, money, sports, family). Doesn't want to see material on current events, racist, sexist, four letter words. First time buyer.

How to Contact: Submit minimum of 10 gags/jokes per batch on 8½ × 11 paper. For first contact, send cover letter and sample material. Reports back only if interested. Returns materials if accompanied by a SASE. Does not file materials. Buys all rights. Pays $8 minimum.

Tips: Two heads are better than one.

CHARLES T. CASTLEMAN, E. 1311 Glass, Spokane WA 99207. (509)482-7783. Name of feature: Sunday Painter. Began selling cartoons in 1987. 98% of cartoons are written by gag/joke writers or outside sources. Cartoons have recently appeared in *Saturday Evening Post, Official Detective, Sun, Globe, National Examiner* and *Home Life.*

How to Contact: Submit cover letter and sample gags; 10 gags/jokes per batch on 3 × 5 cards. Looking for gags on following subjects: detective, animals, artists, generals. Doesn't want to see any x-rated and nudes. Reports in 1 week. Returns material only if provided with SASE. Pays writers 25% of total fee paid for cartoon.

Tips: The secret to a great gag/joke is the unexpected surprise. The single best tip to an aspiring cartoonist or gag writer is to "be persistent and don't give up."

Just for Laughs: The funniest cartoon ever published is: "Sign on deck of Noah's Ark (to Noah): 'Tell the cicada's to shuddup.' If I weren't a cartoonist, I'd probably be a mortician. The single best use for a rejection slip is papering unpainted, unsightly areas of basement walls."

W. J. CHAMBERS, 416 W. Division, Villa Park IL 60181. (812)832-7113. Began selling cartoons in 1959. 50% of cartoons are written by gag/joke writers or outside sources. Cartoons have recently appeared in *Computer World, Professional Electronics, Nebraska Farmer.*

How to Contact: Submit cover letter; 12 gags/jokes per batch on 3 × 5 cards. Looking for gags on following subjects: any kind of trade journal gags. Reports in 3 days. Returns material only if provided with SASE. Pays writers 25% of total fee paid for cartoon; $10-$300.
Tips: The secret to a great gag/joke is a topical or fresh gag. The single best tip to an aspiring cartoonist or gag writer is to send gags you promise, don't dash off a batch of junk.

DON COLE, 12 Lehigh St., Dover NJ 07801. (201)328-9153. Began selling cartoons in 1954. 50% of cartoons are written by gag/joke writers or outside sources. Cartoons have recently appeared in *McCall's, Woman's World, Medical Economics, Sun, Globe.*
How to Contact: Submit gags only; 6-12 gags/batch on 3 × 5 slips. Looks for anything funny. The wholesome, positive or cute sell best. Doesn't want to see off-color material. Reports in 1-5 days. Returns material only if provided with a SASE. Pays writers 25% of total fee paid for cartoon.
Tips: The single best tip to an aspiring gag writer is "Concentrate on great gags. Anything else is a waste of time. Please do not send out the same idea on multiple gag slips, by merely changing a minor element."

RON COLEMAN, Route 5 Box 166C, Salem IN 47167. (812)883-2193. Began selling cartoons in 1958. 5% of cartoons are written by gag/joke writers or outside sources, "but I hope to use more." Cartoons have recently appeared in *Dental Economics, Popular Electronics, Radio Electronics, Computer Edge, Wedding Photographer, Union Communication News, Banjo Newsletter* and others.
How to Contact: Submit sample gags and SASE; send gags/jokes on 3 × 5 cards or 3 × 5 slips of paper. Looking for gags on following subjects: trade journal gags, electronics, computers, medical, dental. "I will assist interested gag writers in learning to slant to my markets." Reports in 1 week. Returns material only if provided with SASE. Pays writers 25% of total fee paid for cartoon. Gags may be marketed to more than one publication, which would increase writer's commission.
Tips: The secret to a great gag/joke is surprise, reactions of supporting characters. The single best tip to an aspiring gag writer is "learn to slant material to trade journals and technical markets. There is a good demand for slanted material and too few cartoonists or writers take the time to develop this ability."

THOMAS W. DAVIE, 28815 4th Place S., Federal Way WA 98003. (206)941-6307. Began selling cartoons in 1963. 30% of cartoons are written by gag/joke writers or outside sources. Cartoons have appeared in *Saturday Evening Post, National Enquirer, King Features.*
How to Contact: Submit 15 gags/jokes per batch on 3 × 5 slips. Looking for gags on generals, medicals, mild sex, hunting and fishing. Doesn't want to see pornography. Reports in 3 weeks. Returns material only if provided with SASE. Pays writers 25% of total fee paid for cartoon.
Tips: The single best tip to an aspiring gag writer is "Originality. Study the markets. Don't overproduce (quality is better than quantity); keep gag batches small, be brief, be neat."
Just for Laughs: Funniest cartoon ever published: "Costume party. Satisfied Uncle Sam leaving disheveled Indian maiden. She says, 'Well, there's history repeating itself.' (Jack Cole—*Playboy*)."

ED DAVIS/SOUTHWEST HUMOR, P.O. Box 460327, Houston TX 77056-8327. (713)785-2618. Began selling cartoons in 1961. 25% of cartoons are written by gag/joke writers or outside sources. Cartoons have recently appeared in *Hustler, National Enquirer, Iron Horse.*

How to Contact: Submit cover letter and sample gags. 10 gags/jokes per batch on 3×5 cards. Looking for gags on any subject "because you can develop a market. Most successful are adult, medical, business, computer." Reports in 1 week. Returns material only if provided with SASE. Pays writers 25% of total fee paid for cartoon. "Can work out different arrangement with proven source of acceptable (to my thinking) material."

Tips: The secret to a great gag/joke is that it's "short or doesn't need captions. Develop unique style, work discipline and marketing persistence. Keep your idea as short as possible and get it across."

Just for Laughs: "The funniest cartoon ever published is Saxon's cartoon depicting two men being served martini's by nude, over-the-hill, spectacled waitress with the gag line: 'Of course, Albuquerque isn't NY, but we try to keep up with things.' If I weren't a cartoonist, I'd probably be a 'millionaire (there are editors who think I'm not a cartoonist anyway).'"

SANDY DEAN, 742 N. Citrus, Pensacola FL 32505. (904)432-4364. Began selling cartoons in 1969. 40% of cartoons are written by gag/joke writers or outside sources. Cartoons have recently appeared in *Star, National Review, Accent on Living*.

How to Contact: Submit 20 gags/jokes per batch on 3×5 cards. Looking for gags on following subjects: farm, outdoor, church, animals. Doesn't want to see porno or "girlie." Reports within 1 week. Returns material only if provided with SASE. Pays writers 25% of total fee paid for cartoon.

Tips: "Slant to subjects I need, not subjects writer likes." The secret to a great gag/joke is surprise. The single best tip to an aspiring cartoonist or gag writer is to "draw, draw, draw, mail, mail, mail."

Just for Laughs: "The funniest cartoon ever published is 'workman glares as fox runs over fresh concrete, doesn't see coming a pack of hounds followed by 20 mounted fox hunters.' If I weren't a cartoonist, I'd probably be a clerk in a pet shop. The single best use for a rejection slip is writing notes to gag writers."

ERIC DECETIS/DECETIS CARTOONS, 2717 Harkness St., Sacramento CA 95818. Began selling cartoons in 1983. 10% of cartoons are written by gag/joke writers or outside sources. Cartoons have recently appeared in *Penthouse, Omni, National Lampoon, Los Angeles Magazine, Campus Life*.

How to Contact: Submit sample gags; 10-20 gags/jokes per batch on 3×5 cards. Looking for quality gags on following subjects: off beat, adult, sight gags. Reports in 2-4 weeks. Returns material only if provided with SASE. Pays writers 25% of total fee paid for cartoon.

Tips: The secret to a great gag/joke is simple gags, "prefer sight gags or ones with short cut lines." The single best tip to an aspiring cartoonist or gag writer is to "have small bones."

Just for Laughs: "The funniest cartoon ever published is almost anything by Charles Addams. If I weren't a cartoonist, I'd probably high-impact divorce attorney or an astronaut. The single best use for a rejection slip is to complete an underwear collection (with rejection bra and panties)."

STEVE DELMONTE, 328 W. Delavan Ave., Buffalo New York 14213. (716)883-6086. FAX: (716)883-9182. Began selling cartoons in 1977. 40% of cartoons are written by gag/joke writers or outside sources. Cartoons have recently appeared in *McCalls, Psychology Today, Woman's World, Diversion*.

How to Contact: Submit cover letter and sample gags; 15-20 gags/jokes per batch on 3×5 cards. Looking for gags on "everything." Reports in 1 month. Returns material only if provided with SASE. Pays writers 25% of total fee paid for cartoon one time.

Tips: The secret to a great gag/joke is a surprise ending/twist. The single best tip to an aspiring cartoonist or gag writer is "don't give up."
Just for Laughs: "The funniest cartoon ever published is where a woman throws up all over a guy on a boat; he says 'bless you!' "

STAN FINE, 125 Montgomery Ave. A-2, Bala Cynwyd PA 19004. (215)667-2045. 60% of cartoons are written by gag/joke writers or outside sources. Cartoons have recently appeared in *Saturday Evening Post, Woman's World, Good Housekeeping, National Enquirer, First, Medical Economics, King Features, McCalls.*
How to Contact: Submit cover letter, sample gags and resume; 12-15 gags/jokes per batch on 3×5 cards. Looking for gags on following subjects: family, kids, school, working women. Doesn't want to see far-out, implausible subject matter. Reports in 1 week. Returns material only if provided with SASE. Pays writers 25% of total fee paid for cartoon.
Tips: The secret to a great gag/joke is "anything that gives me an audible chuckle and relates to everyday happenings." The single best tip to an aspiring cartoonist or gag writer is "if you are attaining positive results, work even harder to consolidate your toehold. Avoid any distractions, read, watch and observe the world around you. Know what is really funny and be able to slant material."
Just for Laughs: "The funniest cartoon ever published is woman skiing, tracks go around each side of tree and continue downhill (by Charles Addams)."

RANDY GLASBERGEN, Box 736, Sherburne NY 13460. Began selling cartoons in 1972. Number of cartoons written by gag writers or outside sources varies. Cartoons have recently appeared in *National Enquirer, Good Housekeeping, McCall's, Woman's World, Better Homes & Gardens, Saturday Evening Post, New Woman, Cosmopolitan,* (all of the top markets, over 12,000 sales).
How to Contact: Submit cover letter, sample gags and resume; 10-20 gags per batch on 3×5 cards. Looking for gags on following subjects: "all kinds—I sell everywhere!" Reports in 1 week. Returns material only if provided with SASE. Pays writers 25% of total fee paid for cartoon; sometimes more for best writers.
Tips: The single best tip to an aspiring cartoonist or gag writer is "be yourself—totally original."

H. GLASSMAN, Box 46664, Los Angeles CA 90046. Uses gag/joke writers for stand-up. "I submit the subjects after I see your sample gags."
How to Contact: Submit 6-10 one-liners per batch on 8½×11 paper. For first contact send cover letter and sample material/jokes/gags. Repots back within 3 weeks. Returns material if accompanied by SASE. Pays $15.
Tips: "Jokes must fit my style and be performable."

STUART GOLDMAN, 2318 Manning St., Philadelphia PA 19103. (215)732-5106. Name of strip: "Eavesdrawings." Began selling cartoons in 1975. 15-20% of cartoons are written by gag/joke writers or outside sources. Cartoons have recently appeared in newspapers, (weekly features for lifestyle sections); also write for performance comedy.
How to Contact: Submit sample gags and tearsheets (with first submission); no less than 5 gags/jokes per batch, presentation is unimportant. Prefers to work with gag/joke writers who have fax capabilities. Looking for gags on following subjects: urban/suburban, working/family life with the main concentration on yuppie lifestyle, business, dating and entertainment. "Also desire to look at scripts for comedy club—have need for sketch material and bits from 2-8 minutes duration, payment varies. Doesn't want to see any bedroom talk—talk about it yes, but not in it." Reports in 2 weeks. Returns material only if provided with SASE. Pays writers $15 minimum depending on where the material is used.

Tips: The secret to a great gag/joke is "conversational continuity and believability." The single best tip to an aspiring cartoonist or gag writer is study body language and develop an ear for conversation.

Just for Laughs: "Favorite cartoon ever published is William Hamilton's autobiographic cartoon—elegant folks at dining table—young woman leans over towards tuxedoed male—'Do you do any *real* art?' The single best use for a rejection slip is to practice your 3-point wastepaper basket shots so you can go to art school on an athletic scholarship."

GEORGE HAESSLER/CONCEPT REALIZATION, 4216 Bishop Rd., Detroit MI 48224. (313)882-3916. Names of cartoons: Georgio, Ritzy Rat. Began selling cartoons in 1961. Cartoons have recently appeared in *Phase Two.*
How to Contact: Submit cover letter, tearsheets; 3 gags/jokes per batch. Looking for sophisticated gags. Reports in 10 days.
Tips: The secret to a great gag/joke is spontaneity. The single best tip to an aspiring cartoonist or gag writer is to "get into another field."
Just for Laughs: "If I weren't a cartoonist, I'd probably be a plumber."

BRIAN HANSEN/CARTOON SOURCE, 2909 Tincup Cir., Boulder CO 80303. (303)494-0220. Began selling cartoons is 1981. 5% of cartoons are written by gag/joke writers or outside sources. Cartoons have recently appeared in *Infoworld, Computerworld, Personal and Professional.*
How to Contact: Submit sample gags on 3×5 cards, 8½×11 paper, or any other form. Looking for gags on following subjects: office, sophisticated, computers, "off-the-wall." Doesn't want to see "adult" material. Reports in 4 weeks. Returns material only if provided with SASE. Pays writers 50% of total fee paid for cartoon.
Tips: The secret to a great gag/joke: "A gag that requires both pictures and words—where neither words nor pictures alone can express the idea. Thousands of cartoons are sold each week—even bad ones. If you can be clever enough to find out who might want to buy them you can sell your cartoons."
Just for Laughs: Roz Chast: "The three certainties of life—death, taxes and Bobo." The single best use for a rejection slip: "Certain occult and extremist organizations pay up to 5¢ per name for referrals and valid addresses."

JONNY HAWKINS, 25375 Basin 118, Southfield MI 48034. (313)356-6317. Began selling cartoons in 1977. 5% of cartoons are written by gag/joke writers or outside sources. Cartoons have recently appeared in *Leadership, Farm and Ranch, The Lutheran, Michigan Farmer, Freeway.*
How to Contact: Submit short intro letter; 10-50 gags on 3×5 slips of paper. Looking for gags on following subjects: generals; "I do quite a few farm cartoons as well as church/pastor gags. I need captionless animal gags for a developing project, though. Doesn't want to see girlie material or anything sick or offensive. I certainly welcome the strange and absurd, but nothing pornographic or blasphemous." Reports usually within a week. Returns material only if provided with SASE. Pays writers 25% of total fee paid for cartoon. After 5 sales with same writer it goes up to 30%; after 10 to 32%.
Tips: The secret to a great gag/joke is "that irony is captured in the fewest possible words, or if the thought of it leaves your spleen hanging on the floor." The single best tip to an aspiring cartoonist or gag writer is be persistent. "Don't let a few rejections sink your ship. Learn from the ones who are successful, but be *yourself!* Do you! Do what *you* think is funny and work on developing it to perfection. Don't send me a gag situation rehashed in 8 different situations—I can do that. Realize that your perspective is needed in this nutty world and, by golly, I'd like to see it if it matches my style."
Just for Laughs: "If I weren't a cartoonist, I'd probably be married. The single best use for a rejection slip is for proof in court that shooting the editor was in self-defense."

BRUCE HIGDON, 2631 Birdsong Ave., Murfreesboro TN 37129. (615)893-6653. Began selling cartoons in 1962. Cartoons have recently appeared in *Army, Soldiers, Saturday Evening Post, Modern Maturity.*
How to Contact: Submit sample gags; 10-15 gags/jokes per batch on 3 × 5 cards. Looking for gags on following subjects: family, military, school and office situations. Doesn't want to see material that is sexist, profane or in poor taste. Reports in 2 weeks. Returns material only if provided with SASE. Pays writers 40% of total fee paid for cartoon.
Tips: The secret to a great gag/joke is that it's quick and to the point. The gag must be fresh to work well with the drawing. The single best tip to an aspiring cartoonist or gag writer is "believe in yourself, then work at making yourself and your humor believable. Think . . . read . . . listen . . . study human nature. Find the laughs in everyday life."
Just for Laughs: "The single best use for a rejection slip is stuffing your clothes and shoes in the winter time."

DAVID R. HOWELL, Box 170, Porterville CA 93258. (209)781-5885. Began selling cartoons in 1973. 50% of cartoons are written by gag/joke writers or outside sources. Cartoons have recently appeared in *National Enquirer, TV Guide, Women's Enterprise, Judicature, True Detective.*
How to Contact: Submit sample gags and resume; at least 10 gags/jokes per batch on 3 × 5 cards. Looking for gags on following subjects: law and crime, TV, electronics, computer, medical, retailing. Doesn't want to see sex, politics or topical. Reports in 2 weeks. Returns material only if provided with SASE. Pays writers 25% of total fee paid for cartoon.
Tips: The secret to a great gag/joke is combination of good, brief line with funny drawing. The single best tip to an aspiring cartoonist or gag writer is "don't ever give up. Watch the humor trends closely."

DALE HUNT, 2414 Otto Dr., Stockton CA 95209. (209)957-6419. Began selling cartoons in 1982. Cartoons have recently appeared in *Stockton Record, Lincoln Chronicle, Delta Impact, Delta Digest Magazine.*
How to Contact: Submit "some kind of idea" on 8½ × 11 paper. Looking for gags on following subjects: medical, fishing. Doesn't want to see kid's cartoons and cars. Reports in a few months "due to editors." Returns material only if provided with SASE. Pays writers 25% of total fee paid for cartoon "only if they sell."
Tips: The secret to a great gag/joke is as soon as you read it, a picture hits your head and you laugh. The single best tip to an aspiring cartoonist or gag writer is "draw all day, spend time studying other cartoonists and listen to your inner mind. Watch for situations around you and watch comedy shows. Sometimes you can get ideas from them but follow the example but don't steal."
Just for Laughs: "The funniest cartoon ever published is Charles Addams' cartoon of the skier going through the tree (captionless)."

FRANK JOHNSON, 18 Holiday Rd., Fairfield CT 06432. (203)372-3398. Names of strips: Boner's Ark, Bringing up Father. Began selling cartoons in 1953. 30% of cartoons are written by gag/joke writers or outside sources.
How to Contact: Submit 10 rough gags/jokes per batch. Looking for gags slanted towards the strip with character's personality. Reports in 2 weeks. Returns material only if provided with SASE. Pays writers outright $5 + maximum.
Tips: The single best tip to an aspiring cartoonist or gag writer is study the top features.
Just for Laughs: "If I weren't a cartoonist, I'd probably be a pro golfer (ha ha)."

MILO KINN, 1413 S.W. Cambridge St., Seattle WA 98106. Began selling cartoons in 1942. 50% of cartoons are written by gag writers or outside sources. Cartoons have recently appeared in *Pet Health News, Legal Economics, American Machinist, Nebraska Farmer, Nutrition Health Review, Machinists Blue Book*.
How to Contact: Submit sample gags; 10-20 gags per batch on 3×5 cards or paper. Looking for gags on following subjects: office, lawyers, farm, machine shop, family, general (of course), medical, woman. Doesn't want to see "girly" gags. Reports in 2 weeks. Returns material only if provided with SASE. Pays writers 25% of total fee paid for cartoon.
Tips: "The secret to a good gag/joke is it makes a funny picture (even without a gagline). Cartoonists should keep drawings simple. Gag writers should write situations without too much description. Keep gag settings uncomplicated."

THOMAS L. LAIRD, 128 South Second St., Philipsburg PA 16866. (814)342-2935. Began selling cartoons in 1982. A small percentage of cartoons are written by gag/joke writers or outside sources. Cartoons have recently appeared in *State College, The Magazine* and *The Office*.
How to Contact: Submit cover letter; minimum of 6 gags/jokes per batch on 3×5 cards or 8½×11 paper. "I really need ideas dealing with holiday themes! Although I am wide open to subject and/or type of gag, I feel that ideas with broad appeal are easiest to move. Children, working, paying taxes/bills, eating, household budgets—etc." Reports in 2 weeks. Returns material only if provided with SASE. Pays writers 25% of total fee received up to $100.
Tips: "Present yourself honestly. If you have never sold before, don't lie about it. There is nothing wrong with just getting started—only never starting. I wish I could say exactly what makes a great gag. I think it's a combination of things that just sort of seem 'right' together. 'I may not know art, but I know what I like.' Let a little of yourself show through in your gags and captions, as well as your characters. Also, don't concentrate on just the majors. Consistently selling to smaller publications often pays more in the long run. In trying to work with gag writers, I've found that writers often don't set up the situation or scene enough or the caption is not clear and concise. Correct that and you'll go far."
Just for Laughs: "A sign on a tree states, 'Do not feed the bears!' Beside the tree, a moose wears sign stating 'I am not a bear.' If I weren't a cartoonist, I'd probably be a '(kindly) third-world dictator or perhaps a hous-husband."

FRANK LENGEL, 900 K Ave., Cayce SC 29033. Began selling cartoons in 1980. 50% of cartoons are written by gag/joke writers or outside sources. Cartoons have recently appeared in *National Enquirer, Saturday Evening Post, Good Housekeeping, King Features, American Legion, Medical Economics*.
How to Contact: Submit sample gags; 10-20 gags/jokes per batch on 3×5 cards. Looking for gags on following subjects: family, business, humor which includes cars, medical humor. Doesn't want to see satire, political humor or multi-panel gags. Reports in 1-2 weeks. Returns material only if provided with SASE. Pays writers 33% of total fee paid for cartoon.
Tips: The secret to a great gag/joke is the "gagline is not a joke. It needs visual (cartoon) action to give it the punch that makes it funny. Be disciplined. Work regularly. Be patient. It takes months, sometimes years to sell a cartoon. And sometimes, magazines pay after material is published. It's a slow business and the best way to be patient is to continue turning out work."

LEOLEEN-DURCK CREATIONS, LEONARD BRUCE DESIGNS, Box 2767, #226, Jackson TN 38302. (901)668-1205. Contact Eileen Bruce. Names of strips: Leotoons, Fred, Peggy and Sue, The McNabs. Began selling cartoons in 1981. 25% of cartoons are written by gag/joke writers or outside sources. Cartoons have recently appeared in *Starlog, Space Age Times.*

How to Contact: Submit cover letter, sample gags, resume, tearsheets and cartoons; 18 gags/jokes per batch on 3×5 cards. Looking for gags on following subjects: off-the-wall, alien-type humor, senior citizen humor, sister to sister humor. Reports in 10 days. Returns material only if provided with SASE. Pays writers 10% of total fee paid for cartoon.

Tips: The secret to a great gag/joke is timely humor in a familiar setting. The single best tip to an aspiring cartoonist or gag writer is "submit, practice and never give up. Look at joke books to see what is funny.

Just for Laughs: "The single best use for a rejection slip is to line your cat box."

LIEBE/PIPWYKK & CO., 2765 W. 5th St., Brooklyn NY 11224. (718)996-1480. Began selling cartoons in 1978. 75% of cartoons are written by gag/joke writers or outside sources. Cartoons have recently appeared in *National Enquirer, Good Housekeeping, New Woman, Cosmopolitan.*

How to Contact: Submit sample gags; 15 gag/jokes per batch on 3×5 cards or paper. Looking for gags on following subjects: general, family, children, animals, romance, relationships, working women. Doesn't want to see politics, science fiction, horror. Reports in 1 month. Returns material only if provided with SASE. Pays writers 25% of total fee paid for cartoon.

Tips: The secret to a great gag/joke: "There's a human or universal truth in it that we recognize. This is what can make a classic. Practice, practice, practice and mail out, mail out, mail out. As a matter of fact, instead of answering this questionnaire right now, I should be drawing."

Just for Laughs: The funniest cartoon ever published is "The annual Peanuts strip where Lucy sets up Charlie Brown to kick the football and then pulls it away. I love the way Schulz has played with this basic element of a relationship over the years. If I weren't a cartoonist, I'd probably be a 'very sorry woman.' The single best use for a rejection slip: I've never used them for toilet paper—too scratchy—but I would imagine that's the best. They make pretty good wallpaper if you don't overdo it. That could get depressing."

AL LIEDERMAN, 1700 St. Johns Ave., Merrick NY 11566. (516)379-6091. Name of strip: Double Duty. Began selling cartoons in 1950. 80% of cartoons are written by gag/joke writers or outside sources. Cartoons have recently appeared in *King Features, Saturday Evening Post, National Enquirer, Journal of Commerce.*

How to Contact: Submit sample gags; 20 gags/jokes per batch on 3×5 cards. Looking for gags on following subjects: office situations, politics, working women. Reports in 6 days. Returns material only if provided with SASE. Pays writers 25% of total fee paid for cartoon.

Tips: The secret to a great gag/joke: "I wish I knew! If it sold, it was a 'great gag!' Don't send (to the cartoonist) any old gag in hopes it'll go. 99 times it won't."

ART McCOURT, Box 210346, Dallas TX 75211. (214)339-6865. Began selling cartoons in 1952. 90% of cartoons are written by gag/joke writers or outside sources. Cartoons have recently appeared in *National Enquirer, The Star, King Features, Reader's Digest, American International Syndicate.*

How to Contact: Submit sample gags; 15-20 gags/jokes per batch on 3×5 cards. Looking for gags on following subjects: farm, medical, hunting, fishing, office situations, working women, sophisticated and computers. Doesn't want to see male, politics. Returns material only if provided with SASE. Pays writers 25% of total fee paid for cartoon.

Tips: The secret to a great gag/joke is make it simple, don't get complicated. The single best tip to an aspiring cartoonist or gag writer is "work at your craft, read a lot. See what others are doing. Be current, be aware and no puns."

Just for Laughs: "The funniest cartoon ever published is Charles Addams' in *New Yorker* where you see ski tracks separated by a tree. If I weren't a cartoonist, I'd probably be a stud, con man or cowboy."

THERESA McCRACKEN/McHUMOR, 910 Constitution Ave. NE, Washington DC 20002. (202)547-1373. Began selling cartoons in 1981. 15% of cartoons are written by gag/joke writers or outside sources. Cartoons have recently appeared in *American Medical Association News, American Bar Association, King Features, Ski, Adweek, California Computing, Chemtech, CEO.*

How to Contact: Submit sample gags; 15 gags/jokes per batch on 3×5 cards. "I use gag writers for trade journals I work with, and these range from computer to auto repair to refereeing magazines. *No general gags* please. I do all of my own generals." Reports in 1 month. Returns material only if provided with SASE. Pays writers 25% of total fee paid for cartoon.

Tips: The secret to a great gag/joke: "My favorites are captionless ones, ones that you get instantly, but then want to look at again carefully." Target material to a publication. Don't overwhelm a cartoonist with hundreds of gags at a time."

REX F. MAY, ("BaLOO"), Box 3108, West Layfayette IN 47906. (317)743-6772. Began selling cartoons in 1975. 1% of cartoons are written by gag/joke writers or outside sources. Cartoons have recently appeared in *Wall Street Journal, Good Housekeeping, National Enquirer, Woman's World, National Review, Leadership, World Monitor, Cavalier, Parts Pups, Medical Economics.*

How to Contact: Submit cover letter, sample gags by mail; no limit on gags/jokes per batch on 3×5 slips of paper. Reports in 7 days. Returns material only if provided with SASE. Pays writers 20% of total fee paid for cartoon.

Tips: "I'm a gagwriter first, cartoonist second, so I use other writers sparingly, but I'm always in the market to work with other cartoonists as writers. The secret to a great gag/joke is humor has to *surprise* and therefore must be original. The fresher the better." The single best tip to an aspiring cartoonist or gag writer is "keep it simple, there should be nothing in the cartoon that doesn't contribute to getting the gag across. Get the spelling and punctuation right!"

Just for Laughs: "The funniest cartoon ever published is two sleepy gurus atop a mountain drinking coffee. One to other: 'I can see it's going to be one of those days—my doughnut just rolled down the mountain.' If I weren't a cartoonist, I'd probably be a political activist."

ANDRÉ NOEL, 161 Hilltop Acres, Yonkers NY 10704. (914)476-1263. Began selling cartoons in 1986. 75% of cartoons are written by gag/joke writers or outside sources. Cartoons have recently appeared in *Saturday Evening Post, National Enquirer, Woman's World, Cosmopolitan.*

How to Contact: Submit sample gags; 20 gags/jokes per batch on 3×5 cards. Looking for gags on following subjects: office situations, working women, sophisticated, family type and off-the-wall types of gags. "Some may be spicy but not X-rated." Doesn't want to see "X-rated, ethnic and macho crap." Reports in 3-4 weeks. Returns material only if provided with SASE. Pays writers 30% of total fee paid for cartoon.

Tips: The secret to a great gag/joke: "It's no secret—keep it simple. Persist and keep good records on sales, holds, gags, etc. Keep your eyes and ears open, listen to people."

Just for Laughs: The funniest cartoon ever published is "A dozey-looking man stands on street corner. Passers-by watch as a huge hand descends from a cloud to 'flick' him. (George Booth). If I weren't a cartoonist, I'd probably be a 'basket-case.' The best use for a rejection slip is to 'start a collection as an incentive to 'break' those particular markets."

TIM OLIPHANT-OLLIE FEATURES, (Ollie, pen name), 200 Mehs Dr. 2-K, Lewisburg TN 37091. (615)359-7430. Freelance humorous illustration. Began selling cartoons in 1981. 10% of cartoons are written by gag/joke writers or outside sources. Cartoons have recently appeared in *Woman's World* and *Highlights for Children*.
How to Contact: Submit cover letter, sample gags, resume and tearsheets; 8 gags/jokes per batch on 3×5 cards. Looking for general material. Doesn't want to see dirty jokes or obscene magazine material. Reports in 2 weeks. Returns material only if provided with SASE. Pays writers 25% of total fee paid for cartoon.
Tips: "A great joke takes a situation from real life and makes a humorous situation out of it so someone says, 'that happened to me' or 'I know someone like that.'"
Just for Laughs: "It's impossible to name the funniest ever cartoon. I've seen so many. Very possibly though, it was something I saw in 'Calvin & Hobbes.' A cartoonist is the only thing I ever wanted to be."

RICHARD ORLIN CARTOONS, 9147 Chesley Knoll Ct., Gaithersburg MD 20879. (301)921-0315. Name of strip: TV Toons. Began selling cartoons in 1980. 5% of cartoons are written by gag/joke writers or outside sources.
How to Contact: Submit sample gags; 25 gags/jokes per batch on 3×5 cards. Looking for gags on following subjects: family, sophisticated, science, computers, television. Doesn't want to see raunchy material. Reports in 5 days. Returns material only if provided with SASE. Pays writers 25% of total fee paid for cartoon. For other television gags makes outright purchase of $25.
Tips: The single best tip to an aspiring cartoonist or gag writer is "don't give up."
Just for Laughs: The funniest cartoon ever published is "Anything Charles Addams' did. If I weren't a cartoonist, I'd probably be dead."

STEVE PHELPS, 613 N. Elizabeth, Santa Maria CA 93454. (805)937-4314. Began selling cartoons in 1984. 50% of cartoons are written by gag/joke writers or outside sources. Cartoons have recently appeared in *Good Housekeeping, Better Homes and Gardens, Saturday Evening Post, TV Guide, Woman's World, King Features, National Enquirer*.
How to Contact: Submit cover letter; 10-20 gags/jokes per batch on 3×5 paper. Looking for gags on following subjects: religious, soaps, generals, youth. Doesn't want to see porn, girlies or suggestive material. Reports within 1 week. Returns material only if provided with SASE. Pays writers 25% of total fee paid for cartoon.
Tips: The secret to a great gag/joke is "fresh new slants, not same old gags over and over, something that can be drawn simply." The single best tip to an aspiring cartoonist or gag writer is "draw, submit — draw, submit. Think funny. Send new cartoonist a few first looks to see if you're worth your salt."
Just for Laughs: "If I weren't a cartoonist, I'd probably be a ski bum. The single best use for a rejection slip is a coaster on my table or a spit wad."

TOM PRISK, Nelson St., HCR-1 Box 741, Michigamme MI, 49861. Began selling cartoons in 1977. 25% of cartoons are written by gag/joke writers or outside sources. Cartoons have recently appeared in *Woman's World, Writer's Digest, Byline Mag, Sun, Globe* and the *National Examiner*.
How to Contact: Submit cover letter and sample gags. 10-20 gags/jokes per batch on 3×5 cards. "I need gags about writers and the writing life. I will not consider pornography or racist material." Reports in 2 weeks. Please *do not* submit material from June 1st through September 1st. Will return material is SASE is included. Pays writers 25% of total fee paid for cartoon.

Tips: I think the secret to a really great gag would be looking at an idea from a different point of view, a new perspective on an old theme. An aspiring cartoonist must *practice* and *never* quit! A gag writer should study published material, see what makes it funny and always strive for originality.

DAN RILEY, 7735 High Pine Rd., Orlando FL 32819. Dan Riley has been in the business for 10 years and has performed at Ceasers, Radio City, Universal Amphitheater, Bally's, Harrah's, Walt Disney World. Act is primarily guitar/comic. Uses gag/joke writers for TV appearances, live act/routine, public appearances, and developmental projects on all subjects except blue material. Buys 50 gags/jokes/one liners per year.
How to Contact: Submit any number of gags/jokes per batch on 8½×11 paper. For first contact send cover letter, resume, credits, sample material/jokes/gags and audio tape. Reports back in 6 weeks only if interested. Returns material, only if requested and if accompanied by SASE. Negotiates rights purchased. Pays $5-100.

DAN ROSANDICH, Box 410, Chassell MI 49916. (906)482-6234. Name of strip: The Golden Daze. Began selling cartoons in 1976. 50% of cartoons are written by gag/joke writers or outside sources. Cartoons have recently appeared in *National Enquirer, Saturday Evening Post, Star, King Features, Swank, Gallery, Sun, Examiner, Globe, Cavalier.*
How to Contact: Submit cover letter; 20-25 gags/jokes per batch on 3×5 cards or slips. Looking for gags on following subjects: "only captionless gags relating to any subjects a person could conjure up." Reports in 3 days. Returns material only if provided with SASE. Pays writers 25% of total fee paid for cartoon or makes outright purchase of $1 minimum.
Tips: The secret to a great gag/joke is "the shorter the gagline, the sweeter to get the idea across." The single best tip to an aspiring cartoonist or gag writer is "persistence and study cartoons previously published."
Just for Laughs: The funniest cartoon ever published is, "After vomiting on a bar patron, drunk says 'Sure glad I didn't do that in my car!' If I weren't a cartoonist, I'd probably be a printer or ditchdigger! The single best use for a rejection slip is taking it to an outhouse."

HARLEY SCHWADRON, Box 1347, Ann Arbor MI 48106. (313)663-1368. Name of features: free-lance magazine cartoons and syndicated panels Big Biz and Grimsly's Day. Began selling cartoons in 1972. 20% of cartoons are written by gag/joke writers or outside sources. Cartoons have recently appeared in *Punch, Wall Street Journal, Woman's World, Woman, Penthouse, Cosmopolitan, Good Housekeeping.*
How to Contact: Submit sample gags on 3×5 paper. Looking for gags on following subjects: general, topical, business. Reporting time varies. Returns material only if provided with SASE. Pays writers 25% of total fee paid for cartoon.
Tips: The secret to a great gag/joke is "gags that have visual elements are best, or ones that tie into some current event or cultural phenomenon." The single best tip to an aspiring cartoonist or gag writer is "keep plugging away."
Just for Laughs: "The single best use for a rejection slip is something not to pad one's resume with."

SUZANNE STEINIGER, 9373 Whitcomb, Detroit MI 48228. (313)838-5204. Began selling cartoons in 1982. 80% of cartoons are written by gag/joke writers or outside sources. Cartoons have recently appeared in *Women, The Farmer, The Nebraska Farmer, The Chronicle of the Horse, Highlights for Children.*
How to Contact: Submit sample gags on 3×5 cards. Looking for animal gags with forest and farm animals for a variety of magazines. "Porno is a taboo with me." Reports in 6 weeks. Pays writers 25% of total fee paid for cartoon.

Tips: "Simplicity in scene and saying is the secret to a great gag." The single best tip is to "keep practicing. Draw everything so you can be versatile. Read all kinds of material from a variety of magazines, especially from *The New Yorker*."
Just for Laughs: "If I weren't a cartoonist, I'd probably be a forest ranger."

JOHN STINGER, Box 350, Stewartsville NJ 08886. (201)859-1005. Began selling cartoons in 1965. 10% of cartoons are written by gag/joke writers or outside sources. Cartoons have recently appeared in syndicated business features worldwide.
How to Contact: Submit sample gags; 10 gags/jokes per batch on 3x5 cards. Looking for gags on office situations only. Doesn't want to see off-color stuff. Reports in 1 week. Returns material only if provided with SASE. Pays writers 15% of total fee paid for cartoon.
Tips: The single best tip to an aspiring cartoonist or gag writer is "think like a gag writer or cartoonist."
Just for Laughs: The funniest cartoon ever published is "woman on knees at door to bill collector. 'Sorry, my mommy is not home.' If I weren't a cartoonist, I'd probably be a gagwriter or movie star. The single best use for a rejection slip is use as a floor mat for my wife's chicken house."

GARY R. SUTHERLAND, 4413 37th SW, Seattle WA 98126. (206)932-5313. Began selling cartoons in 1967. 100% of cartoons are written by gag/joke writers or outside sources. Cartoons have recently appeared in Mount News, KMPS Radio, KRPM Tune-in.
How to Contact: Submit tearsheets, sample gags and resume. One gag/joke per batch on a 3×5 card. I'd like to see *everyday* people. Doesn't want to see pornography and "hippie material." Reporting time is several days.

FRANK TABOR; CARTOON ART STUDIO, 2817 NE 292nd Ave, Camas WA 98607. (206)834-3355. Began selling cartoons in 1946. 98% of cartoons are written by gag/joke writers or outside sources. Cartoons have recently appeared in *Good Housekeeping, Post, American Legion, First, For Women, Star, Globe, Sun.*
How to Contact: Submit sample gags; 10-20 gags/jokes per batch on file slips. Looking for gags on following subjects: home and family, metal shop manufacturing, macabre. Doesn't want to see "raw sex." Reports 1 day after receiving material. Returns material only if provided with SASE. Pays writers 33% of total fee paid for cartoon to steady writers; 25% to occasional submissions.
Tips: The secret to a great gag/joke is "finding an editor who thinks it's funny." The single best tip to an aspiring cartoonist or gag writer is "draw and submit, draw and submit, draw and submit. Write in volume. I sell the most for those who send me the most."

BOB THAVES, Box 67, Manhattan Beach CA 90266. Name of feature: Frank and Ernest. Began selling cartoons in the early 1950's. ". . . nothing would make me happier than to have a brilliant gagwriter writing everything for me!"
How to Contact: Submit any number of gag/jokes per batch on any form of submission. Looking for gags on following subject: offbeat. Reports in 2 weeks. "Will return [material] once without SASE, but not a second time. Why should I pay the costs to return material people are trying to sell to me?" Variable pay—depends on frequency and quality of submission, and varies by use (that is, syndicated feature, licensed product, etc.).
Tips: The secret to a great gag/joke: "I wish I knew, but the point of the gag should be something unexpected. Be yourself—don't try to mimic what's 'hot' today. 1) Don't plagiarize; 2) avoid 'talking heads' gags; 3) avoid the same old, tried, stock situations. Try to do something different and distinctive."
Just for Laughs: The best use for a rejection slip: "Gee. What's a rejection slip?"

MORRIE TURNER, Box 30045 S. Berkeley Station, Berkeley CA 94703. Name of strip: Wee Pals. Began selling cartoons in 1957. 15% of cartoons are written by gag/joke writers or outside sources.
How to Contact: Submit sample gags; 10-12 gags/jokes per batch on 3×5 cards. Reports in 2 weeks. Returns material only if provided with SASE. Pays writers 25% of total fee paid for cartoon.

CHUCK VADUN, 14814 Priscilla St., San Diego CA 92129. (619)672-0212. Began selling cartoons in 1965. 50% of cartoons are written by gag/joke writers or outside sources. Cartoons have recently appeared in *Kiwanis, Good Housekeeping* and *Wall Street Journal*.
How to Contact: Submit sample gags; 10-20 gags/jokes per batch on 3×5 cards. Wants to see gags on anything except smut. Reports in 1 week. Returns material only if provided with SASE. Pays writers 25% of total fee paid for cartoon.
Tips: Neither art nor caption can stand alone. "There is no best use for a rejection slip unless, of course, you save them up until you have enough to wallow in self-pity."

KAREN WEST, Rt. 2 Box 224, Seneca MO 64865. Began selling cartoons in 1978. 30-40% of cartoons are written by gag/joke writers or outside sources. Cartoons have recently appeared in *Saturday Evening Post, Easyriders, Family Circle, Compete Woman, The Mirror* and many minor markets.
How to Contact: Submit sample gags; 12 gags/jokes per batch on 3×5 cards. Looking for gags on following subjects: mostly family, work, general types. Doesn't want to see "girlies" or political. Reports in 10-14 days. Returns material only if provided with SASE. Pays writers 25% of total fee paid for cartoon.
Tips: "Please, no long, drawn out gags that would take 3 panels to explain—I like pungent, off-the-wall, immediate humor! Fresh, potent situations—simple is best—gags that are three sentences long are rarely funny. The single best tip to an aspiring cartoonist or gag writer is hang in there, don't give up—know your markets—don't send a batch blindly—be professional in your approach. If it's funny to you, genuinely funny, it's a good gag. Forced gags just don't get it. Be yourself in your gags."
Just for Laughs: "If I weren't a cartoonist, I'd probably be a mental patient. The single best use for a rejection slip is soak up grease under french fries."

KEVIN WEST, 13601 Ventura Blvd., Suite 354, Sherman Oaks CA 91423. (818)989-1040. Management: Kathy Lymberopoulos/Lymberpoulos, Inc. Kevin West has performed in clubs all over the country, lots of talk shows and comedy shows, movies, TV series, commercials (big commercial star). Act is primarily stand-up, improvisation. Uses gag/joke writers for TV appearances and live act/routine on everything except political.
How to Contact: Submit up to 20 gags/jokes per batch on 8½×11 paper. For first contact send cover letter, resume and credits. Reports back in 2 weeks. Returns material only if provided with SASE. Does not file material. Buys all rights. Pays $50.
Tips: The benefits of working with gag/joke writers: "someone to bounce off of."

JOSEPH F. WHITAKER, 2522 Percy Ave., Orlando FL 32818. Began selling cartoons in 1959. 40% of cartoons are written by gag/joke writers or outside sources. Cartoons have recently appeared in *National Enquirer, Woman, New Woman, Saturday Evening Post, Moose, National Catholic News, Dartnell, Parts Pups, Collision* and trade journals.
How to Contact: Submit sample gags; 15 gags/jokes per batch on 3×5, 20% bond paper. Looking for gags on following subjects: office situations, working women, sophisticated, computers. Doesn't want to see sex gags. Reports in 1 week. Returns material only if provided with SASE. Pays writers 25% of total fee paid for cartoon.
Tips: The secret to a great gag/joke is "be brief and to the point."

Greeting Cards and Paper Products

Who exactly benefits from all these holidays?

When I was growing up, all you had to worry about buying were a couple birthday cards a year, maybe an anniversary card for mom and dad and a get well card for Uncle Murray's inflamed gall bladder.

But today, it seems as if everybody and everything have become national holidays. Grandparents' Day, Mother-in-Law's Day—even Secretary's Day. You think October 14 is just one of 365 fairly innocuous days of the year? Wrong—it's Boss' Day!

Well, you're not the only one who wonders if the plethora of holidays is a well orchestrated plot conceived by the folks at Hallmark to boost paper product sales.

But if holidays have multiplied like fertility-drugged bunnies, then so has the need for freelance art and writing services. Greeting card companies are excellent, receptive markets for humor. They have an almost constant need for humorous illustration and copy, and with the advent of studio card lines, they afford a considerable amount of editorial freedom for the humorous illustrator and writer.

Yet each company tries to put its own, distinctive "spin" on its line. While one publisher may be receptive to "put down" greetings, another may not. Company ABC may prefer airy humorous illustration styles that do not compete with copy. Company XYZ might seek outlandish art busier than a fallout shelter at Armageddon.

Keep in mind that you are filling a need for a greeting card company—they are not satisfying your whims. Find out what they are looking for. You may have some terrific copy for birthday cards, but they may be overstocked with such material. Instead they may have a pressing need for anniversary cards written from a wife-to-husband point of view. Writing material suited to their needs increases your chances of making a sale.

Similarly, before submitting art, study the greeting card company's line to determine what samples might be appropriate and can best demonstrate your stylistic compatibility. If a greeting card company's idea of humor is cute teddy bears with heart-like pupils, perhaps you should refrain from submitting grotesque samples of characters who could make Basil Wolverton's Leena The Hyena look like Christie Brinkley.

Don't lose sight of the fact that humor is a funny, but serious, business. A professional presentation attests to the recipient that you care enough to put some effort behind your submission. While freelance resource managers at greeting card companies have limited time to chat, a quick post-submission phone call is good policy.

You'd be amazed at what you can accomplish in one minute on the telephone. Almost immediately you can determine the client's receptiveness to your work, their potential as a market and whether or not you should update them with other samples of your work. If your work is inappropriate, you will know this quickly, cut your losses and, for everyone's benefit, move on.

Trends

I'd like to say that market trends aren't important, that funny is funny, but when it comes to greeting cards, trend is spelled with a capitol "T." According to Paul Vitale, freelance humor art coordinator at Paramount Cards, the graphic trend is towards white.

"Simple, plain white or soft backgrounds," says Vitale, "and more angular features to the human characters—anything that gets away from the traditional look of flowers on colored backgrounds. We produce alternative card designs which try to keep pace in a highly competitive market."

When it comes to freelance humorous illustration, Vitale "looks at a lot of terrific stuff—there's some tremendous talent out there." But humor writing is another matter. "You'd be amazed," he laments, "at the kind of writing that crosses my desk. I mean, the cover letters are better prepared than the actual greeting card copy—we've even received copy submissions which seem to have been written in crayon!"

Happily, we all like to laugh, and greeting card companies understand the importance of a good sense of humor. So the next time you moan while having to buy a Thanksgiving card for the Fenwicks, just remember: the more holidays, the more freelance art and writing assignments.

AMBERLEY GREETING CARD CO., 11510 Goldcoast Dr., Cincinnati OH 45249. (513)489-2775. FAX: (513)489-2857. Estab. 1966. Publishes greeting cards for anniversary, get well, congratulatory, non-occasion, birthday and retirement. Needs humorous greeting cards (writing only).
Humorous Illustration: Uses local artists only. Reports back in 1 month. Returns materials if accompanied by SASE. Buys all rights. Pays $60 minimum. Also assigns local freelance humorous illustration/cartoon duties. Assigns approximately 10 jobs per month. When considering freelance humorous illustrators, considers skill; ability to take art direction well; humor; marketability of drawing style and dependability. Pays $60 minimum.

Humor Writing: Looking for humorous greeting card writing that is short and to the point, not subtle. For first contact send in editorials (ideas) to Ned Stern, Editor. Reports back within 1 month. Returns materials if accompanied by SASE. Buys all rights. Pays $40. When assigning freelance humorous writing, considers skill and effective use of humor. Tips: If a humorous writer wants to sell his work, he should "see what's in the stores."

AMERICAN GREETINGS CORPORATION, 10500 American Rd., Cleveland OH 44144. (216)252-7300. Estab. 1906. Publishes greeting cards, calendars, books/booklets, paper plates/partyware, gifts and gift wrap for all occasions. Needs humorous illustration for all product categories. Needs humor writing for greeting cards.
Humorous Illustration: For first contact send cover letter and resume to Lynne Shlonsky, Director of Creative Recruitment. "We do not accept unsolicited ideas." Reports back within 1 month. Keeps materials on file. Makes outright purchase. Considers skill, ability to take art direction well, and humor of artist when assigning freelance humorous illustration. If a cartoonist/humorous illustrator wants to sell his work, he should inquire with resume and cover letter. Do not send samples.
Humor Writing: For first contact send cover letter and resume to Lynne Shlonsky, Director of Creative Recruitment. "We do not accept unsolicited ideas." Considers skill, ability, effective use of humor and experience when assigning freelance humorous writing.

CAROLYN BEAN PUBLISHING, 2230 W. Winton Ave., Hayward CA 94611. (415)732-9320. Publishes/manufactures greeting cards and postcards for Christmas, anniversary, get well, Mother's Day, Hanukkah, Easter, Halloween, congratulatory, Father's Day, non-occasion, birthday, retirement, New Year's and Valentine's Day. Needs humorous illustration for greeting cards, postcards; humorous greeting card series (illustration and writing).
Humorous Illustration: Looking for humorous greeting cards/illustrations that are eye-catching, unique and interesting, but not too complicated. Doesn't want to see cards that rely on old jokes. For first contact send cover letter, tearsheets, promo piece, slides to Art Director. To query with specific greeting card ideas, submit in rough format, with one finished to show final art, to Art Director. Reports back within 6 weeks. Returns materials if accompanied by a SASE. Keeps materials on file. Negotiates rights purchased. Pays outright $100-250. Infrequently assigns freelance humorous illustration/cartooning duties. When considering freelance humorous illustrators, considers skill; humor; ability to take art direction well; "marketability" of drawing style. Payment for assigned humorous illustrations: $100-200 by the project.
Humor Writing: Looking for humorous greeting card writing that "approaches 'card giving' occasions in a new way." Doesn't want to see cards that rely on old jokes. For first contact send cover letter and writing samples to the Editor. To query with specific greeting card ideas, submit idea in 3×5 card format, labeled with name, address and phone number on the back to the Editor. Reports back within 6 weeks. Returns materials if accompanied by a SASE. Keeps materials on file. Buys all rights. Pays $25 maximum. When assigning freelance humorous writing, considers skill; ability to work well with our editors; and effective use of humor. Pays for assignments by the project: $25-50 per accepted lines.

BRILLIANT ENTERPRISES, 117 W. Valerio St., Santa Barbara CA 93101. (805)682-0531. Estab. 1967. Provides postcards, books, licensing, syndication. Publishes greeting cards, books/booklets for non-occasion. Needs humorous illustration for postcards, humorous greeting card series (illustrations and writing) and humor writing for postcards.

Humorous Illustration: "Looking for humorous greeting cards/illustrations that conform with our established line and combine words with illustration." For first contact send $2 and SASE for our catalogue of samples to Ashleigh Brilliant, Humor Editor. Reports back within 2 weeks. Returns materials if accompanied by a SASE. Buys all rights. Pays $40 minimum.

Humor Writing: Looking for humorous greeting card writing that conforms with our established line and is submitted camera-ready with illustration. For first contact send $2 and SASE for our catalogue and samples to Ashleigh Brilliant. Reports back within 2 weeks. Returns materials if accompanied by a SASE. Buys all rights. Pays $40 minimum. Tips: "We strive to make our line different from anything else on the market. Freelancers will only be wasting their time and ours unless they study it carefully first. We supply a catalogue and samples for $2 and SASE."

CLASS PUBLICATION, 71 Bartholomew Ave., Hartford CT 06106. (203)951-9200. FAX: (203)951-4084. Estab. 1983. Publishes posters for college market. Needs humorous illustrations for posters.

Humorous Illustration: Looking for humorous illustrations that "have a lot going on in the picture." For first contact send cover letter, color tearsheets and slides (dupe) with a SASE for return to Leo Smith, Art Director. Reports back within 10 days only if interested. Returns materials if accompanied by a SASE. Buys one-time and reprint rights. Pays $500-800 or 7% royalty for three years. When considering freelance humorous illustrators, considers skill; humor; and "marketability" of drawing style.

COMSTOCK CARDS, INC., Suite 18, 600 S. Rock Blvd., Reno NV 89502. (702)333-9400. FAX: (702)333-9406. Estab. 1986. Publishes greeting cards, postcards, notepads and invitations with the sophisticated buyer in mind. Publishes/manufactures greeting cards, gifts, promotional products, notepads, invitations and postcards for Christmas, anniversary, get well, Hanukkah, Halloween, congratulatory, non-occasion, birthday, Valentines Day and retirement. Needs humorous greeting card series writing for notepads and invitations. For first contact send cover letter to David Delacroix, Art Director. Reports back within 3 weeks. Returns materials if accompanied by a SASE. Buys all rights. Pays $50-60/cartoon. Also assigns freelance humorous illustration/cartooning duties. Assigns approximately 50 jobs/year for greeting cards and notepad designs. When considering freelance humorous illustrators, considers "marketability" of artist's drawing style. Pays $50-60/project per line or image.

Humor Writing: Looking for humorous greeting card writing that contains outrageous humor, double entendres and sexual connotations (although not too blatant). Doesn't want to see rhymes or ho-hum writing. For first contact send cover letter with SASE to David Delecroix. To query with specific greeting card ideas, submit idea in format on a 3×5 card. Reports back within 3 weeks. Returns materials if accompanied by a SASE. Keeps copies of materials on file. Buys all rights. Pays $50-60 for outright purchase. When assigning freelance humorous writing, considers writer's effective use of humor. "Keep away from blatant sexuality and from using animals in people situations."

CONTEMPORARY DESIGNS, 213 Main St., Gilbert IA 50105. (515)232-5188. Estab. 1977. Paper products company that provides paper products related to professions (teachers, secretaries, etc.), special people (Mom, Dad, Grandma), campers and Jewish. Publishes/manufactures some greeting cards, novelties, books/booklets, gifts and promotional products for Christmas, anniversary, get well, Mother's Day, Hanukkah, Easter, Halloween, congratulatory, Father's Day, birthday, New Year's and Grandparent's Day. Needs writing for humorous greeting card series for kids who go to camp, Jewish market. Also needs humor writing for memo pads and gift items.

Humor Writing: For first contact send cover letter, resume, client list and writing samples to Sallie Akelsen, President. Reports back only if interested. Returns materials if accompanied by a SASE. Pays for outright purchase. When assigning freelance humorous writing, considers writer's effective use of humor. Pays $25/project.

CONTENOVA GIFTS INC., Box 69130 Station K, Vancouver BC V5K 4W4 Canada. (604)253-4014. FAX: (604)253-4014. Estab. 1965. Wholesale, manufacturer and distributor of impulse novelty products including mugs, plaques and greeting cards. Publishes greeting cards, novelties, gifts, promotional products, mugs, plaques and magnets for Christmas, anniversary, get well, Mother's Day, congratulatory, Father's Day, birthday, retirement, Grandparent's Day and Valentine's Day. Needs humorous illustration for greeting cards; humorous greeting card series (illustrations and writing); and humor writing for mugs, plaques, buttons, bumper stickers and fun signs.
Humorous Illustration: "We have used only local artists up to this time but since our demand has been increasing, we would be willing to look at other artists' work." For first contact send cover letter, resume, client list, tearsheets and color promo piece to Jeff Sinclair, Creative Director. Reports back in 3 weeks. Returns materials if accompanied by a SASE. Buys all rights. Pays $75 minimum. Also assigns freelance humorous illustration/cartooning duties. Assigns approximately 2 jobs per month for greeting cards. When considering freelance humorous illustrators, considers skill; ability to take art direction well; and "marketability" of artist's drawing style.
Humor Writing: Looking for humorous greeting card writing that is short and humorous but not too risqué. Doesn't want to see outdated material or writing that is too wordy gags. For first contact send writing samples to Jeff Sinclair. To query with specific greeting card ideas, submit in 3x5 card format. Reports back within 3 weeks. Returns materials if accompanied by a SASE. Buys all rights. Pays $50 minimum. When assigning freelance humorous writing, considers skill and writer's effective use of humor.

EARTH CARE PAPER INC., Box 3335, Madison WI 53704. (608)256-5232. Estab. 1983. Greeting card publisher and paper products company that manufacturers note cards and greeting cards on recycled paper for people who support environmental protection and appreciate nature. Publishes greeting cards, posters, gift wrap, note cards and stationery for Christmas, non-occasion and birthday. Needs humorous illustration for cards and humorous greeting card series (illustrations and writing). Will only consider following themes: nature, environmental protection, peace and justice.
Humorous Illustration: Looking for humorous greeting cards/illustration that fits one of these themes: nature, environmental protection, peace and justice. For first contact send tearsheets and slides to Barbara Budig, Art Director. To query with specific greeting card ideas, submit slides or reproductions to keep on file. Reports back within 2 months. Does not return materials; keeps materials on file. Negotiates rights purchased. Pays 5% royalty for life of card. Also assigns freelance humorous illustration/cartooning duties. Assigns approximately 20 jobs per year for greeting cards. When considering freelance humorous illustrators, considers skill, humor and experience of artist; ability of artist to take art direction well and "marketability" of artist's drawing style. Payment for assigned humorous illustrations: offers a royalty basis of 5% for life of the product; $100 minimum advance on royalties.
Humor Writing: Looking for humorous greeting card writing that fits one of these themes: nature, environmental protection, peace and justice. For first contact send writing sample to Barbara Budig. To query with specific greeting card ideas, submit in 3x5 card format. Reports back within 2 months. Does not return materials; keeps materials on file. Negotiates rights purchased. Pays $30 minimum, negotiable for outright purchase. Also assigns approximately 20 other freelance writing jobs. These include: greeting cards with environmental humor theme. When assigning freelance humorous writing, considers skill of writer, ability of writer to work well with our editors, writer's

effective use of humor, and experience of writer. Pays $30 minimum.

EASY ACES, INC., 387 Charles St., Providence RI 02504. (401)272-1500. FAX: (401)272-1503. Estab. 1977. Giftware and stationery items for original children's items, seasonal novelties, party goods, birthday items, stationery goods. Publishes/manufactures novelties, puzzles and gifts. Needs humor writing for miscellaneous items and humorous product concepts.

Humor Writing: Looking for humorous greeting card writing that embodies original product concepts. Doesn't want to see writing "which depends on puns!" For first contact send cover letter and writing sample to Fred Roses, President. Reports back only if interested. Returns materials only if requested. Negotiates rights purchased. Pays 5% for life or by negotiation. Also assigns approximately 6 other freelance writing jobs per year. When assigning freelance humorous writing, considers writer's effective use of humor.

ELDER CARDS, INC., P.O. Box 202, Piermont NY 10968. (914)359-7137. FAX: (914)365-0841. Estab. 1983. "We currently create, publish and market antique, photographic greeting cards but will soon expand to include postcards, t-shirts, stationery, wrapping paper and calendars. Publishes/manufactures greeting cards, calendars, posters, gift wrap, postcards, stationery, t-shirts and calendars for all holidays, nonholidays such as Secretary's Day, corporate needs such as customer correspondence and all consumer moods and needs. Needs humorous illustration for greeting cards, postcards, stationery, t-shirts, calendars, etc.; caricatures for greeting cards, postcards, calendars, t-shirts; spot cartoons for greeting cards, postcards, stationery, t-shirts; humorous greeting card series (illustrations and writing); humor writing for greeting cards, postcards, stationery, t-shirts, notepads, buttons; humorous writing and illustrations for greeting cards, postcards, stationery, t-shirts, notepads, buttons, bookmarks, matchbooks and balloons.

Humorous Illustration: Looking for humorous greeting cards/illustration which show people in funny situations, or making light of a "trying" situation like the break-up of a relationship or birthdays, invitations, get wells, weddings and birth announcements and congratulations of all kinds. Doesn't want to see cards which are not funny, too wordy and try too hard. For first contact send cover letter and tearsheets to Steve Epstein, President. To query with specific greeting card ideas, submit in format cover letter and b&w or color tearsheets to Steve Epstein. Reports back within 10 days. Returns materials if accompanied by a SASE. Doesn't keep materials on file. Buys all rights. Pays 5% royalty for life of card. Also assigns freelance humorous illustration/cartooning duties. Assigns approximately 3 jobs/year based on the ideas of both publisher and cartoonist. When considering freelance humorous illustrators, considers skill, humor and experience of artist; ability of artist to take art direction well; "marketability" of drawing style, sendability (i.e. is there a reason to send the card) and speed with which artist can submit concepts and artwork. Payment for assigned humorous illustrations is 5% for life of product. "Greeting cards currently focus on 'moods' in addition to holidays and birthdays, anniversaries, etc. Still birthdays are the 'heart' of the industry and must be included in at least 50% of any greeting card submissions. For all types though, humor and sex always sell."

Humor Writing: Looking for humorous greeting card writing that is short and to the point. Doesn't want to see writing that requires too much thinking. For first contact send cover letter, writing sample and SASE to Steve Epstein. To query with specific greeting card ideas, submit material to Steve Epstein. Reports back within 10 days. Returns materials if accompanied by a SASE. Buys all rights. Pays 5% for life of card. Also assigns approximately 3 jobs per year based on the ideas of both publisher and cartoonist. When assigning freelance humorous writing, considers skill, experience and effective use of humor of writer; ability of writer to work well with our editors; and quickness and reliability to meet deadlines. Pays for assignments 5% royalty for life of the product.

EPHEMERA BUTTONS, 275 Capp St., San Francisco CA 94110. (415)552-4199. Estab. 1979. Novelty button producer. "Produces outrageous, provocative and irreverent buttons for all markets from the 'hip' and trendy to the convenience store crowd." Needs humorous illustration, caricatures and (mainly) humor writing for novelty buttons.

Mom Never Had These in Her Button Box: *Humor, good old-fashioned we-may-have-to-call-the-cops humor is alive and well and festering in San Francisco. Ephemera Buttons, a polite name for an irreverent purveyor of slogans, one-liners, sayings and philosophic doubletalk to pin on your duds, proves that funny is funny—even if most of it does manage to alienate 86% of the population. To be sure, we can't even print their most hilarious button slogans within these pages. Ephemera is picky about what they ultimately use, but they do solicit written humor for buttons—and pay $25 per slogan.*

Humorous Illustration: Looking for humorous greeting cards/illustration that is "bold, graphic line art that will reduce down very small." Doesn't want to see buttons which have old clichés. For first contact send cover letter, SASE and b&w line art to Ed Polish, Editor. To query with specific greeting card ideas submit to Ed Polish. Reports back within 2 weeks. Returns materials if accompanied by a SASE. Buys all rights. Pays $25 outright purchase.

Humor Writing: Looking for humorous button writing which is "bold, shocking, concise, high impact, weird, rude, funny, outrageous." Doesn't want to see writing consisting of tired old clichés. For first contact send list of slogans and SASE to Ed Polish. Reports back within 2 weeks. Returns material if accompanied by a SASE. Buys all rights. Pays $25 per slogan for outright purchase. Paid when produced (3 times a year). Tips: "Send a SASE for our guidelines. Send 3 first-class stamps for our complete retail catalog."

FREEDOM GREETINGS, P.O. Box 715, Bristol PA 15007. (215)545-3300. FAX: (215)547-0248. Publishes greeting cards. Needs humorous illustration for all occasion and seasons, and humorous greeting card series (illustrations and writing).

Humorous Illustration: For first contact send promo piece and ideas to J. Levitt, Vice President. To query with specific greeting card ideas, submit in rough draft format. Reports back within 7 days. Returns materials if accompanied by a SASE. Buys all rights for greeting cards. Pays $250-300 for outright purchase. Also assigns freelance humorous illustration/cartooning duties. Assigns approximately 300 jobs per year. When considering freelance humorous illustrations, considers skill, humor and experience of artist.

Humor Writing: Looking for humorous greeting card writing that "is not the same as everything else that comes my way." For first contact send to J. Levitt. To query with specific greeting card ideas, submit material to J. Levitt. Reports back within 7 days. Returns materials if accompanied by a SASE. Buys all rights.

GRAPHIC CREATIONS, 94-02 148 St., Jamaica NY 11435. (718)687-5050. FAX: (718)688-8009. Estab. 1979. Paper products company. Publishes bookcovers for back to school, elementary to high school. Needs humorous illustration, caricatures, spot cartoons and humor writing, all for bookcovers.

Humorous Illustration: For first contact send promo piece. Does not return materials. Negotiable payment.

IMAGINEERING INC., Box 11859, Phoenix AZ 85061. (602)272-6713. FAX: (602)278-7461. Estab. 1964. Manufactures and develops theatrical and novelty items for the Halloween and toy market. Manufactures theatrical makeup, dress-up accessories, seasonal novelty goods and masks for the mass market. Manufactures paper products for the following: Easter, Halloween, Valentine's Day and St. Patrick's Day. Needs humorous illustration and humor writing for packaging, catalogs and ads.

Humorous Illustration: Looking for humorous greeting cards/illustrations that best describe the fun of our products. For first contact send cover letter, client list and promo piece to James N. Sauter, Art Director. Negotiates rights purchased. Also assigns freelance humorous illustration/cartooning duties. Assigns approximately 2-3 jobs per year for packaging. When considering freelance humorous illustrators, considers skill; ability to take art direction well; humor; "marketability" of drawing style; and experience. Pays by the project.

Humor Writing: For first contact send cover letter, client list and writing samples to James N. Sauter. To query with specific greeting card ideas, request disclosure form first. Reports back only if interested. Keeps materials on file. Negotiates rights purchased. Also assigns approximately 2-3 other freelance writing jobs per year. When assigning freelance humorous writing, considers skill; ability to work well with our editors; effective use of humor and experience. Tips: "We currently have a good creative staff, but products do occasionally come up that we 1) have no time to execute or 2) do not have enough fresh ideas. We will use outside talent on a limited basis."

INTERCONTINENTAL GREETINGS LTD., 176 Madison Ave., New York NY 10016. (212)683-5830. FAX: (212)779-8564. Estab. 1967. Sells design and reproduction rights to card, paper and giftware industries. Provides design, artwork and humorous illustration with text to publishers and manufacturers. Color separated film and reproduction rights on a per country, per product basis. Publishes/manufactures greeting cards, calendars, posters, puzzles, gifts and gift wrap. Publishes Christmas, get well, non-occasion and birthday. Needs humorous illustration for cards. Humorous greeting card series (illustrations and writing) and humor writing for licensing series.

Humorous Illustration: Looking for humorous greeting cards/illustrations that "can be used for a card series that might lead to a licensing character." Doesn't want to see cards which are "done badly, not funny, too 'cartoon-y' and without color." For first contact send cover letter, resume, client list, tearsheets, color tearsheets, color promo piece and slides to Robin Lipner, Art Director. To query with specific greeting card ideas submit to Robin Lipner. Reports back within 4 weeks. Returns materials if accompanied by a SASE. Keeps materials on file. Buys all rights for contract period or negotiates rights purchased. Pays royalty, 20% for life of card. When considering freelance humorous illustrators, considers skill of artist, humor and "marketability" of artist's drawing style. Pays for reproduction rights $35-500 per project. Offers royalty 20% for life of product. Tips: "If a cartoonist/humorous illustrator wants to sell his work, he should have a clear, concise and thoughtful presentation. Explore all available avenues to market it. Insults and racial/ethnic/sexist humor are *out*."

Humor Writing: For first contact send cover letter, resume, client list, clips and writing and artwork samples to Robin Lipner. To query with specific greeting card ideas, submit idea in format to Robin Lipner. Reports back within 3 weeks only if interested. Returns material if accompanied by a SASE. Keeps materials on file. Buys all rights and negotiates rights purchased during the 2 year contract period. Pays for outright purchase $30-500, 20% royalty for life of card. Also assigns approximately 10 jobs per year. These include writing for humorous illustration without texts. When assigning freelance humorous writing, considers skill, ability to work well with our editors and writer's effective use of humor. Payment for assignments is $10-500 per project. Royalties: 5-20% for life of product.

MAINE LINE COMPANY, P.O. Box 947, Rockland ME 04841. (207)594-9418. FAX: (207)594-9420. Estab. 1979. Greeting card publisher. Publishes/manufacturers greeting cards, gifts, mugs, buttons, key rings, magnets, gift bags, postcards, bookmarks, pocketcards, impulse gifts, social expression items, etc. for anniversary, get well, non-occasion and birthdays. *No seasonal cards*. Needs humorous greeting card series and other novelty items (illustrations and writing) and humor writing for buttons, mugs, magnets, keyrings.

Humorous Illustration: Looking for humorous greeting cards/illustration that are attractive, well-drawn with good characters — also good writing with non-cliché messages. Doesn't want to see greeting cards which are unoriginal, old hat. For first contact send cover letter, resume, color tearsheets, color promo piece and slides to Perri Ardman, President. To query with specific greeting card ideas, submit in format either 5×7 vertical or 6⅛×4½ horizontal (not both) to Perri Ardman. Reports back within 3 months. Returns materials if accompanied by a SASE. Keeps materials on file if there might be interest in the future. Buys all rights. Pays $25-200 for outright purchase. Also assigns freelance humorous illustration/cartooning duties. Assigns approximately 10-25 jobs/year. When considering freelance humorous illustrators, considers skill of artist and "marketability" of artist's drawing style. Payment for assigned humorous illustrations $25 minimum depending on number of pieces in project. Greeting cards are put out in series of 24-32 cards.

Humor Writing: Looking for humorous greeting card writing "that is not nasty or rude. Cute double entendres OK." Doesn't want to see writing that is vulgar and crude. For first contact send writing sample. Best to send specific ideas for cards or other products to Perri Ardman. To query with specific greeting card ideas, submit idea and material in format to Perri Ardman. Reports back within 3 months. Returns materials if accompanied by a SASE. Keeps materials on file if there might be interest in the future. Buys all rights. Pays $25-100. Also assigns other freelance writing jobs, approximately 25 jobs/year. When assigning freelance humorous writing, considers skill; effective use of humor; ability to work well with our editors; and ability to write marketable cards/slogans, etc. Pays by the project. Tips: "Good communication and writing that sounds like what a person would actually say are important in humor writing."

MERLYN GRAPHICS CORPORATION, Box 9087, Canoga Park CA 91309. (818)349-2775. Estab. 1987. Greeting card publisher. "We need lines/verse only for greeting cards. We publish very funny, risque, trendy greeting cards for everyday occasions. No holidays except Valentine's and Christmas." Publishes greeting cards for get well, non-occasion and birthday. Needs humorous greeting card series (writing) and humor writing for greeting cards only. "We do not want artwork of any kind. We are 100% photographic."

Humor Writing: Looking for humorous greeting card writing that lends itself to women's interests. Should have a twist to it. "We like offbeat, unpredictable humor—double entendre and very witty." Doesn't want to see cards that are predictable or cliché, cards that are hearts and flowers, or cards that just are not funny. For first contact send #10 SASE for guidelines to ATTN: Editor. To query with specific greeting card ideas, submit idea in format one idea/line per index card to editor. Reports back within weeks. Returns materials if accompanied by SASE. Keeps materials on file. Buys all rights. Pays $50 outright purchase.

Tips: "Don't forget that women buy 97% of all greeting cards."

NEW HEIGHTS, Box 2368, Menlo Park CA 94025. (415)429-1452. Estab. 1987. Greeting card publisher. Publishes humorous greeting cards and postcards for all markets. Publishes greeting cards for all occasions. Needs humorous illustration for cards, caricatures for cards, humorous greeting card series.

Humorous Illustration: For first contact send slides and portfolio to Alison Mayhew, President. Reports back within 30 days. Returns materials if accompanied by SASE. Does not file materials. Negotiates rights purchased. Pays 10% royalty for life of card. When considering freelance humorous illustrators, considers skill, humor and "marketability" of artist's drawing style.

Humor Writing: For first contact, send cover letter, resume and writing samples to Alison Mayhew. To query with specific greeting card ideas, submit idea to Alison Mayhew. Reports back within 30 days. Returns material if accompanied by SASE. Negotiates rights purchased. Pays 10% royalty for life of card.

OATMEAL STUDIOS, Box 138, Rochester VT 05767. (802)767-3171. FAX: (802)767-9890. Estab. 1979. "We publish humorous greeting cards, magnetic notepads, and post-it notes for Christmas, anniversary, get well, Mother's Day, Hanukkah, Easter, Halloween, congratulatory, Father's Day, non-occasion, birthday, retirement, St. Patrick's Day, Rosh Hashanah, Valentine's Day and all other holidays." Needs humorous illustration for cards, humorous greeting card series (illustrations and writing) and humor writing for cards.

Humorous Illustration: Looking for humorous greeting cards/illustration that are fresh looking, fun and original. Doesn't want to see a repeat of lines in the industry. For first contact send color tearsheets, color promo piece and slides to Helene Lehrer, Creative Director. To query with specific greeting card ideas, submit to Helene Lehrer. Reports back within 3 weeks. Returns materials only if requested and accompanied by a SASE. Keeps materials on file. Negotiates rights purchased. Also assigns freelance humorous illustration/cartooning duties. When considering freelance humorous illustrators, considers skill; ability to take art direction well; humor and "marketability" of artist's drawing style.

Humor Writing: For first contact send writing samples and request our guidelines. To query with specific greeting card ideas, submit in 3×5 index card format with name and address on back to David Stewart, Editor. Reports back within 6 weeks. Returns materials if accompanied by a SASE. Does not file materials. Negotiates rights purchased.

Tips: "The writing must be fresh and original. We see lots of ideas that have been on the market for years. I don't feel there are any trends—a well-written card can be on the market for years."

O'B STUDIOS, 940 VanEss N.W., Grand Rapids MI 49504. (616)453-8820. FAX: (616)791-1124. Estab. 1985. Photo caption stickers and photo postcards. Makes photo postcards and humorous photo caption stickers for one hour minilabs, card shops, and camera stores. Manufactures photo caption stickers and photo postcards. "Photo postcards allow photographer to customize greetings for all occasions. Use your own photos." Needs photo caption (balloon) stickers.

Humor Writing: Looking for humorous greeting card writing that is "outrageous — saying must be able to be applied to a wide variety of photographs (not too specific)." For first contact send cover letter and writing sample to Dave O'Brien, President/Owner. To query with specific greeting card ideas, submit idea in format to Dave O'Brien. Reports back within 5 days. Returns materials only if requested. Rights purchased negotiable.

PAPER MOON GRAPHICS, Box 34672, Los Angeles CA 90034. (213)645-8700. FAX: (213)645-4238. Estab. 1976. Specializes in greeting cards and stationery products. Publishes greeting cards for Christmas, anniversary, get well, Hanukkah, Easter, congratulatory, non-occasion and birthday. Needs humorous illustration for greeting cards and humorous greeting card series (illustrations and writing).

Humorous Illustration: Looking for humorous greeting cards/illustration that appeals to a contemporary market and also adheres to a specific card sending situation or occasion. Doesn't want to see predictable, insulting or offensive material that is unprintable. For first contact send cover letter, tearsheets, promo piece, color promo piece and slides to Robert Fitch, Art Director. To query with specific greeting card ideas, submit on 4⅝ × 6¾ folded card mock-up. Reports back within 2 months only if interested. Returns materials if requested and accompanied by a SASE. Buys reprint rights. Pays $100-150 for outright purchase. Also assigns freelance humorous illustration/cartooning duties. When considering freelance humorous illustrators, considers skill; ability to take art direction well; humor; "marketability" of artist's drawing style; and experience of artist. Pays by the project $100-150. Tips: "Trends are friendly, off-the-wall female oriented, which deal with contemporary issues that are shared by all women both working and non."

Humor Writing: Looking for humorous greeting card writing "that embraces receiver, in a humorous and friendly way, not too saccharin or heavy." Doesn't want to see predictable writing that looks like it was done six years ago. For first contact send cover letter and writing samples to Michael D. Conway. To query with specific greeting card ideas, submit in 4⅝ × 6¾ folded card mock-up format. Reports back within 2 months. Returns materials only if requested and accompanied by a SASE. Buys reprint rights. Pays $100-150 for outright purchase. When assigning freelance humorous writing, considers skill; ability to work well with our editors; and effective use of humor. Pays by the project $100-150. Tips: "Submit work often and be sure that the writing speaks directly to someone, as opposed to stand-up comedy one-liners."

PARAMOUNT CARDS, INC., Box 6546, Providence RI 02940-6546. Estab. 1906. Full-line greeting card company offering cards for everyday and seasonal captions. Also gift wrap, candles and buttons for Christmas, anniversary, get well, Mother's Day, Hanukkah, Easter, Halloween, congratulatory, Father's Day, nonoccasion, birthday, retirement, New Year's, Grandparent's Day, graduation, Thanksgiving, Valentine's Day and St. Patrick's Day. Needs humorous illustration for greeting cards, humor writing for greeting cards and all occasions.

Humorous Illustration: Looking for humorous greeting cards/illustration that set or follow trends in an alternative style; new looks, funny and cute-looking characters can sell a card. Doesn't want to see emulation of studio-card art. For first contact send cover letter and portfolio to Paul Vitali, Editorial, Freelance Humor Art Coordinator. To query with specific greeting card ideas, submit sketch and copy on index or other card

Close-up

Robert Fitch
Creative Director
Paper Moon Graphics

Paper Moon Graphics began with an old garage for an office and only three employees. After 12 years and hundreds of greeting cards, Paper Moon is a thriving, up-and-coming company that is constantly updating existing card lines and exploring new concepts in humorous greeting cards.

"When I came to the West Coast and found Paper Moon in 1978, it was a very young company—only one month old," says Robert Fitch, Paper Moon's Creative Director. It's just grown up since then ... we basically learned the business from the ground up." A far cry from the garage in which it was first headquartered, Paper Moon now has 24 employees and produces about 500 different greeting cards per year.

According to Fitch the company has changed with the times and altered its products and approaches to appeal to a broader public. Paper Moon's major modification was to offer more humorous cards. "We originally started out with the primary interest of illustration and photography. We've switched from a more formal approach to absolutely having all our interest in humor."

Fitch describes the company's cards as "alternative although not radical." But he stresses the importance of being "consistently inconsistent" in the greeting card field in order to remain competitive. "We are not hung into one attitude. We may come out with a line that sticks around for a couple of years (and we may add to that line), but we're always looking for new attitudes and direction of cards."

Because he is always looking for new creative ideas and new angles to old ideas, Fitch says it is a necessity for him to receive materials from a variety of freelancers. Small greeting card companies are inherently an excellent outlet for freelance writers, artists and illustrators for two primary reasons: economics and creativity. Economically, Fitch explains, small companies simply cannot afford to have many inhouse people. And from a creative standpoint, those companies that do not use freelancers become "too inbred to be competitive," says Fitch. "Freelancers will continue in this business because you can always get fresh ideas and approaches. It's better for us to work with people from a variety of [geographic] areas and people who have different outlooks because we're selling to many types of clients."

A former freelancer himself, Fitch says Paper Moon works with 20 to 30 freelance writers and 5 to 10 out-of-house artists per year, but the competition for freelance work is fierce and the rate of attrition is extremely low. According to Fitch, "It's rare for someone to have a 10% acceptance rate—RARE!" And although some may think writing a greeting card would be an easy task, Fitch assures that it is not and offers the overall low acceptance rate as proof.

To appeal to Fitch's critical eye, there are a few things a freelancer must do. First and foremost, "Make a clean presentation," he says. "Don't throw your stuff into an envelope and wing it off. Don't make me spend a lot of time reworking the presentation."

Freelancers should also allow ample time for review of their material. "Don't get upset and ask for your work back, even after a couple of months," says Fitch. Small companies have small staffs, and with a high volume of material, there just aren't enough people to quickly reject/accept submissions.

He suggests people work as a creative team—a writer and an illustrator together—who can prolifically develop an entire line of cards instead of one or two individual card ideas. Paper Moon rarely purchases "one-of" cards, unless the idea is good for another card line or happens to really stand out by itself, so it is beneficial to have the writing and artwork synchronized.

If Fitch sees promise in a freelancer's work he will occasionally attempt to guide the work to fit his company's needs. "I'll give people direction and make comments on their work and see if we can help them do better and have a higher rate of acceptance." In the long run this not only helps the freelancer, but it enables Paper Moon to produce more cards that are versatile and marketable to greeting card markets.

—Brian C. Rushing

A card from Paper Moon's Graphically Speaking line. The card's inside message, Neither do the rest of us. Happy Birthday, is written by Ray Scantlin. The illustration is by Michael D. Conway.

in format; very little inside art to Attn: Paul Vitali. Reports back within 2 weeks. Returns materials if accompanied by a SASE. Keeps materials on file but not all material is filed. Buys all rights. Pays $175 for outright purchase. Also assigns freelance humorous illustration/cartooning duties. Assigns approximately 30 jobs per year for page one designs, all captions/seasons, deadlined. When considering freelance humorous illustrators, considers skill; ability to take art direction well; experience; dependability and suitability of style for assignment. Pays $175.

Tips: Send samples demonstrating diversity, or typical "look", and apply it to greeting cards of any kind; "understand that we do most work in-house, so be patient . . . receptive and cooperative artists with flair work best for us. The alternative market look is the future, and that market/look is wide open with respect to a definitive style. We want new and interesting approaches."

Humor Writing: Looking for humorous greeting card writing that is fresh, clever, intelligent, and sendable; which lends itself to visual interpretation; and which indicates that the writer is up-to-date on current humor themes, trends, and treatments. Doesn't want to see the obviously derivative, which merely rehashes outdated formulas; and which is illegible, ungrammatical, and rife with misspellings. For first contact send humorous card ideas to Paul Vitali. To query with specific greeting card ideas, submit in 3x5 card format with name, address, Social Security number and SASE. Reports back within 1 week. Returns materials if accompanied by a SASE. Buys all rights. Pays $75-125 for outright purchase. Also assigns approximately 10 other freelance writing jobs per year. These include: "rush jobs where we need to fill certain captions by a deadline." When assigning freelance humorous writing, considers skill; effective use of humor and dependability, consistency and promptness. Tips: "Don't waste time trying to impress us with a fancy cover letter, but simply send us 10-15 of your best humorous card ideas. The best cards are attuned to the unique relationship between the sender and recipient. Topicality is important. Cards that are gross or lewd may garner lots of laughs, but are often poor sellers."

*PEACHTREE COMMUNICATIONS, INC., Box 3146, Pompano Beach FL 33072. (305)941-2926. FAX: (305)491-6290. Estab. 1988. Greeting card publisher (and calendars). Publishes booklets, greeting cards and calendars for the mass market. Publishes greeting cards for Christmas, anniversary, get well, Mother's Day, Hanukkah, Easter, Halloween, congratulatory, Father's Day, Birthdays, nonoccasion, birthday, retirement, New Year's, Grandparent's Day. Needs humorous illustration for greeing cards and calendars; spot cartoons for booklets; humorous greeting card series (writing); humor writing for short stories on subjects assigned.

Humorous Illustration: Looks for greeting cards/illustrations which appeal to the whole family. Doesn't want to see greeting cards which "are Blah! Need humorous greeting cards which are really funny without being X-rated or offensive." For first contact, send cover letter, resume, client list and tearsheets to George Spencer, Art Director. To query with specific ideas, request disclosure agreement first. Reports back only if interested. Returns material if accompanied by SASE; keeps material on file. Pays $50-250 for life of card. Assigns freelance humorous illustration cartooning duties; 32 jobs per year. When hiring freelance humorous illustrator, considers skill; humor; ability to take art direction well; "marketability" of artist's drawing style; meeting assignments deadlines. Pays $50-250/project. Send query letter with samples of previous work for file.

Humor Writing: For first contact, send cover letter, resume, client list, clips and writing sample to Fred Chapin, Editor. To query with specific ideas, request disclosure form first. Reports back only if interested. Returns material if accompanied by SASE; keeps materials on file. Negotiates rights purchased. Pays $50-250 for life of card. Also assigns other freelance writing jobs for greeting cards in specific category on assignment.

PEACOCK PAPERS, INC., 273 Summer St., Boston MA 02210. (617)423-2868. FAX: (617)423-9033. Estab. 1982. Gift and party manufacturer that produces and distributes contemporary typographically designed paper and party and apparel products. Manufactures greeting cards, partyware, gifts, gift bags, T-shirts, sweatshirts, boxers, cover-ups, mugs, buttons and keytags for Christmas, anniversary, get well, Mother's Day, Hanukkah, Easter, Halloween, congratulatory, Father's Day, non-occasion, birthday, retirement, New Year's, Grandparent's Day, Valentine's Day, St. Patrick's Day and graduation. Needs humorous work for all occasions.
Humor Writing: Looking for humor in short messages and one-liners. Needs fresh current trend subject matter as well as special occasion related. Also subjects including golf, aging, boating and birthdays. Doesn't want to see mundane or unoriginal material. For first contact send cover letter and writing samples to Carol Snow, New Product Manager. Reports back within 3-4 weeks. Returns materials only if requested. Keeps materials on file. Buys outright purchase. Pays $25-50 for selected lines depending on product usage. Negotiates. Most of these jobs are an ongoing process. When assigning freelance humorous writing, considers originality, appeal of line and application to product.

PLUM GRAPHICS INC., Box 136 Prince Station, New York NY 10012. (212)966-2573. Estab. 1983. Publishes greeting cards for birthdays. Needs humor writing for greeting cards.
Humor Writing: Looking for humorous greeting card writing that is easily understood and doesn't limit the market. For first contact send SASE with request for guidelines to Yvette Cohen, President. Reports back only if interested. Returns materials if accompanied by a SASE. Pays $40-500.

ROCKSHOTS, INC., 632 Broadway, New York NY 10012. (212)420-1400. Estab. 1979. Paper products company that publishes greeting cards, humorous and sexy calendars, invitations, post cards and giftwrap for Christmas, get well, Mother's Day, Easter, Halloween, non-occasion and birthday. Needs humor writing for birthday, Christmas and all occasion.
Humorous Illustration: For first contact send promo piece to Bob Vesce, Editor. Submit in format to Bob Vesce. Reports back within 1 month. Returns materials if accompanied by a SASE. Buys all rights. Pays $50-100. When considering freelance humorous illustrators, considers skill and humor.
Humor Writing: Looking for humorous greeting card writing that is risque, sexy, geared to younger set. Doesn't want to see messy submissions. For first contact send writing samples and SASE to Bob Vesce. Lines should be submitted on index cards. To query with specific greeting card ideas, request disclosure form first. Reports back within 1 month. Returns materials if accompanied by a SASE. Buys all rights. Pays $50 for outright purchase. When assigning freelance humorous writing, considers writer's effective use of humor. Tips: "Sexy, sarcastic humor sells here."

SILVER VISIONS, Box 49, Newton MA 02161. (617)244-9504. Estab. 1981. Greeting card and paper products company that publishes photographic cards, calendars and posters for Christmas, anniversary, get well, Mother's Day, Hanukkah, Easter, Halloween, congratulatory, Father's Day, non-occasion, birthday, retirement, New Year's, Grandparent's Day and Judaic. Needs humorous greeting card series (writing).
Humor Writing: Looking for humorous greeting card that works well with a photograph and also Jewish cards. Doesn't want to see put-downs, bad puns, smut, studio cards or crass. For first contact send cover letter, writing samples and assurance of ownership and right to submissions to B. Kaufman, President. To query with specific greeting card ideas, submit in 3x5 index card format to B. Kaufman. Reports back only if interested. Returns materials if accompanied by a SASE. Negotiates rights purchased. Pays $35.

When assigning freelance humorous writing, considers skill, effective use of humor and ability to distill an idea to work with a photograph easily executed. Tips: "Current trends are reality humor, difficulty of life situations and relationships."

SPRINGBROOK PUBLICATIONS, INC., 34111 Doreka Dr., Fraser MI 48026. (313)294-4260. Estab. 1975. Paper products company that publishes gift-greeting products (i.e., wall-scrolls and table-top plaques) for the mass market for anniversary, Mother's Day, non-occasion and birthday. Needs humor writing for plaque products.
Humor Writing: Looking for humorous greeting card writing that "pokes fun at people (parodies) and life situations." For first contact send cover letter and writing samples to Larry Stevens, Creative Director. To query with specific greeting card ideas, request disclosure form first or submit idea in format to Larry Stevens. Reports back within 1 month only if interested. Returns materials if accompanied by a SASE. Does not file materials. Negotiates rights purchased. Pays $75. When assigning freelance humorous writing, considers skill; effective use of humor; and experience of writer. Pays 5% royalty for life of product.

SUNRISE PUBLICATIONS, INC., 1145 Sunrise Greetings Ct., Bloomington IN 47401. (812)336-9900. FAX (812)336-8712. Estab. 1973. Greeting card publisher geared towards the alternative card market for Christmas, anniversary, get well, Mother's Day Hanukkah, Easter, Halloween, congratulatory, Father's Day, non-occasion, birthday, New Year's, baby, wedding, thank-you, Thanksgiving, graduation, St. Patrick's Day, and Valentine's Day. Needs humorous illustrations for cards, caricatures for cards, spot cartoons for cards and humorous greeting card series (illustrations and writing).
Humorous Illustration: Looking for humorous greeting cards/illustration that tie in very well to an editorial message and to a specific sending occasion. Doesn't want to see risque. For first contact send tearsheets, color tearsheets and slides to Lorraine Farrell, V.P. Creative Services. To query with specific greeting card ideas, submit to Lorraine Farrell. Reports back within 3 weeks. Always returns materials. Keeps materials on file. Negotiates rights purchased. Pays $200-500 or 3% royalty for life of card. Also assigns freelance humorous illustration/cartooning duties. Assigns approximately 150 jobs per year. When considering freelance humorous illustrators, considers skill; ability to take art direction well; humor and "marketability" of artist's drawing style. Pays $200-500. Offers royalty of 3% for life of the product. Tips: "Submit art, slides or transparencies. Art is going very minimal so there is more reliance on editorial. We are interested in artistic humor."
Humor Writing: Looking for humorous greeting card writing that is good-natured. Doesn't want to see risque. For first contact send writing samples and SASE to Kim Turner/Lori Teesch, Product Managers. To query with specific greeting card ideas, submit to Kim Turner/Lori Teesch. Reports back within 4 weeks. Returns materials if accompanied by a SASE. Keeps materials on file. Buys all rights. Pays $25-125. Also assigns various amounts of other freelance writing jobs. When assigning freelance humorous writing, considers writers effective use of humor; and how readily can the editorial be illustrated. Pays $25-125. Tips: Send editorial one idea per 3x5 card. Group cards in 20's and enclose a SASE. We may be somewhat interested in cynical humor (most recently there have been many cynical cards which portray the modern, cynical woman).

TLC GREETINGS, 615 McCall Rd., Manhattan KS 66502. (913)776-4041. FAX: (913)776-4041 Ext. 232. Estab. 1986. Greeting card publisher. "We publish and design humorous greeting cards directed to women from 18-50 years old. Could use positive humor." Publishes/manufactures greeting cards for anniversary, get well, congratulatory, non-occasion and birthday. Needs humorous illustration for greeting cards, caricatures for greeting cards, humorous greeting card series (illustrations and writing) and humor writing for greeting cards.

Humorous Illustration: Looking for humorous greeting cards/illustrations that are pleasing, use soft colors, simple lines and apply to women. For first contact, send cover letter, resume, tearsheets and color tearsheets to Michele Johnson, Creative Director. To query with specific greeting card ideas, request disclosure agreement first to Michele Johnson. Reports back on submissions within 3 weeks. Returns materials if accompanied by SASE. Keeps materials on file if interested in work. Negotiates rights purchased. Pays $50-200 for outright purchase. Also assigns freelance humorous illustration/cartooning duties. Assigns approximately 1 job/month or 10-30 jobs/year for humorous illustrations. When considering freelance humorous illustrators, considers skill of artist, ability to take art direction well, humor and "marketability" of artist's drawing style. Payment for assigned humorous illustrations $10-12/hour, $50-200/project. Tips: "Prepare an original, unique tearsheet of your work. Show both color and b&w design. Our success is with fun illustrations with soft colors. Keep your ideas simple, yet clever."

Humor Writing: Looking for humorous greeting card writers who can look at what we've published and produce ideas which reflect our style. For first contact, send cover letter, resume and writing sample to Michele Johnson. To query with specific greeting card ideas, request disclosure form first and submit material to Michele Johnson. Reports back within 3 weeks. Returns material if accompanied by SASE. Pays for ideas upfront. Buys all rights. Pays $25-75 outright purchase. Also assigns approximately 3 jobs/month, 40 jobs/year for 30-40 ideas for a set fee. When assigning freelance humorous writing, considers skill, ability to work well with editors, and writer's effective use of humor. Pays $10-15/hour, $25-200/project. Tips: "Send humorous ideas which fit the company's product line. We publish no risque work. Unique ideas only. First impressions are very important. Send your best ideas or illustrations. Be confident."

VAGABOND CREATIONS, INC., 2560 Lance Drive, Dayton OH 45409. (513)298-1124. FAX: (513)298-1124. Estab. 1957. Greeting card and paper products company that publishes illustrated stationery, calendars (small size) and greeting cards for Christmas, anniversary, get well, Mother's Day, congratulatory, Father's Day, non-occasion, Valentine's Day, graduation and birthday.

Humorous Illustration: For first contact send cover letter only. Returns materials if accompanied by a SASE. Buys all rights. Pays $15-30 for outright purchase.

WEST GRAPHICS, 238 Capp St., San Francisco CA 94114. (415)621-4641. FAX: (415)621-8613. Estab. 1980. Greeting card publisher. Alternative greeting card publisher of off-the-wall humor and illustration (cartoons) for birthdays, anniversaries and other categories. Publishes/manufactures greeting cards and books/booklets. Publishes products for Christmas, anniversary, get well, Mother's Day, Hanukkah, Easter, Halloween, congratulatory, Father's Day, Friendship, non-occasion, birthday and retirement. Needs humorous illustrations and caricatures for cards. Humorous greeting card series (illustrations and writing).

Humorous Illustration: Doesn't want to see cards which are cute and cliché. For first contact send cover letter, tearsheets and slides to Tom Drew, Art Director. Reports back within 3 weeks. Returns materials if accompanied by a SASE. Pays outright purchase of $200 or 5% royalty for life of card. Also assigns freelance humorous illustration/cartooning duties. Assigns approximately 5 jobs per year. When considering freelance humorous illustrators, considers skill, humor, ability to take art direction well and "marketability" of artist's drawing style. Payment for assigned humorous illustrations by the project $200 minimum or 5% for the life of the product.

Humor Writing: For first contact send cover letter, writing sample and SASE to Editorial Department. To query with specific greeting card ideas, submit idea on 3×5 index cards to Editorial Department. Reports back within 3 weeks. Returns materials if accompanied by a SASE. Negotiates rights purchased. Pays outright purchase of $60. Tips: "Submit for review 3×5 cards with name, address, phone on each."

CAROL WILSON FINE ARTS, INC., Box 17394, Portland OR 97217. (503)281-0780. Estab. 1982. Greeting card publisher. Publishes humorous cards for the contemporary card market and also publishes fine arts cards. Publishes/manufactures greeting cards and postcards for Christmas, anniversary, get well, Mother's Day, Hanukkah, Easter, Halloween, congratulatory, Father's Day, non-occasion, birthday, retirement, Valentine's, friendship, "love" and most everyday occasions. Needs humorous greeting card series (illustrations and writing) and humor writing for greeting cards and postcards.

Humorous Illustration: Looking for humorous greeting cards/illustrations that are clever but upbeat and positive, humor which is not only funny but conveys a "sendable" sentiment. Doesn't want to see cards which rely on trite puns, old age jokes, or are funny but not "sendable" as a greeting card from one person to another. For first contact send slides of photocopies of artwork and writing on small cards to Gary Spector, President, Art Director. Reports back within 3-4 weeks. Returns material if accompanied by SASE. Negotiates rights purchased. Pays $50-150 outright purchase, negotiable. When considering freelance humorous illustrators, considers skill, humor, experience, ability to take art direction well, and "marketability" of artist's drawing style."I think humorous illustrations for greeting cards are going to be more positive, less 'raunchy.' "

Humor Writing: Looking for humorous greeting card writing that is clever, funny, positive in attitude and very "sendable." It is a card that is "from me to you." Imagine the buyer purchasing the card to send to someone the buyer knows. Doesn't want to see cards that are trite or that don't relate to the situation of actually buying and sending cards. For first contact send writing samples to Gary Spector. To query on specific greeting card ideas submit material to Gary Spector. Reports back within 2-4 weeks. Returns materials if accompanied by SASE. Negotiates rights purchased. Pays $50-80 outright purchase. Tips: Trends in the market are "more positive, less 'wordy.' "

© Rowland B. Wilson

Hasn't the Surgeon General Cautioned Against Hand Kissing? *Rowland B. Wilson may be best known for his work in the "My insurance company? New England Life, of course. Why?" advertising campaign, but the Rancho La Costa, California-based cartoonist keeps busy with other assignments. This is one of 54 spot cartoons for a calendar—the drawing, a visual depiction of the meaning of the word 'obsequious.' Contracted by Peter Vatsures, an art director for The Drawing Board, Wilson was given two months to complete the 54 spots and a four figure advance on royalties from sales of the calendar.*

Browsing through the plethora of publications at your local newsstand, one has to wonder if Americans truly are reading less, as the experts say.

Magazines

Without a doubt, magazines remain the most receptive markets to freelance humor. Many seek everything—from gag cartoons to humorous illustration, humorous fiction to humorous nonfiction.

Nonetheless, it is of extreme importance to understand a particular magazine's editorial format, slant or philosophy before submitting material. You wouldn't, for example, submit risque gag cartoons to the wholesome _Saturday Evening Post_. On the other hand, angelic cartoons about church bake sales probably don't stand a snowball's chance in hell at _High Society_. There's no better way to waste postage than to blindly submit inappropriate material—and remember, there's not a speck of nutritional value in stamp licking.

Illustration

When it comes to humorous illustration, put together a package of your work (self-promotion page, client list, tearsheets, etc.), send it off to the appropriate art buyer and ask him to keep it on file. The _last_ thing you want is to have the material returned. Let the art director keep your stuff—it's the thing they have to remember you by when the right assignment comes up.

Another thing to stress: While your illustration attests to your artistic talent, a well-written, professional cover letter convinces the art director of your intelligence. Humorous illustration, after all, is much more than the physical pushing around of pen on paper. In your cover letter, tell the art director about your ability to conceptualize, your knack for solving tough graphic problems and your other, nonartistic skills.

Writing

For the writer of humor, both fiction and non, it is always best to query a potential market with your story idea. Remember that editors must read through stacks of unsolicited material. Therefore, you serve yourself better if you keep your presentation succinct. Give the editor a taste and leave them salivating for more.

Payment and rights

The only thing more diverse than publications' editorial slants is the payment scale. Major consumer magazines pay top dollar for humorous writing and art, while the smallest trade publications may pay a small stipend and guarantee you a 50 yard line seat in Heaven. The latter publications are banking on your need for tearsheets and, if you're just starting out, these printed pieces *are* important and attest to your status as a published humorist.

Rights and usages will vary drastically as well. With art, a first time or one time usage fee will usually be paid, but the rights purchased for writing tend to be broader. First North American Serial Rights seem to be the most commonly negotiated terms for writing, though all rights, reprint rights, etc. may be contracted.

Generally speaking, there are many more publications which pay inadequately than those which pay well and it is a highly competitive field. The up side is magazine publishing's editorial diversity. Just written a hilarious fiction piece from a poodle's point of view? Thanks to magazine publishing's sense of humor, chances are good that someone will want to publish it. And I'd certainly want to read it.

ABOARD, Suite 220, 100 Almeria Ave., Miami FL 33134. (305)441-9744. FAX: (305)441-9739. Estab. 1976. Bimonthly inflight magazine. Circ. 100,000. Needs humorous illustration, humorous writing and gag cartoons for Latin American audience. Accepts previously published cartoons and humorous articles.
Gag Cartoons: Prefers gag cartoons on travel and related themes. No political jokes or "play on words." Doesn't want to see gag cartoons on planes. Preferred gag cartoon format is with gagline and color wash. Submit to Editorial Department. Reports back within 2 months. Returns material only if requested. Negotiates rights purchased. Pays $20 minimum for b&w; $20 for color. Pays on publication.
Humorous Illustration: Buys approximately 3 humorous illustrations/year for articles. When hiring a freelance humorous illustrator, these abilities are considered: a truly unique drawing style; effective use of humor; ability to "fun up" an otherwise "flat" manuscript. For first contact send cover letter, resume, slides, portfolio and specify price and rights to Editorial Department. Looks for good quality for printing, bright, humorous and no controversy. Reports back if interested. Samples are filed; returned if requested with SASE. Negotiates rights purchased. Pays $20 minimum/b&w page; $25 for color.
Humorous Writing: Buys approximately 2 humorous pieces/year. Needs humorous fiction, humorous anecdotes, "fillers." Length: 1,500 words; 800 for filler. To query make sure article is appropriate and study writer's guidelines. Send SASE for copy. For first contact send cover letter, outline of proposed story and writing sample to Editorial

Department. Reports back within 2 months. Samples are filed or returned if requested. Negotiates rights purchased. Pays $100 for 1,500 words.

Tips: "Use clear language, go to the point, describe situation. We need humor for Latin American readers — ours is a bilingual magazine."

ABYSS MAGAZINE, 3716 Robinson Ave., Austin TX 78722. (512)472-6534. Estab. 1979. Bimonthly topical magazine. Circ. 2,200. Needs comic strips, spot cartoons and humorous writing.

Gag Cartoons: Buys 1-3 gag cartoons/issue; 15-20/year. Prefers gag cartoons on science fiction, fantasy and horror. Doesn't want to see gag cartoons on Dungeons and Dragons. Preferred gag cartoon formats are single panel, double panel, multi-panel, b&w line art and b&w wash. Query with 5-7 rough drawings/batch to D. Nalle, Editor. Reports back within 6 weeks. Reports only if interested. Returns material only if requested and accompanied by a SASE. Buys one-time rights. Pays $3-8 for b&w. Pays on publication. Tips: "To succeed in this market, a gag cartoonist should look at the magazine first and know the markets he/she is working."

Humorous Illustration: Buys 2 humorous illustrations/issue; 10/year for articles and spots. When hiring a freelance humorous illustrator, these abilities are considered: has a truly unique drawing style, ability to conceptualize well and clever ideas — good use of metaphors, a clean, graphically pleasing drawing style; a bold, powerful, attention-getting drawing style, effective use of humor and flexibility, broad potential in drawing style. For first contact send cover letter, b&w tearsheets and b&w promo piece to P. Nalle, Editor. Reports back within 6 weeks. Samples are filed, returned if requested, returned by SASE. Buys one-time rights. Pays $2-8 for b&w page; $20-30 for b&w cover. Pays on publication.

Humorous Writing: Buys approximately 1 humorous piece/issue; 5 humorous pieces/year. Needs humorous nonfiction, humorous fiction and cartoon stories. Subject matter includes fantasy, science fiction, horror, gaming and dark humor. Length: 1,000-2,000 words. "In querying our magazine, we advise that you familiarize yourself with our magazine, that your article be appropriate for us and study our writer's guidelines first." Send $3 and SASE for copy of guide and latest issue. For first contact send cover letter, query, outline of proposed story and manuscript to D. Nalle, Editor. Reports back within 1½ months. Samples are returned with SASE only if requested. Buys one-time rights. Pays 1-3¢/word. Tips: "Be funny, not just silly."

ACCENT ON LIVING, Box 700, Bloomington IL 61702. (309)378-2961. Estab. 1956. Quarterly consumer magazine. Circ. 20,000. Needs humorous writing and gag cartoons. Accepts previously published cartoons and humorous articles.

Gag Cartoons: Buys 10-15 gag cartoons/issue; 40-60/year. Prefers gag cartoons on disability issues. Preferred gag cartoon format is b&w line art, 5 × 7 format. Send submissions to Betty Garee, Editor. Reports back in 2 weeks. Returns material if accompanied by SASE. Buys first time rights. Pays $20 minimum/b&w. Pays on acceptance.

Humorous Writing: Buys approximately 1 humorous piece/issue. Needs humorous nonfiction, humorous "slice-of-life" and humorous fiction. Subject matter includes disability. Length: 500-1,000 words. Study writer's guidelines first; send $2.50 and SASE for copy of magazine. For first contact send query and outline of proposed story to Betty Garee, Editor. Reports back in 2 weeks. Samples returned with SASE. Buys first time rights. Pays 10¢/word.

ALASKA OUTDOORS, Box 190324, Anchorage AK 99519. (907)276-2672. FAX: (907)258-6027. Estab. 1978. Monthly consumer magazine. Circ. 300,000. Needs humorous writing.

Is That a Fez on Your Head or Are You Just Glad to See Me? *"Read the manuscript and fax us some ideas." Those were the instructions given to Greg Clarke by Carole Erger-Fass, Executive Art Director for ADWEEK. A Los Angeles-based graphic humorist, Clarke's visual objective was to show "magazine publishing's practice of producing personalized editions to meet different subscriber interests." Hence the use of the "many hats" allusion. Clarke was paid $200 for one time rights to the art.*

© Greg Clarke

Humorous Writing: Buys approximately 1 humorous piece/issue; 12 pieces/year. Needs humorous nonfiction, humorous "slice-of-life" and humorous fiction. Subject matter includes Alaska outdoor recreation humor. Length: 1,200-1,500 words. To query: be familiar with magazine; make sure article is appropriate; study writer's guidelines. Send SASE for copy of guidelines. For first contact send cover letter, query, outline of proposed story and writing sample to Diane Clawson, Managing Editor. Reports back in 3 weeks. Samples are filed or returned with SASE. Buys first time and reprint rights. Pays $75-150 for 1,200-1,500 words. Offers 50% kill fee.

ALIVE! A MAGAZINE FOR CHRISTIAN SENIOR ADULTS, Box 369, West Chester OH 45069. (513)825-3681. Estab. 1988. Quarterly newsletter. Publishes news, features of interest to Christian Seniors—55 and up. Humorous articles and stories acceptable. Circ. 5,000. Accepts previously published cartoons and humorous illustrations.
Gag Cartoons: Prefers gag cartoons and spot cartoons on retirement. Preferred gag/spot cartoon format is single panel, of national appeal. When hiring a freelance humorous illustrator, "we look for the ability to read a manuscript and come up with a strong visual idea as opposed to our supplying illustration idea." For first contact, send b&w tearsheets and portfolio to A. June Lang, Office Editor. Reports back in 1 month. Returns material if accompanied by SASE. Buys first time rights and reprint rights. Pays $25 for spot cartoons.
Humorous Writing: Needs humorous fiction and anecdotes, humorous "fillers" for "Heart Medicine" section. Subject matter includes subjects of interest to over-55 age group and retirees. Length: 200-1,200 words. Submit manuscript with SASE. For first contact, send manuscript and published tearsheets to A. June Lang, Office Editor. Unsolicited material is returned with SASE. Buys first time rights and reprint rights. Pays 3¢/word for 200-1,200 words.

ALL ABOUT BEER, 4764 Galacia Way, Oceanside CA 92056. (619)724-4447. Estab. 1979. Bimonthly consumer magazine. Circ. 43,000. Needs gag cartoons, humorous illustration, humorous writing and spot cartoons. Accepts previously published cartoons and humorous articles.
Gag Cartoons: Buys 10 gag cartoons/year. Prefers gag cartoons revolving around beer. For us, the "dream" gag cartoon would be in the upscale, sophisticated style of *New Yorker* magazine. Preferred gag cartoon format is single panel, b&w line art, with gagline, b&w wash, with balloons. Query with 6 rough drawings/batch to Mike Bosak, Publisher. Reports back in 2 weeks only if interested. Returns material if accompanied

by SASE. Buys first time and one-time rights. Pays $20 minimum/b&w. Pays on publication.

Tips: A gag cartoonist should "have an interesting style, imaginative ideas, upscale and sophisticated feel, not crude."

Humorous Illustration: Buys approximately 12 humorous illustrations/year for covers and articles. Works on assignment only. When hiring a freelance humorous illustrator, these abilities are considered: a truly unique drawing style; conceptualizes well and has clever ideas—good use of metaphors; a clean, graphically-pleasing drawing style; a bold, powerful, attention-getting drawing style; a subtle, understated drawing style; uses humor effectively; does not exaggerate or distort too much; shows flexibility, broad potential in drawing style; can "fun up" an otherwise "flat" manuscript; is businesslike, meets deadline and is responsive to publisher's needs; "all illustrations must involve beer in some manner." Send submissions to Mike Bosak.

Humorous Writing: Buys approximately 12 humorous pieces/year. Needs humorous nonfiction, interviews, "slice-of-life," fiction, cartoon stories and humorous anecdotes, "fillers." Subject matter must involve beer in some manner. Length: 100-1,000 words. To query: be familiar with magazine; make sure article is appropriate; study writer's guidelines. Send $3 and SASE for copy. For first contact, send cover letter, manuscript and published tearsheets to Mike Bosak. Reports back in 3 weeks. Samples not filed are returned with SASE. Buys first time and one-time rights. Pays $55/printed page if b&w, $75 if color.

AMAZING HEROES, 7563 Lake City Way NE, Seattle WA 98115. (206)524-1967. FAX: (206)524-2104. Estab. 1981. Monthly trade journal and comics fan magazine. Circ. 10,000. Needs humorous illustration and writing, spot illustration, gag cartoons and spot cartoons.

Gag Cartoons: Buys up to 3 gag cartoons/issue. Prefers gag cartoons on adventure comic book themes only. Doesn't want to see gag cartoons on *Batman*. "We get lots of super hero jokes. It's refreshing to see take-offs on other comic book genres (science fiction, western, fantasy, etc.)." Preferred gag cartoons format is single panel, without gagline, b&w line art, b&w wash. Query with 3-5 camera ready drawings/batch to Lynette Alcorn-McCubbin, Art Director. Reports back within months. Returns material if accompanied by SASE. Buys first time rights. Pays $5 minimum/b&w. Pays on publication.

Tips: A gag cartoonist should "know adventure comic books but have broader art skills than can be obtained just from reading comics. Also present submissions in a neat, reprodtucable way."

Humorous Illustration: Buys approximately 10 humorous illustrations/issue, 120/year for spots. When hiring a freelance humorous illustrator, these abilities are considered: a truly unique drawing style; conceptualizes well and has clever ideas—good use of metaphors; a clean, graphically-pleasing drawing style; a bold, powerful, attention-getting drawing style; uses humor effectively, shows flexibility, and broad potential in drawing style. For first contact, send b&w tearsheets to Lynette Alcorn-McCubbin. Reports back within months. Samples are not filed; returned by SASE. Buys first time rights. Pays $5 minimum/b&w page. Pays on publication. "We also accept non-humorous comic book character studies. Be original, be satirical; explore other comic book genres besides super-heroes."

Humorous Writing: Buys approximately 1 humorous piece/issue; 10 pieces/year. Needs humorous nonfiction. Subject matter is comic book related material. Length: 2,000-10,000 words. To query: be familiar with magazine; make sure article is appropriate. For first contact send cover letter and query to Thomas Harrington, Managing Editor. Reports back in weeks. Samples are filed; returned only if requested. Pays 15¢/word.

Tips: "Our best humor pieces come from work where the writer discovers some obscure but intriguing facet of the comic book hobby (real or made up) and lets the topic speak for itself."

AMELIA MAGAZINE, 329 E Street, Bakersfield CA 93304. (805)323-4064. Estab. 1983. Quarterly literary magazine. Circ. 1,250. Needs humorous illustration, humorous writing, gag cartoons, spot cartoons and 3-5 panel cartoon spreads. Accepts previously published cartoons.

Gag Cartoons: Buys 3-8 gag cartoons/issue; 12-32/year. Prefers gag cartoons on virtually any theme pertinent to a literate audience. Doesn't want to see gag cartoons on wishing wells and anthropomorphic "doodads". "For us the 'dream' gag cartoon would be one that draws an immediate laugh out loud." Preferred gag cartoon formats are single panel without gagline b&w line art, double panel with gagline b&w wash and multi-panel. Query with 3-6 rough drawings/batch to Frederick A. Raborg, Jr., Editor. Reports back within 2 weeks. Returns material if accompanied by a SASE. Buys first time rights and one-time rights. Pays $5-25 for b&w.

Humorous Illustration: Buys approximately 2 humorous illustrations/issue; 8-10/year for spots and articles. When hiring a freelance humorous illustrator, these abilities are considered: a truly unique drawing style; conceptualize well and has clever ideas—good use of metaphors; a clean, graphically-pleasing drawing style; a subtle, understated drawing style; effective use of humor; flexibility, broad potential in drawing style; ability to "fun up" an otherwise "flat" manuscript; businesslike attitude—meets deadlines and is responsive to editor's needs. For first contact send cover letters, b&w tearsheets, resume, b&w promo piece, samples of offered work to Frederick A. Raborg, Jr. In reviewing humorous illustration we look for uniqueness and effect on attention span. Reports back within 2 weeks. Samples are filed or returned with SASE. Buys first time rights and one-time rights. Pays $15 minimum/b&w page, $50 minimum/b&w cover, $100 minimum/color cover. Pays on acceptance for cover; on publication for inside spots.

Tips: "We like wit in addition to humor; we like to know the illustrator has some knowledge of what we tend to use."

Humorous Writing: Buys approximately 2 humorous pieces/issue; 8/year. Subject matter includes same themes as for fiction—all types, including science fiction, Gothic romance and mainstream. Length: 1,000-2,500 words. To query: be familiar with magazine; make sure article is appropriate; study writer's guidelines. Send SASE for copy. For first contact send cover letter, manuscript to Frederick A. Raborg, Jr. Reports back within 2 weeks. Samples are not filed; returned with SASE. Buys first time rights. Pays $10-35 for 1,000-2,500 words. Offers 50% kill fee.

Tips: "Try out the material on responsive listeners or readers before submitting. Humor writing should sound humorous as well as read so, just as good dialogue must sound true. A good humor writer must think in universal terms. So much humor is regionally slanted and is lost on the majority of the readers. Be catholic in your approaches, more liberal than conservative."

AMERICAN ATHEIST, Box 140195, Austin TX 78714-0195. (512)458-1244. FAX: (512)467-9525. Estab. 1958. Monthly cause magazine. Circ. 30,000. Needs comic strips, humorous illustration, caricatures, and spot cartoons. Accepts previously published cartoons and humorous articles.

Gag Cartoons: Buys 2-5 gag cartoons/issue; 30/year. Prefers gag cartoons on the difficulties of an atheist in a religious culture; "what's wrong with religion". Doesn't want to see gag cartoons on Noah's ark. Preferred gag cartoon format is single panel, b&w line art. Query with 5-10 rough drawings/batch to R. Murray-O'Hair, Editor. Reports back in 2 months only if interested. Returns material if accompanied by SASE. Buys first time rights. Pays $15/b&w. Pays on acceptance.

Tips: A gag cartoonist should "have an understanding of the atheist position."
Humorous Illustration: Buys approximately 10 humorous illustrations/year for articles and spots. When hiring a freelance humorous illustrator, these abilities are considered: an ability to conceptualize well and clever ideas—good use of metaphors; not too much exaggeration or distortion; flexilbility, broad potential in drawing style; ability to "fun up" an otherwise "flat" manuscript. For first contact send cover letter, b&w tearsheets, and "samples of work that apply to our special needs" to R. Murray-O'Hair. Reports back in 2 months only if interested. Samples are filed or returned with SASE. Buys first time rights. Pays $25/b&w page. Pays on acceptance.
Humorous Writing: Buys approximately 10 humorous pieces/year. Needs humorous nonfiction, humorous fiction, humorous anecdotes and "fillers." Humorous material must be pertinent to Atheism or state/church separation. Length: 1,000-3,000 words. To query: be familiar with magazine; make sure article is appropriate; study writer's guidelines. For first contact, send cover letter to R. Murray-O'Hair. Reports in 2 months. Samples are filed or returned with SASE. Buys first time rights. Pays $15/ thousand words.

THE AMERICAN BAPTIST, Box 851, Valley Forge PA 19482-0851. (215)768-2000. Estab. 1803. Monthly consumer magazine and company magazine. Circ. 65,000. Needs comic strips, humorous illustration, humorous writing, cartoon narratives, caricatures, spot cartoons. Accepts previously published cartoons and humorous articles. Prefers working with freelancers who have fax capabilities.
Gag Cartoons: Buys 6-8 gag cartoons/year. Prefers gag cartoons with religious themes. Preferred gag cartoon format is single panel, with gagline, color wash. Query with 8-10 rough drawings/batch to Ronald J. Arena, Managing Editor. Reports back in 2 weeks. Returns material only if requested. Negotiates rights purchased. Pays up to $50/b&w, $75/color. Pays on acceptance.
Tips: A gag cartoonist should "Meet deadlines, make me laugh, submit material suitable for a church-related magazine."
Humorous Illustration: Buys approximately 4-6 humorous illustrations/year for articles and spots. Works on assignment only. When hiring a freelance humorous illustrator, these abilities are considered: ability to conceptualize well and clever ideas—good use of metaphors; a clean, graphically-pleasing drawing style; effective use of humor; ability to "fun up" an otherwise "flat" manuscript; businesslike attitude—meets deadlines and responsive to editor's needs. For first contact send cover letter, color promo piece, and color tearsheets to Ronald J. Arena. In reviewing humorous illustration we look for "clean, graphically pleasing drawing style and something that makes me laugh—or at least smile." Reports back in 2 weeks. Samples returned if requested. Negotiates rights purchased. Pays $150/b&w page, $300/color page; $300/b&w cover, $400/color cover. Pays on acceptance.

AMERICAN RETAILER, 21 West Delilah Rd., Pleasantville NJ 08232. (609)646-2063. FAX: (609)646-2692. Estab. 1987. Bimonthly trade journal. Circ. 100,000. Needs humorous illustration, humorous writing, cartoon narratives, caricatures, gag cartoons and spot cartoons. Accepts previously published cartoons and humorous articles.
Gag Cartoons: Buys 1 gag cartoon/issue; 6/year. Preferred gag cartoon formats are single panel without gagline b&w line art, double panel with gagline b&w wash and multi-panel with balloons. Send to Dan Kramer, Editor. Returns material only if requested. Buys one-time rights. Pays $50 minimum for b&w. Pays on publication.
Humorous Illustration: Buys approximately 1 humorous illustration/issue; 6/year for articles. Works on assignment only. When hiring a freelance humorous illustrator, these abilities are considered: conceptualize well and clever ideas—good use of metaphors; effective use of humor; ability to "fun up" an otherwise "flat" manuscript; businesslike attitude—meets deadlines and responsive to editor's needs. For first contact send cover

letter and b&w tearsheets to Dan Kramer. Reports back within days if interested. Samples are filed. Buys one-time rights. Pays $15 minimum b&w page; $120 minimum b&w cover. Pays on publication.

ARETE MAGAZINE, Suite 418, 405 W. Washington St., San Diego CA 92103. (619)237-0074. FAX: (619)237-9366. Estab. 1988. Bimonthly consumer magazine. Circ. 40,000. Needs humorous writing.
Humorous Writing: Buys approximately 2 humorous pieces/year. Needs humorous nonfiction. "Our subject matter is wide open. We ask only that it be intelligent, well-written and, of course, funny." Length: 1,000-1,500 words. To query: be familiar with magazine; make sure article is appropriate. For first contact send cover letter and manuscript to Mathew C. Burns, Humor Editor. Reports back in weeks. Samples are not filed; returned with SASE. Buys first time rights. Pays $200-600 for 1,000-2,500 words. Offers 15% kill fee.
Tips: "We're looking for intelligent, well-written humor articles that are both clever and original. Avoid being too cute or too goofy. You can have excellent ideas and still fail because not enough thought has gone into the writing itself. You must be a writer first and humorist second."

ISAAC ASIMOV'S SCIENCE FICTION MAGAZINE, 380 Lexington Ave., New York NY 10017. (212)557-9100. Estab. 1977. Thirteen times/year science fiction consumer magazine. Circ. 90,000. Needs spot cartoons. Accepts previously published cartoons.
Gag Cartoons: Prefers gag cartoons on science fiction, fantasy or science—uses cartoons as fillers. Send submissions to Sheila Williams, Managing Editor. Reports back within 2 months. Returns material if accompanied by a SASE. Buys first time rights. Pays minimum $35/b&w. Pays on acceptance.
Tips: "Remember that we only use cartoons as fillers and buy very few cartoons each year. Cartoonists should read our magazine so that they are aware of what we publish. We are only interested in cartoons which deal with the same themes that our magazine does (i.e., science fiction, fantasy, and science). Any artist interested in working for us should be able to illustrate an entire range of stories from the humorous to the dramatic and should be very interested in science fiction."

ATARI EXPLORER, 7 Hilltop Rd., Mendham NJ 07945. Estab. 1978. Bimonthly consumer magazine. Circ. 50,000. Needs gag cartoons. Accepts previously published cartoons.
Gag Cartoons: Buys 4-5 gag cartoons/issue; 20-30/year. Prefers gag cartoons on personal computers, particularly Atari computers. Doesn't want to see gag cartoons on computer dating, computer-replaces-employee, computer-talks-back. and cartoons depicting giant 30 year-old mainframe computers with tape reels (usually improperly threaded). Preferred gag cartoon format is single panel b&w line art. Query with rough drawings to Elizabeth B. Staples, Editor. Reports back within 10 days. Returns unused material. Buys one-time rights. Pays $20 minimum for b&w. Pays on acceptance.
Tips: "Really understand personal computers and the people who use them."

ATLANTIC INSIGHT/ATLANTIC BUSINESS, 5502 Atlantic St., Halifax, Nova Scotia B3H 1G4 Canada. (902)421-1214. FAX: (421)425-8758. Estab. 1979. Monthly consumer magazine. Circ. 100,000. Accepts previously published humorous articles.
Gag Cartoons: Reports back within 6-8 weeks. Returns material only if requested. Pays on publication.
Tips: "Have an intense Atlantic Canadian focus. We only publish material relevant to the four Atlantic provinces."
Humorous Illustration: For first contact send cover letter, resume and b&w tearsheets to Bob LeDrew, Assistant Editor. Reports back within 6-8 weeks. Samples are not filed. Pays $50 minimum/b&w page, cover, color page and color cover. Pays on publication.

Humorous Writing: Needs nonfiction. Subject matter includes only Atlantic Canadian topics. Length: up to 1,000. To query: be familiar with magazine; make sure article is appropriate; study writer's guidelines. Send SASE for copy. For first contact send cover letter, query, published tearsheets, resume and writing samples to Bob LeDrew, Assistant Editor. Reports back within 6-8 weeks. Samples are not filed. Buys first time rights. Pays 30-35¢/word.

BAJA TIMES, Box 5577, Chula Vista CA 92012. (706)612-1244. Estab. 1978. Monthly newspaper and tabloid. Circ. 60,000. Needs humorous illustration and writing.
Gag Cartoons: Prefers gag cartoons on the positive aspects of Mexico. Preferred gag cartoon formats are single panel, b&w line art with gagline, b&w wash, multi-panel with balloons. Query with 2-4 rough drawings/batch to John W. Utley, Editor. Reports back in 4 weeks. Returns material only if requested and if accompanied by SASE. Buys one-time rights. Pays $10/b&w on publication.
Humorous Illustration: Buys humorous illustration for articles. When hiring a freelance humorous illustrator, these abilities are considered: ability to conceptualize well and clever ideas—good use of metaphors; ability to "fun up" an otherwise "flat" manuscript. For first contact, send cover letter and b&w tearsheets to John W. Utley. Reports back in 4 weeks. Samples are filed; returned if requested by SASE. Buys one-time rights. Pays $10/b&w page on publication.
Humorous Writing: Buys approximately 1 humorous piece/issue, 12 pieces/year. Needs humorous nonfiction and "slice-of-life." Subject matter has to reflect Baja Calfornia, Mexico. "Our publication is tourist oriented." Length: 1,500 words. To query: make sure article is appropriate. Send $1 and SASE for copy. For first contact, send cover letter, manuscript and writing sample to John W. Utley. Reports back in 1 month. Samples are filed or returned with SASE. Buys one-time rights. Pays $35-60/piece for 900-1,500 words. No kill fee—no assigned articles.
Tips: "We are more interested in articles than art, although properly oriented art with articles would certainly be considered. We are a tourist oriented publication catering to the Baja California, Mexico (adjacent to San Diego, CA) market area of Tijuana, Rosarito and Ensenada. This is a specialized market and all material must reflect favorably on Mexico. No Bandido types, corrupt police, etc."

THE BARKEATER, Box 33, North River NY 12856. (518)251-2661. Estab. 1982. Quarterly consumer magazine. Circ. 6,000. Needs comic strips, humorous illustration, humorous writing, gag cartoons and spot cartoons. Accepts previously published cartoons and humorous articles.
Gag Cartoons: Buys 2 gag cartoons per/issue; 8/year. Prefers gag cartoons on sportsman's themes, fishing, hunting, trapping, and back-woods living. Preferred gag cartoon formats are single panel with b&w line art, double panel with gagline, and multi-panel with balloons. Query with 2-3 rough drawings/batch to Jeff Fosdick, Publisher/Editor. Reports back (sometimes) within 2 weeks. Returns material if accompanied by a SASE. Buys first time rights. Pays $10-15 minimum for b&w. Pays on publication.
Tips: A gag cartoonist should be "humorous but not offensive to any party. Good humor is often a good laugh at one's self."
Humorous Illustration: Buys approximately 4 humorous illustrations/year for articles and spots. When hiring a freelance humorous illustrator, these abilities are considered: ability to conceptualize well and clever ideas—good use of metaphors; a clean, graphically-pleasing drawing style; effective use of humor; ability to "fun up" an otherwise "flat" manuscript; businesslike attitude—meets deadlines and is responsive to editor's needs. For first contact send cover letter, b&w tearsheets and b&w promo piece to Jeff Fosdick. In reviewing humorous illustration we look for drawing style and ability to enhance the humor of an article in an illustration. Reports back within 2 weeks. Samples

are filed or returned with SASE. Buys first time rights and one-time rights. Pays $10-20 minimum for b&w page. Pays on publication.

Tips: "Facial expressions should be appropriate/simplicity."

Humorous Writing: Buys approximately 1 humorous piece/year; 4 humorous pieces/year. Needs humorous nonfiction and fiction, humorous interviews, humorous "slice-of-life", cartoon stories, humorous anecdotes, and "fillers." Subject matter includes Sportsman Magazine, Adirondack-related, fishing, hunting, trapping, crafts and country life. Length: 1,000-1,500 words. To query: be familiar with magazine, and make sure article is appropriate. For first contact send cover letter, manuscript, writing sample, query, outline of proposed story to Jeff Fosdick. Reports back within 2 weeks. Samples are filed or returned with a SASE. Buys first time rights and one-time rights. Pays $20-50 for 1000-1500 words.

BARTENDER, Box 158, Liberty Corner NJ 07938. (201)766-6006. FAX: (201)766-6607. Estab. 1979. Bimonthly trade journal. Circ. 140,000. Needs comic strips, humorous illustration, humorous writing, cartoon narratives, caricatures and gag cartoons. Accepts previously published cartoons and humorous articles. Prefers working with freelancers who have fax capabilities.

Gag Cartoons: Buys 3 gag cartoons/issue.

BELIEVERS, Box 109, Traverse City MI 49685-0109. (616)943-4926. Estab. 1987. Quarterly consumer magazine. Circ. 10,000. Needs cartoons narratives and humorous writing. Accepts previously published cartoons and humorous articles.

Gag Cartoons: Buys 1 gag cartoon/year. Prefers gag cartoons that are "tastefully religious or family cartoons." Preferred gag cartoon format is single panel, b&w line art, with gagline. Query with 2-6 rough drawings/batch to Ms. Pat Murphy, Editor/Publisher. Reports back in 2 weeks. Returns material if accompanied by SASE. Buys first time rights. Pays $7.50/b&w on publication.

Humorous Illustration: Buys approximately 1 humorous illustration/issue; 4/year for articles. When hiring a freelance humorous illustrator, these abilities are considered: ability to conceptualize well and clever ideas—good use of metaphors; a subtle, understated drawing style; effective use of humor; ability to "fun up" an otherwise "flat" manuscript; businesslike attitude—meets deadlines and responsive to editor's needs. For first contact send cover letter, b&w tearsheets, client list, b&w promo piece, (b&w only) to Pat Murphy. In reviewing humorous illustration we look for "an effective message." Reports back in 2 weeks. Samples are filed; returned by SASE if requested. Buys first time rights. Pays $7.50/b&w page on publication.

Tips: "Read the story carefully, and let God send you the picture we need."

Humorous Writing: Buys approximately 1 humorous piece/issue; 4 pieces/year. Needs humorous "slice-of-life," humorous anecdotes and "fillers." Subject matter includes Christian slant, written on 6th-8th grade level. Length: 1,500-3,000 words. To query: send $2.50 and SASE for copy. For first contact send cover letter and manuscript to Pat Murphy. Reports back in 2 weeks. Samples returned with SASE. Buys first time rights. Pays $2-20 for 20-3,000 words.

Tips: "When writing Christian humor we can have fun but we don't show a preacher as stupid, we show him as human. We want humor that will not offend our Christian readers. It should deliver a message. It should make them stop and think."

BIRD TALK, Box 6050, Mission Viejo CA 92690. (714)855-8822. FAX: (714)855-3045. Estab. 1983. Monthly consumer magazine. Circ. 175,000. Needs gag cartoons and humorous writing. Accepts previously published cartoons and humorous articles.

Gag Cartoons: Buys 4-7 gag cartoons/issue; 75/year. Prefers gag cartoons on pet birds. Doesn't want to see gag cartoons on "Polly want a cracker." Preferred gag cartoon format is single panel with/without gagline b&w line art. Query with 3-10 good line drawings per batch to Karyn New, Editorial Director. Reports back within 1 month. Returns material if accompanied by a SASE. Buys one-time rights. Pays $35 minimum for b&w. Pays on publication.

Tips: Understand the personalities of pet birds.

Humorous Writing: Buys approximately 1 humorous piece/issue; 15/year. Needs humorous nonfiction, "slice-of-life" and anecdotes. Subject matter includes personal experiences detailing humorous and unusual things pet birds do. Length: 500-2,500 words. To query: be familiar with magazine, make sure article is appropriate and study writer's guidelines. Send $3.50 and SASE for copy. For first contact send cover letter, manuscript, query to Karyn New. Reports back within 1 month. Samples are not filed; returned with SASE. Buys one-time rights. Pays 5-15¢/word.

Tips: "Please make the humor in the actions of the bird, not in exaggeration. No pseudo-Erma Bombeck pieces."

BIRD WATCHER'S DIGEST, Box 110, Marietta OH 45750. (614)373-5285. FAX: (614)373-8443. Estab. 1978. Bimonthly consumer magazine. Circ. 75,000. Needs gag cartoons. Accepts previously published cartoons.

Gag Cartoons: Buys 1-3 gag cartoons/issue. Prefers gag cartoons on wild birds/wild bird watching. Preferred gag cartoon format is single panel, b&w line art. Query with 2-7 rough drawings/batch to Mary Bowers, Editor. Reports back in 6-8 weeks. Returns material if accompanied by SASE. Buys one-time rights. Pays $15/b&w on publication.

BOSTONIA, 10 Lenox St., Brookline MA 02146. (617)353-9711. Estab. 1900. Bimonthly consumer magazine. Circ. 140,000. Needs humorous illustration and writing. Prefers working with freelancers who have fax capabilities.

Gag Cartoons: Returns material only if accompanied by a SASE. Buys first time rights. Pays minimum $200/b&w; $300/color.

Humorous Illustration: Buys approximately 6 humorous illustrations/issue; 20/year for covers, articles and spots. Works on assignment only. When hiring a freelance humorous illustrator, these abilities are considered: a truly unique drawing style; ability to conceptualize well and clever ideas—good use of metaphors; a clean, graphically-pleasing drawing style; a bold, powerful, attention-getting drawing style; a subtle, understated drawing style; effective use of humor; flexibility, broad potential in drawing style; businesslike attitude—meets deadlines and responsive to editor's needs. For first contact send cover letter, b&w or color tearsheets, b&w or color promo piece, slides to Douglas Parker, Art Director. "In reviewing humorous illustration we look for originality and communication skills." Reports back if interested. Samples are filed or returned by SASE. Buys first time rights. Pays minimum $300/b&w page; $500/color. Pays on publication.

Tips: "Illustration should be an aid to reading comprehension."

Humorous Writing: Buys approximately 1-2 humorous pieces/issue; 6-12/year. Needs humorous nonfiction/fiction and humorous "slice-of-life". Length: 500-1,000 words. To query be familiar with magazine. For first contact send cover letter and manuscript to Lori Calabro, Managing Editor. Reports back within 6 months if interested. Samples are filed or returned with SASE. Buys first time rights. Pays $200-400 for 500-1,000 words. Offers 25% kill fee.

THE CALIFORNIA HIGHWAY PATROLMAN, 2030 V St., Sacramento CA 95818. (916)452-6751. Estab. 1937. Monthly consumer magazine. Circ. 18,000. Needs humorous writing and spot cartoons. Does not accept previously published cartoons.

Gag Cartoons: Buys 5-6 gag cartoons/issue; 60 gag cartoons/year. Gag cartoons must be California Highway Patrol-related. Preferred gag cartoon formats are single panel, b&w line art, double panel, with gagline, with balloons. Query with finished cartoons to Carol Perri, Editor. Returns material if accompanied by SASE. Buys one-time rights. Pays $15/b&w on publication.

Tips: "Keep our audience in mind."

Humorous Writing: Buys approximately 6-10 humorous pieces/year. Needs humorous nonfiction and humorous "slice-of-life." Length: short—under 1,000 words. To query: be familiar with magazine; make sure article is appropriate; study writer's guidelines. For first contact, send cover letter and manuscript to Carol Perri. Reports back in 3-6 months. Samples are not filed; returned with SASE. Buys one-time rights. Pays 2½¢/word.

Tips: "Send complete manuscript. Can't tell humorous writing quality from a query."

CALIFORNIA JOURNAL, 1714 Capitol Avenue, Sacramento CA 95814. (916)444-2840. Estab. 1980. Monthly consumer magazine. Circ. 18,000. Needs humorous illustration and caricatures.

Humorous Illustration: Buys approximately 4 humorous illustrations/issue; 36/year for articles. Works on assignment only. When hiring a freelance humorous illustrator, these abilities are considered: ability to conceptualize well and clear ideas—good use of metaphors; a clean, graphically-pleasing drawing style; flexibility, and broad potential in drawing style. For first contact send cover letter, resume, b&w or color tearsheets and b&w or color promo piece to Richard Zeiger, Editor. "In reviewing humorous illustrations we look for illustrations that have political content." Samples are filed. Buys all rights. Pays $100 minimum/b&w page, $300 color cover. Pays on publication.

CALIFORNIA LAWYER, Suite 1016, 1390 Market St., San Francisco CA 94102. (415)558-9888. Estab. 1976. Monthly trade journal. Circ. 110,000. Needs gag cartoons and spot cartoons. Accepts previously published cartoons and humorous articles. Prefers working with freelancers who have fax capabilities.

Gag Cartoons: Buys 2 gag cartoons/issue; 24/year. Prefers gag cartoons on legal issues. Preferred gag cartoon format is single panel. Query with 5-10 rough drawings/batch to Gordon Smith, Art Director. Reports in 3-4 weeks only if interested. Buys one-time rights. Pays $75 for b&w. Pays on publication.

Tips: "Have a tight drawing style—no frizzy stuff."

CAMPUS LIFE, 465 Gundersen Drive, Carol Stream IL 60188. (708)260-6200. FAX: (708)260-0114. Estab. 1943. Monthly consumer magazine (10 times a year, combined issues—July-Aug., May-June). Circ. 130,000. Needs humorous writing, gag cartoons, spot cartoons. Accepts previously published humorous articles.

Gag Cartoons: Buys 5 gag cartoons/issue; 50/year. Prefers gag cartoons on teen themes that laugh with teens—not at them. Doesn't want gag cartoons on silly puns or worn clichés. For us, the "dream" gag cartoon would be "funny, bizarre, something kids will laugh at and hang up in their lockers." Preferred gag cartoon format is single panel, b&w line art. Submit 5-10 rough drawings/batch to Chris Lutes, Cartoon Editor. Reports back in 5-6 weeks. Returns material if accompanied by SASE. Buys first time rights. Pays $50/b&w on acceptance.

Tips: A gag cartoonist should "understand current youth contemporary style; avoid sounding like a parent. Don't send cartoons that look like they were drawn in the 50's."

Humorous Illustration: Buys approximately 3 humorous illustrations/issue; 30/year for articles, spots and departments. Works on assignment only. When hiring a freelance humorous illustrator, these abilities are considered: a truly unique drawing style; ability to conceptualize well and clever ideas—good use of metaphors; a clean, graphically-pleasing drawing style; effective use of humor; not too much exaggeration or distortion; flexibility, broad potential in drawing style; ability to "fun up" an otherwise "flat" manuscript; businesslike attitude—meets deadlines and responsive to editor's needs; no need for a lot of direction. For first contact, send b&w and color tearsheets, color and b&w promo piece to Jeff Carnehl, Art Director.

Tips: "I enjoy trying out new artists and tend to look for more original styles."

Humorous Writing: Buys approximately 3-5 humorous pieces/year. Needs humorous nonfiction, humorous teen "slice-of-life," humorous fiction, cartoon stories — *Mad* style. Subject matter includes anything that covers the high-school experience. Length: 500-1,000 words. To query: be familiar with magazine; make sure article is appropriate; study writer's guidelines. Send $2 and SASE for copy of the magazine. For first contact send writing sample, query, outline of proposed story, published tearsheets to Chris Lutes. Reports back in 60 days only if interested. Samples are returned with SASE. Buys first time rights. Pays $125-300 for 750-2,000 words.

Tips: "Must be carefully targeted to high school students, should attempt to reflect current humor trends. For style, think the "clean side" of David Letterman, also a Dave Berry style for high school students would work."

CANADIAN CARTOONIST MAGAZINE, Box 725, New Westminster, British Columbia V3L-4Z3 Canada. (604)524-5585. Estab. 1989. Quarterly trade journal. Circ. 500. Needs profiles on cartoonists and how to cartooning. Accepts previously published humorous articles.

Humorous Writing: Buys approximately 4 humorous pieces/issue. Needs humorous interviews. Subject matter includes profiles, "how to", and organizational updates. Length: 500-1,000 words. To query: be familiar with magazine, make sure article is appropriate and study writer's guidelines. Send $5.00 and SASE for copy. For first contact send cover letter and outline of proposed story to Charles B. Walker, Editor. Reports back within 2 months. Samples are returned with SASE. Buys first time rights. Pays $20-30 for 500-1,000 words.

Tips: "I need articles about Canadian cartoonists and cartooning in general in Canada."

CARTOON MARKETS, Suite One, 90 W. Winnipeg Ave., St. Paul MN 55117-5428. Estab. 1963. Monthly newsletter. Circ. 600. Needs gag cartoons.

Gag Cartoons: Buys 4 gag cartoons/issue; 48/year. Prefers gag cartoons on the humor of creating humor. Doesn't want to see gag cartoons unrelated to our theme. For us the "dream" gag cartoon would be "muse to frowning cartoonist at art table: 'You can't get the right slant because your table is at the wrong angle.' " Preferred gag cartoon format is single panel b&w line art with gagline. Query with 1-15 rough drawings/batch to Loanne Engen, Art Director; only full-year subscribers qualify to submit cartoons. Reports back within 1 month. Returns material if accompanied by a SASE. Buys first time rights. Pays $10 minimum for b&w. Pays on acceptance.

Tips: "Read and understand the needs of our publication, which goes to professional cartoonists and gagwriters. To encourage beginners, we accept only their work for publication, but a full-year subscription is required. $25/year; $2.50/sample copy."

CARTOON WORLD, Box 30367, Lincoln NE 68503. (402)435-3191. Estab. 1936. Monthly newsletter. Circ. 300. Needs only articles on cartooning and gagwriting.

Tips: This publication is only published to find new markets for cartoonists and has articles on "How to Cartoon," and "How to Write Gag Ideas" only. For sample, $5.

CASINO DIGEST, Suite 123, 1901-G Ashwood Ct., Greensboro NC 27408. (919)375-6358. Estab. 1984. Monthly consumer tabloid newsletter. Circ. 40,000. Needs humorous illustration, cartoon narratives, caricatures, gag cartoons, spot cartoons and political/editorials. Accepts previously published cartoons and humorous articles.

Gag Cartoons: Buys 1 gag cartoon/issue; 12/year. Prefers gag cartoons on Casino gambling, political (for news purposes) plus editorial. Doesn't want to see gag cartoons on gambling games. For us the "dream" gag cartoon would be "one that reflects the

Close-up

Larry Sloman
Executive Editor
National Lampoon

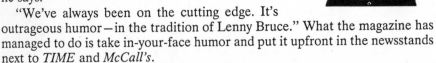

National Lampoon humor, says Executive Editor Larry Sloman, is parody pure and simple. But it's biting parody. Indeed, nothing is sacred and no one is safe from the magazine's scathing satire. "We're like a bunch of kids let loose with pea shooters," he says.

"We've always been on the cutting edge. It's outrageous humor—in the tradition of Lenny Bruce." What the magazine has managed to do is take in-your-face humor and put it upfront in the newsstands next to *TIME* and *McCall's*.

"We made our kind of humor palatable for the mass audience. Today you can see it everywhere—on HBO and Cinemax. The challenge we now face is to try to top ourselves and that isn't easy," he says.

In the seventies, the magazine was famous for its jabs at the system, politicians and "pompous stuffed shirts" in particular. In the early eighties, says Sloman, "humor became more mean-spirited. Shows like Letterman's exemplified this yuppie or me-decade spirit of putting down the people beneath you.

"But we're already noticing a swing back. Humor, like anything else in society, is cyclical. Now you've got professional nice guys like Arsenio Hall and the target has shifted back to the big guys. But we've always gone after the big guys."

Sloman continues to try to keep the magazine one step ahead of itself. And this means a constant search for new, fresh material. "Lately, I've brought in stand up comics like Gilbert Gottfried, Richard Belzer and Emo Phillips, to write for us."

The magazine parodies everything from the Yellow Pages to the latest bestseller. "We try to take the topical approach, even with social issues, but it's difficult to do with a bimonthly publication." Although the magazine went bimonthly a few years ago, plans are already in motion for its return as a monthly sometime by the end of this year. In fact, with new owners and a new publisher, *National Lampoon* is undergoing a complete restructuring.

For a time, Sloman was discouraging submissions because so much of it was inappropriate for the magazine or simply not funny. "You can train someone in basic journalism, but it's hard to try to teach someone to write funny. Humor takes a lot of mental preparation. Writers need to think about it before committing anything to paper. To get just the right twist, you need to think it through."

Although Sloman accepts only about one in every 200 unsolicited submissions, he insists there are several different ways a writer can break into the magazine. The "Letters to the Editor" section is the most accessible, but he is also looking for parodies of short news pieces and ideas for longer material. The magazine also accepts clippings for its "True Facts" section, a compilation of true, but bizarre items. "We also accept regular short fiction, list pieces, photo essays, movie and magazine parodies and comics in a host of different forms." Sloman likes to see the manuscript for short submissions. For longer pieces, send a query letter with clips, especially for humorous material.

Writers should also research the market before submitting. "I cannot stress enough the importance of knowing your market. It's insulting to get a piece so wrong it's obvious the writer has not looked at the magazine."

Be original and avoid the obvious, adds Sloman, and don't forget the basics. "I'm amazed at how many writers forget that they have to hook a reader into a piece with the first few paragraphs. If I'm reading an unsolicited manuscript and nothing happens for the first three or four paragraphs, I won't finish it. You've got to have a strong opening and a strong ending."

Much of the material in *National Lampoon* is heavily illustrated and writers who are also artists are prized. Yet even if the writer cannot draw, Sloman encourages writers to suggest art treatment. "It's definitely a good idea to think visually."

Above all, be original, he says. "Push the humor to the edge. This does not mean add a lot of cuss words. It means take an adventurous perspective. Deflate pomposity!"

—Robin Gee

---

consumers, and the casinos, feelings toward given situations . . . from both in and out of the casino." Preferred gag cartoon formats are single panel with/without gagline b&w line art, double panel with gagline b&w wash and multi-panel with balloons. Query with 2-4 rough drawings/batch to Joe Lawless, Publisher/Editor. Reports back within 1 month. Returns material if accompanied by a SASE. Negotiates rights purchased. Pays minimum $50 for b&w. Pays on publication.

Tips: "Have a keen sense of the casino gambling world, not a stereotype, and be aware of what motivates casino patrons both in thought and in action. Should also be well-informed on the viewpoints of the casino operators and express them in articulate form both in drawing and captions."

Humorous Illustration: Buys approximately 1 humorous illustration/issue; 12/year for articles, spots and editorials. Works on assignment only. When hiring a freelance humorous illustrator, these abilities are considered: a truly unique drawing style; ability to conceptualize well and clever ideas — good use of metaphors; a clean, graphically-pleasing drawing style; a bold, powerful, attention-getting drawing style; effective use of humor; not too much exaggeration or distortion; flexibility, broad potential in drawing style; businesslike attitude — meets deadlines and responsive to editor's needs; and draw serious editorial cartoons for news. For first contact send cover letter, b&w tearsheets, client list, b&w promo piece if available and examples of serious and humorous cartoons to Joe Lawless. "In reviewing humorous illustrations we look for sophistication of the drawing, how well the idea is presented and communicated." Reports back within 1 month. Samples are filed or returned by SASE. Negotiates rights purchased. Pays $50 minimum b&w/page.

Tips: "Realistic people and situations are the key. A person standing in front of a slot machine or at a gambling table is old hat ... unless it makes a unique point."

Humorous Writing: Buys approximately 1 humorous piece/issue; 12/year. Needs humorous nonfiction/fiction, interviews, "slice-of-life" and humorous editorial and/or political. Subject matter must be in direct relation to casino gambling in some way; other forms of gambling do not apply. Length: 500-1,000. To query: be familiar with magazine and that make sure article is appropriate. For first contact send cover letter, outline of proposed story and published tearsheets to Joe Lawless. Absolutely no phone calls. Reports back within 1 month. Samples are filed or returned with SASE. Negotiates rights purchased. Pays $.10/word for 500-1,000 words. Offers 50% kill fee.

Tips: "The more you know about casino gambling (not stereotype) from both the patrons' and casino operators' viewpoints, the more successful you will be. Being able to draw editorial cartoons for serious articles will enhance your portfolio. Poor communication, ideas and drawing are the main reasons a cartoon of this type will be turned down. This market is WIDE OPEN to both humorous and serious cartoonists and writers. But bought only if subject matter is dealt with in both style and realism. Stereotype cartoonists abound in this industry. No more, please! Cartoons should have one of two characteristics: (1) drawn and presented in the fashion of the *Saturday Evening Post* and *New Yorker* or (2) to suit the serious nature of the editorial sections of any major daily newspaper. EXAMPLE OF THE LATTER: a patron is sitting at a non-smoking blackjack table in a casino. He shows a *large bankroll* while lighting a cigarette. The Pit Boss says 'You can't play here. The smoking blackjack tables are across the room.' In the second panel the patron picks up his bankroll and says 'No thank you, I'll go across the street.' "

A CASUAL CARTOON REVIEW, 511 Warwick Ave., Warwick RI 02888. Estab. 1989. Quarterly or occasional low-grade photocopied zine. Circ. 30-40. Needs humorous illustration and humorous writing of animation angle. Accepts previously published cartoons and humorous articles.

Gag Cartoons: Reports back in days. Returns material if accompanied by SASE. Buys one-time rights. Pays for copies (5) on publication.

Humorous Illustration: Buys humorous illustrations for articles. When hiring a freelance humorous illustrator, these abilities are considered: a clean, graphically-pleasing drawing style; ability to illustrate with animated character. For first contact send samples to Steve Ahlquist. Reports back within days. Samples are filed or returned with SASE. Buys one-time rights. Pays for copies (5) on publication.

Humorous Writing: Needs humorous nonfiction and articles on animation. Subject matter includes animation articles with a light, well-researched, offbeat touch. Length: any length, "Quality over quantity." To query: be familiar with magazine; make sure article is appropriate. For first contact, send manuscript, writing sample and query to Steve Alhquist. Reports back within days. Samples are filed or returned with SASE. Buys one-time rights. Pays for 5 copies.

Tips: "Not exactly a humor magazine but I do not take the enterprise seriously either. It would be very difficult to meet my standards, but I'll publish anything, even that which falls below my standards."

CAT FANCY, Box 6050, Mission Viejo CA 92690. (714)855-8822. Estab. 1965. Monthly consumer magazine. Circ. 332,000. Needs humorous illustration and writing, gag cartoons and spot cartoons.

Gag Cartoons: Buys 12-15 gag cartoons/year on cats. Doesn't want to see gag cartoons that "are hostile about or negative toward cats." Preferred gag cartoon format is single panel, with/without gagline, b&w line art. Send submissions to K.E. Segnar, Editor.

and SASE for copy. For first contact send cover letter, query, outline of proposed story and published tearsheets (if available) to Cynthia Foley. Reports back within 2 weeks. Samples are returned. Buys first time rights. Pays $25-200/article.

Tips: "Know horses and horse people. You must be involved in the sport to understand these people. We love good humor and are very picky."

© Harley Schwadron

"You guys are in big trouble. This is my lawyer. I burned my mouth on your porridge."

It's Never Like This on "L.A. Law": *Just when you thought every Three Bears gag had been done, Harley Schwadron of Ann Arbor, Michigan comes up with this gem. The perfect example of art and writing working together—the dialogue is completely believable and the minimalist drawing isn't too overbearing (ahem). One-time rights to the cartoon were purchased by the* National Law Journal *and the cartoon was then reprinted in a legal textbook (and you thought lawyers didn't know how to laugh).*

Sent → Sent 2ND BATCH

THE CLERGY JOURNAL, Box 162527, Austin TX 78716. (512)327-8501. Estab. 1924. Monthly trade journal. Circ. 16,000. Needs gag cartoons and spot cartoons.

Gag Cartoons: Buys 5 gag cartoons/issue, 40/year. Prefer gag cartoons on religion. For us, the "dream" gag cartoon would be "about preaching." Preferred gag cartoon format is single panel, b&w line art, with gagline. Query with 5-10 rough drawings/batch to Manfred Holck Jr., Editor. Reports back in 2 weeks. Returns material if accompanied by SASE. Buys first time rights. Pays $10/b&w on acceptance.

Tips: "Remember that ministers are our primary audience."

CLUBHOUSE, Box 15, Berrien Springs MI 49103. (616)471-9009. Estab. 1951. Bi-monthly. Circ. 15,000. Needs humorous illustration, gag cartoons and spot cartoons. Accepts previously published cartoons.

Gag Cartoons: Buys 3 gag cartoons/issue; 18/year. Prefers gag cartoons on kid's problems with parents, kids and pets, school, kids and other related topics. Preferred gag cartoon formats are single panel with/without gagline and b&w line art. Query with 10 rough drawings/batch to Elaine Trumbo, Editor. Reports back within 6 weeks. Returns material if accompanied by a SASE. Buys first time rights, reprint rights and one-time rights. Pays $12 minimum for b&w.

Tips: "Remember to submit cartoons that are amusing to kids — not cartoons in which adults find the frailties of children funny."

Humorous Illustration: Buys humorous illustrations for stories. Works on assignment only. When hiring a freelance humorous illustrator, these abilities are considered: ability to conceptualize well and clever ideas — good use of metaphors; a clean, graphically-pleasing drawing style; effective use of humor; ability to "fun up" an otherwise "flat" manuscript; businesslike attitude — meets deadlines. For first contact send b&w tearsheets to Elaine Trumbo. In reviewing humorous illustration "we look for a style that kids will enjoy." Reports back within 6 weeks if interested. Samples are filed; returned by SASE if requested. Buys first time rights. Pays $25 minimum b&w page.

Tips: "Loose, vibrant, playful style preferred."

Humorous Writing: Needs humorous nonfiction and humorous "slice-of-life". Subject matter includes topics that relate to kids and children in a favorable light. Length: 1,200 words. To query: be familiar with magazine; study writer's guidelines. For first contact send manuscript to Elaine Trumbo. Reports back within 6 weeks. Samples are returned with SASE. Buys first time rights, reprint rights and one-time rights. Pays $25-35 for 800-1,400 words.

Tips: "We usually prefer 1st person when writing in this style. *Clubhouse* prefers material which makes children seem funny, wise, brave, etc. Our goal is to have a child feel good about who he (and his kind) is/are and to encourage him to know we are on his side. We buy all material in the spring. Send manuscripts in April or May."

COLLEGIATE MICROCOMPUTER, Rose-Hulman Institute Technology, Terre Haute IN 47803. Estab. 1983. Quarterly scholarly journal. Circ. 1,500. Needs gag cartoons and spot cartoons.

Gag Cartoons: Buys 5 gag cartoons/issue, 25/year for uses of microcomputers at college level. Preferred gag cartoon format is single panel, b&w line art. Send submissions to Brian J. Winkel, Editor. Reports back within days. Returns material if accompanied by SASE. Buys one-time rights. Pays $25/b&w on acceptance.

COMPLETE WOMAN, 1165 N. Clark, Chicago IL 60610. (312)266-8680. Estab. 1980. Bimonthly consumer magazine. Circ. 100,000. Needs humorous illustration, gag cartoons and spot cartoons.

Gag Cartoons: Buys 12 gag cartoons/issue; 72/year. Prefers gag cartoons on women/men, work, etc. Preferred gag cartoon format is gagline b&w wash. Query with 10-12 rough drawings/batch to Bonnie Krueger, Editor. Reports back within 3 weeks. Returns material if accompanied by a SASE. Buys one-time rights. Pays $20 minimum for b&w. Pays on publication.

Tips: "Know about women and don't stereotype them."

Humorous Illustration: Buys approximately 10 humorous illustrations/issue for articles. Works on assignment only. When hiring a freelance humorous illustrator, these abilities are considered: ability to conceptualize well and clever ideas — good use of metaphors; a clean, graphically-pleasing drawing style; effective use of humor; not too much exaggeration or distortion; businesslike attitude — meets deadlines and responsive to the magazine's needs. For first contact send cover letter and b&w tearsheets to Julie Kotar, Art Director. In reviewing humorous illustration we look for style and appeal to women. Reports back within 3 weeks. Samples are returned by SASE. Buys one-time rights. Pays $50 minimum/b&w page.

Tips: "Review our magazine prior to sending in."

Humorous Writing: Buys approximately 1 humorous piece/issue. Needs humorous nonfiction, humorous interviews and humorous "slice-of-life." Subject matter includes information geared towards women. Length: 800 words. To query: be familiar with magazine; make sure that article is appropriate. For first contact send cover letter, writing sample, query, published tearsheets to Susan Handy, Senior Editor. Reports back within 3 weeks. Samples are returned with SASE. Buys one-time rights. Pays approximately 10¢/word.

Tips: "Research our magazine and position story to appeal to our market."

CONSTRUCTION PUBLICATIONS, P.O. Box 1689, Cedar Rapids IA 52406. (319)366-1597. FAX (319)364-4853. Estab. 1948. Bimonthly trade journal. Circ. 70,000. Needs gag cartoons and spot cartoons.

Gag Cartoons: Buys 10 gag cartoons/issue; 60/year. Prefers gag cartoons on heavy construction industry. For us, the "dream" gag cartoon "makes construction people feel good about themselves." Preferred gag cartoon format is single panel with gagline, b&w line art and b&w wash. Reports back with 3 weeks. Returns material if accompanied by a SASE. Buys all rights. Pays $15 b&w. Pays on acceptance.

Tips: Relate to the industries served by the publication."

CREATING EXCELLENCE, Box 2048, S. Burlington VT 05407. (802)655-7200. Estab. 1986. Bimonthly business-oriented magazine—Vermont. Circ. 20,000. Needs humorous illustration, humorous writing and spot cartoons. Accepts previously published cartoons and humorous articles.

Gag Cartoons: Buys 1-2 gag cartoons/issue; 6-10/year. Prefers gag cartoons on specific article content. Doesn't want to see gag cartoons on general business. Preferred gag cartoon formats are single panel b&w line art and multi-panel. Query with 1-15 rough drawings/batch to David Robinson, Editor. Reports back within 1 month if interested. Returns material if accompanied by a SASE. Buys first time rights, reprint rights, one-time rights or negotiates rights purchased. Pays up to $50 for b&w. Pays on publication.

Humorous Illustration: Buys approximately 1-2 humorous illustrations/issue for articles. When hiring a freelance humorous illustrator, these abilities are considered: a clean, graphically-pleasing drawing style; not too much exaggeration or distortion; businesslike attitude—meets deadlines and responsive to editor's needs. For first contact send cover letter and b&w tearsheets to David Robinson. In reviewing humorous illustrations we look for clean style, sensitivity to subject and taste. Reports back within 1 month if interested. Samples are filed or returned by SASE if requested. Buys first time rights, reprint rights, one-time rights or negotiates rights purchased. Pays up to $75/b&w page. Pays on publication.

Humorous Writing: Buys approximately 1-5 humorous piece/issue. Needs humorous nonfiction. Length: 1,500 words. To query: be familiar with magazine; make sure article is appropriate; study writer's guidelines. For first contact send cover letter, query and published tearsheets to David Robinson. Reports back within 1 month; if interested or not. Samples are filed or returned with SASE. Buys first time rights, reprint rights, one-time rights or negotiates rights purchased. Pays 10¢/word or $50-$250 for 500-2,500 words. Offers 40% kill fee.

Tips: "It's best to query specific articles by letter."

CURRENT COMEDY, Suite 4D, 165 W. 47th St., New York NY 10036. Estab. 1954. For "speakers, toastmasters, business executives, public officials, educators, public relations specialists and communication professionals. We are looking for funny, performable one-liners and short jokes that deal with happenings in the news, fads, trends and other topical subjects. The accent is on laugh-out-loud comedy. We are particularly interested in material that can be used by speakers and toastmasters: lines for beginning a speech, ending a speech, acknowledging an introduction, specific speaking occasions—any clever, original comments that would be of use to a person making a speech. We are also in the market for jokes used to respond to specific speaking situations (microphone feedback, broken air conditioning, hecklers). Short, sharp comment on business trends and events is also desirable." Submit 25 gags/jokes per batch. Preferred format is 8½×11 paper. For first contact, send sample material/jokes/gags. Reports back in 3-4 weeks. Returns material if accompanied by SASE. Keeps materials on file. Buys all rights. Pays $12/joke.

Tips: "Different people see familiar subjects in unique ways. I write half the jokes, but outside writers make up half of the material in *Current Comedy*."

CURRENTS, 314 N. 20th St., Colorado Springs CO 80904. (719)473-2466. Estab. 1979. Quarterly magazine for whitewater river enthusiasts. Circ. 10,000. Needs humorous illustration, humorous writing and spot cartoons.

Humorous Illustration: Buys approximately 2-4 humorous illustrations/year for articles and spots. When hiring a freelance humorous illustrator, these abilities are considered: ability to conceptualize well and clever ideas—good use of metaphors; a bold, powerful, attention-getting drawing style; effective use of humor; not too much exaggeration or distortion; knowledge of the subject matter. For first contact, send cover letter, b&w tearsheets or inquiry letter with roughs of proposed illustrations to Eric Leaper, Editor. In reviewing humorous illustrations we look for "illustrations pertaining to whitewater rivers/river running. We need people who have done their 'homework' on what is going on in the sport of river running and who are readers of past issues of *Currents* and have professional artistic skills." Reports back in 2 weeks. Samples are returned by SASE. Buys first time rights. Pays $10/b&w page; Does not publish color.

Humorous Writing: Buys approximately 1 humorous piece/year. Needs humorous fiction/nonfiction and interviews. Subject matter must pertain to whitewater rivers/river running. Length: 600-1,200 words. To query: be familiar with magazine; make sure article is appropriate; study writer's guidelines. Send $1 for sample copy and guidelines. For first contact, send cover letter, manuscript, query, published tearsheets, outline of proposed story to Eric Leaper. Reports back in 2-4 weeks. Samples are returned with SASE. Buys first time rights. Pays $25.

Tips: "It is very difficult to be published in *Currents*. You must know subject matter well. Our readers are experienced paddlers and politically knowledgeable. Be sure to read a copy of *Currents* to get a feel for what we our readers care about."

DAKOTA COUNTRY, Box 2714, Bismark ND 58502. (701)255-3031. Estab. 1979. Monthly consumer magazine. Circ. 10,350. Needs comic strips, humorous writing and spot cartoons. Accepts previously published cartoons and humorous articles.

Gag Cartoons: Buys 2-3 gag cartoons/issue, 24-30/year on hunting and fishing. Preferred gag cartoon format is single panel b&w line art. Query with 10-30 rough drawings/batch to Bill Mitzel, Publisher. Reports back in 2 weeks. Returns material if accompanied by SASE. Buys reprint rights. Pays $10/b&w on acceptance.

Humorous Illustration: Buys approximately 1-2 humorous illustrations/issue, 5-6/year for articles. When hiring a freelance humorous illustrator, these abilities are considered: a truly unique drawing style, ability to conceptualize well and clever ideas—good use of metaphors; a clean, graphically-pleasing drawing style; effective use of humor; ability to "fun up" an otherwise "flat" manuscript. For first contact send b&w tearsheet to Bill Mitzel. In reviewing humorous illustration we look for originality and humor. Reports back in 2 weeks. Samples are returned by SASE. Buys reprint rights. Pays $25/b&w page on acceptance.

Humorous Writing: Buys 1 humorous piece/issue, 3-4/year. Needs humorous fiction/nonfiction, interviews, "slice-of-life," anecdotes, "fillers" and cartoon stories. Subject matter includes hunting and fishing. Length: 1,200 words. To query, make sure article is appropriate. For first contact, send manuscript and published tearsheets to Bill Mitzel, Publisher. Reports back in 2 weeks. Samples are returned with SASE. Buys reprint rights. Pays $30-50 for 1,200-1,500 words.

DOG FANCY, Box 6050, Mission Viejo CA 92690. Estab. 1969. Monthly consumer magazine. Needs gag cartoons and spot cartoons. Accepts previously published cartoons and humorous articles.

Gag Cartoons: Buys 2 gag cartoons/issue; 24/year. Prefers gag cartoons on dogs. Preferred gag cartoon format is single panel b&w line art with gagline. Query with 5-10 rough drawings/batch to Kim Thornton, Editor. Reports back within 6 weeks. Returns material if accompanied by a SASE. Buys one-time rights. Pays $35 minimum for b&w. Pays on publication.

Tips: "Truly know dogs. A lot of people think they know about dogs, but unless they are really familiar with dog breeds, activities, actions and personalities, their cartoons aren't very funny at all."

Humorous Illustration: Buys approximately 1 humorous illustration/year for articles. When hiring a freelance humorous illustrator, these abilities are considered: ability to conceptualize well and clever ideas — good use of metaphors; not too much exaggeration or distortion; ability to "fun up" an otherwise "flat" manuscript; businesslike attitude — meets deadlines and responsive to editor's needs. Samples are filed or returned by SASE. Buys one-time rights.

Humorous Writing: Buys approximately 1 humorous piece/year. Needs humorous nonfiction. To query: be familiar with magazine; make sure article is appropriate; study writer's guidelines. Send $3.50 and SASE for copy. For first contact send query to Kim Thornton. Reports back within 6 weeks. Samples are filed or returned with SASE. Buys one-time rights. Pays $50-150 for 500-1,500 words.

EAP DIGEST (EMPLOYEE ASSISTANCE PROGRAM), Performance Resource Press, 2145 Crooks Rd., Troy MI 48084. (313)643-9580. FAX: (313)643-4435. Estab. 1980. Bimonthly trade journal. Circ. 20,000. Needs gag cartoons. Accepts previously published cartoons.

Gag Cartoons: Buys 1 gag cartoon/issue, 4-6/year, on employees' personal problems, primarily substance abuse, and other problems an employee might seek help for, especially help from an employee assistance counselor. Preferred gag cartoon formats are single panel, double panel with gagline, with/without balloons. Query with any number of rough drawings/batch to Janet M. Hearle, Managing Editor. Reports back in 4 weeks. Returns material only if requested. Buys first-time rights and one-time rights. Pays $15-30/b&w on publication.

EARTHWATCH MAGAZINE, 680 Mount Auturn St., Watertown MA 02272. (617)926-8200. FAX: (617)926-8532. Estab. 1971. Bimonthly consumer magazine. Circ. 50,000. Needs humorous illustration, cartoon narratives, caricatures, gag cartoons and spot cartoons. Accepts previously published cartoons.

Gag Cartoons: Send submissions to Thomas W. Knowlton, Director of Publications. Reports back within 2 weeks. Returns material if requested. Buys first time rights. Pays $150/b&w page minimum; $250/color. Pays on acceptance.

Humorous Illustration: Send submissions to Thomas W. Knowlton. Reports back within 2 weeks. Buys first time rights. Pays $150 minimum/b&w page; $250/color. Pays on acceptance.

ENVIRONMENT, Suite 400, 4000 Albemarle St. NW, Washington DC 20016. (202)362-6445. Estab. 1958. Monthly consumer magazine and trade journal. Circ. 12,000. Needs spot cartoons. Accepts previously published cartoons.

Gag Cartoons: Buys 1 gag cartoon/issue, 10-12/year on environmental topics—acid rain, ozone hole, deforestation, pollution, etc. Preferred gag cartoon format is single panel, without gagline, b&w line art, with gagline, b&w wash. Query with 10-20 rough drawings/batch to Ann Rickerich, Production/Graphics Manager. Reports back in 2 months. Returns material if accompanied by SASE. Buys first time rights. Pays $35/ b&w on publication.
Tips: "We only publish witty cartoons on environmental subjects. Stay away from anything too judgemental or negative."

EQUILIBRIUM[10], Box 162, Golden CO 80401. Estab. 1984. Monthly consumer magazine. Circ. 15,000. Needs comic strips, humorous illustration, humorous writing, cartoon narratives, caricatures, gag cartoons, spot cartoons and specials on opposites and equilibrium. Accepts previously published cartoons and humorous articles.
Gag Cartoons: Buys 10 gag cartoons/issue; 150/year. Preferred gag cartoon formats are single panel without gagline b&w line art, double panel with gagline b&w wash and multi-panel. Query with 3-5 rough drawings/batch to Art Department. Reports back within 180 days if interested. Returns material if accompanied by a SASE. Negotiates rights purchased. Pays $20 minimum for b&w and $40 minimum for color. Pays on publication.
Tips: Query for author's guidelines first. "Read our literature and enter the official author's cheapstakes sweepstakes contest."
Humorous Illustration: Buys approximately 5 humorous illustrations/issue; 50/year for articles and spots. When hiring a freelance humorous illustrator, these abilities are considered: a truly unique drawing style; ability to conceptualize well and clever ideas— good use of metaphors; a clean, graphically-pleasing drawing style; a bold, powerful, attention-getting drawing style; a subtle, understated drawing style; not too much exaggeration or distortion; ability to "fun up" an otherwise "flat" manuscript; businesslike attitude—meets deadlines and responsive to editor's needs. For first contact send cover letter, b&w or color tearsheets, slides and client list to current Art Editor. In reviewing humorous illustration we look for material that fits the style of our magazine. Reports back within 6 months if interested. Samples are filed for 2 years maximum if undecided or returned by SASE. Negotiates rights purchased. Pays $100 minimum/b&w page. Pays on publication.
Humorous Writing: Buys approximately 10 humorous piece/issue; 50/year. Needs humorous fiction/nonfiction, cartoon stories and humorous anecdotes, "fillers." Length: under 1,200 words. To query: be familiar with magazine and study writer's guidelines. Send $4.00 and SASE for copy. For first contact send cover letter "with a processing fee of $5 (submissions will be omitted if not included)" and query to Art Editor. Reports back within 6 months. Samples are filed until published or returned with SASE. Negotiates rights purchased. Pays $10-100 for 50-1,200 words. Offers 10% kill fee.

FAIRFIELD COUNTY WOMAN, 15 Bank St., Stanford CT 06901. (203)323-3105. Estab. 1982. Monthly consumer magazine (and tabloid). Circ. 50,000. Needs comic strips (possibly), humorous illustration, humorous writing and spot cartoons. Accepts previously published cartoons and humorous articles.
Humorous Illustration: Buys approximately 2 humorous illustrations/issue, 20/year for articles and spots. Works on assignment only. When hiring a freelance humorous illustrator, these abilities are considered: a truly unique drawing style, conceptualizes well and has clever ideas—good use of metaphors; a clean, graphically-pleasing drawing style; uses humor effectively; can "fun up" an otherwise "flat" manuscript; is businesslike, meets deadlines and is responsive to editor's needs. For first contact, send cover letter, b&w and color tearsheets and slides to Joan Honig. Reports only if interested. Samples are returned by SASE. Buys first time rights. Pays $25/b&w page, $150/color cover.

Humorous Writing: Buys approximately 2 humorous pieces/issue, 24/year. Needs humorous nonfiction and humorous "slice-of-life." Subject matter includes women's issues, monthly column on man's point of view, family, children, relationships and career. Length: 1,000 words. To query: be familiar with magazine; study writer's guidelines. Send $1.50 and SASE for copy. For first contact, send cover letter, writing sample and published tearsheets to Joan Honig, Editor. Reports only if interested. Samples returned with SASE. Buys first time rights. Pays $35-65 for 600-1,200 words.

FARM & RANCH LIVING, 5400 South 60th Street, Greendale WI 53129. (414)423-0100. FAX: (414)423-0138. Estab. 1978. Bimonthly consumer magazine. Circ. 350,000. Needs gag cartoons. Accepts previously published cartoons.

Gag Cartoons: Buys 6-7 gag cartoons/issue; 36-42/year. Prefers gag cartoons on farm and ranch situations. Preferred gag cartoon formats are single panel b&w line art, gagline with b&w wash and balloons. Send to Bob Ottum, Editor. Reports back within approximately 3 weeks. Returns material if accompanied by a SASE. Buys one-time rights. Pays $35 minimum for b&w. Pays on acceptance.

FFA NEW HORIZONS, P.O. Box 15160, Alexandria VA 22309. (703)360-3600. FAX (703)360-5524. Estab. 1952. Bimonthly association magazine. Circ. 420,000. Needs gag cartoons, humorous illustration and spot cartoons. Accepts previously published cartoons.

Gag Cartoons: Buys 2 gag cartoons per/issue. Prefers gag cartoons on teenagers, agriculture, school dating and teachers. Doesn't want to see gag cartoons on stereotypical farm kids/farmers. For us, the "dream" gag cartoon would be "youthful, hip and very funny." Preferred gag cartoon format is single panel, b&w line art with gagline. Query with 8 rough drawings/batch to Andrew Markwart, Managing Editor. Reports back with weeks. Buys one-time rights. Pays $20 b&w. Pays on acceptance.

Humorous Illustration: Buys approximately 2 humorous illustrations/issue for articles. Works on assignment only. When hiring a freelance humorous illustrator, these abilities are considered: ability to conceptualize well and clever ideas—good use of metaphors, humor effective use of humor, flexibility, broad potential in drawing style. For first contact send cover letter and b&w tearsheets to Andrew Markwart. Reports back within weeks. Samples are filed. Buys all rights. Pays minimum $50 b&w page. Pays on acceptance. Tips: "Many of our cartoonists have been around awhile, so we're ready for some fresh ideas and styles!"

FIELD & STREAM, 2 Park Ave., New York NY 10016. Estab. 1895. Monthly consumer magazine. Circ. 2 million. Needs humorous illustration, humorous writing and gag cartoons.

Gag Cartoons: Prefers gag cartoons on hunting and fishing. Doesn't want to see gag cartoons on talking animals. Preferred gag cartoon format is single panel. Send submissions to Duncan Barnes, Editor. Reports back in 6-8 weeks. Returns material. Buys first time rights. Pays $100/b&w.

Tips: "Be familiar with the magazine and its subject matter."

Humorous Illustration: Buys approximately 1 humorous illustration/issue, 12/year for articles and spots. Works on assignment only. When hiring a freelance humorous illustrator, these abilities are considered: ability to conceptualize well and clever ideas—good use of metaphors; effective use of humor; not too much exaggeration or distortion; flexibility, broad potential in drawing style; businesslike attitude—meets deadlines and responsive to editor's needs. For first contact, send color tearsheets and color promo pieces to Mindy Stanton, Associate Art Director. In reviewing humorous illustration we look for style, ideas and drawing technique. Samples are filed. Buys first time rights. Pays $700/color page, $150-200/b&w spots. Pays on acceptance.

Humorous Writing: Buys approximately 12 humorous pieces/issue. Needs humorous nonfiction. Subject matter must be humor that relates to fishing or hunting. "See our magazine." Length: 1,000-1,500 words. To query: be familiar with magazine (most important) and make sure article is appropriate. For first contact send cover letter and manuscript to Duncan Barnes. Reports back in 6-8 weeks. Samples are not returned. Buys first time rights. Pays $800 for 1,000-1,500 words.

FILMCLIPS, Box 1335, New York NY 10013. (718)899-3947. Estab. 1988. Quarterly newsletter. Circ. 500. Needs humorous writing, caricatures and gag cartoons. Accepts previously published cartoons and humorous articles.

Gag Cartoons: Buys 15 gag cartoons/year on film industry and movie memorabilia. Preferred gag cartoon formats are single panel b&w line art, with gagline, b&w wash, with balloons. Query with 1-10 rough drawings/batch to Dan Karpf, Editor. Reports back in 30 days. Returns material if accompanied by SASE. Buys first time rights, reprint rights and one-time rights. Pays $5/b&w on publication.

Tips: "Know memorabilia collecting and/or the film industry."

Humorous Illustration: Buys approximately 10 humorous illustrations/year for spots. When hiring a freelance humorous illustrator, these abilities are considered: ability to conceptualize well and clever ideas—good use of metaphors; a bold, powerful, attention-getting drawing style; effective use of humor; ability to "fun up" an otherwise "flat" manuscript. For first contact, send cover letter, b&w tearsheets and b&w promo pieces to Dan Karpf. In reviewing humorous illustration we look for an "understanding of our newsletter and its contents." Reports back in 30 days. Samples are returned by SASE. Buys first time rights, reprint rights and one-time rights. Pays $5/b&w page. Pays on publication.

Humorous Writing: Buys approximately 1 humorous piece/issue, 5/year. Needs humorous nonfiction, humorous interviews, humorous "slice-of-life" and humorous anecdotes and "fillers." Subject matter includes entertainment industry and/or movie memorabilia collecting. Length: 200-600 words. To query, make sure article is appropriate for us. For first contact, send manuscript and query to Dan Karpf. Reports back in 30 days. Samples are returned with SASE. Buys first time rights, reprint rights and one-time rights. Pays 1¢/word.

THE FINAL EDITION, P.O. Box 294, Rhododendron OR 97049. (503)622-4798. Estab. 1982. Monthly company magazine. Circ. 8,000. Needs comic strips, humorous illustration, humorous writing, cartoon narratives, caricatures, gag cartoons, spot cartoons and portfolios. "We can feature one artist per month. It is something new that we are trying out!" Accepts previously published cartoons and humorous articles. Preferred gag cartoon format is single panel, double panel, multi-panel, without gagline, with gagline, with balloons and b&w line art. Query with 10-15 rough drawings/batch to Michael P. Jones, Editor. Reports back within 2 months. Returns material if accompanied by a SASE. Buys first time rights. Pays in published copies.

Humorous Illustration: When hiring a freelance humorous illustrator, these abilities are considered: a truly unique drawing style, ability to conceptualize well and clever ideas—good use of metaphors; bold, powerful, attention-getting drawing style; a subtle, understated drawing style; effective use of humor; not too much exaggeration or distortion; flexibility, broad potential in drawing style; ability to "fun up" an otherwise "flat" manuscript and businesslike attitude—meets deadlines and responsive to my needs. For first contact send cover letter, resume, client list, b&w tearsheets and portfolio to Michael P. Jones, Editor. "Just starting to incorporate into publication, but we'll be looking for new and interesting ways of dealing with real life issues." Reports back within 2 months. Samples are returned by SASE. Buys first time rights. Pays in published copies. Tips: "Give us enough samples of your work so that we can see the real artist within you."

Humorous Writing: Needs humorous nonfiction, fiction, interviews, cartoon stories, humorous "slice-of-life" and humorous anecdotes, "fillers." Subject matter includes anti-racism, anti-pollution, anti-hunting, anti-logging and other environmental and social issues. For first contact send cover letter, published tearsheets and writing sample to Michael P. Jones, Editor. Reports back within 2 months. Samples are returned with SASE. Buys first time rights.

Tips: "Be yourself! Don't copy someone else's style. Develop your own individualized style. And, stay away from what's in 'vogue' today—your work should be timeless, just like fine art."

FLORIDA LEADER, Box 14081, Gainesville Fl 32604. (904)373-6907. Estab. 1982. Quarterly consumer magazine. Circ. 27,000. Needs comic strips and spot cartoons.

Gag Cartoons: Buys 3 gag cartoons/issue on school subjects. Preferred gag cartoon format is single panel, with gagline, multi-panel, with balloons. Query with 3-5 rough drawings/batch to Jeffrey Riemersma, Art Director. Reports back in 2 weeks. Returns material if accompanied by SASE. Buys reprint rights. Pays $25/b&w and $35/color on acceptance.

Humorous Illustration: Buys approximately 3 humorous illustration/issue for articles. Works on assignment only. When hiring a freelance humorous illustrator, these abilities are considered: a truly unique drawing style, ability to conceptualize well and clever ideas—good use of metaphors; effective use of humor; ability to "fun up" an otherwise "flat" manuscript; businesslike attitude—meets deadlines and responsive to editor's needs. For first contact, send cover letter and portfolio to Jeffrey Riemersma, Art Director. In reviewing humorous illustration "we look for ability to work with college-related subject matter." Reports back in 2 weeks. Samples are returned by SASE. Negotiates rights purchased. Pays $25/b&w page, $35/color page, $50/color cover. Pays on acceptance.

FLOWER & GARDEN MAGAZINE, 4251 Pennsylvania Ave., Kansas City MO 64111. (816)531-5730. Estab. 1957. Bimonthly consumer magazine. Circ. 600,000.

Humorous Illustration: Buys approximately 2-3 humorous illustrations/issue for spots. In reviewing humorous illustration we look for gardening humor. Reports back in 6 weeks. Samples not filed are returned. Buys first time rights. Pays $20+ page on acceptance.

Tips: "Positive humor appreciated (no nagging housewife humor, for example). Must be garden-related."

FORUM, 208 W. Pensacola Street, Tallahassee FL 32399-1700. (904)224-1161. Estab. 1982. Quarterly trade journal. Circ. 53,000. Needs humorous writing, gag cartoons and spot cartoons. Accepts previously published cartoons and humorous articles.

Gag Cartoons: Prefers gag cartoons on educational, political or generic topics. For us, the "dream" gag cartoon would be pro-education, pro-union. Preferred gag cartoon format is single panel b&w line art, or double panel with gagline b&w wash. Query with 3 rough drawings/batch to Carey McNamara, Art Director. Reports back if interested. Returns material if accompanied by a SASE. Buys one-time rights. Pays $10 minimum for b&w. Pays on publication.

Humorous Illustration: Buys humorous illustrations for spots. When hiring a freelance humorous illustrator, these abilities are considered: a truly unique drawing style; ability to conceptualize well and clever ideas—good use of metaphors; businesslike attitude—meets deadlines and responsive to editor's needs. For first contact send cover letter, b&w tearsheets and client list to Carey McNamara. In reviewing humorous illustrations "we look for distinct style—tight concept." Reports back if interested. Samples are filed or returned by SASE. Buys one-time rights. Pays $100 minimum for b&w page.

Humorous Writing: Buys approximately 6 humorous pieces/year. Needs humorous nonfiction/fiction, humorous interviews, humorous "slice-of-life", cartoon stories and humorous anecdotes. "fillers." Subject matter is education-related. Length: under 200 words. To query: make sure article is appropriate and study writer's guidelines. For first contact send cover letter, writing sample and published tearsheets to April Herrie, Editor. Reports back within 3 weeks. Samples are filed. Negotiates rights purchased. Pays $5-20 for a piece.

THE FREEDONIA GAZETTE, Darien 28, New Hope PA 18938-1224. (215)862-9734. Estab. 1978. Semi-annual fanzine. Circ. 400. Needs comic strips, humorous illustration, humorous writing, caricatures, gag cartoons and spot cartoons. Accepts previously published cartoons and humorous articles.

Gag Cartoons: Buys 1-2 gag cartoons/issue, 2-4/year. Prefers gag cartoons on the Marx Brothers and their films; use of "groucho glasses" as a disguise. For us, the "dream" gag cartoon would be "funny and relevant to the effect of Marx films on the world at large." Preferred gag cartoon formats are single panel without gagline, b&w line art only, double panel, with gagline, multi-panel, with balloons. Query with 1-2 rough drawings/batch to Neal Gorman, Cartoon Editor. Reports back in 10 days. Returns material if accompanied by SASE. Negotiates rights purchased. Pays $4/b&w on publication.

Tips: "Be original, be funny, have a real sense of appreciation for the humor of the Marx Brothers."

Humorous Illustration: Buys approximately 1-2 humorous illustrations/issue, 2-4/year for covers, articles and spots. When hiring a freelance humorous illustrator, these abilities are considered: a truly unique drawing style, ability to conceptualize well and clever ideas—good use of metaphors; a clean, graphically-pleasing drawing style; a bold, powerful, attention-getting drawing style; a subtle, understated drawing style; and effective use of humor. For first contact, send cover letter, b&w tearsheets and b&w promo piece to Neal Gorman, Art Director. In reviewing humorous illustration we look for originality, "not just a copy from a photograph"; creativity, unique drawing style that stands out from other artists; unusual shapes which can have text filled-in around them. Reports back in 10 days. Samples are filed or returned by SASE. Negotiates rights purchased. Pays $4/b&w page, $8/b&w cover on publication.

Tips: "Don't copy from a photograph; chances are most of our readers also own that photo. Be sure artwork is camera-ready so we can do it justice."

Humorous Writing: Buys approximately 1-2 humorous pieces/issue, 2-4/year. Needs humorous fiction/nonfiction and anecdotes, "fillers." "As you've guessed by now, we're very narrow-minded. Humorous writing must relate to the Marx Brothers and their effect on the writer." Length: 100-1,000 words. To query: make sure that your article is appropriate; and be a fan of the Marx Brothers. For first contact, send cover letter and outline of proposed story to Paul Wesolowski, Editor-in-Chief. Reports back in 10 days Samples are filed or returned with SASE. Negotiates rights purchased. Pays $4-8 for 500-1,000 words.

Tips: "Be original. Be funny. Know the difference between being inspired by the Marxes and lamely copying them. We're a not-for-profit organization so we don't pay editors, writers or artists much except in free copies of any issue their work appears in. But we're willing to work with a submission rather than reject it outright, and the result will be good looking tearsheets which can help land a 'real' assignment from a high-paying publication."

FUNNY BUSINESS HUMOR SERVICE, 210 Hollywood St., Fitchburg MA 01420. (508)342-1074. Estab. 1978. Monthly newsletter and monthly comedy booklet (filled with jokes). Circ. 150. Needs humorous writing and topical one-liners.

Humorous Writing: Buys approximately 1,200 humorous one liners/issue. Needs humorous nonfiction, humorous "slice-of-life," and humorous anecdotes, "fillers"; 5 to 15-word one liners in sentence form. Subject matter includes "dumb friends", the program director, the president and the hottest topic in the news. Length: 5-20 words. To query: study writer's guidelines. Send $1 and SASE for copy. For first contact, send writing sample and one liners on spec. to Jack Raymond, Editor. Reports back in 20 days. Samples are filed. Pays $1-5.

Tips: "We need your best one liners and that means send only the best. Pre-test material on friends and family to make sure it's funny!"

GEM SHOW NEWS, Rt. #2, Box 78, Blue Ridge TX 75004. (214)752-5192. FAX: (214)752-5205. Estab. 1977. Trade journal published 10 times/year. Circ. 12,000-30,000. Needs humorous writing, gag cartoons, spot cartoons, humor gem, jewelry and mineral related. Accepts previously published cartoons and humorous articles.

Gag Cartoons: Buys 1-2 gag cartoons/issue, 12/year on gemstones, jewelry, mineral collecting, security (securiy related must be positive theme). For us, the "dream" gag cartoon would be "a crook not getting away with an attempted hold-up." Preferred gag cartoon formats are single panel, b&w line art, double panel with gagline, multi-panel. Send submissions to Edward J. Tripp, Publisher. Reports back in 2 months. Returns material if accompanied by SASE. Buys first time rights, reprint rights and one-time rights. Pays $8/b&w on acceptance on simple one panel cartoons; 5¢ per word on articles.

Humorous Illustration: Buys approximately 1 humorous illustration/issue, 10/year for spots. When hiring a freelance humorous illustrator, these abilities are considered: businesslike attitude—meets deadlines and responsive to editor's needs. For first contact send finished items only for acceptance/rejection to Edward J. Tripp. Reports back in 2 months only if interested. Samples are returned by SASE if requested. Pays $8/b&w page.

Tips: "Try your best. Don't be discouraged; keep up the good work. Don't take a rejection too seriously, you may get another some day."

Humorous Writing: Buys approximately 5 humorous pieces/year. Needs humorous nonfiction, humorous interviews, humorous "slice-of-life," anecdotes and "fillers." Subject matter includes gem jewelry, mineral collecting. Length: most are 1,000 words; annual issue, 3,000 words. To query: study writer's guidelines. Send 90¢ and SASE (9×12) for copy. For first contact send finished pieces ready for acceptance/rejection to Edward J. Tripp. Reports back in 2 months. Samples are returned with SASE. Pays 5¢/word for 1,000-3,000 words.

GENESIS, 22 W 27th St., New York NY 10001. (212)725-4811. FAX: (212)689-7814. Estab. 1973. Monthly consumer magazine. Circ. 185,000. Needs gag cartoons.

Gag Cartoons: Buys 3-4 gag cartoons/issue; 36/year. Prefers gag cartoons on "risque subjects," sex gags—no gross gags. Doesn't want to see gag cartoons of people at a bar or people in bed with the generic gag line. For us the "dream" gag cartoon would be well-drawn, humorous looking and "off the wall." Preferred gag cartoon format is single panel with/without b&w line art, b&w wash or color wash. Query (no roughs) to Paul J. Maringelli, Art Director. Reports back within 1 week. Returns material if accompanied by a SASE. Buys first time rights. Pays $75 minimum for b&w/$200 minimum for color.

Tips: "I'm always looking for someone new and funny! B&w cartoons should fill a 4½"×4½" box nicely, 4-color cartoons should fill a 9½"×7" box."

GENT, (see *Cavalier*)

Take Me Back to Those Carefree Days of the Spanish Inquisition: *Thanks to his advertisements in illustration directories and high visibility in consumer magazines, the phone in Gary Hallgren's Mastic Beach, New York studio rings with regularity. Recalling work Hallgren did for* New York *magazine,* Seventeen *Associate Art Director Dania Martinez felt that his "free and casual" drawing style would be ideal for an essay about time travel through different eras. But when it came to deadline, Hallgren was given anything but a century to turn around his art—rather, he was only given a week. Martinez accepted Hallgren's final art without changes and purchased one-time rights to the illustration.*

GLASS FACTORY DIRECTORY, Box 7138, Pittsburgh PA 15213. (412)362-5136. Estab. 1912. Annual book. Circ. 1,500. Needs gag cartoons and spot cartoons. Accepts previously published cartoons.

Gag Cartoons: Buys 3-4 gag cartoons/issue, 4-6/year. Prefers gag cartoons on making glass. Doesn't want to see gag cartoons on breaking glass of any kind. For us, the "dream" gag cartoon would be "one that takes the improbable (not the impossible) and makes it visually real." Preferred gag cartoon format is single panel with/without gagline, b&w line art. Query with any number of rough drawings/batch to Liz Scott, Managing Editor. Reports back in 2-4 months. Returns material if accompanied by SASE. Buys all rights. Pays $25/b&w on acceptance (or on publication, depending on situation).

Tips: A gag cartoonist should "learn about making glass—read, visit plants, etc."

GOLF ILLUSTRATED, 3 Park Ave., New York NY 10010. (212)340-4805. FAX: (212)725-3962. Estab. 1985. Monthly consumer magazine. Circ. 450,000. Needs cartoon narratives, caricatures, gag cartoons and spot cartoons.

Gag Cartoons: Buys 1-2 gag cartoons/issue. Prefers gag cartoons on golf. Preferred gag cartoon format is single panel. Query with 3-10 rough drawings/batch to Al Barkow, Editor-in-Chief. Reports back within 7 days. Returns material if accompanied by a SASE. Buys first time rights, negotiates rights purchased. Pays $75 minimum for b&w; $100 minimum color.

Humorous Illustration: Buys approximately 6 humorous illustrations/issue; 20/year for articles. Works on assignment only. When hiring a freelance humorous illustrator, considers these abilities: a truly unique drawing style; ability to conceptualize well and clever ideas—good use of metaphors; effective use of humor; flexibility, broad potential in drawing style; ability to "fun up" an otherwise "flat" manuscript; businesslike attitude—meets deadlines and responsive to editor's needs. For first contact send cover letter, b&w or color tearsheets to Ellen Oxild, Art Director. In reviewing humorous illustration we look for high quality and conceptualization. Reports back within 5 days. Samples are returned by SASE. Buys reprint rights. Pays $500 minimum for color page.

© Gary Hallgren

Humorous Writing: Buys 4-6 humorous pieces/year. Needs humorous nonfiction and humorous anecdotes, "fillers". Subject matter is golf. Length: 750-1,200 words. To query: be familiar with magazine; make sure article is appropriate. For first contact send humorous writing to Al Barrow, Editor-in-Chief. Reports back within 7 days. Samples are returned with SASE. Buys reprint rights. Pays 75¢/word. Offers 10% kill fee.

GOOD READING FOR EVERYONE, Box 40, Sunshine Park, Litchfield IL 62056. (217)324-3425. Estab. 1964. Monthly consumer magazine. Circ. 5,000. Needs spot cartoons.
Gag Cartoons: Buys 1 gag cartoon/issue, 12/year on family, business, weather, sports and seasons. Preferred gag cartoon format is single panel, b&w line art, with gagline. Send finished art. Reports back in 3 months. Returns material if accompanied by SASE. Buys first time rights. Pays $15/b&w on acceptance.
Humorous Writing: Buys approximately 1 humorous piece/issue, 12/year. Needs humorous nonfiction, humorous "slice-of-life" and anecdotes, "fillers." Length: 200 words. To query: study our writer's guidelines. Send 50¢ and SASE for copy. For first contact, send cover letter and manuscript to Editor. Reports back in 3 months. Samples returned with SASE. Buys first time rights. Pays $20 for 200 words.

GUIDELINES MAGAZINE: A ROUNDTABLE FOR WRITERS AND EDITORS, Box 608, Pittsburg MO 65724. (417)993-5544. Estab. 1988. Four newsletters and four consumer magazines. Circ. 700. Needs comic strips, humorous illustration, humorous writing, cartoon narratives, caricatures, gag cartoons and spot cartoons. Accepts previously published cartoons and humorous articles.
Gag Cartoons: Buys 2-3 gag cartoons/issue; 20/year. Prefers gag cartoons on writing and/or editing. Preferred gag cartoon format is single panel without gagline, b&w line art. Query with 2-4 rough drawings/batch to Susan Salaki, Editor. Reports back within 1 month. Returns material if accompanied by a SASE. Buys first time rights and one-time rights. Pays $5-15 for b&w. Pays on publication.
Humorous Illustration: Buys approximately 2 humorous illustrations/issue; 20/year for articles and spots. When hiring a freelance humorous illustrator, these abilities are considered: a truly unique drawing style; ability to conceptualize well and clever ideas—

good use of metaphors; a clean, graphically-pleasing drawing style; a bold, powerful, attention-getting drawing style; a subtle, understated drawing style; effective use of humor; flexibility, broad potential in drawing style; ability to "fun up" an otherwise "flat" manuscript; businesslike attitude—meets deadlines and responsive to editor's needs. For first contact send cover letter and b&w promo piece to Susan Salaki. In reviewing humorous illustration we look for material appropriate to the magazine's writing and editing topics. Reports back within 1 month. Samples are returned by SASE. Buys first time rights and one-time rights. Pays $5-15/b&w page. Pays on publication.

Tips: "The goal of GM is to help writers understand the needs and special problems of editors; likewise, we strive to help editors understand what writers are having problems with as they progress in their writing careers. Cartoonists and illustrators who can capture this interaction effectively are especially needed."

Humorous Writing: Buys approximately 1 humorous piece/issue; 10/year. Needs humorous nonfiction, humorous "slice-of-life", humorous anecdotes, "fillers" but the #1 need is humorous interviews. Subject matter includes writers and the potential creativity derived from dreams, writers of the 19th century and romance from the writer's perspective. Length: 400-800 words. To query: study writer's guidelines. Send $4 and SASE for copy. For first contact send cover letter and manuscript to Susan Salaki. Reports back within 1 month. Samples are returned with SASE. Buys first time rights and one-time rights. Pays $5-30 for 400-800 words. Offers 25% kill fee.

Solidly on Shaky Ground: *Peter Spacek, a New York City-based humorous illustrator popped out this drawing for* Barron's *within the publication's short two day deadline. Spacek was assigned the black-and-white job after showing* Barron's *Art Director Elin Von Spreckeisen his portfolio. Von Spreckeisen briefly explained the gist of the article to Spacek and let the illustrator "do whatever he wanted." "The idea I wanted to convey," says Spacek, "was that people should beware—things may not seem as they really are."*

© Peter Spacek

HEAVEN BONE MAGAZINE, Box 486, Chester NY 10918. (914)469-9018. Estab. 1986. Semi-annual literary magazine. Circ. 500. Needs comic strips and humorous illustration. Accepts previously published cartoons.

Gag Cartoons: Query with 3-10 rough drawings/batch to Steve Hirsch. Reports in 6 months. Returns material if acompanied by SASE. Buys one-time rights. Pays in copies of publication.

Humorous Illustration: "Haven't used any yet, but interested in seeing spots." A freelance humorous illustrator must "understand our needs before submitting." For first contact send cover letter and b&w tearsheets to Steve Hirsch. Reports back in 6 months. Samples are filed or returned by SASE. Buys one-time rights. Pays in copies of publication.

Tips "We like esoteric, literary and spiritual humor."

HIGH SOCIETY MAGAZINE, 801 Second Avenue (10th Floor), New York NY 10017. (212)661-7878. FAX: (212)883-1244. Estab. 1976. Monthly sophisticated men's consumer magazine. Circ. 230,000. Needs comic strips, humorous illustration, caricatures, gag cartoons and spot cartoons.

Gag Cartoons: Buys 5 gag cartoons/issue; 60/year. Prefers gag cartoons on sex and sex-related topics. Preferred gag cartoon formats are b&w line art, multi-panel with balloons. Query with 10-20 rough drawings/batch to Steve Loshiavo, Cartoon Editor. Reports back within 3 weeks if interested. Returns material if accompanied by a SASE. Buys first time rights. Pays $100 minimum for color. Pays on acceptance.

Humorous Illustration: Buys approximately 5 humorous illustrations/year for articles. When hiring a freelance humorous illustrator, these abilities are considered: a clean, graphically-pleasing drawing style; businesslike attitude—meets deadlines and responsive to editor's needs. For first contact send cover letter and color tearsheets to Stephen Loshiavo. Reports back within 2 weeks. Samples are returned by SASE. Buys first time rights. Pays $100 minimum/color page.

Humorous Writing: Buys approximately 5 humorous pieces/issue; 12/year. Needs humorous interviews and humorous anecdotes, "fillers." To query: be familiar with magazine. For first contact send cover letter, writing sample and published tearsheets to Stephen Loshiavo. Reports back within 2 weeks. Samples are returned with SASE. Buys first time rights. Pays $200-400 for 6-8 pages. Offers 10% kill fee.

HIGHLIGHTS FOR CHILDREN, 803 Church St., Honesdale PA 18431. (717)253-1080. FAX: (717)-253-0179. Estab. 1946. Monthly children's magazine (11 issues a year, July/August is combined). Circ. 3,000,000. Needs humorous illustration, humorous writing, gag cartoons and spot cartoons.

Gag Cartoons: Buys 1-2 gag cartoons/issue for *Highlights*, approximately 250/year total for all publications. Doesn't want gag cartoons on flying carpets, snake charmers or kangaroo pouches. Preferred gag cartoon formats are single panel without gagline, b&w line art, double panel with gagline, multi-panel color wash. Send submissions to Kent L. Brown Jr., Editor. "No queries." Reports back in 30 days. Returns material. Buys all rights. Pays $20/b&w on acceptance.

Tips: "Capture humor that will apply to youngsters. Mostly we get adult cartoons."

Humorous Illustration: Buys approximately 3-5 humorous illustrations/issue, 50/year for covers, articles and spots. Works on assignment only. When hiring a freelance humorous illustrator, these abilities are considered: ability to conceptualize well and clever ideas—good use of metaphors; a clean, graphically-pleasing drawing style; effective use of humor; not too much exaggeration or distortion; flexibility, broad potential in drawing style; ability to "fun up" an otherwise "flat" manuscript; businesslike attitude—meets deadlines and responsive to editor's needs. For first contact, send cover letter, b&w or color tearsheets and resume to Roseanne Guararra, Art Director. Reports in 30 days. Samples are filed. Buys all rights. Pays $100 minimum/color page, $425 minimum/color cover. Pays on acceptance.

Humorous Writing: Buys approximately 2 humorous pieces/issue, 22/year. Needs humorous fiction/nonfiction, quizzes, games, puzzles and cartoon stories. No derogatory, violent or anti-authority humor. Length: very short—to 900 words. To query: be familiar with magazine, make sure article is appropriate and study free writer's guidelines. For first contact send cover letter (optional) and manuscript to Greg Linder, Assistant Editor. Reports back in 30 days. Samples are not filed; returned with SASE. Buys all rights. Pays 14¢/word.

Tips: "Humor at the expense of the child is not acceptable. We are looking for tasteful humor which makes children laugh. Humorous writing need not exclude warmth, realism and emotion."

HOME, 1776 Lake Worth Rd., Lake Worth FL 33460. (407)582-2099. FAX: (407)582-4667. Bimonthly consumer/controlled publication. Circ. 80,000-100,000. Needs humorous writing and spot cartoons. Accepts previously published humorous articles.

Humorous Writing: Buys approximately 1-2 humorous pieces/issue, 12/year. Needs humorous nonfiction, humorous "slice-of-life" and humorous anecdotes, "fillers" (rarely). "As a general interest publication, just about any subject is okay." Length: 600-1,200 words. To query: be familiar with magazine; study free writer's guidelines. For first contact send cover letter, query and manuscript to Richard Champlin, Editor. Samples are filed; returned only if requested. Buys first time rights, reprint rights (rarely) and one-time rights. Pays 30¢/line or $25 for 600-1,200 words.

Tips: "Don't use 'sophisticated' words as a basis of humor. A smooth, friendly tone must be maintained as if you were relating a humorous occurence that actually happened."

HOME EDUCATION MAGAZINE, Box 1083, Tonasket WA 98855. (509)486-1351. Estab. 1983. Bimonthly consumer magazine. Circ. 5,200. Needs humorous illustration and writing, caricatures, gag cartoons and spot cartoons. Accepts previously published cartoons and humorous articles.

Gag Cartoons: Buys 4-6 gag cartoons/year and "would use more if we could find good ones!" Prefers gag cartoons on home schooling only. For us, the "dream" gag cartoon would be "one that relates to home schooling with understanding of what it is." Preferred gag cartoon formats are single panel without gagline b&w line art, double panel with gagline b&w wash, multi-panel with balloons. Query with 4-6 rough drawings/batch to Helen Hegener, Managing Editor. Reports back in 2-4 weeks. Returns material only if accompanied by SASE. Buys one-time rights and "often negotiates reprint rights for our anthologies." Pays $5/b&w on acceptance.

Humorous Illustration: Buys approximately 2-4 humorous illustrations/issue for articles and spots. Works on assignment only. When hiring a freelance humorous illustrator, these abilities are considered: ability to conceptualize well and clever ideas — good use of metaphors; a clean, graphically-pleasing drawing style; a subtle, understated drawing style; effectivle use of humor; not too much exaggeration or distortion; flexibility, broad potential in drawing style; ability to "fun up" an otherwise "flat" manuscript; business-like attitude — meets deadlines and responsive to editor's needs; knowledge of the subject (home schooling). For first contact send cover letter and b&w tearsheets to Helen Hegener. Reports back in 2-4 weeks. Samples are not filed; returned only by SASE. Buys one-time rights and "often negotiates reprint rights when we publish collections from our magazine." Pays $100/b&w page on acceptance.

Tips: "Illustrations must relate to topic! Rarely use full page illustrations, usually only ⅙ to ⅓ page sizes."

Humorous Writing: Buys approximately 1-2 humorous pieces/issue. Needs humorous nonfiction, humorous interviews and humorous "slice-of-life." Subject matter must relate to home schooling. Length: 500-2,000 words. To query: be familiar with magazine; make sure article is appropriate; study writer's guidelines. Send $4.50 and SASE for copy. For first contact, send cover letter, query and manuscript to Helen Hegener. Reports back in 2-4 weeks. Samples are not filed; returned with SASE only. Buys one-time rights; "we often negotiate reprint rights for our anthologies." Pays $10 for 500 words.

Tips: "We can never find enough good humor pieces!"

HOUSEWIFE-WRITER'S FORUM, HOUSEWIVES' HUMOR: WOMEN'S HUMOR JOURNAL, Drawer 1518, Lafayette CA 94549-1518. (415)932-1143. Semi-annual digest. Circ. 1,000 (printed). Needs comic strips, humorous illustration and writing, caricatures, gag cartoons and spot cartoons. Accepts previously published cartoons and articles.

Gag Cartoons: Buys 2-3 gag cartoons/issue, 4-6/year on children, spouses, women's daily lives, domestic situations and career topics. Preferred gag cartoon formats are single panel without gagline b&w line art, double panel with gagline, multi-panel with balloons. Query with 1-5 rough drawings/batch to Deborah Haeseler, Editor/Publisher. Reports back in 2 months. Returns material if accompanied by SASE. Buys one-time rights. Pays $1/b&w on acceptance.

Tips: A gag cartoonist should "have strong artistic and humor writing skills. We don't match artists with writers due to time constraints."

Humorous Illustration: Buys approximately 1-3 humorous illustrations/issue, 2-6/year for covers and spots. When hiring a freelance humorous illustrator, these abiilties are considered: ability to conceptualize well and clever ideas—good use of metaphors; a clean, graphically-pleasing drawing style; a bold, powerful, attention-getting drawing style; a subtle, understated drawing style; effective use of humor; not too much exaggeration or distortion; flexibility, broad potential in drawing style; businesslike attitude— meets deadlines and responsive to editor's needs. "I like to publish a variety of artistic and humorous styles." For first contact, send cover letter and b&w tearsheets to Deborah Haeseler. "I prefer to see submissions sent directly." In reviewing humorous illustration we look for clean, understandable and reproducible art. Reports back in 2 months. Samples are not filed; returned by SASE. Buys one-time rights. Pays $1/b&w page or b&w cover on acceptance.

Tips: "Humorous illustrations must stand on their own since I don't (at this point) match artists with writers. I may incorporate your artwork into a humorous article or short story, so keep it generic."

Humorous Writing: Buys approximately 10-20 humorous pieces/issue, 20-40/year. Needs humorous fiction/nonfiction, humorous "slice-of-life," anecdotes, "fillers," cartoon stories and "columns, but I don't buy continuing columns that are self-syndicated." Subject matter includes women's lives at home or work, children, spouses, family relationships, pet peeves, personal experiences. All types presented vividly, wryly, perhaps sardonically. Length: 25-2,000 words, average of 500-750 words. To query: be familiar with magazine; make sure article is appropriate; study writer's guidelines. Send $4 and SASE for copy. For first contact, send cover letter, manuscript and published tearsheets to Deborah Haeseler. "I don't assign humorous stories on the basis of a proposal or query since humor is so difficult to predict." Reports back in 2 months. Samples are not filed; returned with SASE. Buys one-time rights. Pays ¼¢/word or $1-10 for 25-2,000 words.

Tips: "The most important thing to recognize is the difference between what's funny to you and what's funny to the majority of readers. Humor is one of the most difficult genres to write, but it is also one of the most rewarding. Adding to the complications of writing humor is the fact that the competition is fierce. Once a writer is established, selling humor is relatively easy, but new writers should recognize that the editorial doors don't open quickly, because while editors may be receptive to fresh ideas and novel approaches, the reading audience quickly identifies with humorists whose work they enjoy and they develop a ravenous appetite for more of the same from the same writer. *Housewives' Humor* is a good beginner's market because our goal is to introduce the reading audience to new humorists on an ongoing basis."

HUMOR: INTERNATIONAL JOURNAL OF HUMOR, English Department, Purdue University, West Lafayette IN 47907. (317)494-3780. Estab. 1982. Professional journal.

Humorous Writing: Needs humorous nonfiction for scholary articles on all subjects. For first contact, send entire manuscript to Victor Raskin, Editor. Accepts submissions via modem, fax or disk. Returns materials if accompanied by SASE.

THE INSTRUMENTALIST, 200 Northfield Rd., Northfield IL 60093. (708)446-5000. Estab. 1944. Monthly trade journal. Circ. 20,000. Needs gag cartoons.
Gag Cartoons: Buys 5 gag cartoons/issue, 60/year. Prefers positive cartoons on music (especially classical). Doesn't want to see gag cartoons on how nerdy musicians are or what a trial it is to have a child who plays an instrument. Preferred gag cartoon formats are single panel without gagline b&w line art, double panel with gagline b&w wash. Query with 1-10 rough drawings/batch to Elaine Guregian, Editor. Reports back in 1 month. Returns material. Buys all rights. Pays $20/b&w on publication.
Tips: A gag cartoonist should "enjoy music so he can be funny and not insult those in the profession."

INTERNATIONAL BOWHUNTER MAGAZINE, Box 67, Rt. 1, Box 41E, Pillager MN 56473-0067. (218)746-3333. Estab. 1983. Seven times/year consumer magazine. Circ. 57,000. Needs comic strips, humorous illustration and humorous writing.
Gag Cartoons: Buys 20 gag cartoons/year. Prefers gag cartoons on bowhunting. Preferred gag cartoon formats are single panel b&w line art, double panel with gagline and multi-panel. Send submissions to Johnny E. Boatner, Editor. Reports back within 6 weeks. Returns material if accompanied by a SASE. Buys first time rights. Pays $10 minimum for b&w. Pays on publication.
Humorous Illustration: Buys approximately 20 humorous illustrations/year for spots.
Humorous Writing: Needs humorous "slice-of-life," humorous fiction and humorous anecdotes, "fillers." Subject matter includes bowhunting. Length: 600-900 words. To query: make sure article is appropriate. For first contact send manuscript to Johnny E.Boatner. Reports back within 6 weeks. Samples are returned with SASE. Buys reprint rights. Pays $50-100 for 600-900 words.
Tips: Bowhunting; use "dry humor."

JAPANOPHILE, Box 223, Okemos MI 48864. (517)349-1795. Estab. 1974. Quarterly literary magazine. Circ. 800. Needs humorous writing and gag cartoons. Accepts previously published humorous articles.
Gag Cartoons: Buys 1 gag cartoon/issue, 3/year. Prefers gag cartoons on Japan and Japanese Culture. Preferred gag cartoon format is single panel b&w line art, with gagline. Query with 1-2 rough drawings/batch to editor. Reports back in 2 months. Returns material if accompanied by SASE. Buys one-time rights. Pays $5/b&w on publication.
Humorous Illustration: Buys approximately 1 humorous illustration/issue, 3/year for articles. When hiring a freelance humorous illustrator, these abilities are considered: a clean, graphically-pleasing drawing style; effective use of humor. For first contact, send cover letter and b&w tearsheets.

JOURNAL OF READING, Box 8139, Newark DE 19714. (302)731-1600. Estab. 1956. Monthly (October through May) professional membership journal. Circ. 20,000. Needs cartoons about reading, language, libraries and literacy among high schoolers and adults. Accepts previously published cartoons.
Gag Cartoons: Preferred gag cartoon formats are single panel without gagline, b&w line art, double panel with gagline, multi-panel. "Horizontal drawings are preferred (wider than high). We're 8½″ × 11″ format with two columns 20 picas wide, page 42 picas wide. Cartoons are fitted in at the end of articles, centered on page." Query with 1-10 rough drawings/batch to editor. Reports back in 2 weeks. Returns material. Buys one-time rights. Pays $25/b&w on acceptance.
Tips: "Stick to our topic, do not put down teachers or kids."

JUDICATURE, Suite 1600, 25 E. Washington, Chicago IL 60602. (312)558-6900. Estab. 1917. Bimonthly scholarly journal. Circ. 20,000. Needs humorous illustration and gag cartoons. Accepts previously published cartoons.

Gag Cartoons: Buys 4 gag cartoons/year. Prefers gag cartoons on law, judges and especially court related themes. Preferred gag cartoon format is single panel b&w line art with gagline. Query with 5-6 rough drawings/batch to David Richert, Editor. Reports back in 1 week. Returns material if accompanied by SASE. Buys one-time rights. Pays $35/b&w on publication.

Humorous Illustration: Buys approximately 4 humorous illustrations/year for covers and articles. Works on assignment only. When hiring a freelance humorous illustrator, these abilities are considered: ability to conceptualize well and clever ideas—good use of metaphors; a clean, graphically-pleasing drawing style; effective use of humor; not too much exaggeration or distortion; ability to "fun up" an otherwise "flat" manuscript; businesslike attitude—meets deadlines and reponsive to editor's needs. For first contact, send cover letter and b&w tearsheets to David Richert, Editor. Reports back in 2 weeks. Samples are filed or returned by SASE. Buys one-time rights. Pays $175/b&w page, $250/b&w cover on publication.

JUGGLER'S WORLD, Box 443, Davidson NC 28036. (704)892-1296. FAX: (704)892-2625. Estab. 1947. Quarterly consumer magazine. Circ. 3,500. Needs comic strips, humorous illustration, cartoon narratives, caricatures, gag cartoons and spot cartoons. Accepts previous published cartoons and humorous articles.

Gag Cartoons: Buys 4 gag cartoons/year. Prefers gag cartoons on juggling. Doesn't want to see gag cartoons on chain saw juggling. Preferred gag cartoon format is single panel b&w line art, with gagline or multi-panel. Query with 1-3 rough drawings/batch to Bill Giduz, Editor. Reports back in 1 week. Returns material. Buys first time rights, reprint rights; negotiates rights purchased. Pays $25/b&w on acceptance.

Humorous Illustration: Buys approximately 2 humorous illustrations/issue for articles and spots. When hiring a freelance humorous illustrator, these abilities are considered: a truly unique drawing style; ability to conceptualize well and clever ideas—good use of metaphors; a clean, graphically-pleasing drawing style; businesslike attitude—meets deadlines and reponsive to editor's needs. For first contact, send cover letter and b&w tearsheets to Bill Giduz. Reports back in 1 week. Samples are filed or returned. Buys first time rights and reprint rights; negotiates rights purchased. Pays $25/b&w page on acceptance.

Humorous Writing: Buys approximately 2 humorous pieces/issue. Needs humorous fiction/nonfiction, humorious interviews, anecdotes, and humorous "fillers." Subject matter includes juggling. Length: 250-750 words. To query: make sure article is appropriate; study writer's guidelines. Send $2 and SASE for copy. For first contact send cover letter and writing sample to Bill Giduz, Editor. Reports back in 1 week. Samples are filed or returned. Buys first time rights and reprint rights; negotiates rights purchased. Pays $25-75 for 250-750 words. Offers 100% kill fee.

KASHRUS MAGAZINE, Box 96, Parkville Station, Brooklyn NY 11204. (718)998-3201. Estab. 1980. Bimonthly consumer magazine. Circ. 10,000. Needs humorous writing, cartoon narratives, gag cartoons and spot cartoons.

Gag Cartoons: Prefers gag cartoons on Kosher food and other Jewish themes. Preferred gag cartoon formats are single panel b&w line art, double panel with gagline, multi-panel. Query with 2 rough drawings/batch to Rabbi Wikler, Editor. Reports in 2 weeks only if interested. Returns material if accompanied by SASE. Buys first-time rights and all rights; negotiates rights purchased. Pays $75/b&w on publication.

Tips: "Read our magazine, understand the market, call us to discuss the matter."

Humorous Illustration: Buys humorous illustrations for articles and spots. Works on assignment only. When hiring a freelance humorous illustrator, these abilities are considered: "an understanding of our concept and audience." For first contact send for a copy of *KASHRUS* for $2 (no SASE necessary); then call if it interests the freelancer." For first contact, send query and published tearsheets to Rabbi Wikler. Reports back only if interested. Samples are filed or returned with SASE. Buys first time rights, reprint rights, one-time rights and all rights; negotiates rights purchased. Pays $100-150 for 750-1,200 words. Offers 50% kill fee.

Tips: "Writer must understand our readers—Kosher, observant Jews—and our subject—kosher food, food production and technology."

KENTUCKY HAPPY HUNTING GROUND, Department of Fish and Wildlife Resources, #1 Game Farm Rd., Frankfort KY 40601. (502)564-4336. FAX: (502)564-6508. Estab. 1945. Bimonthly state government conservation magazine. Circ. 35,000. Needs humorous writing and gag cartoons. Accepts previously published cartoons and humorous articles.

Gag Cartoons: Buys 1 gag cartoon/issue, 6/year. "Cartoons must be related to wildlife, conservation and nature." Doesn't want to see gag cartoons on a man and woman in a boat. For us, the "dream" gag cartoon would be "something that, while humorous, at the same time makes a serious point about wildlife conservation." Preferred gag cartoon format is single panel, b&w wash or color wash. Send submissions to John Wilson, Cartoon Editor. Reports back in 2 months only if interested. Returns material if accompanied by SASE. Buys one-time rights. Pays $30/b&w, $50/color on publication.

Tips: A gag cartoonist should "make a point about conservation using humor."

Humorous Writing: Buys approximately 2-3 humorous pieces/year. Needs humorous fiction/nonfiction, humorous "slice-of-life," humorous anecdotes and "fillers." "Subject matter must relate to wildlife, natural resources conservation, the out-of-doors." Length: 1,500 words. To query: be familiar with magazine; make sure article is appropriate. For first contact, send query and manuscript to John Wilson. Reports back in 2 months. Samples are not filed; returned with SASE. Buys one-time rights. Pays $50-250 (maximum pay only if accompanied by illustrations) for 800-2,000 words.

Tips: "My publication—a state wildlife conservation magazine—is basically serious. Often I think it's serious to the point of being dull. There's a great potential for the use of humor to enliven publications with basically serious concerns."

KITE LINES, Box 466, Randallstown MD 21133-0466. (301)922-1212. Estab. 1977. Quarterly consumer magazine. Circ. 13,000. Needs humorous illustration and writing, and spot cartoons. Accepts previously published cartoons.

Gag Cartoons: Buys 1-2 gag cartoons/year. Only uses cartoons on kites, kiteflying and kitemaking. Doesn't want to see gag cartoons on "kite-eating trees" or UFO similes. For us, the "dream" gag cartoon would be "based on real-life kiteflying experience." Preferred gag cartoon format is single panel with/without gagline or with balloons, b&w line art. Query with 3-6 rough drawings/batch to Valerie Govig, Publisher/Editor. Reports back in 2 weeks. Returns material if accompanied by SASE. Buys first time rights. Pays $15 minimum on acceptance.

Tips: A gag cartoonist should "know kites and kiteflying and draw well—especially draw the kite correctly."

Humorous Illustration: Buys approximately 1 humorous illustration/year for articles. Works on assignment only. When hiring a freelance humorous illustrator, these abilities are considered: ability to conceptualize well and clever ideas—good use of metaphors; flexibility, broad potential in drawing style; businesslike attitude—meets deadlines and responsive to editor's needs. For first contact send client list, b&w promo piece, including at least one kite drawing to Valerie Govig. In reviewing humorous illustration we look for ability to understand and respond to our problem. Reports back in 2 weeks. Samples are filed or returned by SASE. Buys first time rights. Pays $50/b&w page minimum for an assigned job. Pays on acceptance.

Humorous Writing: Buys approximately 1 humorous piece/year and "would like more." Needs humorous nonfiction, humorous "slice-of-life" and humorous anecdotes, "fillers." "Subject matter is always kites, kitemaking and kiteflying. Humor comes from

the way the writer looks at the subject. Can't specify, but we like short pieces better." To query: be familiar with magazine; make sure article is appropriate; "we do have guidelines, free with SASE, but they are not directed to humor particularly." For first contact, send manuscript to Valerie Govig. Reports in 2 weeks. Samples are filed or returned with SASE. Buys first time rights. Pays $30-100 for 1-2 published pages.
Tips: "Perhaps humor about any subject always takes a special tune of mind, a real talent for human observation. As a quarterly, *Kitelines* is probably not really a "market" in the best meaning of the term. But we certainly appreciate humor about kites and want to see and use more of it."

LIGHT & LIFE PRESS, Box 535002, Indianapolis IN 46253. Estab. 1897. Sunday school take-home quarterly in weekly parts. Circ. 30,000. Needs gag cartoons and spot cartoons. Accepts previously published cartoons and humorous articles.
Gag Cartoons: Buys 10 gag cartoons/year. Preferred gag cartoon format is single panel b&w line art, with gagline. Query with 10-20 rough drawings/batch to Vera Bethel, Editor. Reports back in 4 weeks. Returns material if accompanied by SASE. Buys one-time rights and reprint rights. Pays $10/b&w on publication.

LISTEN, 1350 North Kings Road, Nampa ID 83687. (208)465-2592. FAX: (208)465-2531. Estab. 1948. Monthly consumer magazine. Circ. 70,000. Needs humorous illustration, caricatures and spot cartoons. Accepts previously published cartoons if they illustrate one of the articles directly.
Humorous Illustration: Buys approximately 3 humorous illustrations/issue; 36/year for articles. Works on assignment only. When hiring a freelance humorous illustrator, these abilities are considered: a truly unique drawing style; a bold, powerful, attention-getting drawing style (our magazine is marketed to a teen audience); businesslike attitude—meets deadlines and responsive to editor's needs. For first contact send b&w or color tearsheets, b&w or color promo piece and slides to Merwin Stewart, Art Director. In reviewing humorous illustration we look for a drawing style which is "different than anything I'm already buying." Reports back only if interested. Samples are filed or returned by SASE if requested. Buys first time rights and one-time rights. Pays $150 minimum/b&w page; $300+/color. Pays on acceptance.
Tips: "Being able to work within a two-week time frame, long-distance and meeting the deadline are essential to receiving on-going projects for *Listen* magazine. *Listen* is marketed to a teen audience."

LIVING AMONG NATURE DARINGLY, 4466 Ike Mooney Rd., Silverton OR 97381. (503)873-8829 or 873-6585. Estab. 1986. Five times/year consumer magazine. Circ. 1,000. Needs comic strips, caricatures and political satire. Accepts previously published cartoons.
Gag Cartoons: Query with 1-3 rough drawings/batch. Reports back within 3 weeks with SASE required. Returns material if accompanied by a SASE. Buys first time rights, reprint rights, one-time rights, all rights and negotiates rights purchased. Pays $10 minimum for b&w. Pays on publication.
Humorous Illustration: Buys approximately 1 humorous illustration/issue; 5/year for articles and spots. When hiring a freelance humorous illustrator, these abilities are considered: a truly unique drawing style; ability to conceptualize well and clever ideas—good use of metaphors; a clean, graphically-pleasing drawing style; has a bold, powerful, attention-getting drawing style; effective use of humor. For first contact send cover letter, b&w promo piece to Bill Anderson, Editor/Publisher. Note: "Material is published from paid subscribers only, although we will review submissions from non-subscribers. Subscriptions cost $9 for 1 year, $15 for 2 years." In reviewing humorous illustrations "we look for a good chuckle and wholesomeness." Reports back within 3 weeks with SASE required. Samples are not filed; returned by SASE.

Tips: "Probably the best cartoonist of a sort we're looking for is Trudeau of *Doonesbury* fame, he reminds us of what we can make America—make the reader want to think socially for a better America."

Humorous Writing: Buys approximately 1 humorous piece/issue; 5/year. Needs humorous nonfiction. Subject matter includes current national and international events, from a slightly liberal, strongly populist viewpoint. Length: 150-500 words. To query: be familiar with magazine; make sure that your article is appropriate; study our writer's guidelines. Send $2.50 and SASE for copy. For first contact send cover letter and outline of proposed story to Bill Anderson. Reports back within 3 weeks with SASE required. Samples are returned with SASE. Negotiates rights purchased. Pays $7.50-20 for 150-500 words.

Tips: "Study Mike Royko or Art Buchwald, but tone it down two decibels. No anti-religious material of any sort, (Jewish, Moslem, Christian, etc.). *Land* magazine specializes in showing people how to farm the old-fashioned way to break loose from dependence on a system which enslaves people to make ever-more money and ever-rising debts. This bourgeois mode can be depicted with caricatures of any visible politician or financier or. . . . only when we stop keeping up with the Jones' can enough pressure be taken off that drug abuse can stop."

MACINTOSH NEWS, 600 Community Dr., Manhasset NY 11030. (516)562-5447. FAX: (516)-562-5474. Estab. 1988. Bimonthly consumer magazine. Circ. 40,000. Needs humorous illustration, caricatures, gag cartoons and spot cartoons. Accepts previously published cartoons.

Gag Cartoons: Buys 6 gag cartoons/year. Prefers gag cartoons on business, computers, finances and technology. Doesn't want to see gag cartoons on computers breaking down. For us, the "dream" gag cartoon would be "how a computer really affects your life (love, hate, 100% of your time, 'smartass')." Preferred gag cartoon format is single panel, with gagline, color wash. Query with 3-6 rough drawings/batch to Teresa Carboni, Art Director. Reports only if interested. Returns material only if requested. Buys one-time rights. Pays $150/color on publication.

Humorous Illustration: Buys approximately 6 humorous illustrations/issue for articles and spots. When hiring a freelance humorous illustrator, these abilities are considered: a truly unique drawing style; ability to conceptualize well and clever ideas—good use of metaphors; ability to "fun up" an otherwise "flat" manuscript. For first contact, send cover letter, resume, color tearsheets, color promo piece to Teresa Carboni. In reviewing humorous illustration we look for instant humor. Reports only if interested. Samples are filed. Buys one-time rights. Pays $150/color page on publication.

Tips: "Remember this is a business publication, but we like fun and good art too."

MAGAZINE ISSUES, Feredonna Communications, Drawer 9808, Knoxville TN 37940. (615)-584-1918. Estab. 1982. Bimonthly trade journal. Circ. 13,000. Needs comic strips, humorous illustration, caricatures, gag cartoons and spot cartoons.

Gag Cartoons: Prefers gag cartoons on publishing—all aspects. Preferred gag cartoon formats are single panel b&w line art, b&w wash and multi-panel. Send submissions to Michael Scott Ward, Editor. Reports back if interested. Does not return material. Negotiates rights purchased. Pays $25 minimum for b&w. Pays on publication.

Humorous Illustration: Buys approximately 3 humorous illustrations/year for covers, articles and spots. When hiring a freelance humorous illustrator, these abilities are considered: a clean, graphically-pleasing drawing style; effective use of humor; businesslike attitude—meets deadlines and responsive to editor's needs. For first contact send b&w tearsheets or b&w promo piece to Michael Scott Ward. In reviewing humorous illustration "we look for style and appropriateness." Reports back only if interested. Samples are filed. Negotiates rights purchased. Pays $75 minimum/b&w page; $100/color; $240 color cover (covers by assignment only). Pays on publication.

Humorous Writing: Buys approximately 1 humorous piece/issue; 4/year. Needs humorous nonfiction, humorous interviews and humorous "slice-of-life." Subject matter includes magazine publishing, "inside of business." Length: 1,000-2,000 words. To query: make sure article is appropriate. For first contact send manuscript, query and outline of proposed story to Michael Scott Ward. Reports back only if interested. Samples are filed. Negotiates rights purchased. Pays $50-150 for 1,000-2,000 words.

MANAGEMENT ACCOUNTING, 10 Paragon Drive, Montvale NJ 07645. (201)573-6269. FAX: (201)573-8185. Estab. 1919. Monthly trade journal. Circ. 85,000. Needs gag cartoons. Accepts previously published cartoons.
Gag Cartoons: Buys 1 gag cartoon/issue; 12/year. Prefers gag cartoons on business, finance and accounting. Doesn't want to see gag cartoons on "dumb secretaries" or sexist themes. For us the "dream" gag cartoon would be "New Yorker style with high level satire." Preferred gag cartoon format is single panel with gagline. Query with 1-10 rough drawings/batch to Robert F. Randall, Editor. Reports back within 1 week. Returns material if accompanied by a SASE. Buys first time rights. Pays $25 minimum for b&w. Pays on acceptance.

MATURE YEARS, Box 801, 201 8th Ave. S., Nashville TN 37202. (615)352-3240. Estab. 1967. Quarterly church-related magazine. Circ. 80,000. Needs humorous writing (brief), cartoon narratives and gag cartoons.
Gag Cartoons: Buys 1-2 gag cartoons/issue, 4-6/year. Prefers gag cartoons on older persons and the church. Preferred gag cartoon format is single panel b&w line art, with gagline. Send submissions to Norma Bates, Assistant Editor. Returns material if accompanied by SASE. Buys all rights. Pays $25/b&w on acceptance.
Humorous Illustration: Buys approximately 5 humorous illustrations/issue, 20/year for articles. Works on assignment only. When hiring a freelance humorous illustrator, these abilities are considered: not too much exaggeration or distortion. For first contact, send b&w tearsheets to Dave Dawson, Art Procurement Director. Pays $50/b&w page on acceptance.
Humorous Writing: Buys approximately 2 humorous pieces/year. Needs humorous fiction/nonfiction, humorous interviews, humorous "slice-of-life," humorous anecdotes and humorous "fillers." Length: 1,000-2,000 words. To query: be familiar with magazine; make sure article is appropriate; study writer's guidelines. Send $2.50 and SASE for copy. For first contact send query and outline of proposed story to Donn C. Downall, Editor. Reports back in 6 weeks. Buys all rights and negotiates rights purchased. Pays 4¢/word.

METRO, 410 S. First St., San Jose CA 95113. (408)298-8000. Weekly newspaper. Circ. 55,000. Needs comic strips, humorous illustration, gag cartoons and spot cartoons. Accepts previously published cartoons and humorous articles. Prefers working with freelancers who have fax capabilities.
Gag Cartoons: Buys 10-20 gag cartoons/year. Preferred gag cartoon format is b&w line art. Query with 5-10 rough drawings/batch to Michael S. Gant, Arts Editor. Reports back only if interested. Does not return material. Buys one-time rights. Pays $10/b&w on publication.
Humorous Illustration: Buys approximately 5-10 humorous illustrations/year for articles. Works on assignment only. When hiring a freelance humorous illustrator, these abilities are considered: ability to conceptualize well and clever ideas—good use of metaphors; a bold, powerful, attention-getting drawing style; businesslike attitude—meets deadlines and responsive to editor's needs. For first contact, send cover letter, b&w tearsheets and resume to Michael S. Gant. In reviewing humorous illustration we look for originality and graphic design. Reports back only if interested. Samples are not returned. Buys one-time rights. Pays $15/b&w page, $50/b&w cover on publication.

Humorous Writing: Buys approximately 5 humorous pieces/year. Needs humorous nonfiction and humorous "slice-of-life." Subject matter includes political satire, but not heavy-handed propaganda. Length: 750 words. To query: be familiar with magazine. For first contact, send cover letter, query, published tearsheets, resume and writing sample to Michael S. Gant, Arts Editor. Reports back only if interested. Samples are not returned. Buys one-time rights. Pays 5¢/word. Offers 50% kill fee.

MILITARY MARKET, 6883 Commercial Dr., Springfield VA 22159. Estab. 1950. Monthly trade journal. Circ. 9,800. Needs gag cartoons.
Gag Cartoons: Buys 4 gag cartoons/issue, 48/year. Prefers gag cartoons on department store and supermarket situations from point of view of managers, suppliers and in-store workers. Doesn't want to see gag cartoons on "bimbos." Preferred gag cartoon format is single panel, b&w line art, with/without gagline. Query with 5-20 rough drawings/batch to Nancy Tucker, Editor. Reports back in 4-6 months. Returns material if accompanied by SASE. Buys one-time rights. Pays $25/b&w on acceptance.

MINNE HA! HA!, "THE TWIN CITIES' SORELY NEEDED HUMOR MAGAZINE", P.O. Box 14009, Minneapolis MN 55414. (612)729-7687. Estab. 1978. Quarterly tabloid. Circ. 20,000. Needs comic strips, humorous illustrations, humorous writing, cartoon narratives, caricatures, gag cartoons, spot cartoons and humorous photos. Accepts previously published cartoons and humorous articles.
Gag Cartoons: Buys 5-10 gag cartoons/issue. Prefers gag cartoons on the arts, skateboarders, street gangs, Scandinavians, new age, politics, environment, media and yuppies. For us the "dream" gag cartoon would be "lampooning authority figures and other cartoonists, modern living and/or gangs and crime—anything urban." Preferred gag cartoon format is single panel without gagline b&w line art and multi-panel. Query with 10-25 rough drawings/batch to Lance Anger, Editor. Reports back if interested. Does not return material. Buys one-time rights. Pays $10 minimum for b&w; $20 minimum for color. Tips: "Be sarcastic and satirical about modern cities, especially crime and street gangs—also a plus to know Minnesotan Scandinavian culture."
Humorous Illustration: Buys approximately 2 humorous illustrations/issue; 8/year for covers and articles. When hiring a freelance humorous illustrator, these abilities are considered: unique drawing style; bold, powerful, attention-getting drawing style; effective use of humor; businesslike attitude—meets deadlines and responsive to my needs. For first contact send b&w or color tearsheets, b&w or color promo piece, resume and client list to Lance Anger. Reports back if interested. Samples are filed and not returned. Buys one-time rights. Pays $25 minimum b&w page; $50 minimum color page; $40 minimum b&w cover; $70 minimum color cover. Pays on publication. Co-op payment schedule, "we pay more if advertising is up in that issue."
Humorous Writing: Buys approximately 2 humorous pieces/issue; 8/year. Needs humorous fiction/nonfiction, humorous interviews, humorous "slice-of-life", cartoon stories and humorous anecdotes, "fillers." Length: up to 2,000 words. Short pieces more likely to be used. "In querying our magazine, we advise that your article be appropriate for us." For first contact send manuscript, writing sample, published tearsheets and outline of proposed story to Lance Anger. Reports back if interested. Samples are filed and not returned. Buys one-time rights. Pays $25-100 for 100-2,000 words. Offers 25% kill fee.
Tips: "Minneapolis is a small city going through the scary process of becoming a big urban mess. Fear of gangs, crime is taking over. We need a humorous viewpoint to help keep perspective on this. We like 'laugh-out-loud' gut-slamming humor, hilarity, more than subtle *New Yorker* style stuff. This is a Midwestern culture that likes to think of itself as a small New York, but really is not. Play off of that successfully and you'll have a place to get your work published!"

MODERN CARTOONING AND GAGWRITING, Box 1142, Novato CA 94947. Estab. February 1989. Monthly trade journal. Circ. 250 + . Needs comic strips, humorous illustration, humorous writing, cartoon narratives, caricatures, gag cartoons and spot cartoons. Accepts previously published cartoons and humorous articles.

Gag Cartoons: Buys 2-3 gag cartoons/issue; 20-36/year. Prefers gag cartoons on cartoon and humor biz, trade journal related, especially with *Modern Cartooning* title used. Doesn't want to see gag cartoons on rejection slip theme. For us the dream gag cartoon would be "camera-ready, drawn according to guidelines, SASE's are used." Preferred gag cartoon format is single panel b&w line art, with gagline. Query with 3-6 rough drawings/batch to Raymond Moore, Editor. Reports back in one month. Returns material if accompanied by a SASE. Buys first time rights and reprint rights. Pays $10 minimum for b&w. Pays on acceptance.

Tips: Submit work according to guideline specifications, using SASE for any expected material return.

Humorous Illustration: Buys approximately 2 humorous illustration/issue; 24 humorous illustrations/year for covers, articles and spots. When hiring a freelance humorous illustrator, these abilities are considered: a truly unique drawing style; ability to conceptualize well and clever ideas—good use of metaphors; a clean, graphically-pleasing drawing style; effective use of humor; flexibility, broad potential in drawing style; ability to "fun up" an otherwise "flat" manuscript; businesslike attitude—meets deadlines and responsive to editor's needs. Send submissions to Raymond Moore. In reviewing humorous illustrations look for articles that contain humor/intelligence/holds readers interest, meets guideline specifications, neat/clean. Reports back within one month. Samples are returned by SASE. Buys first time rights and reprint rights. Pays $10 minimum/b&w page. Pays on acceptance.

Tips: "Avoid sending 'how-to' articles; aim with the professional cartoonist/gagwriter in mind."

Humorous Writing: Buys approximately 2 humorous pieces/issue; 24/year. Needs humorous nonfiction, humorous interviews and cartoon stories. Subject matter includes biographies from professional cartoonists/gagwriters. Length: not to exceed 3-typed pages. To query: be familiar with magazine; make sure article is appropriate; study writer's guidelines. Send $5 for sample copy. For first contact send writing sample and query to Raymond Moore. Reports back within one month. Samples are returned with SASE. Buys first time rights and reprint rights. Pays $10 maximum/page. Offers $10 kill fee.

Tips: "Avoid temper flares with editor if he doesn't reply ASAP. Avoid repetition in articles."

MODERN DRUMMER, 870 Pompton Ave., Cedar Grove NJ 07009. (201)239-4140. FAX: (201)239-7139. Estab. 1977. Monthly consumer magazine. Circ. 50,000. Needs humorous illustration, humorous writing, gag cartoons and spot cartoons. Accepts previously published cartoons.

Gag Cartoons: Buys 6 gag cartoons/year. Prefers gag cartoons on drummer-oriented gags. Preferred gag cartoon format is single panel b&w line art. Query with 6-12 rough drawings/batch to R. Spagnardi, Editor. Reports back within 2 weeks. Returns material if accompanied by a SASE. Buys all rights. Pays $25 minimum for b&w. Pays on publication.

Humorous Writing: Buys approximately 5 humorous pieces/year. Needs humorous nonfiction and humorous interviews. Subject matter includes music industry, specifically from a drummer's point of view. "Call magazine editor to see what editorial needs are."

Humorous Illustration: Buys approximately 3 humorous illustrations/year for articles. Works on assignment only. When hiring a freelance humorous illustrator, these abilities are considered: ability to conceptualize well and clear ideas—good use of metaphors; a clean, graphically-pleasing drawing style; effective use of humor; not too much exaggeration or distortion. For first contact send cover letter, b&w tear sheets and b&w promo tearsheets to R. Spagnardi. Reports back within 2 weeks. Buys all rights. Pays $25 minimum b&w page. Pays on publication.

MONROE MAGAZINE, 477 N. Dixie, Monroe MI 48161. (313)242-8788. FAX: (313)242-5973. Estab. 1988. Monthly consumer magazine. Circ. 20,000. Needs humorous writing. Accepts previously published humorous articles.
Humorous Writing: Buys approximately 1-2 humorous pieces/year. Needs humorous fiction, humorous anecdotes and "fillers." Length: 25-250 words. To query: be famliar with magazine; make sure article is appropriate. For first contact, send cover letter and outline of proposed story to David Meagher, Editor. Reports back only if interested. Samples not filed are returned with SASE. Buys first time rights. "We pay $25 for an article that we use." Offers 10% kill fee.

MOTHER EARTH NEWS, Box 70, Hendersonville NC 28793. (704)693-0211. Estab. 1970. Bimonthly consumer magazine. Circ. 700,000. Needs humorous writing. Accepts previously published humorous articles.
Humorous Writing: Buys approximately 4-5 humorous pieces per year. Needs humorous "slice-of-life" and humorous fiction. Subject matter includes how-to, country life, environmental issues, regional humor, folksy humor and rural humor. Length: 800 words. To query: be familiar with magazine; make sure article is appropriate for our Last Laugh column. For first contact send manuscript, query and outline of proposed story to Last Laugh. Reports back within weeks/months. Samples are returned. Buys first time rights. Pays $500+ for 800-1,000 words.
Tips: "It can be first person, a well-strung collection of jokes, 'how I screwed up'— whatever, as long as it's appropriate to our subject areas and is really funny (not just cute)."

MOUNTAIN FAMILY CALENDAR, Box 294, Rhododendron OR 97049. (503)622-4798. Estab. 1984. Monthly general interest magazine. Circ. 7,000. Needs comic strips, humorous illustration and writing, cartoon narratives, caricatures, gag cartoons and spot cartoons. Accepts previously published cartoons and humorous articles.
Gag Cartoons: Buys 4 gag cartoons/issue, 60/year. Prefers gag cartoons on Oregon Trail, outdoor recreation, nature and logging. Doesn't want to see gag cartoons on sex. For us, the "dream" gag would be "pioneers crossing over the Oregon Trail." Preferred gag cartoon formats are single panel without gagline b&w line art, double panel with gagline, multi-panel with balloons. Query with 5-12 rough drawings/batch to Michael P. Jones, Editor. Reports back in 1 month (hopefully). Returns material only if requested and accompanied by SASE. Buys first time rights. Pays in copies, upon publication.
Tips: "Be flexible and willing to try new things. If work has merit and if we are interested, then we will ask the illustrator to work on a book project with us."
Humorous Illustration: Buys approximately 3 humorous illustrations/issue, 26/year for spots. When hiring a freelance humorous illustrator, these abilities are considered: a truly unique drawing style; ability to conceptualize well and clever ideas—good use of metaphors; a clean, graphically-pleasing drawing style; has a bold, powerful, attention-getting drawing style; has a subtle, understated drawing style; effective use of humor; not too much exaggeration or distortion; flexibility, broad potential in drawing style; ability to "fun up" an otherwise "flat" manuscript; businesslike attitude—meets deadlines and responsive to editor's needs; "is patient and flexible. If you're a demanding primadonna, don't bother us." For first contact, send cover letter, b&w or color tearsheets, b&w or color promo piece, resume, slides, client list and portfolio to Michael P. Jones. In reviewing humorous illustration "we look for the potential to do new things with their talent." Reports back in 1 month. Samples not filed are returned if requested by SASE. Buys first time rights. Pays in copies, on publication.

Tips: "Be flexible and try new things with talent."

Humorous Writing: Buys approximately 1 humorous piece/issue, 12/year. Needs humorous fiction/nonfiction, humorous interviews, humorous "slice-of-life," cartoon stories, anecdotes and "fillers." Subject matter includes anit-logging, nature, fish and wildlife, outdoor recreation and travel. Length: open. To query: study writer's guidelines. Send 45¢ and SASE for copy. For first contact send cover letter, manuscript, writing sample, query, outline of proposed story, published tearsheets, resume to Michael P. Jones. Reports back in 1 month. Samples are returned with SASE only if requested. Buys first time rights. Pays in copies on publication.

Tips: "Keep it clean! We are a family-oriented publication."

MTL MAGAZINE, 8270 Mountain Sights #201, Quebec H4P 2B7 Canada. (514)731-9449. FAX: (514)731-7459. Estab. 1988. Monthly consumer magazine. Circ. 50,000. Needs humorous illustration.

Humorous Illustration: Buys approximately 10 humorous illustrations/issue; 100/year for articles, editorial page and listings. Works on assignment only. When hiring a freelance humorous illustrator, these abilities are considered: a truly unique drawing style; ability to conceptualize well and clever ideas — good use of metaphors; has a clean, graphically-pleasing drawing style; a bold, powerful, attention-getting drawing style; effective use of humor; not too much exaggeration or distortion; flexibility, broad potential in drawing style; ability to "fun up" an otherwise "flat" manuscript; is businesslike, meets deadlines and responsive to editor's needs. For first contact send cover letter, resume, portfolio to Ava Chisling, Managing Editor. In reviewing humorous illustration "we look for originality and intelligence." Reports back if interested. Samples are returned by SASE. Negotiates rights purchased. Pays $400 minimum/color page (Canadian dollars). Pays on publication.

Tips: "Please read the text you are to illustrate; a professional doesn't take suggested changes to heart; vary your styles so as not to be 'typecast.' "

Humorous Writing: Buys approximately 1 humorous pieces/issue; 10/year. Needs humorous interviews. Subject matter includes humorous interviews with celebrities. Length: 1,500 words. To query: be familiar with magazine. For first contact send cover letter, writing sample, published tearsheets, outline of proposed story and resume to Ava Chisling. Reports back only if interested. Samples are returned with SASE. Negotiates rights purchased. Pays $75 Canadian per 250 words (or one typed page). Offers 50% kill fee.

Tips: "Must be applicable to the Montreal market; or an interview with a notable celebrity with something to say we haven't heard before. I believe the key to good humor writing is not to only make yourself laugh; be original. Humor illustrations should be subtle and wise; most of all, don't underestimate your audience and understand the editorial you'll illustrate."

MUSCLE MAG INTERNATIONAL, Unit Two, 52 Bramsreele Rd., Brampton ON L6W3M5 Canada. (416)457-3030. FAX: (416)791-4292. Estab. 1974. Monthly consumer magazine. Circ. 150,000. Needs comic strips, humorous writing, caricatures and gag cartoons.

Gag Cartoons: Buys 25 gag cartoons/year. Prefers gag cartoons on bodybuilding. Doesn't want to see gag cartoons that are poorly drawn. For us, the "dream" gag cartoon would be "a strong drawing with a strong caption." Preferred gag cartoon formats are single panel b&w line art, double panel b&w wash, color wash. Query with 6-10 rough drawings/batch to Robert Kennedy, President. Reports back in 30 days. Returns material with postage. "We are Canadian, so Canadian stamp only or $3 cash for return postage." Buys first time rights. Pays $50/b&w, $100/color; payment varies according to quality. Pays on acceptance.

Tips: "Be professional. Don't ever submit work that is shakily drawn, dirty, folded or poorly executed. No cartoonist should submit work unless he or she is properly trained or diligently self-taught."

Humorous Illustration: Buys approximately 6 humorous illustrations/year for articles. When hiring a freelance humorous illustrator, these abilities are considered: a truly unique drawing style; ability to conceptualize well and clever ideas—good use of metaphors; a bold, powerful, attention-getting drawing style; effective use of; flexibility, broad potential in drawing style. For first contact, send cover letter and b&w tearsheets to Robert Kennedy. Reports back in 10 days only if interested. Samples are not filed; returned if requested. Buys first time rights.

Humorous Writing: Buys approximately 6 humorous pieces/year. Needs humorous fiction, anecdotes and "fillers." Subject matter includes body builders or editors and publishers of bodybuilding publications. Length: 1,000-8,000 words. To query: be familiar with magazine; make sure article is appropriate. For first contact, send cover letter and manuscript to Robert Kennedy. Reports back in 10 days only if interested. Samples are not filed; returned with Canadian postage or $3 cash. Buys first time rights. Pays $150-400.

Tips: "Humor writing should enable readers to relate to the quirks relative to bodybuilders. Humor work must be honed and reworked more than regular fiction or nonfiction because balance is most important to make the humor stand out as humor."

NATIONAL GARDENING, 180 Flynn Ave., Burlington VT 05401. Estab. 1979. Monthly membership magazine. Circ. 185,000. Needs humorous illustration and writing.

Humorous Illustration: Buys approximately 1 humorous illustration/issue for articles. Works on assignment only. When hiring a freelance humorous illustration, these abilities are considered: a truly unique drawing style; ability to conceptualize well and clever ideas—good use of metaphors; ability to "fun up" an otherwise "flat" manuscript; businesslike attitude—meets deadlines and reponsive to editor's needs; knowledge of gardening. For first contact, send cover letter, b&w and color tearsheets, color promo piece to Linda Provost, Art Director. "Send me a letter and enough work in any form (that I can keep on file) to give me an idea of your style and range." In reviewing humorous illustration we look for imagination, fluidity, not straight cartooning or corniness. Reports back only if interested. Samples are filed or returned by SASE. Buys one-time rights; negotiates rights purchased. Pays $250/b&w page, $350/color page on acceptance + 30 days.

Humorous Writing: Buys approximately 4 humorous pieces/year. Needs humorous nonfiction. Subject matter includes garden-related topics. Length: 650 words. To query: be familiar with magazine; make sure article is appropriate. For first contact, send cover letter and manuscript to Vicky Congden, Assistant Editor. Reports back in 4-6 weeks. Samples not filed are returned with SASE. Buys one-time rights. Pays $150-300 for 600-1,000 words.

NEW BLOOD MAGAZINE, 1843 E. Venton St., Covina CA 91724. Estab. 1986. Quarterly magazine. Circ. 15,000. Needs comic strips, humorous illustration, gag cartoons and spot cartoons. Accepts previously published cartoons and humorous articles.

Gag Cartoons: Buys 1-2 gag cartoons/issue, 12/year. Gag cartoons on any subject accepted. "The more controversial, the better." Preferred gag cartoon formats are single panel b&w line art, double panel with gagline b&w wash, multi-panel, with balloons color wash. Query with 5-10 rough drawings/batch to Chris Lacher, Editor. Reports back in 3 weeks. Returns material if accompanied by SASE. Buys first time rights. Pays $10-100/b&w, negotiates payment for color. Pays half on acceptance, half on publication.

Humorous Illustration: Buys approximately 1-2 humorous illustrations/issue, 12/year for articles. When hiring a freelance humorous illustrator, these abilities are considered: a clean, graphically-pleasing drawing style; effective use of humor; businesslike attitude—meets deadlines and responsive to editor's needs. For first contact, send cover letter and b&w tearsheets to Chris Lacher. "Especially interested in new talents—hence the title." Reports back in 3 weeks. Samples are filed; samples not filed are returned by SASE if requested. Buys first time rights. Pays $10-100/b&w page. Pays half on acceptance, half on publication.

Tips: "Follow our guidelines, don't be averse to a few suggestions for changes and you'll do well at NB."

Humorous Writing: Buys approximately 1 humorous piece/issue, 1-4/year. Needs humorous fiction/nonfiction, humorous interviews and humorous anecdotes, "fillers." Open to all subjects; the more volatile the piece, the better. Length: up to 5,000 words. To query: be familiar with magazine; make sure article is appropriate; study writer's guidelines. For first contact, send cover letter and manuscript to Chris Lacher. Reports back in 3 weeks. Samples are filed or returned with SASE if requested. Buys first time rights. Pays 5¢/word. Offers 50% kill fee.

Tips: "Buying cartoons/humorous writing is a new field for *New Blood*, so we're not impressed with many names, since we don't know them. The things we've seen so far impress us, and we're sure yours will too, so submit soon."

NEW YORK HABITAT, Suite 1105, 928 Broadway, New York NY 10010. (212)505-2030. FAX: (212)254-6795. Estab. 1982. Trade journal published 8 times a year. Circ. 10,000. Needs humorous illustration.

Gag Cartoons: Buys 1-2 gag cartoons/issue, 8-10/year. Prefers gag cartoons on "situations dealing specifically with NYC co-ops and condos (our market)." Doesn't want to see gag cartoons on Glasnost. Preferred gag cartoon format is single panel without gagline, b&w line art. Query with 3-4 rough drawings/batch to Lloyd Chrein, Managing Editor. Reports back in 3 weeks only if interested. Returns material if accompanied by SASE. Buys first time rights. Pays $75/b&w on publication.

Tips: A gag cartoonist should "know the audience and have a sense of irony."

Humorous Illustration: Buys approximately 1-2 humorous illustration/issue, 8-10/year for articles. Works on assignment only. When hiring a freelance humorous illustrator, these abilities are considered: a truly unique drawing style; ability to conceptualize well and clever ideas—good use of metaphors; a clean, graphically pleasing drawing style; a bold, powerful, attention-getting drawing style; effective use of humor; not too much exaggeration or distortion; flexibility, broad potential in drawing style; ability to "fun up" an otherwise "flat" manuscript; businesslike attitude—meets deadlines and responsive to editor's needs. For first contact, send b&w tearsheets and client list to Lloyd Chrein. Reports back in 3 weeks. Samples are returned by SASE. Buys first time rights. Pays $75/b&w page.

Tips: "Pick up and read the magazine."

THE NEW YORKER, 25 W. 43rd St., New York NY 10036. (212)840-3800. Estab. 1925. Weekly consumer magazine. Circ. 650,000. Needs gag cartoons.

Gag Cartoons: Buys 25 gag cartoons/issue, 780/year. Prefers gag cartoons on anything fresh, original and graphically distinguished. Doesn't want to see gag cartoons on husbands and wives. For us, the "dream" gag cartoon would be "a complete surprise." Preferred gag cartoon format is single panel. Query with 8-20 rough drawings/batch to Art Editor. Reports back in 3 weeks. Returns material if accompanied by SASE. Buys all rights. Pays $500/b&w on acceptance.

Close-up

Lee Lorenz
Cartoon Editor
The New Yorker

If Lee Lorenz offers you a word of encouragement, don't pack up your bags and move to New York just yet.

As cartoon editor for *The New Yorker* magazine, Lorenz sifts through thousands of cartoons a week, and while he rejects the vast majority of them, there are those that offer a glimmer of hope. When that happens, Lorenz may even get on the phone and call the cartoonist.

"When it becomes apparent there is something promising about a cartoonist," says Lorenz, "it's important for me to encourage him early on. On the other hand, I have to be cautious. At the slightest word of encouragement, he could mortgage his house, move to New York and camp out on the doorstep of *The New Yorker*."

But could you really blame the cartoonist? There is no more important forum for the single panel or "gag" cartoon. *The New Yorker* is a journal that recognizes the importance of the gag cartoon and treats such with uncommon respect. Having your cartoons published in *The New Yorker* is like shooting a hole-in-one—a rare feat and even tougher to improve upon.

In decades past, gag cartoonists were afforded more markets like *The New Yorker* (*Collier's*, *Look*, *The Saturday Evening Post*) which would publish general interest cartoons. In recent years, the market has narrowed considerably. "Now," says Lorenz, "you have special interest magazines that want targeted cartoons for their particular readership (women, skiing, business, etc.), so it is very difficult to draw general interest cartoons and recirculate them. You have to be much more of an entrepreneur today to make a living at gag cartooning— a cartoonist must learn to be very resourceful."

A tight, highly-competitive business, gag cartooning is a profession from which few actually making a living. "Even out of the 100 members of the Cartoonist's Association, I doubt that more than half make a living from cartooning."

Inundated with the deluge of cartoons, Lorenz continues to be surprised— usually for the wrong reasons. "You'd be amazed," he says, "at how much material comes in that isn't presented in a professional manner. It's not fair to me and it's not fair to the cartoonists who are in this as a profession. It's easy enough to find out how the material should be properly submitted. I have to stress that this a profession—it's not a spare time activity, a hobby or something you do when you retire. I do get impatient with people who feel they might just sell a few cartoons to *The New Yorker* to pick up some spare change!"

A cartoonist himself for 31 years, Lorenz thinks many cartoonists have unrealistic expectations about *The New Yorker*. "What we are looking for in terms of style, point of view and consistency," he stresses, "comes very slowly—even to people who are gifted. Everybody doesn't start out with the skills and the kind of experience they need to be successful in this market."

Every week Lorenz weeds out the good from the bad of 3,000 cartoon submissions. "Everything that I think has even remote possibilities," says Lorenz, "I put aside (this could mean as many as 200 cartoons). Then two or three times a week, I go through everything I've held and select 50 or so cartoons which I take down to Bob Gottlieb (*New Yorker* editor). When I first look at the cartoons, I try to be as generous as possible."

Lorenz advises that gag cartoonists know their market. "From an economic standpoint," he says, "it's silly to send material to a market that is obviously not receptive. On the other hand, I don't think cartoonists should go too far in trying to shape themselves for an existing market—the best cartoonists create a market for themselves. Before we started using Roz Chast, we had never published anything like that. If she had looked at the magazine and said, 'Well, I don't see anything like my stuff, so I guess I shouldn't submit,' she would never be in *The New Yorker* today."

Ultimately, Lorenz insists that a cartoonist must have confidence. "If your work is good," he says, "people will start responding to it. Be patient, but be resourceful."

—Bob Staake

Drawing by Lorenz; © 1989

The New Yorker Magazine, Inc.

NORTH AMERICAN HUNTER, Box 3401, Minnetonka MN 55343. (612)936-9333. FAX: (612)-936-9333. Estab. 1979. Bimonthly North American Hunting Club official publication. Circ. 225,000. Needs gag cartoons. Accepts previously published humorous articles.

Gag Cartoons: Prefers hunting related cartoons. Doesn't want to see gag cartoons on dumb wives who don't hunt or understand hunting. For us, the "dream" gag cartoon would be "a humorous hunting experience that all hunters can relate to." Preferred gag cartoon format is single panel, with gagline. Query with 6-12 rough drawings/batch to Debra Morem, Senior Editorial Assistant. Reports back in 7 days. Returns material if accompanied by SASE. Buys all rights. Pays $15/b&w on acceptance.

Humorous Writing: Buys approximately 6 humorous pieces/year. Needs humorous hunting related stories from NAHC members only. For first contact, send cover letter and query to Bill Miller, Editor. Reports back in 2 weeks. Samples are returned with SASE. Buys all rights.

THE NORTHERN LOGGER, Box 69, Old Forge NY 13420. (315)369-3078. FAX: (315)-369-3736. Estab. 1952. Monthly trade journal. Circ. 14,000. Needs humorous illustration, gag cartoons and spot cartoons. Accepts previously published cartoons.

Gag Cartoons: Buys 1 gag cartoon/issue, 12/year. Doesn't want to see gag cartoons on beavers. Preferred gag cartoon format is gagline, b&w line art. Query with 1 rough drawing/batch to Eric Johnson, Editor. Reports back in 1 month. Returns material if accompanied by SASE. Buys one-time rights. Pays $15/b&w on acceptance.

NOW AND THEN (East Tennesee State University), Box 19180 A, ETSU, Johnson City TN 37614. (615)929-5348. Estab. 1984. Published 3 times a year. Circ. 2,000. Needs comic strips, humorous illustration and writing, cartoon narratives, caricatures, gag and spot cartoons.

Gag Cartoons: Buys 3 gag cartoons/year. "We only take gag cartoons on life in Appalachia or other related themes." Preferred gag cartoon format is single panel, double panel, multi-panel, with/without gagline, with balloons, b&w line art, b&w wash. Query with 1-8 rough drawings/batch to Pat Arnow, Editor. Reports back in 4 months. Returns material if accompanied by SASE. Buys one-time rights. Pays $25/b&w on publication.

Humorous Illustration: "Never have bought humorous illustration, but we would, if something comes up we like." Works on assignment only. When hiring a freelance humorous illustrator, these abilities are considered: businesslike attitude — meets deadlines and responsive to editor's needs; is very familiar with Appalachian region. For first contact, send cover letter, client list and samples to Pat Arnow. In reviewing humorous illustration looks for "appropriateness to our publication; no mindless stereotypes." Reports back in 4 months. Samples are filed or returned by SASE. Buys one-time rights. Pays $25/b&w page or b&w cover on publication.

Tips: "Would be nice if illustrator were familiar with our publication and interested in what we are trying to do, which is to show a full range of life in Appalachia, not just the poverty."

Humor Writing: Buys approximately 1 humorous piece/issue, 3/year. Needs humorous fiction and cartoon stories. Subject matter is Appalachian-oriented. Length: less than 2,000 words. To query: be familiar with magazine; make sure article is appropriate. Writer's guidelines free. Sample issue $3.50. For first contact, send cover letter, manuscript and list of some credits in cover letter to Pat Arnow. Reports back in 4 months. Samples are returned with SASE. Buys one-time rights. Pays $50 for any length.

Tips: "We are not interested in humor that insults the region; stereotypes are entirely unwelcome. Irony about the stereotypes, yes; making fun of hillbillies, no, no, no."

NUGGET, (see *Cavalier*)

NUTRITION HEALTH REVIEW, 171 Madison Avenue, New York City NY 10016. (212)679-3590. Estab. 1976. Quarterly consumer magazine, tabloid and newsletter. Circ. over 100,000. Needs comic strips, humorous illustration, caricatures, gag cartoons and spot cartoons.

Gag Cartoons: Buys 15 gag cartoons/issue. Prefers gag cartoons on medicine, food psychology, domestic relations, nutrition, mental health. Doesn't want to see gag cartoons on weight loss/gain or fractures. Preferred gag cartoon format is single panel with gagline. Send to Frank Ray Rifkin. Reports back within 30 days. Returns material only if requested. Buys first time rights. Pays $15 minimum for b&w. Pays on acceptance.

OUR FAMILY, Box 249, Battleford ST S0M-0E0 Canada. (306)927-7771. FAX: (306)937-7644. Estab. 1949. Monthly consumer magazine. Circ. 13,000. Needs humorous illustration and writing. Accepts previously published cartoons and articles.

Gag Cartoons: Buys 30 gag cartoons/year. Prefers gag cartoons on family, marriage and religion. Preferred gag cartoon format is single panel, with gagline, b&w line art. Query with 5 rough drawings/batch to Nestor Gregoire, Editor. Reports back in 4 weeks. Returns material if accompanied by SASE. Buys first time rights. Pays $15/b&w on acceptance.

Humorous Illustration: Works on assignment only.

Humorous Writing: Buys approximately 6 humorous pieces/year. Needs humorous nonfiction, humorous "slice-of-life" and humorous anecdotes, "fillers." Subject matter includes family and church. Length: 100-500 words. To query: make sure article is appropriate. Send SASE for copy. For first contact send manuscript to Nestor Gregoire. Reports back in 4 weeks. Samples not filed are returned with SASE. Buys first time rights and reprint rights. Pays 7¢/word.

OUTDOOR AMERICA, Level B, 1401 Wilson Blvd., Arlington VA 22209. (703)528-1818. FAX: (703)528-1836. Estab. 1922. Quarterly association magazine. Circ. 50,000. Needs comic strips, humorous illustration and writing and spot cartoons. Accepts previously published cartoons and humorous articles.

Gag Cartoons: Buys varying number of gag cartoons/issue. Prefers gag cartoons on fishing, hunting, outdoor ethics and conservation issues. Preferred gag cartoon formats are single panel, double panel with b&w line art. Query with 2-5 rough drawings/batch to Kristin Merriman, Editor. Reports back within 3 weeks. Returns material if accompanied by SASE. Buys one-time rights. Pays $50/b&w, $75/color on publication.

Tips: A gag cartoonist should "avoid sexist and ethnic jokes; focus primarily on outdoor ethics and conservation issues."

Humorous Illustration: Buys varying number of humorous illustrations/issue; 8-10/year for articles and spots. When hiring a freelance humorous illustrator, these abilities are considered: ability to conceptualize well and clever ideas-good use of metaphors; a clean, graphically pleasing drawing style; effective use of humor; flexibility, broad potential in drawing style; ability to "fun up" an otherwise "flat" manuscript; businesslike attitude — meets deadlines and responsive to editor's needs. For first contact, send cover letter, resume, b&w and color tearsheets to Kristin Merriman. In reviewing humorous illustration looks for "something that makes me smile, such as a humorous way of looking at something ordinary." Reports back in 3 weeks. Samples are filed or returned by SASE. Buys one-time rights. Pays $50-150/b&w page, $75-150/color page.

Tips: "Introduce yourself to me. Let me know if you are an outdoor lover, what your hobbies are and what your specialty is."

Humorous Writing: Buys approximately 1 humorous piece/issue, 4-6/year. Needs humorous nonfiction and outdoor stories. Subject matter includes hunting, fishing, camping, the senior citizen outdoor lover, conservation and outdoor ethics. Length: 750-1,000 words. To query: be familiar with magazine; make sure article is appropriate; study writers' guidelines. Send SASE for free copy of guidelines; $1.50 for sample magazine.

For first contact, send cover letter, manuscript, published tearsheets, resume and writing sample to Kristin Merriman. Reports back within 3 weeks. Samples are filed or returned with SASE. Buys one-time rights. Pays 10-20¢/word.

OVERSEAS, Kolping St. 1, 6906 Leimen, West Germany. (011)49-6224-7060. FAX: (011)49-6224-70616. Estab. 1971. Monthly consumer magazine. Circ. 83,000. Needs comic strips, humorous illustration and writing, cartoon narratives, gag and spot cartoons. Accepts previously published cartoons and humorous articles.
Gag Cartoons: Buys 3 gag cartoons/issue, 36-50/year. Prefers gag cartons on living in Europe, being a tourist in Europe and working in U.S. military. Preferred gag cartoon formats are single panel, double panel, multi-panel, with or without gagline, with balloons, b&w line art. Query with finished photocopied cartoon to Charles Kaufman, Editorial Director. Reports back in 2-3 weeks. Returns material only if requested and if accompanied by SASE. Buys first time rights. Pays $20/b&w on publication.
Humorous Illustration: Buys approximately 10 humorous illustrations/year for articles and spots. Works on assignment only. When hiring a freelance humorous illustrator, these abilities are considered: a clean, graphically-pleasing drawing style; businesslike attitude — meets deadlines and is responsive to editor's needs. For first contact, send cover letter and b&w tearsheets to Charles Kaufman. In reviewing humorous illustration looks for good style. Reports back in 2-3 weeks. Samples are filed or returned, if requested, by SASE. Buys first time rights. Pays $25/b&w page.
Tips: "Follow up. We get bombarded by new illustrators weekly. To get an assignment, be at the right place at the right time."
Humorous Writing: Buys approximately 30-40 humorous pieces/issue. Needs humorous fiction/nonfiction, humorous "slice-of-life" and humorous anecdotes, "fillers." Subject matter includes being a tourist in Europe, living in Europe and working in U.S. military. Length: 50-100 words. To query: make sure article is appropriate. For first contact, send cover letter, query, outline of proposed story and manuscript to Charles Kaufman, Editorial Director. Reports back in 2-3 weeks. Samples are filed or returned by SASE if requested. Buys first time rights. Pays $35-150 for 50-200 words. Offers 25-50% kill fee.
Tips: "We want short, satirical, punchy humor; no Readers Digest-type humor. No sex, drugs or bodily functions jokes."

PACIFIC RIM RIZA, Suite 1801, 6290 Sunset Blvd., Los Angeles CA 90028. (213)856-9338. FAX: (213)462-8271. Estab. 1988. A magazine for people interested on the Pacific Rim. Needs humorous illustration and humorous writing.
Humorous Illustration: For first contact send resume, client list and portfolio to Rose Thomas, Associate Publisher. Reports back within 5 days. Returns materials only if requested. Negotiates rights purchased. Pays $15 minimum/hour.
Humorous Writing: Works with one humorous writer/year. For first contact send resume, client list and writing samples. Reports back within 5 days. Returns materials. Negotiates rights purchased. Pays $100 minimum/project.

PARISH FAMILY DIGEST, 200 Noll Plaza, Huntington IN 46750. (219)356-8400. FAX: (219)356-8472. Estab. 1945. Bimonthly religious (Roman Catholic), family oriented. Circ. 150,000. Needs humorous writing, gag cartoons and spot cartoons.
Gag Cartoons: Buys 3 gag cartoons/issue; 18/year. Prefers gag cartoons on family life, religious life ("all in good taste, please"). Preferred gag cartoon format is single panel b&w line art with gagline. Send submissions to George P. Foster, Editor. Reports back within 2 weeks. Returns material if accompanied by a SASE. Buys first time rights. Pays $10 minimum for b&w. Pays on acceptance.

Humorous Writing: Buys approximately 1 humorous piece/issue; 6/year. Needs humorous nonfiction, humorous "slice-of-life" and humorous anecdotes, "fillers". Subject matter includes family or religious life from a Catholic perspective. Length: 400-1,000 words for articles; 100-word maximum for fillers. To query: be familiar with magazine; make sure article is appropriate; study writer's guidelines. Send 6 x 9 SASE and two first-class stamps for writer's guidelines and sample copy. For first contact send manuscript to George P. Foster. Reports back within 3-4 weeks. Samples are not filed; returned with SASE. Buys first time rights. Pays 5¢ per word or $20-50 for 400-1,000 words.

PENNSYLVANIA MAGAZINE, Box 576, Camphill PA (717)761-6620. Estab. 1981. Bimonthly consumer magazine. Circ. 40,000. Needs humorous writing and spot cartoons. Accepts previously published cartoons and humorous articles.
Gag Cartoons: Just starting to buy gag cartoons. Preferred gag cartoon format is single panel b&w line art. Topics must be related to or based within the state of Pennsylvania. Query with 5-10 rough drawings/batch to Editor. Reports back within 2 weeks. Returns material if accompanied by a SASE. Buys one-time rights. Pays $10-25 b&w. Pays on acceptance.
Tips: Deal with a subject in or unique to Pennsylvania.
Humorous Illustration: Just starting to buy humorous illustrations for spots. For first contact send b&w promo piece and samples to Editor. In reviewing humorous illustrations looks for art skill and ideas pertaining to Pennsylvania. Reports back within 2 weeks. Samples are filed or returned by SASE if requested. Buys one-time rights. Pays $10-25 for b&w page. Pays on acceptance.
Humorous Writing: New. Needs humorous nonfiction and humorous anecdotes, "fillers". Subject matter includes anything based in Pennsylvania. Length: 50-200 words. To query: be familiar with magazine; make sure article is appropriate; study writer's guidelines. Send $3 for copy of magazine; SASE for writer's guidelines. For first contact send samples to Editor. Reports back within 2 weeks. Samples are filed or returned with SASE. Buys one-time rights. Pays $.15 per word or $10-35 for 50-200 words.
Tips: "We are interested in items we can use in a "life in Pennsylvania" department, and in cartoons for spot use. All materials must pertain to our state."

THE PERSONALITY PAGE, Suite 390, 2899 Agoura Rd., Westlake Village, CA 91361. (805)388-2026. Estab. 1987. Biweekly comedy sheet for radio announcers. Circ. 60. Needs humorous writing.
Humorous Writing: Buys approximately 200 humorous pieces/month; 2,000/year. Needs humorous nonfiction/fiction and one-liners. Subject matter includes jokes on current events, funny astrological forecasts, one-liners and observational humor. May be sarcastic, ironic, cynical, reality-based. "We buy some puns." Length: 15-120 words. To query: be familiar with magazine. Send $1 and SASE for copy. For first contact send writing sample to Mark Wheeler, Owner/Editor. Reports back only if interested. Samples are not returned. Buys all rights. Pays $1 for 15-120 words.

PERSONNEL MAGAZINE, AMERICAN MANAGEMENT ASSOCIATION, 135 W. 50th St., New York NY 10020. FAX: (212)903-8168. Monthly company magazine. Circ. 22,000. Needs humorous illustration and spot cartoons. Prefers working with freelancers who have fax capabilities.
Humorous Illustration: Buys approximately 1 humorous illustration/issue, 8/year for articles and spots. Works on assignment only. When hiring a freelance humorous illustrator, these abilities are considered: a truly unique drawing style; ability to conceptualize well and clever ideas — good use of metaphors; a clean, graphically-pleasing drawing style; effective use of humor; ability to "fun up" an otherwise "flat" manuscript; businesslike attitude — meets deadlines and is responsive to editor's needs. For first contact

send b&w and color tearsheets, b&w and color promo pieces to Seval Newton, Art Director. In reviewing humorous illustration looks for good drawing style and humor. Reports back only if interested. Samples are filed or returned by SASE. Buys one-time rights. Pays $100/b&w, ⅓-½ page.

PHENOMENEWS, Suite 111, 28545 Greenfield, Southfield MI 48076. (313)569-3888. Estab. 1978. Monthly newspaper and tabloid. Circ. 36,000. Needs comic strips and gag cartoons. Accepts previously published cartoons.

Gag Cartoons: Buys 1-2 gag cartoons/issue. Prefers gag cartoons on New Age (astrology, crystals, past lives, palmistry, etc.), holistic health, human potential movement. For us, the "dream" gag cartoon would be "cute, well-drawn characters not putting down New Age philosophies but can poke fun, also with a positive message." Preferred gag cartoon formats are single panel, double panel, with balloons, b&w line art. Query with 2-5 rough drawings/batch to Cindy Saul, Editor. Does not report back. Returns material if accompanied by SASE. Pays $15/b&w on publication.

Tips: A gag cartoonist should "have a good working knowledge of the New Age and what's 'hot' at the moment. Have a positive, non-sexist outlook on life and be able to convey it in their work."

PHI DELTA KAPPAN, Box 789, Eighth & Union, Bloomington IN 47402-0789. (812)339-1156. Estab. 1915. Professional education journal published 10 times/year (Sept.-June). Circ. 150,000. Needs humorous illustration and gag cartoons. Accepts previously published cartoons.

Gag Cartoons: Buys 20 gag cartoons/issue, 200+/year. Prefers well-drawn cartoons on education. For us, the "dream" gag cartoon would be of *New Yorker* quality. Preferred gag cartoon format is single panel, with gagline, with balloons, b&w line art, b&w wash. Query with 10-15 finished cartoons, no more, to Terri Hampton, Permissions. Reports back in 3 weeks. Returns material if accompanied by SASE. Buys one-time rights. Pays $25/b&w on acceptance.

Tips: A gag cartoonist should "be original; draw well and understand education issues and themes; develop a recognizable, personal style. We review as many as 300 cartoons a week. Please send only your very best. Keep track of your submissions and don't resubmit work. Don't take rejection personally—it's a competitive field. We'll let you know clearly if we find your work unsuitable for our publication, otherwise keep trying."

Humorous Illustration: Buys approximately 1-5 humorous illustrations/issue for articles and spots. Works on assignment only. When hiring a freelance humorous illustrator, these abilities are considered: a truly unique drawing style; ability to conceptualize well and clever ideas—good use of metaphors; a clean, graphically-pleasing drawing style; effective use of humor; does not exaggerate or distort too much; ability to "fun up" an otherwise "flat" manuscript; businesslike attitude—meets deadlines and is responsive to editor's needs; willing to take direction and make needed changes. For first contact, send cover letter, b&w or color tearsheets, client list and b&w promo piece to Carol Bucheri, Design Director. "Ballpark your fee range or indicate willingness to work within our fees. Send some samples for me to keep on file and send examples of the kind of work you like to do (what you feel comfortable with) in your preferred media. In reviewing humorous illustration we look for editorial experience, personal style, 'good' drawing, intelligent humor and technical knowledge (i.e., what will reproduce)." Reports back only if interested. Samples are filed or returned by SASE. Buys first time rights and one-time rights. Pays $150/b&w page on acceptance.

Tips: "Give the art director feedback about your needs for freedom or direction in developing concepts and compositions."

Yeah, But Which Came First — The Chicken or the Egg? *When it comes to self-promotion, Randy Glasenbergen prefers to take the direct mail approach. "I've used* **American Showcase** *and* **The Creative Black Book** *somewhat," says Glasenbergen, "but these are very expensive gambles for anyone." Instead, the Sherburne, New York-based cartoonist promotes his "fun, friendly and unique" style via the mail. The result was an assignment from Kris Herzog, art director for* **Phi Delta Kappan** *magazine. Glasenbergen then proceeded to draw his "eye catching embellishment of the message conveyed in the article." Herzog purchased one-time rights to the art, drawn in Flair pen and gray marker, for $300.*

PREVENTION MAGAZINE, 33 E. Minor St., Emmaus PA 18098. (215)967-5171. FAX: (215)967-3044. Estab. 1940. Monthly consumer magazine. Circ. 3½ million. Needs humorous illustration, caricatures, spot cartoons. Accepts previously published cartoons. **Gag Cartoons:** Buys 12-15 gag cartoons/year. Prefers gag cartoons on health and fitness and losing weight. Preferred gag cartoon format is single panel, with gagline, b&w line art, b&w wash. Query with 5-25 rough drawings/batch to Wendy Ronga, Executive Art Director. Reports back in 1 month only if interested. Returns material. Buys first time rights. Pays $250/b&w on acceptance.
Humorous Illustration: Buys approximately 4 humorous illustrations/issue for articles and spots. Works on assignment only. When hiring a freelance humorous illustrator, these abilities are considered: a truly unique drawing style; ability to conceptualize well and has clever ideas — good use of metaphors; a clean, graphically-pleasing drawing style; uses humor effectively; ability to "fun up" an otherwise "flat" manuscript; businesslike attitude — meets deadlines and is responsive to editor's needs. For first contact, send cover letter, client list, b&w or color tearsheets and b&w promo piece to Wendy Ronga. In reviewing humorous illustration looks for concepts and style. Reports back in 2 weeks. Samples are filed or returned. Buys first time rights. Pays $500/b&w page, $1,000/color page on acceptance.

PRIME TIME SPORTS & FITNESS, 228 Greenwood, Evanston IL 60201. (312)864-8113. Estab. 1981. Consumer magazine published 8 times a year. Circ. 64,000. Needs comic strips, humorous writing, cartoon narratives, gag cartoons and spot cartoons. Accepts previously published cartoons and humorous articles.

Gag Cartoons: Buys 20 gag cartoons/year. Prefers gag cartoons on any sports, health or fitness theme. For us, the "dream" gag cartoon would be "oriented toward the woman fitness freak." Preferred gag cartoon formats are single panel, double panel, multi-panel or with balloons. Query with 1-10 rough drawings/batch to Dennis Dorner, Editor. Reports back in 4-6 weeks only if interested. Returns material only if requested and if accompanied by SASE. Negotiates rights purchased. Pays $20/b&w, $50/color on publication.

Tips: A gag cartoonist should "know, very well, the fitness club scene and the true sports feeling of pro sports."

Humorous Illustration: Buys approximately 3 humorous illustrations/year for covers. When hiring a freelance humorous illustrator, these abilities are considered: a clean, graphically-pleasing drawing style; a bold, powerful, attention-getting drawing style; businesslike attitude—meets deadlines and is responsive to editor's needs. For first contact, send cover letter and b&w tearsheets to Dennis Dorner, Editor. In reviewing humorous illustration "we look for basically a clean, detailed style with lifelike drawings." Reports back in 2 months only if interested. Samples not filed are returned, if requested, by SASE. Negotiates rights purchased. Pays $25/b&w page, $50/color page, $50/b&w cover, $500/color cover. Pays on publication.

Tips: "Use good shadings and depth texture in your style."

Humorous Writing: Buys approximately 3 humorous pieces/issue, 25/year. Needs humorous fiction/nonfiction, humorous interview, humorous "slice-of-life," cartoon stories and anecdotes, "fillers." Subject matter includes sports and health, fitness. Length: 300-2,000 words, prefers lower word count. To query: make sure article is appropriate. For first contact send cover letter and manuscript to Dennis Dorner, Editor. "Do not send queries or resume. We don't care about past work." Reports back in 4-6 weeks. Samples are not filed, returned only if requested. Negotiates rights purchased. Pays 25¢/word or $50-500 for 300-2,000 words.

Tips: "Do people know what is humorous? Some supposedly 'funny' articles are insults to people and people's intelligence. What we need, and so do others, are brightly written articles that can make fun of things and people with some taste and sophistication, but not the supposedly smart aleck New York style of writing which is a true mistake for submission to any magazine."

THE PLAYER-AMERICA'S GAMING GUIDE, 2524 Arctic Avenue, Atlantic City NJ 08401. (609)344-9000. FAX: (609)345-3469. Estab. 1988. Monthly consumer magazine. Circ. 200,000. Needs unpublished and spot cartoons.

Gag Cartoons: Buys 14 gag cartoons/year. Prefers gag cartoons on casino gaming, lottery, horse racing. Preferred gag cartoon format is single panel. Send to Glenn Fine, Publisher. Reports back within 30 days if interested. Returns material if accompanied by a SASE. Negotiates rights purchased. Pays $25 minimum for b&w; $45 minimum for color.

Tips: "Know the gambling consumer and what is amusing to him."

PRODUCTION, Suite 7324, 6311 Romaine St., Hollywood CA 90038. (213)460-4494. Estab. 1986. Monthly trade journal and business magazine. Circ. 60,000. Needs comic strips, humorous illustration and writing, cartoon narratives, caricatures, gag cartoons, spot cartoons and feature writing.

Gag Cartoons: Prefers gag cartoons on film/video. Preferred gag cartoon formats are single panel, double panel, multi-panel, with or without gagline, with balloons, b&w line art, b&w wash, color wash. Send submissions to David M. Latt, Publisher. Reports back only if interested. Returns material if accompanied by SASE. Negotiates rights purchased. Pays on publication.

Humorous Illustration: Buys approximately 50-100 humorous illustrations/year for covers, articles, spots, features and ads. Works on assignment only. When hiring a freelance humorous illustrator, these abilities are considered: a truly unique drawing style; ability to conceptualize well and clever ideas—good use of metaphors; a clean, graphically-pleasing drawing style; a bold, powerful, attention-getting drawing style; a subtle, understated drawing style; uses humor effectively; ability to "fun up" an otherwise "flat" manuscript; businesslike attitude—meets deadlines and is responsive to editor's needs. For first contact, send cover letter, resume, client list and copies of work or portfolio to David M. Latt. "In reviewing humorous illustration we look for style." Reports back only if interested. Samples are filed or returned by SASE. Negotiates rights purchased. Pays on publication.

Humorous Writing: Buys approximately 30 humorous pieces/year. Needs humorous anecdotes, "fillers." All articles must be assigned. Subject matter includes film/video. Length: varies. To query: "find out what we want for a particular month." For first contact, send cover letter, query, resume and writing sample to David M. Latt. Reports back only if interested. Samples are filed or returned with SASE. Negotiates rights purchased.

QUARANTE, P.O. Box 2875, Arlington VA 22202. (202)223-1512. Estab. 1984. Quarterly consumer magazine. Circ. 50,000. Needs spot cartoons. Accepts previously published cartoons.

Gag Cartoons: For us, the "dream" gag cartoon would be "showing the pretentiousness of affluence and materialism, also hypocrisy among 'society women' and illustration showing conflicts between young women climbing the corporate ladder and older women execs who are already successful. We'll look at anything." Query with any number of rough drawings to Georgia James, Humor Editor. Reports in 2 months. Returns material with SASE. Buys one-time rights. Pays $25-50/b&w on publication.

Humorous Illustration: Buys humorous illustrations for articles. Doesn't have to relate to a particular topic. When hiring a freelance humorous illustrator, these abilities are considered: ability to conceptualize well and clever ideas—good use of metaphors; a clean, graphically-pleasing drawing style; effective use of humor. For first contact, send b&w tearsheets and other examples of work to Georgia James. In reviewing humorous illustration "we look for elegance and sophistication." Reports back in 2 months. Samples not filed are returned by SASE. Buys one-time rights. Pays $25-50/b&w page.

Humorous Writing: Needs humorous "slice-of-life" and cartoon stories. To query: study magazine. Send $3, $1.60 postage and SASE for copy of magazine. Samples returned with SASE. Buys one-time rights. Pays $50.

RADIANCE, The Magazine for Large Women, P.O. Box 31703, Oakland CA 94604. (415)482-0680. Estab. 1984. Quarterly consumer magazine. Circ. 25,000. Needs comic strips, humorous illustration and writing, cartoon narratives, caricatures and spot cartoons. Accepts previously published cartoons and humorous articles.

Gag Cartoons: Query with 2-6 rough drawings/batch to Alice Ansfield, Editor. Reports back in 6 weeks. Returns material if accompanied by SASE. Buys one-time rights. Pays $25-100 on publication.

Tips: A gag cartoonist should "know the magazine philosophy and read the article she/he is drawing for."

Humorous Illustration: Buys approximately 1 humorous illustration/issue, 4/year for articles and spots. When hiring a freelance humorous illustrator, these abilties are considered: a clean, graphically-pleasing drawing style; ability to "fun up" an otherwise "flat" manuscript; businesslike attitude—meets deadlines, is responsive to editor's needs, "listens well to what we are trying to get across and comes up with good ideas." For first contact, send cover letter, b&w tearsheets and b&w promo piece to Alice Ansfield. In reviewing humorous illustration "we look for style, design, clarity." Reports back in 6 weeks. Samples are filed or returned by SASE. Buys one-time rights. Pays $25-100.

Humorous Writing: Buys approximately 1 humorous piece/issue, 4/year. Needs humorous nonfiction, interviews, "slice-of-life," fiction and cartoon stories. Subject matter includes stories about being a large woman in today's society, anecdotes about daily life events, shopping, relationships, etc., fantasy/fiction with large-sized heroines and characters. Length: 800-2,000 words. To query: be famliar with magazine; make sure article is appropriate; study writer's guidelines. Send $2 and SASE for copy. For first contact, send cover letter, query, outline of proposed story, manuscript, published tearsheets and writing sample to Alice Ansfield. Reports back in 6 weeks. Samples are filed or returned with SASE. Buys one-time rights. Pays $50-75 for 800-2,000 words. Offers 50% kill fee.

Tips: "The writer should be familiar with the large woman—have sensitivity, compassion, insight into her before writing for us. Humor is a good vehicle for us to give our readers greater perspective on what is often a hard life to live as a fat person."

READ ME, 1118 Hoyt Ave., Everett WA 98201. (206)259-0804. Estab. 1988. Quarterly tabloid. Circ. 1,000-1,500. Needs humorous writing, gag cartoons and covers. Accepts previously published cartoons.

Gag Cartoons: Buys 6-10 gag cartoons/issue; 30/year. Prefers gag cartoons on reading, books, bookstores, libraries, war between sexes and general. For us the "dream" gag cartoon would be a knee slapper which is memorable. Preferred gag cartoon format is single panel with/without gagline. Query with 6-12 rough drawings/batch to Ron Fleshman, Editor/Publisher. Reports back within 1 month if interested. Returns material if accompanied by a SASE. Buys first time rights and reprint rights. Pays $5/b&w. Pays on acceptance.

Tips: Study *New Yorker.*

Humorous Illustration: Buys approximately 4 humorous illustrations/year for covers. When hiring a freelance humorous illustrator, these abilities are considered: ability to conceptualize well and clever ideas—good use of metaphors; a clean, graphically-pleasing drawing style; a bold, powerful, attention-getting drawing style; uses humor effectively; businesslike attitude—meets deadlines and is responsive to editor's needs. For first contact send cover letter and b&w tearsheets to Ron Fleshman. Looks for wit, quality of thought and execution. Reports back within 1 month. Samples are returned by SASE. Buys first time rights. Pays $15/b&w page. Pays on acceptance.

Humorous Writing: Buys approximately 10 humorous pieces/issue; 40/year. Needs humorous fiction/nonfiction and humorous anecdotes, "fillers." Subject matter includes "mild to sharp Juvenalian styles; no rehashed Bombeck; humorists are, at heart, great moralists. Work should have that spirit." Length: 250-1,500 words. "In querying our magazine, we advise that you familiarize yourself with our magazine." Send $1.50 for copy. For first contact send cover letter and manuscript to Ron Fleshman. Reports back within 3 months. Samples are returned with SASE. Buys first time rights and reprint rights. Pays $1-3 short filler; $2.50 cartoon setup gags; $4-20 essays, stories, etc. (250-1,500 words). Does not pay by word but by quality of thought and execution. The less rewriting required for "our" slant, the higher the check. SASE imperative for an answer to anything.

Tips: Study Bergson, then go look in the mirror.

ROAD KING MAGAZINE, P.O. Box 250, Park Forest IL 60466. (708)481-9240. FAX: (708)481-1063. Estab. 1963. Bimonthly consumer magazine. Circ. 210,000. Needs humorous writing about trucking and spot cartoons.

Gag Cartoons: Buys 1 gag cartoon/issue; 4-6/year. Prefers gag cartoons on trucking over-the-road. Doesn't want to see gag cartoons on non-trucking. Preferred gag cartoon format is b&w line art with gagline. Query with 4-6 rough drawings/batch to Kevin

Warren, Associate Editor. Reports back within 3 months if interested. Returns material if accompanied by a SASE. Buys all rights. Pays $25 minimum for b&w. Pays on publication.

Humorous Writing: Buys approximately 1-2 humorous pieces/year. Needs humorous fiction on trucking. Length: 1,200 maximum. In querying our magazine, "we advise that you familiarize yourself with our magazine and that your article be appropriate for us." For first contact send copy of manuscript to Kevin Warren. Reports back within 3 months if interested. Samples are returned with SASE. Buys all rights. Pays $200-400 for 1,000-1,200 words.

Tips: "Have an understanding of the long-haul trucker market. No sex or violence."

RURALITE, P.O. Box 558, Forest Grove OR 97116. (503)357-2105. Estab. 1954. Monthly consumer magazine. Circ. 260,000. Needs humorous illustration and writing. Accepts previously published humorous articles.

Humorous Illustration: Buys approximately 11 humorous illustrations/year for articles. Works on assignment only. When hiring a freelance humorous illustrator, these abilities are considered: ability to conceptualize well and clever ideas—good use of metaphors; a clean, graphically-pleasing drawing style; uses humor effectively; can "fun up" an otherwise "flat" manuscript; businesslike attitude—meets deadlines and is responsive to editor's needs. For first contact, send cover letter, b&w tearsheets and b&w promo piece to Walt Wentz, Feature Editor. In reviewing humorous illustration looks for clarity, expression, modeling, ingenuity. Reports back in 3 days. Samples are returned by SASE. Buys first time rights, reprint rights and one-time rights. Pays $30-45/b&w page on acceptance.

Tips: "Illustrations are for assigned stories only and writer should be able to pick out possibilities and generate his own humorous concept, unless otherwise negotiated. Promptness is appreciated."

Humorous Writing: Buys approximately 1 humorous piece/issue, 11/year. Needs humorous nonfiction, "slice-of-life" and fiction. Subject matter includes anything that will appeal primarily to a rural and small-town audience; settings in Northwestern part of the country. Easy-reading style. Length: 800-1,000 words. To query: be familiar with magazine; make sure article is appropriate; study writer's guidelines. Send SASE for copy. For first contact, send query to Walt Wentz. Reports back in 3 days. Samples are returned with SASE. Buys first time rights, reprint rights and one-time rights. Pays $40-75 for 800-1,000 words.

Tips: "Humor writing needs a deft, confident touch, with easy mastery of the language; brisk, clear delineations of character and situation; no telegraphing of humor—if it has to be explained, it isn't funny. Humor is one of the most difficult of writing forms. We've received endless Irma Bombeck imitations, some Dave Barry knockoffs, and even one Patrick Manus pastich. Problem is, of course, that those people do a better job of writing like themselves than anybody else. A humor style can be derivative without being slavishly imitative; these we have no objection to. We really prefer, however, an independent, distinctive style developed by somebody who writes as easily as he/she speaks."

SAGEBRUSH JOURNAL/CAROLINA VETERANS NEWS, 430 Haywood Rd., Asheville NC 28806. (704)253-7175. Estab. 1985. Bimonthly consumer magazine. Circ. 5,000. Needs comic strips, humorous illustration and writing, cartoon narratives, caricatures, gag cartoons and spot cartoons. Accepts previously published cartoons and humorous articles.

Gag Cartoons: Buys 10 gag cartoons/year. Prefers gag cartoons on cowboys, entertainment and military. Preferred gag cartoon format is single or double panel with a gagline. Send submissions to Linda Hagan. Does not report back. Returns material if accompanied by SASE. Buys all rights. Pays $1/b&w on publication.

Humorous Illustration: Buys approximately 1 humorous illustration/issue, 8/year for spots. Send submissions to Linda Hagan. Does not report back. Samples are returned by SASE. Buys all rights. Pays $1/b&w page on publication.

Humorous Writing: Buys approximately 1 humorous piece/issue, 5/year. Needs humorous nonfiction, interviews, "slice-of-life," anecdotes and "fillers." Subject matter includes entertainment, western, military. To query: be familiar with magazine; make sure article is appropriate; study writer's guidelines. For first contact, send manuscript to Linda Hagan, Editor. Does not report back. Samples are filed or returned with SASE. Buys all rights. Pays 25¢/column inch or $1.

THE SATURDAY EVENING POST, Box 567, Indianapolis IN 46202. (317)636-8881. Consumer magazine published 9 times a year. Circ. 700,000. Needs gag cartoons and spot cartoons.

Gag Cartoons: Buys 30 gag cartoons/issue, 270/year. Prefers gag cartoons on kids, family, pets and jobs. Doesn't want to see gag cartoons on overweight people or the homeless. Preferred gag cartoon format is single panel. Query with 10-15 rough drawings/batch to Steven Pettinga, Cartoon Editor. Reports in 6 weeks. Returns material if accompanied by SASE. Buys all rights. Pays $125 on publication. Tips: A gag cartoonist should "have patience."

Humorous Illustration: Buys approximately 30 humorous illustrations/issue, 270/year for spots. Works on assignment only. When hiring a freelance humorous illustrator, these abilities are considered: a truly unique drawing style; a clean, graphically-pleasing drawing style; uses humor effectively.

Used with permission of The Saturday Evening Post

"Tom and I still haven't worked out our wedding plans. I want a formal ceremony and a catered reception, and he doesn't want to get married."

But He Does Want Me to Sign His Pre-Nuptial Agreement: *Aaron Bacall of Staten Island, New York drew on the subject of marriage for* **The Saturday Evening Post.** **Post** *Cartoon Editor, Steven C. Pettinga, purchased all rights to Bacall's pen, ink and wash drawing.*

SCHOOL MATES, 186 Route 9W, New Windsor NY 12553. (914)562-8350. FAX: (914)561-2477. Estab. 1987. Quarterly juvenile magazine. Circ. 5,000. Needs gag cartoons and spot cartoons.

Gag Cartoons: Prefers gag cartoons on chess. For us the "dream" gag cartoon would be one that also offered chess instruction. Preferred gag cartoon format is single panel, with/without gagline and b&w line art. Send submissions to Jennie L. Simon, Editor. Returns material if accompanied by a SASE. Buys first time rights. Pays $25 minimum for b&w. Pays on publication. Tips: "be a chess player."

Humorous Illustration: Buys approximately 1 humorous illustration/year for articles. For first contact send cover letter and b&w tearsheets to Jennie L. Simon. Samples are returned by SASE. Buys first time rights. Pays $25 minimum/b&w page. Pays on publication.

Humorous Writing: "In querying our magazine, we advise that you familiarize yourself with our magazine, so that the article is appropriate for us; study writer's guidelines."

SCHOOL SHOP/TECH DIRECTIONS, P.O. Box 8623, Ann Arbor MI 48107. (313)769-1211. FAX: (313)769-8383. Estab. 1940. Monthly (Aug.-May) trade journal. Circ. 45,000. Needs gag cartoons.

Gag Cartoons: Buys approximately 2 gag cartoons/issue or 10/year. Prefers gag cartoons on vocational, technical and technology education. Must be a school, not industrial setting. Preferred gag cartoon format is single panel, with or without gagline, b&w line art. Query with 1-10 rough drawings/batch to Susanne Pekham, Editorial Director. Reports back in 1 month. Buys first time rights. Pays $20 on publication.

Tips: "Send us a few examples of cartoons which deal with the industrial education field, with special emphasis on classroom situations."

THE SCIENCES, 622 Broadway, New York NY 10012. (212)838-0230. FAX: (212)260-1356. Bimonthly company magazine. Circ. 70,000. Needs comic strips, cartoon narratives and gag cartoons.

Gag Cartoons: Buys 1 gag cartoon/issue, 10/year. Prefers gag cartoons on science. Preferred gag cartoon formats are single panel, b&w line art, multi-panel, with balloons, b&w wash, color wash. Send submissions to Elizabeth Meryman, Picture Editor. Reports back in weeks. Returns material only if requested. Buys one-time rights. Pays $3-500/color.

SENIOR, 3565 S. Higuera, San Luis Obispo CA 93401. (805)544-8711. Estab. 1981. Monthly tabloid. Circ. 140,000. Needs humorous illustration and writing and caricatures. Accepts previously published cartoons and humorous articles.

Gag Cartoons: Preferred gag cartoon format is single panel with b&w line art. Query with 3-10 rough drawings/batch to George Brand, Editor. Returns material if accompanied by SASE. Buys one-time rights. Pays $10/b&w on publication.

Humorous Illustration: Buys humorous illustration mainly for covers and articles. When hiring a freelance humorous illustrator, these abilities are considered: a truly unique drawing style; ability to conceptualize well and clever ideas—good use of metaphors; a clean, graphically-pleasing drawing style; a bold, powerful, attention-getting drawing style; does not exaggerate or distort too much; businesslike attitude—meets deadlines and is responsive to editor's needs. For first contact, send cover leter and b&w promo piece to George Brand. Reports back in 2 weeks. Samples returned by SASE. Buys one-time rights. Pays $10/b&w page, $20/b&w cover.

Humorous Writing: Buys approximately 3-4 humorous pieces/issue, 20/year. Needs humorous nonfiction, interviews and "slice-of-life." Length: 600-900 words. To query: be familiar with magazine; study writer's guidelines. Send $1.50 and SASE for copy. For first contact, send cover letter and manuscript to George Brand. Reports back in 2 weeks. Samples returned with SASE. Buys one-time rights. Pays $1.50/inch.

SENIOR EDITION USA, Suite 2240, 1660 Lincoln St., Denver CO 80264. (303)837-9100. FAX: (303)837-1921. Estab. 1974. Monthly newspaper. Circ. 30,000. Needs humorous writing.
Humorous Writing: Buys approximately 1-2 humorous pieces/issue, 25-30/year. Needs humorous nonfiction, "slice-of-life," anecdotes, "fillers." Subject matter includes anything of interest or relevance to senior citizens, not stereotypical or condescending to senior citizens. Length: 150-300 words. To query: make sure article is appropriate; study writer's guidelines. Send $1 and SASE for copy. For first contact, send manuscript or writing sample to Rose Beetem, Managing Editor. Reports back. Samples returned with SASE. Buys first time rights. Pays $5-25 for 150-800.
Tips: "We look for true experience — many articles are rejected because they are cliché, denigrate age or seniors, or are irrelevent to our market age group. We also syndicate through Senior Edition USA Writers Group."

SERENDIPITY, 4295 Silver Lake Rd., Pinson AL 35126. (205)681-2259. Estab. 1988. Bimonthly consumer magazine. Circ. 3,000-7,000. Needs comic strips, humorous illustration and writing, cartoon narratives, caricatures, gag cartoons and spot cartoons.
Gag Cartoons: Buys 3-5 gag cartoons/issue, 12-26/year. Prefers gag cartoons on politics, weird stuff, etc. Doesn't want to see gag cartoons on talking animals. For us, the "dream" gag cartoon would be one that is pretty, funny and multi-leveled in its meaning. Preferred gag cartoon formats are single panel, b&w line art, double panel, with gagline, multi-panel, with balloons. Query with 4-6 rough drawings/batch to Joseph Dickerson, Editor. Reports back in 2 months. Returns material if accompanied by SASE. Buys first time rights. Pays $5-15/b&w on publication. Tips: A gag cartoonist should "be very unique, new, fresh and funny."
Humorous Illustration: Buys approximately 1-2 humorous illustrations/issue, 5-12/year for spots. When hiring a freelance illustrator, these abilties are considered: a truly unique drawing style; ability to conceptualize well and clever ideas — good use of metaphors; a clean, graphically-pleasing drawing style; a bold, powerful, attention-getting drawing style; uses humor effectively; does not exaggerate or distort too much; ability to "fun up" an otherwise "flat" manuscript; businesslike attitude — meets deadlines and is responsive to editor's needs. For first contact, send cover letter, resume and b&w tearsheets to Joseph Dickerson. Reports back in 2 months. Samples are filed or returned by SASE. Buys first time rights. Pays $5-15/b&w page on publication.
Humorous Writing: Buys approximately 1-3 humorous pieces/issue, 6-18/year. Needs humorous nonfiction, "slice-of-life," fiction and cartoon stories. Length: 1,500-3,000 words. To query: be familiar with magazine; study writer's guidelines. For first contact, send cover letter and manuscript to Lee Crane, Assistant Editor. Reports back in 3 months. Samples are filed or returned with SASE. Buys first time rights. Pays $10-40 for 1,500-3,000 words. Offers 20% kill fee.

THE SINGLE PARENT, 8807 Colesville Road, Silver Spring MD 20910. (301)588-9354. FAX: (301)588-9216. Estab. 1958. Bimonthly association consumer magazine. Circ. 125,000. Needs humorous writing. Accepts previously published cartoons and humorous articles. Associated with Parents Without Partners, Inc., and readers are mostly members of this organization.
Gag Cartoons: "We haven't bought any in the past year. Not from prejudice, but because no submissions struck the right note." Prefers gag cartoons on single parenting themes. Doesn't want to see gag cartoons on divorce bitterness. Preferred gag cartoon format is single panel, b&w line art with gagline. Query with 5-10 rough drawings/batch to Allan Glennon, Editor. Reports back within 1 month if interested. Returns material if accompanied by a SASE. Buys one-time rights. Pays $10 minimum for b&w. Pays on publication. Tips: "Study the magazine to see the types of materials that interest us. Be understanding of ex-spouse differences."

Humorous Illustration: Buys approximately 12 humorous illustrations/year for articles. Works on assignment only. When hiring a freelance humorous illustrator, these abilities are considered: a truly unique drawing style; ability to conceptualize well and clever ideas—good use of metaphors; a clean, graphically-pleasing drawing style; uses humor effectively; businesslike attitude—meets deadlines and is responsive to editor's needs. For first contact send cover letter and b&w promo piece to Allan Glennon. Looks for clean lines. Reports back within 1 month if interested. Samples are filed or returned by SASE. Buys one-time rights. Pays $75 minimum/b&w page.

Humorous Writing: Buys approximately 1-2 humorous pieces/issue; 7-10/year. Needs humorous nonfiction and humorous "slice-of-life." Subject matter includes raising children as a single parent; dating as a single parent; ex-spouse relationships. Length: 1,500 words. "In querying our magazine, we advise that you familiarize yourself with our magazine, that your article be appropriate for us and study our writer's guidelines." For first contact send cover letter and manuscript to Allan Glennon. Reports back within 1 month. Samples are returned with SASE. Buys one-time rights. Pays $75 for 1,500 words. "We do not assign articles."

Tips: "I'm unable to define what makes me laugh. It's a matter of outlook. We seldom publish gag cartoons, and aren't really looking for them. If one came in that we liked, however, we'd publish it. We are a specialized market, aimed at single parents, and as much of the content of the magazine as possible is geared to that market. An article for *Family Circle* cannot be converted to a *Single Parent* article merely by throwing the words 'single parent' into it periodically. Tongue-in-cheek articles about the children and even the 'exes' fit as well, as long as they don't savage the other parent. Anyone trying us with humorous material, of course, is up against our established contributors. But that's life."

SKI MAGAZINE, 2 Park Ave., New York NY 10016. (212)779-5105. Estab. 1936. Monthly consumer magazine. Circ. 440,000. Needs humorous illustration and writing, gag cartoons and spot cartoons.

Gag Cartoons: Buys 2 gag cartoons/issue, 15/year. Prefers gag cartoons on skiing. Preferred gag cartoon format is with gagline, b&w line art. Query with 5-10 rough drawings/batch to R. Needham, Editor. Reports back in 30 days. Returns material if accompanied by SASE. Buys first time rights. Pays $50/b&w on acceptance.

Humorous Illustration: Buys approximately 2 humorous illustrations/issue for articles. When hiring a freelance humorous illustrator, these abilities are considered: a truly unique drawing style; ability to conceptualize well and clever ideas—good use of metaphors; a clean, graphically-pleasing drawing style; a bold, powerful, attention-getting drawing style; uses humor effectively; ability to "fun up" an otherwise "flat" manuscript; businesslike attitude—meets deadlines and is responsive to editor's needs. For first contact, send cover letter, b&w and color tearsheets and portfolio to R. Needham. Reports back in 1 month. Samples are returned. Buys first time rights. Pays $100/b&w page, $300/color page. Tips: "Use bold colors."

Humorous Writing: Buys approximately 6 humorous pieces/year. Needs humorous nonfiction, "slice-of-life," anecdotes and "fillers." Subject matter includes skiing. Length: 150-1,000 words. To query: be familiar with magazine and make sure article is appropriate. For first contact, send cover letter and manuscript to R. Needham. Reports back in 30 days. Samples are returned with SASE. Buys first time rights. Pays 50¢/word or $1 for 150-1,000 words. Offers 15% kill fee.

SKYDIVING, P.O. Box 1520, DeLand FL 32721. (904)736-9779. Estab. 1979. Monthly magazine. Publishes news about the techniques, events, equipment, people and places of sport parachuting. Circ. 8,300. Accepts previously published cartoons/illustrations.

Gag Cartoons/Humorous Illustrations: Subjects include skydiving. For first contact, send cover letter and b&w tearsheets to Sue Clifton, Editor. Reports back in weeks. Returns material. Buys first time rights. Pays $15-25.
Tips: "Know the sport of parachuting."

SNICKER, 1248 Oak Bark, St. Louis MO 63146. (314)772-7483 or (314)567-5508. Estab. 1987. Quarterly tabloid. Circ. 5,000. Needs cartoon narratives, gag cartoons and spot cartoons. *"Snicker* is a forum for humor, truth and experimentation. Surprise us and your fellow artists. Invent new formats." Accepts previously published cartoons and humorous articles.
Gag Cartoons: Uses numerous gag cartoons/issue. Doesn't want to see "Far Side" clones. "For us, the 'dream' gag would be atomic cowboys." Preferred gag cartoon format is multi-panel narrative. Send submissions to Rich Balducci, Editor. Reports back in 2 weeks only if interested. Returns material if accompanied by SASE. Tips: A gag cartoonist should "use his or her soul as often as his or her pen, brush, rapidograph, pencil, crayon or marker."
Humorous Illustration: Uses approximately 2-3 humorous illustrations/issue, 8-12/year for covers. Sometimes works on assignment. When hiring a freelance humorous illustrator, these abilities are considered: a truly unique drawing style; ability to conceptualize well and clever ideas — good use of metaphors; a bold, powerful, attention-getting drawing style; a subtle, understated drawing style; uses humor effectively. For first contact, send anything to Dillar, creative consultant. Reports back in 2 weeks only if interested. Samples are filed or returned by SASE.
Humorous Writing: Uses approximately 1-2 humorous pieces/issue, 3-4/year. Needs humorous nonfiction, interviews, fiction and cartoon stories. Subject matter includes experimental, underground, environmental, social, anarchist, predatory, contradictory, life and death. Length: 500-1,100 word. To query: be familiar with magazine; study writer's guidelines, "then create your own rules." Send $1 and SASE for copy of *Snicker*. For first contact, send anything to Kathleen Balducci, Co-publisher. Reports back in 2 weeks. Samples are filed or returned with SASE.

SOLUTIONS FOR BETTER HEALTH, (formerly Mature Health), Suite 500, 45 34th St., New York NY 10001. (212)239-0855. Estab. 1989. Consumer magazine published 10 times a year. Circ. 245,000. Needs gag cartoons. Accepts previously published cartoons.
Gag Cartoons: Buys 1 gag cartoon/issue, 10/year. Prefers gag cartoons on health-related subjects only, preferably geared towards older adults, 40-65 years old (or older). Preferred gag cartoon format is single panel, with gagline. Query with any number of rough drawings/batch to David Allikas, Managing Editor. Reports back in 7 days. Returns material if accompanied by SASE. Buys first time rights. Pays $50/b&w on publication.

SOUTHERN BEVERAGE JOURNAL, 13225 S.W. 88 Avenue, Miami FL 33176. (305)233-7230. FAX: (305)252-2580. Estab. 1944. Monthly trade journal. Circ. 30,000. Needs humorous illustration, caricatures, gag cartoons and spot cartoons. Accepts previously published cartoons.
Gag Cartoons: Buy 4 gag cartoons/year. "Prefers gag cartoons on alcohol beverage industry — not drunks!" Preferred gag cartoon format is single panel b&w line art with gagline. Query with 2-4 rough drawings/batch to Jackie Preston, Editor. Reports back within 10 days. Returns material only if requested. Negotiates rights purchased. Pays $100-150 for b&w and $250-350 for color. Pays on acceptance.
Tips: "Understand the problems of retailers, bartenders and restaurant owners concerning anti-alcohol lobby. We never portray alcoholic beverage consumption in a negative manner."

Humorous Illustration: Buys approximately 4 humorous illustrations/year for covers and articles. Just began per issue illustration last year. When hiring a freelance humorous illustrator, these abilities are considered: a truly unique drawing style; ability to conceptualize well and clever ideas — good use of metaphors; a clean, graphically-pleasing drawing style; uses humor effectively; does not exaggerate or distort too much; can "fun up" an otherwise "flat" manuscript; businesslike attitude — meets deadlines and is responsive to our needs. For first contact send cover letter, b&w/color tearsheets and color promo piece to Jackie Preston. Reports back within 10 days. Samples are returned if requested. Negotiates rights purchased. Pays $100-150/b&w page; $250-350/color page and cover. Pays on acceptance.

SOUTHERN SENSATIONS, P.O. Drawer 322, Denmark SC 29042. (803)793-3856. Estab. 1988. Bimonthly consumer magazine. Circ. 25,000. Needs humorous illustration and writing. Accepts previously published cartoons and humorous articles.
Humorous Illustration: Buys approximately 4-6 humorous illustrations/year for articles. When hiring a freelance humorous illustrator, these abilities are considered: a truly unique drawing style; ability to conceptualize well and clever ideas — good use of metaphors; a clean, graphically-pleasing drawing style; a bold, powerful, attention-getting drawing style; a subtle, understated drawing style; uses humor effectively; does not exaggerate or distort too much; shows flexibility, broad potential in drawing style; ability to "fun up" an otherwise "flat" manuscript; businesslike attitude — meets deadlines and is responsive to editor's needs. For first contact, send cover letter and b&w tearsheets to J. Kelley Fairey, Co-publisher. "In reviewing humorous illustration we look for style, reality and whether or not it fits articles." Reports back in days if interested. Samples are filed or returned by SASE if requested. Buys first time rights, one-time rights and all rights. Pays $25-50/b&w page, $50-100/color page. Tips: "We shy away from offering tips to professionals, but illustrator needs to keep 'southern' in mind."
Humorous Writing: Buys approximately 4-6 humorous pieces/year. Needs humorous nonfiction, "slice-of-life," fiction, anecdotes, "fillers." Subject matter should be "down home pure southern." Length: 500-1,400 words. To query: be familiar with magazine; make sure article is appropriate. For first contact, send cover letter, outline of proposed story and writing sample to Evelyn Fairey, Co-publisher. Reports back in days if interested. Samples are filed or returned with SASE if requested. Buys first time rights, one-time rights and all rights. Pays $25-100 for 500-1,400 words.
Tips: Humor writing "should be clean cut and southern."

STARLOG MAGAZINE, STARLOG PRESS, 8th Floor 475 Park Ave. South, New York NY 10016. (212)689-2830. FAX: (212)889-7933. Estab. 1976. Monthly consumer magazine. Needs spot cartoons on science fiction, fantasy, superhero.
Gag Cartoons: Buys 50 gag cartoons/year. Reports back if interested. Returns material if accompanied by a SASE. Buys all rights. Pays $15-25 for b&w; $25-50 color.
Tips: "We publish only a small number of cartoons per issue (4-10), but we are interested in new cartoonists who can take a fun look at science fiction films (routine gags need not apply). It would be helpful if artists have some familiarity with science fiction. We're not a big market but we are a market. Our most prolific cartoonist contributor has sold us about 50 cartoons in two years. So, there are some possibilities here. Do not call. And we will not review portfolios. No time for social chitchat meetings, thanks."

STUDENT ASSISTANCE JOURNAL, Performance Resource Press, 2145 Crooks Rd., Troy MI 48084. (313)643-9580. FAX: (313)643-4435. Estab. 1988. Trade journal published 5 times a year. Circ. 50,000. Needs gag cartoons and spot cartoons. Accepts previously published cartoons.

Gag Cartoons: Buys 1 gag cartoon/issue, 3-5/year. Prefers gag cartoons on students' personal problems, for which they might seek the help of a counselor, especially substance abuse issues. Preferred gag cartoon formats are single or double panel, with/ without gagline, with balloons. Query with any number of rough drawings/batch to Janet Hearle, managing editor. Reports back in 4 weeks. Returns material only if interested. Buys first time rights and one-time rights. Pays $15-30/b&w on publication.

TAMPA BAY MAGAZINE, 2581 Landmark Dr., Clearwater FL 34621. (813)791-4800. Estab. 1986. Bimonthly consumer magazine. Circ. 100,000. Needs humorous illustration, cartoon narratives, gag and spot cartoons. Accepts previously published cartoons.

Gag Cartoons: Buys 3 gag cartoons/issue. Preferred gag cartoon format is single panel b&w line art with gagline. Query with 1-10 rough drawings/batch to Aaron R. Fodiman, Publisher. Reports back if interested. Returns material if accompanied by a SASE. Buys one-time rights. Pays $15 minimum for b&w. Pays on publication.

Humorous Illustration: Buys approximately 3 humorous illustrations/issue for covers and articles. When hiring a freelance humorous illustrator, these abilities are considered: a truly unique drawing style; ability to conceptualize well and clever ideas — good use of metaphors; a bold, powerful, attention-getting drawing style; does not exaggerate or distort too much. For first contact send cover letter b&w tearsheets and promo piece to Aaron R. Fodiman. Reports back if interested. Samples are returned by SASE. Buys one-time rights. Pays $15 minimum/b&w page; $25/color; $50/b&w cover; $100/color cover. Pays on publication.

Humorous Writing: Buys approximately 10 humorous pieces/issue. Needs humorous anecdotes, "fillers". Length: 25 words. In querying our magazine, "we advise that you familiarize yourself with our magazine and that your article be appropriate for us." For first contact send Aaron R. Fodiman. Samples are returned with SASE. Buys one-time rights. Pays $75 minimum for a piece.

TEENAGE MAGAZINE, Box 481, Loveland CO 80539. (303)669-3836. FAX: (303)669-3269. Estab. 1983. Consumer magazine published 10 times a year. Circ. 32,000. Needs comic strips, humorous illustration and writing, cartoon narratives, caricatures. Accepts previously published cartoons.

Humorous Illustration: Buys approximately 1-2 humorous illustrations/issue, 10-20/ year for articles. Works on assignment only. When hiring a freelance humorous illustrator, these abilities are considered: a truly unique drawing style; ability to conceptualize well and clever ideas — good use of metaphors; a clean, graphically-pleasing drawing style; uses humor effectively; shows flexibility, broad potential in drawing style; business-like attitude — meets deadlines and is responsive to editor's needs; creative. For first contact, send cover letter and b&w or color tearsheets to Lisa Kretsch, Art Director. "In reviewing humorous illustration we look for work that is youthful, contemporary and cartoonish." Reports back in 4 weeks. Samples not filed are returned by SASE. Buys first time rights. Pays $25/b&w page, $100/color page, $100/b&w cover, $300/color cover. Pays on acceptance.

Humorous Writing: Buys approximately 1 humorous piece/issue, 10/year. Needs humorous nonfiction, interviews, "slice-of-life," fiction. Subject matter includes teenage issues (school, church, etc.). Length: 500-600 words. To query: be familiar with magazine; make sure article is appropriate; study writer's guidelines. Send $1 and SASE for copy. For first contact, send cover letter, query, outline of proposed story and published tearsheets to Jolene L. Roehlkepartain, Associate Editor. Reports back in 4 weeks. Samples are returned with SASE. Buys all rights. Pays $50-100 for 500-600 words. Offers 25% kill fee.

TENNIS MAGAZINE, 5520 Park Ave., Trumbull CT 06611. Monthly consumer magazine. Circ. 500,000. Needs gag cartoons.

Gag Cartoons: Buys 9-12 gag cartoons/year. Preferred gag cartoon format is single panel, b&w line art. Query with any number of rough drawings/batch to Kathleen Burke, Art Director. Reports back in 1 month only if interested. Returns material if accompanied by SASE. Buys first time rights and reprint rights. Pays $75/b&w on publication.

Tips: A gag cartoonist should "understand the subject; have original concepts; execute concepts professionally; and make us all laugh."

THOUGHTS FOR ALL SEASONS: THE MAGAZINE OF EPIGRAMS, Dept. of Sociology, State University College at Geneseo NY 14454. (716)245-5324. Estab. 1976. Commemorative issue consumer magazine. Circ. 500-1,000. Needs humorous illustration.

Humorous Illustration: Buys approximately 4 humorous illustrations/issue for spots. Works on assignment only. When hiring a freelance humorous illustrator, these abilities are considered: ability to conceptualize well and clever ideas — good use of metaphors; uses humor effectively; businesslike attitude — meets deadlines and is responsive to editor's needs. For first contact send b&w tearsheets to Professor Michael P. Richard, Publisher and Senior Editor. Looks for ability to translate a concept into graphics. Reports back within 1 month if interested. Samples are filed. Buys first time rights. Pays $25 minimum for b&w page. Pays on publication. Tips: "Illustrator must scan manuscript of the forthcoming issue and generate some preliminary sketches."

Humorous Writing: Needs epigrams. Subject matter includes social satire and word play. Length: 1-3 lines each "In querying our magazine, we advise that you familiarize yourself with our magazine." Send $3.75 and $1.25 for postage and handling for a copy. Writer's guidelines free. For first contact send writing sample to Professor Michael P. Richard. Reports back within 1 month. Samples are filed.

Tips: "Must be familiar with the epigram as a literary form."

THRASHER MAGAZINE & THRASHER COMICS, P.O. Box 884570, San Francisco CA 94188-4570. (415)822-3083. FAX: (415)822-8359. Estab. 1981. Monthly skateboarding and rock 'n roll consumer magazine. Circ. 3-400,000. Needs comic strips, humorous illustration, humorous writing, cartoon narratives and illustration.

Gag Cartoons: Buys 4-6 gag cartoons/year. Prefers gag cartoons on skateboarding, punk rock and youth. Send submissions to Kevin Ancell, Cartoon/Comics Editor. Reports back if interested. Returns material if accompanied by a SASE. Buys all rights. Pays $50 minimum for b&w. Pays on publication.

Humorous Illustration: Buys approximately 1-2 humorous illustrations/year for articles. Works on assignment only. When hiring a freelance humorous illustrator, looks for a truly unique drawing style. For first contact send b&w or color tearsheets to Enrico Chandoha, Art Director. Looks for boldness, guts, raw humor and reality. Reports back if interested. Samples are filed or returned if requested. Buys all rights. Pays $100 minimum/b&w page. Tips: "We don't want anything 'cute'."

Humorous Writing: Buys approximately 6-8 humorous pieces/year. Needs humorous nonfiction/fiction, humorous interviews and cartoon stories. Subject matter includes skateboarding and rock 'n roll. Length: 500-1,500 words. "In querying our magazine, we advise that you familiarize yourself with our magazine and that your article be appropriate for us." For first contact send outline of proposed story and writing sample to Kurt Carlson, Copy Editor. Reports back if interested. Samples are filed or returned if requested. Buys all rights. Pays $.15 per word. Offers 50% kill fee.

Tips: "We print pieces that have attitude, sarcasm, satire and wit. We're not above 'strengthening' it a bit. Our magazine is about youth and the street."

THIRD WORLD, Rua da Gloria, 122-Sala 105, Rio de Janeiro RJ Brazil 20241. (5-21)222-1370 or (5-21)242-1957. Estab. 1986. Bimonthly news magazine. Circ. 4,000. Needs humorous illustration, humorous writing, cartoon narratives, caricatures and spot cartoons. Accepts previously published cartoons and humorous articles.

Humorous Illustration: Buys approximately 1-2 humorous illustrations/issue; 5-15/year for covers and articles. When hiring a freelance humorous illustrator, these abilities are considered: ability to conceptualize well and clever ideas—good use of metaphors; a clean, graphically-pleasing drawing style; does not exaggerate or distort too much; shows flexibility, broad potential in drawing style; is sensitive to issues of importance to Third World peoples and/or is from a Third World country. For first contact send cover letter, b&w or color tearsheets to Bill Hinchberger, Editor. Looks for contributors who are from or understand the countries of the South. No First World stereotypes. Reports back within 1 month. Samples are filed and not returned. Negotiates rights purchased. Pays $10 minimum/b&w page; $15 color cover.

Tips: "Write and ask us for a sample copy and read the magazine. We are a good market for young artists and Third World artists who are looking for greater exposure."

Humorous Writing: Buys various amounts of humorous pieces/issue. Needs humorous nonfiction, humorous interviews, humorous anecdotes, "fillers", Op-ed. Subject matter includes humor that doesn't make fun of Third World people and their customs. Interested in pieces that depict the Third World positively. Length: Op-ed 600-700 words, "fillers"; 200-400 words. "In querying our magazine, we advise that you familiarize yourself with our magazine and that your article be appropriate for us." Send for a free copy. For first contact send cover letter, manuscript, writing sample, query and published tearsheets to Bill Hinchberger. Reports back within 1 month. Samples are not filed and not returned. Buys first time rights, reprint rights and one-time rights. Pays $50-100 for a piece. "We only make formal assignments to people in whom we have confidence."

Tips: "*Third World* is not a humor magazine, but we are always open to informative and lively pieces that present the world from a Third World perspective."

TOLE WORLD, P.O. Box 5986, Concord CA 94524. (415)671-9852. FAX: (415)671-0692. Estab. 1977. Bimonthly consumer magazine. Circ. 30,000. Needs topical cartoons with illustration and caption.

Gag Cartoons: Prefers gag cartoons on tole painting, classroom situations and goof-ups. Doesn't want to see gag cartoons on harmless, evocative, hilarious and timeless. Preferred gag cartoon format is single panel, with gagline, b&w line art, b&w wash. Query with 2-10 rough drawings/batch to Zach Shatz, Editor. Reports back in 4 weeks. Returns material if accompanied by SASE. Buys all rights. Pays $25/b&w on acceptance. Tips: A gag cartoonist should "understand the readership, the specifics of the magazine focus and the necessity for lightness in humor."

Humorous Illustration: Buys approximately 1 humorous illustration/issue for spots. When hiring a freelance humorous illustrator, these abilties are considered: ability to conceptualize well and clever ideas—good use of metaphors; a clean, graphically-pleasing drawing style; shows flexibility, broad potential in drawing style. For first contact, send query of possible ideas.

VIRTUE, P.O. Box 850, 548 Sisters Parkway, Sisters OR 97759. (503)549-8261. FAX: (503)549-0153. Estab. 1978. Bimonthly consumer magazine. Circ. 150,000. Needs humorous illustration and writing, cartoon narratives, gag cartoons, spot cartoons and continual feature character. Accepts previously published cartoons.

Gag Cartoons: Buys 2-3 gag cartoons/issue, 15-18/year. Prefers gag cartoons on woman's relationships, family, animal humor, holidays and seasons. Doesn't want to see gag cartoons on religion, domestic conflict. For us, the "dream" gag cartoon would be referring specifically to our features, or to the temperament of our audience. Preferred gag cartoon formats are single panel, double panel, with or without gagline, b&w line art, b&w wash. Query with 5-10 rough drawings/batch to Geoff Sprague, Art Director. Reports back in 60 days. Returns material if accompanied by SASE. Buys one-time rights; negotiates rights purchased. Pays $25/b&w on publication. Tips: "Develop a clean consistent drawing style and work with funny, positive situations. Do not contrive gags. Relate to everyone's experiences. Avoid duplicating Gary Larson."

Humorous Illustration: Buys approximately 1 humorous illustration/issue, 5/year for articles and spots. When hiring a freelance humorous illustrator, these abilities are considered: unique drawing style; conceptualizes well and has clever ideas — good use of metaphors; clean, graphically-pleasing drawing style; bold, powerful, attention-getting drawing style; subtle, understated drawing style; uses humor effectively; does not exaggerte or distort too much; shows flexibility, broad potential in drawing style; can "fun up" an otherwise "flat" manuscript; is businesslike, meets deadlines and is responsive to editor's needs. For first contact, send cover letter, resume, client list, b&w or color tearsheets, b&w or color promo pieces, slides and portfolio to Geoff Sprague. In reviewing humorous illustration we look for "clean style, strong potential for finished art look. Handles human form in a believable way. Capable of a broad range of expression and emotion." Reports back only if interested. Samples are filed or returned by SASE. Buys first time rights. Pays $150/b&w page, $250/color page. Tips: "Develop a clean style. Be willing to work FAST. Make use of fax machines for sending roughs."

Humorous Writing: Buys approximately 1 humorous piece/issue, 6/year. Needs humorous nonfiction, "slice-of-life" and fiction. Subject matter includes family life. Avoid satire and sarcasm. Length: 1,000-1,500 words. To query: be familiar with magazine; make sure article is appropriate; study writer's guidelines. Send SASE for copy of guidelines, $3 (no SASE) for magazine sample. For first contact, send query, outline or proposed story and writing sample to Becky Durest Fish, Editor. Reports back in 4-6 weeks. Samples are not filed, returned if requested. Buys first time rights. Pays 15-25¢/word for 1,000-1,500 words.

WISCONSIN, THE MILWAUKEE JOURNAL MAGAZINE, Box 661, Milwaukee WI 53201. (414)224-2341. Estab. 1969. Weekly Sunday newspaper magazine. Circ. 510,000. Needs humorous writing and gag cartoons. Accepts previously published cartoons and humorous articles.

Gag Cartoons: Buys 2 gag cartoons/issue; 125/year. Prefers gag cartoons on contemporary subjects. Doesn't want to see gag cartoons on wife/mother-in-law themes. For us the "dream" gag cartoon would be something that made an interesting comment on people while being funny. Preferred gag cartoon format is single panel b&w line art. Send submissions to Alan Borsuk, Editor. Reports back within 2 months. Returns material if accompanied by a SASE. Buys one-time rights. Pays $15 minimum for b&w. Pays on acceptance.

Humorous Writing: Buys approximately 1 humorous piece/issue; 35/year. Needs humorous nonfiction and humorous "slice-of-life." Subject matter includes women's personal essays that, below the surface, contain substantial commentary. Wisconsin angle is a strong plus. Length: 750-1,000 words. "In querying our magazine, we advise that you familiarize yourself with our magazine, that your article be appropriate; study writer's guidelines." Free copy. For first contact send manuscript to Alan Borsuk. Reports back within 2 months. Buys one-time rights. Pays $125-175 for 750-1,250 words. Offers a negotiated kill fee.

THE WISCONSIN RESTAURANTEUR, 125 W. Doty, Madison WI 53703. (608)251-3663. FAX: (608)251-3666. Estab. 1933. Monthly trade journal. Circ. 4,200. Needs humorous illustration and writing, gag cartoons and spot cartoons. Accepts previously published cartoons and humorous articles with reprint rights only.

Close-up

Elwood Smith
Humorous Illustrator

If you think Elwood Smith is a funny name, you ought to see his drawings.

Flip through the pages of any major magazine, from *TIME* to *Esquire*, and chances are you'll come across Smith's bubble-bodied, cucumber-nosed, bow-tied, hat-sporting characters—who are almost always walking dogs, cats or even pigs.

But Smith was a late bloomer. It wasn't until he moved to New York City at 35 that he locked into his drawing style: a designy, yet highly derivative form reminiscent of the comics of the 1920s through 40s. An Elwood Smith drawing is proof of the adage that everything old is in fact new again.

"As a kid," recalls Smith, "I used to read 'Barney Google,' 'Krazy Kat,' 'Mutt 'n' Jeff' and 'Pogo.' Years later my influences were more cerebral— Seymour Chwast, Ed Sorel, Milton Glaser—more design-oriented, less cartoony, a little more heady. I even went through a period where I looked a little like Alan E. Cober and R.O. Blechman put in a blender."

Smith is somewhat envious of illustrators who have not gone through periods of artistic idolatry, emulation and stylistic groping. "I've met illustrators," says Smith, "who come full-fledged into the world with a style, but I didn't. Some people just draw and it comes out very naturally, but for me it was always hard work. It's getting easier, though."

While he respects cartoonists, Smith doesn't consider himself one. "I'm a humorous illustrator," Smith asserts, "and it's a different world. I always work on assignment; I always read a manuscript. A cartoonist creates out of his own imagination, but I always need a manuscript or a headline to bounce off of. I'm not very good at working any other way. I tried a comic strip and it failed."

When a magazine art director or editor presents him with a manuscript, Smith almost always demands creative control of the art which he is to render. "As I become more well known in the business, I'm given more and more freedom, so I tend to refuse jobs that don't give me the kind of freedom I want," says Smith. Eight years of art directing and 20 years of illustrating have convinced Smith that when it comes to his work, he knows best. "I think I'm a good judge of what will work and what won't work," says Smith.

Unlike most magazine illustrators who use "thumbnail" sketches to think out various solutions to their graphic problems, Smith does not. "That isn't the way I work," Smith points out. "I give the client one sketch of what I'll draw as the final art. In the exploration of working on the sketch and pushing the pencil around, the idea emerges."

Because of Smith's high editorial visibility, art directors pretty much know how he'll approach their assignment. "They know my style," says Smith, "and they have to rely on me to do the right thing. But sometimes I'll send somebody their sketch and they say that it misses—totally misses. Then I have to determine if I'm willing to take another shot at it or get a (50%) kill fee and let them find somebody else."

Advertising is playing a bigger and bigger role in Smith's career. In years past, agencies and clients would shy away from Smith's self-described "goofy, far-out" style. "Now that my stuff is a little more mainstream, agency art directors find me more acceptable," he says. Still, Smith prefers doing editorial work over advertising gigs. And when it comes to an ink well over a watercolor palette, Smith likes working in color rather than black and white. "I don't feel I'm a real good black and white artist," Smith admits. "When I work in black and white, I have to approach things a little differently. Color helps me think out the spatial relationships."

As successful as he is, Smith has not forgotten the importance of self-promotion. "My philosophy," proclaims Smith, "is that you can't be too visible. Send out interesting mailers that don't take up too much space in an art director's dinky office. Self-promotional consistency is something that is often overlooked. An art director can forget about you, even if your work is good, by the time the right assignment comes up. Don't bombard them but keep reminding them— pretty soon they'll remember you."

Increasingly, technology allows the freelancer to live virtually anywhere he wants, and for Smith that means the small town of Rhinebeck, New York. "But I couldn't live here," explains Smith, "if it weren't for Federal Express and I couldn't get along without the fax machine."

—Bob Staake

**An example of one of Smith's full-color
8½ × 11 self-promotional mailers.**

Gag Cartoons: Buys 1 gag cartoon/issue, 11/year. Prefers gag cartoons on foodservice. Doesn't want to see unrelated subjects. For us, the "dream" gag cartoon would be restaurant or hotel cartoons that involve real problems in the industry. Preferred gag cartoon format is single panel, double panel, multi-panel, with or with gagline, b&w line art. Query with 2-10 rough drawings/batch to Jan LaRue, Editor. Reports back in 30 days only if interested. Returns material if accompanied by SASE. Buys first time rights, one-time rights and all rights. Pays $5/b&w on acceptance. Tips: A gag cartoonist should "never put a restauranteur in a bad light."

Humorous Illustrator: Buys approximately 1 humorous illustration/issue, 11/year for fillers. When hiring a freelance humorous illustrator these abilities are considered: ability to conceptualize well and clever ideas — good use of metahors; clean, graphically-pleasing drawing style; uses humor effectively; does not exaggerate or distort too much; ability to "fun up" an otherwise "flat" manuscript. For first contact, send cover letter, b&w promo piece and b&w tearsheets (if available) to Jan LaRue. Reports back in 30 days. Samples are returned by SASE. Buys first time rights, one-time rights and all rights. Pays $10/b&w page. Tips: "No off-color or off-subject material."

Humorous Writing: Buys approximately 1 humorous piece/issue, 11/year. Needs humorous nonfiction, fiction, anecdotes, "fillers" and cartoon stories. Subject matter includes foodservice or employee-oriented service. Length: 500-1,500 words. To query: be familiar with magazine; make sure article is appropriate; study writer's guidelines. Send SASE for copy. For first contact, send manuscript or writing smaple to Jan LaRue. Reports back in 30 days. Samples are returned with SASE. Buys first time rights, one-time rights. Pays $5-25 for 500-1,500 words.

Tips: "Manuscripts and cartoons should be neat and easy to read. Do not send non-foodservice related material. Do not send previously published copyrighted material unless clearance is provided. Do not send letter-size envelope if requesting a copy of the magazine."

WOMAN'S ENTERPRISE, 28210 Dorothy Drive, Agoura Hills CA 91301. (818)889-8740. FAX: (818)889-4726. Bimonthly consumer magazine. Circ. 100,000. Needs gag cartoons and spot cartoons.

Gag Cartoons: Buys 2 gag cartoons/issue. Prefers gag cartoons on women in small business. Preferred gag cartoon format is single panel with gagline b&w line art and b&w wash. Send submissions to Caryne Brown, Editor. Reports back within 6 weeks. Returns material if accompanied by a SASE. Buys one-time rights. Pays $50 minimum for b&w. Pays on acceptance. Tips: Know the magazine and read editorial guidelines.

WOMEN'S HOUSEHOLD, 306 E. Parr Rd., Berne IN 46711. (219)589-8741. FAX: (219)589-8093. Estab. 1961. Monthly consumer magazine. Circ. 50,000. Needs humorous illustration and humorous writing.

Gag Cartoons: Buys 5 gag cartoons/year. Prefers gag cartoons on pen pals. Doesn't want to see gag cartoons on weight, soaps. For us the "dream" gag cartoon would be a pen pal "series." Preferred gag cartoon format is single panel b&w line art. Query with 2-5 rough drawings/batch to Allison Ballard-Bonfitto, Editor/Art Director. Reports back within 2 months. Returns material. Negotiates rights purchased. Pays $15 minimum for b&w. Pays on publication.

Humorous Illustration: Buys approximately 1 humorous illustration/issue; 10/year for articles. Works on assignment only. When hiring a freelance humorous illustrator, these abilities are considered: clean, graphically-pleasing drawing style; bold, powerful, attention-getting drawing style; uses humor effectively; does not exaggerate or distort too much; ability to "fun up" an otherwise "flat" manuscript; ability to take direction. For first contact send cover letter and b&w tearsheets to Allison Ballard-Bonfitto. Looks for clarity, originality and composition. Reports back within 2 months. Samples are filed or returned. Negotiates rights purchased. Pays $50 minimum/b&w page. Pays on

publication. Tips: "Must be able to work with a script and an art director."
Humorous Writing: Buys approximately 1 humorous piece/issue; 12/year. Needs humorous "slice-of-life" and humorous looks at a homemaker's everyday life. Subject matter includes pen palling, house cleaning, crafts, child raising and man-woman relationships. Length: 1,000 words. In querying our magazine, "we advise that you familiarize yourself with our magazine, that your article be appropriate for us; and study our writer's guidelines." Send $1.50 and SASE for copy. For first contact send cover letter, manuscript and writing sample to Allison Ballard-Bonfitto. Reports back within 2 months. Samples are filed or returned. Negotiates rights purchased. Pays $50-80 for 800-1,000 words. Offers 80% kill fee.
Tips: "Find the humor in everyday situations without being insulting or silly. Show the similarities between women and people in general."

WOMEN'S SPORTS & FITNESS, P.O. Box 2456, Winter Park FL 32789. (407)628-4802. FAX: (407)628-7061. Estab. 1976. Consumer magazine. Circ. 250,000.
Humorous Writing: Buys approximately 3 humorous pieces/year. Needs humorous nonfiction, interviews, "slice-of-life" and anecdotes, "fillers". Subject matter includes stories from the world of sports and fitness by women. Length: 850 words. In querying our magazine, "we advise that you familiarize yourself with our magazine and that your article be appropriate for us." For first contact send cover letter, manuscript, writing sample, query, published tearsheets or outline of proposed story to Lewis Rothlein, Editor. Reports back within 6 weeks. Samples are returned with SASE. Buys first time rights. Pays $150-250 for 850 words. Offers 25% kill fee.
Tips: "Prefer humor based on real life situations rather than based on just cleverness. But this is not to discourage cleverness."

WOODMEN OF THE WORLD MAGAZINE, 1700 Farnam St., NE 68102. (402)342-1890. Estab. 1890. Monthly membership magazine. Circ. 470,000. Needs humorous writing, gag cartoons and spot cartoons. Accepts previously published cartoons and humorous articles.
Gag Cartoons: Buys 1-2 gag cartoons/issue, 18/year. Prefers gag cartoons of interest to the American family. Preferred gag cartoon format is single panel, with or without gagline, b&w line art, b&w wash, color wash. Send submissions to Leland A. Larson, Editor. Reports back in 2 weeks. Returns material. Buys one-time rights. Pays $15/b&w, $20/color on acceptance.
Humorous Writing: "We would buy humorous writing if we could see some good work." Needs humorous nonfiction and "slice-of-life." Subject matter includes material of interest to families. Length: 500-1,500 words. To query: make sure article is appropriate. For first contact, send manuscript to Leland Larson, Editor. Reports back in 2 weeks. Buys one-time rights. Pays 10¢/word or $50-150 for 500-1,500 words.

WORKBENCH, 4251 Pennsylvania, Kansas City MO 64111. (816)531-5730. Estab. 1957. Bimonthly consumer magazine. Circ. 800,000. Needs humorous illustration, gag cartoons and spot cartoons.
Gag Cartoons: Buys 2 gag cartoons/issue, 12/year.

THE WORLD & I, 2850 New York Ave. NE, Washington DC 20002. (202)635-4000. FAX: (202)269-9353. Estab. 1986. Monthly academic magazine. Circ. 30,000. Needs humorous writing.
Humorous Writing: Buys approximately 1 humorous piece/issue; 12/year. Needs humorous nonfiction, interviews; "slice-of-life" and anecdotes, "fillers." Length: 2,000 words. In querying our magazine, we advise that you familiarize yourself with our magazine, that your article be appropriate for us, and study our writer's guidelines. For first contact send cover letter and manuscript to Maureen Spagholo, "Life" section Editor.

Reports back within 1 month. Samples are not filed and returned with SASE. Buys first time rights, one-time rights and all rights. Pays $300-700 for 1,500-2,000 words. Offers 20% kill fee.

WPI JOURNAL, 100 Institute Rd., Worcester MA 01609. (508)831-5609. FAX: 831-5604. Estab. 1898. Quarterly alumni magazine. Circ. 22,000. Needs humorous illustration, gag cartoons and spot cartoons. Accepts previously pubilshed cartoons. Prefers working with freelancers who have fax capabilities.
Gag Cartoons: Buys 1 gag cartoon/issue, 4/year. Prefers gag cartoons on science, technology, higher education. Preferred gag cartoon format is b&w line art, with gagline, b&w wash. Query with 1-10 rough drawings/batch to Michael Dorsey, Editor. Reports back in 2 weeks. Returns material if accompanied by SASE. Buys first time rights. Pays $30 on publication.
Humorous Illustration: Buys 4 humorous illustrations/year for articles. Works on assignment only. When hiring a freelance humorous illustrator, these abilities are considered: truly unique drawing style; conceptualizes well and has clever ideas — good use of metapors; clean, graphically-pleasing drawing style; does not exaggerate or distort too much; shows flexibility, broad potential in drawing style; is businesslike, meets deadlines and is responsive to editor's needs. For first contact send cover letter, resume, client list and b&w tearsheets to Michael Dorsey. Reports back in 2 weeks. Samples are filed. Buys first time rights. Pays $50/b&w page on publication.

WRITER'S DIGEST, 1507 Dana Ave., Cincinnati OH 45207. (513)531-2222. Estab. 1920. Monthly consumer magazine. Circ. 215,000. Needs humorous illustration, humorous writing, gag cartoons and light verse. Accepts previously published cartoons and humorous articles. Prefers working with freelancers who have fax capabilities for illustration.
Gag Cartoons: Buys 2 gag cartoons/issue. Prefers gag cartoons on writing and literary topics. Doesn't want to see gag cartoons on writer's block. For us the "dream" gag cartoon would be "captionless, line drawings; horizontals often fill page layout needs most immediately." Send to Editor. Reports within 2 weeks. Returns material if accompanied by a SASE. Buys first North American serial rights for one-time use. Pays $50 minimum for b&w. Pays on acceptance. Tips: "Keep up-to-date with trends in humor, use an expressive drawing style and always realize that cartooning is an artform in which the illustration is about 55% of the final product."
Humorous Illustration: Buys approximately 3 humorous illustrations/year for articles. Works on assignment only. For first contact send color or b&w promo piece to Carole Winters, Art Director. Reports back only if interested. Samples are not filed and not returned. Buys first North American serial rights for one-time use. Pays $150 minimum/b&w page. Pays on acceptance.
Humorous Writing: Buys approximately 24 short humorous pieces/year and 3 long. Needs nonfiction, "slice-of-life" and anecdotes, "fillers" for our writing life and chronicle sections. Subject matter includes writing and the problems and joys thereof. Avoid the subject rejection. Length: 50-750 words for Writing Life, 2,000 words maximum for Chronicle. In querying our magazine, "we advise that you familiarize yourself with our magazine, that your article be appropriate for us and study our writer's guidelines." For first contact send manuscript to Bill Strickland, Associate Editor. Reports within 2 weeks. Samples are not filed and returned only if requested. Buys first North American serial rights for one-time use. Pays 10¢ per word. Offers 20% kill fee.
Tips: "Humor is tough to shape and mold. Let it flow and find its own shape."

Newspapers

When it comes to humor, newspapers seem to be locked firmly into their own little Catch 22. Almost without exception, they buy their humorous articles, columns, comic strips, editorial cartoons and graphics directly from the syndicates. An Art Buchwald, Gary Larson or Pat Oliphant wouldn't complain about such an arrangement, but a freelancer certainly could.

Yet one can break into the market with success if he understands the realities which face the editor or art director of the daily newspaper.

Let's look at the pie: The syndicates service the daily newspaper with 75% of its humorous art/writing. An additional 20% of exclusive humorous art/writing is handled by the newspaper's fulltime staff. That leaves 5% for the freelancer to claw and scratch at.

Sound discouraging? It need not be.

Approach newspapers with material that has strong local, state and regional appeal. The Op-Ed Editor in Portland, Maine may be inundated with syndicated editorial cartoons about the fall of communism in Eastern Europe when what he'd *like* are cartoons of a more local, parochial nature.

Naturally, the same holds true for written humor.

Newspapers, however, have a little more latitude when it comes to humorous illustration. While they all have fulltime art staffs, many newspapers, especially the larger ones, see benefit in making assignments to freelance humorous illustrators. And with the advent of the fax machine, they're doing so more and more.

BOOK AUTHOR'S NEWSLETTER, 1507 Dana Ave., Cincinnati OH 45207. (513)531-2222. Estab. 1988. Periodic publication that focuses on news items and articles on writing/marketing novels and nonfiction books. Circ. 3,000. Previously published cartoons/humorous illustrations accepted.
Cartoons and Humorous Illustrations: Needs spot cartoons. When buying cartoons/humorous illustrations, considers if artist aims content at the freelance writer. For first contact, send possible cartoons to consider to Kirk Polking, editor. Reports back within 3 weeks. Returns material if accompanied by SASE. Buys one-time rights. Payment for spot cartoons: $10.

CAPITOL COMEDY, Box 25605, Washington DC 20007. (202)333-5852. FAX: (804)422-6378. Estab. 1989. Newsletter of quotable quips with political emphasis on the national and regional level. Circ. 750/month.
Cartoons and Humorous Illustrations: Needs comic strips, editorial cartoons, gag cartoons, single panels of national appeal and Washington DC subjects; humorous illustration; Op-Ed humorous illustrations; caricatures and spot cartoons. When buying cartoons/humorous illustrations considers if artist: can turn around art on short deadline; has ability to read a manuscript and come up with a strong visual idea; uses humor effectively. For first contact send cover letter, b&w tearsheets and b&w promo piece to Elaine Bole. Reports back within 1 month. Returns material if accompanied by SASE. Negotiates rights purchased. Payment for all cartoons/humorous illustrations: $25-200.
Humor Writing: Needs humorous anecdotes, "fillers." "We seek in-the-news humor, topical timely humor and humor a professional speaker could use." Accepts humorous material that has a regional, national or international slant. Length: 1-liners. For first contact, send writing sample. Unsolicited material is returned with SASE. Buys all rights. Payment: $5/joke accepted for publication.

CHICAGO READER, 11 E. Illinois St., Chicago IL 60611. (312)828-0350. Estab. 1971. "Alternative" newspaper. "We are a general interest publication for city dwellers, specializing in features rather than news with emphasis on politics, arts, entertainment, peculiar aspects of city life." Circ. 135,000/week. Accepts previously published humorous articles.

Cartoons and Humorous Illustrations: Needs comic strips, gag cartoons, single panels of national appeal and humorous illustration. When buying cartoons/humorous illustrations, considers if artist has vision that is clearer than a salable concept, sharper than cuddly little characters or cute one-liners. For first contact, send cover letter and b&w tearsheets (photocopies no originals). For editorial cartoons contact Robert McCamant, Art Director; for humorous illustration, spots or comic strips/gag cartoons, contact David Jones, Cartoon Editor. Reports back within 2-4 months. Returns material. Buys first time rights or one-time rights. Payment for humorous illustration or spot cartoons: $10-80. Tips: "Look at our publication, see what our regular cartoonists are doing. Decide what weird corner of the modern cosmos we're not looking into yet. If submitting, send 6-12 samples of most recent work. Be patient."

Humor Writing: Favors humorous "slice-of-life," anecdotes, "fillers." "We aren't looking for 'humor' per se. If we find humor in a piece of writing, that's gravy. Most of our articles should have a Chicago base of some sort." For first contact, send cover letter and manuscript. For humorous feature/article contact Alison True, Associate Editor. Unsolicited material is returned. Buys first time rights. Pays 17¢/word or $185/1,500 words. "For 'casual'-type pieces, exceedingly rare, humorous features could pay up to $1,000." Tips: "We are not a good market for humor submissions. We only slowly, grudgingly add comics as the cartoonist/humorist reveals a fully realized, consistent, peculiar vision of our life and times. We are much less likely to buy strips/serials than singles and gags."

COMEDY ON A STICK, 45 Dunfield #409, Toronto, Ontario M4S 2H4 Canada. (416)481-5026. Estab. 1978. Monthly newsletter. Circ. more than 400. Needs funny one-liners.

Humorous Writing: Buys approximately 20 humorous pieces/issue; 200-300/year. Needs funny one-liners on current trends and topics. Subject matter includes jokes that would be funny when read aloud. "We would like topics of interest to disc jockeys, business people as well as the average Joe." Length: under 40 words. To query: be familiar with magazine. Send $3 for copy. For first contact send jokes and SASE to Steve Shrott, Editor. Reports back within 1-2 weeks if interested. Buys all rights. Pays $5/joke.

Tips: "Make the joke as short as possible, yet still keep the humor. Make the jokes as clear as you can so that it would be understandable to a wide audience. Also, the more jokes you send us, the more chances of making a sale."

COMEDY WRITERS ASSOCIATION NEWSLETTER, P.O. Box 023304, Brooklyn NY 11202-0066. Estab. 1989. Quarterly newsletter.

Humor Writing: Needs short 'how-to' articles on writing and selling jokes, comedy scripts and humorous stories. Short original jokes also wanted. For first contact, send article or jokes to Robert Makinson, Editor.

Humor Writing: Unsolicited material is returned with SASE. Buys all rights. Pays 3¢/word for articles, $1-3/joke. Send SASE for guidelines. Sample issue $4. Remit to Robert Makinson.

FILLERS FOR PUBLICATIONS, 5225 Wilshire Blvd., Los Angeles CA 90036. (213)933-2646. Estab. 1956. Monthly newsletter that focuses on business-related cartoons (nothing pertaining to sex, politics or religion).

Cartoons and Humorous Illustrations: Needs gag cartoons, single panels of national appeal, humorous illustration and spot cartoons. When buying cartoons/humorous illustrations considers if artist uses humor effectively. Must be line drawings. For first contact, send samples. For humorous illustration, spots, contact Lucie Dubovik, Manager.

Reports back within 2 weeks. Returns material if accompanied by SASE. Buys first time rights and one-time rights. Pays $5-10.

INSIDE JOKE, P.O. Box 1609, Madison Sqare Station, New York NY 10159. Estab. 1980. Biquarterly magazine. "A newsletter of comedy and creativity" (emphasis on left-oriented satire). Circ. 150. Previously published cartoons/humorous illustrations accepted but prefers originals made for *Inside Joke*.

Cartoons & Humorous Illustrations: Needs comic strips and editorial cartoons of national appeal; gag cartoons, cover art (write for specs) and general artwork. Does not pay for material. Send #10 SASE for writer/artist guidelines. Send materials to Elyane Wechsler. Returns materials if unused.

Humor Writing: Needs humorous nonfiction, slice-of-life, fiction, feature (series), anecdotes, fillers and political satire, "low-life scum" satire. Length: Under 1,900 words. For first contact send SASE for guidelines. Tips: "Sample issues of *Inside Issue* cost $1.50 each. I recommend sending for an issue before submitting your writing or art. Please make all checks payable to Elayne Wechsler. I cannot affort to pay you, even in free copies, but contributors receive a discount in that they only need pay 3 oz. postage instead of the regular subscription price."

© Philip S. Marden

Bumper to Bumper in Beantown: *"I was trying to show the futile attempt to control traffic in Boston," says Philip S. Marden, a New York City-based humorous illustrator. The job was a direct result of one of Marden's direct mail self-promos. "I sent examples of my work to one or two art directors at the Globe," Marden recalls, "and they must have been passed along to some of the other art directors there." When Marden's work caught the attention of Art Director Jacqueline Berthet, she hired him to illustrate the "Boston Traffic" story, buying one-time usage of the black and white art for $350. The original art was drawn in a felt-tipped pen 4½" × 7½" and two Amberlith overlays were used to achieve the grey line tints.*

INTENSIVE CARING UNLIMITED, 910 Bent Lane, Philadelphia PA 19118. (215)233-4723. Estab. 1983. Bimonthly newsletter that focuses on information and support for families with children with medical or developmental problems. Circ. 3,000. Previously published cartoons/humorous illustrations and humorous articles are accepted.

Cartoons and Humorous Illustrations: Needs comic strips, families with young children subjects, humorous illustration (on assignment). When buying cartoons/humorous illustrations considers line drawings and if artist uses humor effectively. For first contact, send cover letter and b&w tearsheets or sample to Lenette S. Moses, Editor. Reports back within 2 weeks. Returns material if accompanied by SASE. Artist retains all rights. "Ours is a nonprofit newsletter. We can offer no pay, just national publication exposure." Tips: "Query the editor for upcoming article topics."

Humor Writing: Needs humorous nonfiction, interviews, "slice-of-life." "We need humorous articles about how families deal with crises and children in general." Length: approx. 1,000 words. "Query editor for upcoming topics." For first contact, send cover letter and writing sample to Lenette S. Moses. Unsolicited material is filed if applicable or returned with SASE. Author retains all rights. "Ours is a nonprofit newsletter. We offer no pay, just national publication exposure."

LATEST JOKES, P.O. Box 023304, Brooklyn NY 11202-0066. (718)855-5057. Estab. 1974. Monthly newsletter that focuses on short, up-to-date jokes. Circ. 250.

Humor Writing: Needs short, original jokes satirizing modern trends. Send jokes to Robert Makinson, Editor. Pays $1-3 for jokes. Send SASE for guidelines. Sample issue $3. Remit to Robert Makinson.

MCINTOSH PUBLISHING LTD., Box 430 North Battleford, Saskatchewan S9A-245 Canada. (306)445-4401. FAX: 306)445-1977. Estab. 1906. Newsletter, weekly newspaper, "alternative" weekly, trade journal. Circ. 42 million; 20 million for community newspaper. Previously published cartoons/humorous illustrations and articles are accepted. Prefers working with freelancers who have Fax capabilities.

Cartoons and Humorous Illustrations: Needs comic strips, editorial cartoons, wildlife, hunting, skiing and fishing subjects. When buying cartoons/humorous illustrations, considers if artist uses humor effectively. For first contact, send b&w promo piece. For editorial cartoons, op-ed or caricatures, contact Stan Nawakawski, Publisher. Reports back within 4 weeks. Returns material only if requested. Buys reprint rights. Payment for editorial cartoon/humorous illustration: $10-25.

Humor Writing: Needs humorous "slice-of-life," humorous material for hunting, fishing and skiing section. Accepts humorous writing that has a regional slant. For first contact, send cover letter and writing samples to Bill McIntosh, Publisher. Unsolicited material is filed. Buys reprint rights.

MONTREAL MIRROR, 400 McGill, Montreal, Quebec Canada. (514)393-1010. Alternative weekly that focuses on news, feature emphasis and local news culture. Circ. 50,000. Previously published cartoons/humorous illustrations accepted.

Cartoons & Humorous Illustrations: Needs comic strips of regional appeal; editorial cartoons of local appeal; gag cartoons, special subject on food and spot cartoons. For first contact send cover letter, b&w tearsheets, b&w promo piece to B. Weston, News Editor. Reports back if interested. Returns material if accompanied by a SASE. Keeps material on file. Buys one-time rights. Payment for editorial cartoon: $15 minimum.

NEW TIMES, INC., 1201 E. Jefferson, Phoenix AZ 85034. (602)271-0040. FAX: (602)495-9954. Estab. 1970. Weekly newspaper/tabloid that focuses on week's news and arts, encompasses stories of local interest, restaurants, clubs, event listings, events of the week, a children's section, music and record reviews, movie reviews and other listings. Circ. 140,000. Previously published humorous articles accepted. Prefers working with freelancers who have Fax capabilities.

Cartoons & Humorous Illustrations: Needs humorous illustration, op-ed humorous illustrations, caricatures and spot cartoons. When buying cartoons/humorous illustrations considers if artist can draw on local news; can turn around art on short deadline; draws in black and white more often than color style; uses humor effectively and has creative input. For first contact send cover letter, resume, b&w tearsheets, color tearsheets, slides (not mandatory) and/or b&w promo piece to Kenna Stevens, Art Director. For editorial cartoons and humorous illustration/spots contact Kenna Stevens. Reports back within a few days. Returns material only if requested. Keeps material on file. Buys all rights. Payment for humorous illustration: $60-175; for spot cartoons: $50-60; op-ed humor illustration: $175 maximum; cover illustration: $250 maximum.

NORTH MYRTLE BEACH TIMES, P.O. Box 725, 203 North Kings Highway, North Myrtle Beach SC 29597. (803)249-3525. Estab. 1971. Newspaper and tabloid. "We concentrate on local but include some state and national news. We are a locally owned hometown community semiweekly newspaper." Circ. 9,200/issue; special editions circ. 15,000/issue. Accepts previously published submissions "only if not published locally."
Cartoons and Humorous Illustrations: Needs comic strips, editorial cartoons and gag cartoons of local, regional or national appeal; "Especially on sports and golf, since we are the golf capital of world." Also need humorous illustration, op-ed humorous illustrations; caricatures, spot cartoons. When buying cartoons/humorous illustrations, considers if artist can draw on localized news. Send cover letter and tearsheets to editor. Payment for editorial cartoons varies.

NORTHEAST OUTDOORS, Box 2180, Waterbury CT 06722. Estab. 1968. Monthly newspaper that focuses on upbeat, first-person experiences and advice about the "where-to's and how-to's" of camping in the Northeast. Circ. 14,000. Previously published cartoons/humorous illustrations accepted.
Cartoons and Humorous Illustrations: Needs editorial cartoons and gag cartoons of regional appeal, especially about camping. When buying cartoons/humorous illustrations, considers if artist uses humor effectively. For first contact, send cover letter to Jean Wertz, editor. Reports back within 4 weeks. Returns material. Buys one-time rights. Payment for op-ed humor illustration: $20. Tips: "Targets campers (especially RVers) in Northeast."
Humor Writing: Needs humorous nonfiction and "slice-of-life" on camping. Accepts humorous material that has a regional slant. Length: 1,000. For first contact, send cover letter and query for proposed article to Jean Wertz. Unsolicited material is returned. Buys first time rights or one-time rights.

THE ONION, Suite 270, 33 University Square, Madison WI 53715. (608)256-1372. Estab. 1988. Humor-entertainment tabloid that serves the college student population of Madison. Smart, hip and irreverent humor, not afraid of the shocking or disturbing. Circ. 25,000. Previously published cartoons/humorous illustrations and humorous writing accepted, "though we prefer unpublished."
Cartoons & Humorous Illustrations: Needs comic strips or panels of college and national appeal on college life, adult single life and life in general. "We consider buying cartoons/humorous illustrations if we roll over laughing while reading them." For first contact send work, submitted for potential publication to Scott Dikkers, Editor. Reports back within 2 weeks. Returns material only if requested and accompanied by a SASE. Buys one-time rights. Payment for regular cartoon feature: $10-20. "We always pay if we print your work."
Humor Writing: Needs humorous nonfiction, fiction, sports, interviews, features (series), "slice-of-life" and anecdotes, "fillers" with a sardonic edge, satires on college life—or any subject appealing to a college audience. Deviations from these suggestions for comic effect is encouraged. Length: 200-2,000 words. For first contact send typed,

Close-up

Paul Conrad
Editorial Cartoonist
Los Angeles Times

In the 1980s, Paul Conrad half jokingly considered changing the format of his editorial cartoon from a vertical to a horizontal one. The change was entertained *not* for aesthetic or compositional considerations, but to resemble a TV screen.

"Everyone watches television," says Conrad, the three time Pulitzer Prize-winning editorial cartoonist of the *Los Angeles Times*, "and for the most part it's all crap. Nobody reads anymore."

But if Americans are prone to watching rather than reading their news, they still turn to daily newspapers for their editorial cartoons—those clever, sarcastic, even caustic pictorial commentaries in which politicos and issues of the day are skewered by venom-dipped pens.

In fact, nobody skewers better than Conrad, and while the so called "New Breed" of editorial cartoonist uses rim shot humor and shallow Op-Ed one-liners to editorialize, the 66-year-old Conrad prefers attacking the jugular with merciless precision.

"There is too much *illustrating* of the news these days," says Conrad. "I look at many editorial cartoons and I don't know what the cartoonists are *saying* or how they feel about a certain issue. I look and I say, they're *funny*, but I don't know exactly where they're coming from—whether they're for or against a certain issue, and I think that's very important."

Indeed, Conrad views the actual art of his editorial cartoons to be but the vehicle for getting across his philosophically liberal ideas. He even goes so far to say that an editorial cartoon is 90% idea, 10% drawing.

"I've never seen bad drawing destroy a good idea," he points out. "On the other hand, I've never seen a good drawing save a bad idea. It follows that you have to start with an idea and then the drawing comes along to make the whole thing work."

In recent years, Conrad has developed a reduced, even minimalist, graphic approach to his work. While the Conrad of the 1970s used bold, powerful swashes of black for his Watergate-era renderings, the 1990 Conrad resigns to Jerry Brown's "less is more" aphorism.

"Drawing is very important," admits Conrad, "but I've cut out a whole lot of the nonsense—the crosshatching, the shading—I'm not sure it's all that necessary. If I can finish a cartoon in 20 minutes, then that's the ideal editorial cartoon—it's to the point."

Indeed, readers may ignore five written editorials on the Op-Ed page, but read the cartoon. "I have no idea what readership is of written editorials," Conrad offers, "but it doesn't come anywhere close to the readership of editorial cartoons. It's back to TV—people look at *pictures*, so they look at editorial cartoons."

But Conrad stops short of dismissing the editorial cartoon as fast food for a public starved for pictures. "It *is* a peculiar art form," he offers, "but I think it's a necessary art form—and I do believe it's a noble art form. I don't know of a *single* editorial cartoon changing the world, but I do think that over a period of time a *series* of cartoons can. Recently, I think Herblock (of *The Washington Post*) has done a remarkable job of explaining what Civil Rights are all about."

Before attempting to break into the elite and highly specialized profession, Conrad recommends a strong, broad college education. "Read, read, read—the works," he advises. "Take a foreign language to discipline the mind. Take English literature and economics—that's imperative."

College also affords the aspiring editorial cartoonist the all-important forum for expression—the school newspaper. "On the college paper," Conrad says, "that's where you make all your mistakes—hopefully."

While jobs for editorial cartoonists are few and far between, more and more newspapers have recognized the benefit of having their own cartoonist. "A cartoonist," says Conrad, "goes to a small newspaper and he sweats it out there. If he's any good, somebody will notice him and he may get to go to a bigger paper."

The sweat behind him, Paul Conrad remains one of the most respected masters of the art form. For many, Conrad *is* editorial cartooning. Yet in a profession that rewards innocuous gag lines and graphic mimicry, Conrad stands alone—sharpening his pen, spiking his vitriolic ink and waiting for the next unsuspecting politician to walk by.

—Bob Staake

" BUT BURNING THE FLAG GOES TOO FAR ! "

double-spaced writing samples (computer print out is fine too, but please double space) to Scott Dikkers. Unsolicited material is filed or returned if requested only with SASE. Buys one-time rights. Pays $10-60 for a piece 200-2,000 words long. "We don't assign articles."

Tips: "Blow us away with your humor. We're looking for cutting-edge stuff that will turn our office into a gigglefest. Don't waste your time with elaborate queries, cover letters, designer envelopes or scented full-color submissions. Send for our writer's guidelines or a couple issues of *The Onion* (with $1.25 postage) if you'd like, then send us camera-ready column-friendly cartoons, or aptly lengthed written pieces that will make us laugh. Madison is a tremendously ripe market for humor, and yours could gain a large following if you can keep it coming."

PARENTGUIDE NEWS, 2 Park Ave., New York NY 10021. (212)213-8840. Estab. 1983. Monthly newspaper. Circ. 205,000. Needs comic strips, humorous illustration and writing, spot cartoons.
Gag Cartoons: Send submissions to Leslie Elgort, editor. Returns material if accompanied by SASE.

PEACE NEWSLETTER, 924 Burnet Ave., Syracuse NY 13203. (315)472-5478. Estab. 1936. "Alternative" monthly newsletter. "The PNL is the internal organ of the Syracuse Peace Council and a forum for articles which discuss issues of concern to the peace movement." Circ. 4,000. Previously published cartoons/humorous illustrations and articles are accepted.
Cartoons and Humorous Illustrations: Needs comics strips of regional or national appeal; editorial cartoons of local, regional or national appeal; gag cartoons, single panels of regional or national appeal, especially about peace issues (nuclear war, etc.); humorous illustration; op-ed humorous illustrations; caricatures; spot cartoons. When buying cartoons/humorous illustrations, considers if artist can draw on localized news; can turn around art on short deadline; has ability to read a manuscript and come up with strong visual ideas; uses humor effectively. For first contact, send cover letter and b&w tearsheet to PNL Coordinator. Reports back within 2 months only if interested. Returns material if accompanied by SASE (if requested); keeps material on file. "We do not (cannot) pay."
Humor Writing: Needs humorous interviews, op-ed pieces. "All humorous writing should have a peace movement slant." Accepts humorous material that has a regional, national and international angle. Length: 500-800 words. For first contact, send cover letter, resume, outline of proposed article and writing sample to PNL Coordinator. Unsolicited material is filed or returned with SASE if requested. "We cannot pay."

THE PLAIN DEALER, 1801 Superior Ave., Cleveland OH 44139. (216)344-4800. FAX: (216)344-4122. Estab. 1842. Daily newspaper. Circ. 450,000. Previously published cartoons/humorous illustrations and humorous writing accepted.
Cartoons & Humorous Illustrations: Needs editorial cartoons of local, regional and national appeal; humorous illustration, op-ed humorous illustrations and caricatures. When buying cartoons/humorous illustrations considers ability to read a manuscript and come up with a strong visual idea. For first contact send cover letter, b&w tearsheets and slides. For editorial cartoons, contact Jim Strang, Deputy Editorial Director or Gloria Millner, Associate Editor; for humorous illustration/spots contact Christine Jindra, Features Editor. Reports back within 2 weeks. Returns material only if requested and accompanied by a SASE. Does not file material. Buys first time rights and reprint rights. Payment for editorial cartoon: $25 minimum; humorous illustration: $25 minimum; spot cartoons: $25 minimum; op-ed humor illustration: $25 minimum.

Humor Writing: Needs humorous op-ed pieces, humorous "slice-of-life" and humor for our Sunday magazine. Accepts humorous material that has a local, regional, national or international angle. Length: 800-1,200 words. For first contact send cover letter, query for proposed article and writing sample. For humorous op-ed piece contact Jim Strang; for humorous feature/article contact Christine Jindra; for humorous piece for Sunday magazine contact Clint O'Connor, Sunday Magazine Editor. Unsolicited material is not filed and returned only if requested with SASE. Buys first time rights or negotiates rights purchased. Pays $75- (inside feature pages) $200 (op-ed pieces).

REPORTER–YOUR EDITORIAL ASSISTANT, 7015 Prospect Pl. NE, Albuquerque NM 87110. (505)884-7636. Estab. 1956. Monthly newsletter that focuses on teen-related cartoons.
Cartoons and Humorous Illustrations: Needs gag cartoons of national appeal, humorous illustration; nothing pertaining to sex, politics or religion. When buying cartoons/humorous illustrations, considers if artist uses humor effectively. Must be line drawings. For first contact, send samples to Lucie Dubovik, Manager. Reports back within 2 weeks. Returns material if accompanied by SASE. Buys first time rights and one-time rights. Payment is $5-10.

Two Heads Are Better Than One, But This is Ridiculous! *There's a pleasing, even reassuring spontaneity to Keith Bendis' humorous illustrations—he makes the art of drawing funny pictures look so easy. Gerald Sealy, Art Director for the Philadelphia Inquirer Magazine gave the Lake Peeksill, New York-based Bendis a manuscript, complete creative freedom and a ten day deadline. Paying homage to his artistic influences, Bendis describes his drawing style as a "loose, cartoonish, Steinbergish, Steadmanlike, Searle-influenced, Steigish pencil technique." Bendis advertises in* American Showcase *and his agent nurtures a high profile, three times a year ad campaign for the humorous illustrator on the back cover of* Art Direction *magazine.*

© Keith Bendis

STUDENT PRESS LAW CENTER REPORT, Suite 504, 1735 Eye Street NW, Washington DC 20006. (202)466-5242. Estab. 1974. Triannual magazine that focuses cases and controversies involving free press rights of student journalists. Illustrations used to advocate student press freedom and condemn censorship. Circ. 7,000. Previously published cartoons/humorous illustrations accepted.
Cartoons & Humorous Illustrations: Needs comic strips, editorial cartoons, gag cartoons and single panels of regional and national appeal; op-ed humorous illustration, caricatures and spot cartoons. When accepting cartoons/humorous illustrations considers if artist can turn around art on short deadline; and if the artist is a high school or college student. For first contact send cover letter and b&w tearsheets. Reports back within 1 month. Returns material only if requested. All illustrations/cartoons are contributed by volunteer students with an interest in press freedom issues.

SUNRISE, P.O. Box 6767, Seeger Square Station, Saint Paul MN 55106-0767. (612)774-4971. FAX: (612)770-9187. Estab. 1977. Monthly tabloid that focuses on neighborhood news. Circ. 15,000. Previously published cartoons/humorous illustrations and articles are accepted.
Cartoons and Humorous Illustrations Needs comic strips and editorial cartoons of local appeal, gag cartoons, single panels of local appeal, humorous illustration, op-ed humorous illustration, caricatures, spot cartoons. When buying cartoons/humorous illustrations, considers if artist can draw on localized news and can turn around art on short deadline. For first contact, send cover letter, b&w tearsheets, b&w promo piece and resume to editor. Reports back only if interested. Does not return or file material. Buys all rights. Payment for editorial cartoon, humorous illustration, spot cartoons and op-ed humor illustration: $10-15.
Humor Writing: Needs all types of humorous writing. Accepts humorous material that has a local or regional slant. Length: 500-600 words. For first contact, send cover letter, resume, query for proposed article and outline of proposed article to editor. Unsolicited material is not filed or returned. Buys all rights.
Tips: "Be very local."

TREASURE CHEST, Suite 211A, 253 W 72 St., New York NY 10023. (212)496-2234. Estab. 1988. Monthly tabloid focusing on antiques and collectibles. Provides information source and marketplace for collectors and dealers. Circ. 50,000. Previously published cartoons/humorous illustrations and articles are accepted.
Cartoons and Humorous Illustrations: Needs humorous illustration, caricatures and spot cartoons that are positive and upbeat and focus on antiques and collectibles. When buying cartoons/humorous illustrations, considers if artist has ability to read a manuscript and come up with a strong visual idea and uses humor effectively. For first contact, send b&w tearsheets and sketches to Howard Fischer, Editor. Reports back in 1 month. Returns material if accompanied by SASE. Negotiates rights purchased. Payment for humorous illustration and spots cartoons: $10-25.
Humor Writing: Needs humor writing relating to antiques and collectibles. Subject matter includes auction scenes, antique shop buyers and sellers, collectors and his/her collections—all upbeat and positive. Length: 500-1,000. For first contact, send manuscript to Howard Fischer, Editor. Unsolicited material returned with SASE. Negotiates rights purchased. Pays $15-25 for 500-1,000 words. Tips: "Those interested in working with *Treasure Chest* should send $1 for sample copy and writers' and artists' guidelines in order to better understand what we seek."

WDS FORUM, 1507 Dana Ave., Cincinnati OH 45207. (513)531-2222. Estab. 1970. Quarterly publication that focuses on writing and marketing articles/stories. Circ. 13,000. Previously published cartoons/humorous illustrations are accepted.
Cartoons and Humorous Illustrations: Needs spot cartoons. When buying cartoons/humorous illustrations, considers if artist aims content at the freelance writer. For first contact, send possible cartoons to Kirk Polking, Editor. Reports back within 3 weeks. Returns material if accompanied by SASE. Buys one-time rights. Payment for spot cartoons: $10.

WISCONSIN, THE MILWAUKEE JOURNAL MAGAZINE, Box 661, Milwaukee WI 53201. (414)224-2341. Estab. 1969. Weekly newspaper. Circ. 510,000. Needs humorous writing and spot cartoons. Previously published cartoons/humorous articles accepted.
Gag Cartoons: Buys 1-2 gag cartoons/issue, 75/year. Prefers gag cartoons on contemporary living. Doesn't want to see gag cartoons on wife, mother-in-law, women. "For us, the dream gag cartoon would be something funny but with some underlying social comment." Preferred gag cartoon format is single panel, b&w line art. Send submissions

to Alan Borsuk, Editor. Reports back within 2 months. Returns material. Buys one-time rights. Pays $15/b&w on acceptance.

Humorous Writing: Buys approximately 1 humorous piece/issue, 30/year. Needs humorous nonfiction and "slice-of-life." Length: 800-1,000. To query: be familiar with magazine; make sure article is appropriate. For first contact, send manuscript to Alan Borsuk. Reports back in 2 months. Samples are filed or returned with SASE. Buys one-time rights. Pays $125-175 for 800-1,000. Kill fee is negotiated.

"Well, maybe this isn't the right address, but you have to admit — we delivered it promptly!"

NATIONAL ENQUIRER

Neither Rain, nor Snow, nor I.Q. Lower Than Your Shoe Size: *Who would sign their cartoons "Baloo?" Rex May. In fact, Rex does. Confused? We all are. You see, "Baloo" is the pen name of Rex May, a West Lafayette, Indiana-based gag writer/cartoonist who claims to have written over 157,000 gags (imagine the filing cabinet!). First time rights to this one were bought by Michelle Cooks, Cartoon Editor of National Enquirer for $300. "I wanted to show the ordinary American getting whipsawed by the government," says Baloo, "and being offered the usual excuses—this time made funny, to help us both bear it." Actively selling gag cartoons since 1974, Baloo "just sends batches of cartoons to editors and sees what happens. I've broken into many markets that way. No cover letter. Just cartoons and SASE."*

WOMEN'S AMERICAN ORT REPORTER, 16th Floor, 315 Park Ave. S., New York NY 10010. (212)505-7700. Estab. 1966. Quarterly newspaper and tabloid. Circ. 120,000. Needs humorous illustration and writing, caricatures and spot cartoons. Previously published cartoons and humorous articles are accepted. Prefers working with freelancers who have Fax capabilities.

Gag Cartoons: Buys 2 gag cartoons/year. Prefers gag cartoons on Jewish and women. Preferred gag cartoon format is single panel, b&w line art. Query with 2-4 rough drawings/batch to Eve Jacobson, Editor. Reports back in 3 months. Returns material if accompanied by SASE. Buys first time rights and reprint rights.

Humorous Illustration: Buys approximately 2 humorous illustrations/year for articles and spots. Works on assignment only. When hiring a freelance humorous illustrator, these abilities are considered: has a truly unique drawing style; conceptualizes well and has clever ideas—good use of metaphors; has a clean, graphically-pleasing drawing style; has a bold, powerful, attention-getting drawing style; shows flexibility, broad potential in drawing style; is businesslike, meets deadlines and is responsive to editor's needs. For first contact, send cover letter, resume and b&w tearsheets to Eve Jacobson. Reports back within 3 months. Samples are filed and returned by SASE. Buys first time rights and reprint rights. Pays $75/b&w page, $150/b&w cover on publication.

Humorous Writing: Buys approximately 1 humorous piece/issue. Needs humorous nonfiction and interviews. Subject matter includes Jewish, women's. Length: 1,000 words. To query: be familiar with magazine; make sure article is appropriate. For first contact, send cover letter, manuscript, published tearsheets and resume to Eve Jacobson. Reports back within 3 months. Samples are returned with SASE only if requested. Buys first time rights and reprint rights.

© Mark Rosenthal

the Game — Marc Rosenthal

Rah Rah Rah! Sis Boom Bah! *Mark Rosenthal of Malden Bridge, New York drew on the subject of Harvard football for the* **Boston Globe.** *"I was given a deadline of about four days," recalls Rosenthal, "and the Globe gave me total latitude on the assignment—just handing me the manuscript and the size." Rosenthal promotes himself in such illustration resources as* **American Showcase** *and the* **ADWEEK** *Portfolios and "sends out mailings three or four times a year to anyone who has used or called me."*

Some say it is easier to break into Fort Knox than it is to break into syndication. After all, you only need a mini-van filled with TNT and a double digit I.Q. to crack Fort Knox, but becoming syndicated requires talent, perseverance and comic strip characters which can be manufactured as a line of plush toys, though not necessarily in that order.

To be sure, the merchandising of comic strips has become a big business. And while most syndicates give priority to the comic strip itself, they license their characters for everything from coffee mugs to greeting cards, note pads to calendars. Think about "Garfield."

Still this trend does not dissuade countless aspiring cartoonists from creating strips and panels, their heads spinning with dreams of becoming card-carrying phenoms of pop culture. Strips are conceived off hours by shoe salesmen, housewives and busboys and submitted to the syndicates for the thumb up or thumb down. The latter being the more common outcome, "Don't quit the day job" is the credo which should be tattooed into the aspirant's gray matter.

However, a writer hoping to make a mark in syndication better first make his mark as a newspaper staffer. With rare exception, syndicates tend to distribute regular humor columns written by established writers. Sure, an Erma Bombeck will slip through the cracks, but this phenomenon is occasional—sort of like a meteor crashing into a trailer home.

Some syndicates have a steady need for short features, articles and other writing which could be of a humorous nature. It would be best to inquire about a specific syndicate's freelance writing needs with a succinct cover letter, a resume or client list and, of course, a short writing sample.

It is also rare for a syndicate to distribute the editorial cartoons of a cartoonist who is not staffed at a daily newspaper. Since cartoonists are notorious for conveniently forgetting deadlines, the syndicates prefer distributing the graphic commentary of cartoonists who are under the thumb of an editor. They then distribute three, four, five or even six of their cartoons a week to subscribing newspapers.

Nevertheless, if syndicates see promise in young editorial cartoonists, they have been known to effectively place them at newspapers. The newspapers then have their own editorial cartoonists who are placed into a structured environment — and the syndicates now feel comfortable about distributing their work.

If you want to give a syndicate a solid look at your editorial cartoons, give them 10 or 12 copies to mull over. The subject matter of the cartoons should be of a national or international nature, but give them a couple which tackle strictly local issues. A cartoon on a regional, state or local concern will demonstrate your ability to handle more parochial matters. Naturally, you'll also want to enclose a cover letter and a resume which outlines your schooling and print experience.

After you've created the next "Calvin and Hobbes," "Far Side" or "Peanuts" you'll need to submit it to see if it sinks, swims or needs mouth-to-mouth. Some syndicates may want to see 14 days worth of the strip, while others may want 21 individual strips. Don't make the mistake of sending pencilled, yet uncompleted, copies of the strips — print reproduction is of paramount importance in the distribution process and the syndicates want to see your inked work to determine how well it will reduce and appear in newsprint.

Include a succinct cover letter and a SASE. You also have no reason to submit to only one syndicate at a time. Simultaneous submission to 10, 15, even 20 syndicates at a time is standard, accepted practice. (Wouldn't it be great if three syndicates at once wanted to distribute your feature and they had to mud wrestle for it?)

Syndication is a volume business. Ideally, the syndicate salespeople have one objective in mind — to get your feature in as many papers as possible. A top strip with mass appeal could be in 2,000 papers internationally, a 3-time-a-week humor column might be in 600 papers in North America alone. The rate a newspaper pays for a feature is determined by its circulation. A newspaper with a daily circulation of 1,713,000 will pay much more for "Doonesbury" than will a paper tossed onto 78,000 front lawns.

In the end, the syndicate and the creator split the net profit made on the feature and a successful comic strip can easily reward a cartoonist with a fat six figure income. The licensing of the feature can bring in much more revenue than that.

However, the syndicates are extremely picky when it comes to signing new properties. Although a syndicate may be queried with over 5,000 new comic strip ideas a year, they may only elect to syndicate two to four in that same period.

But as you sit at the word processor or drawing board, resist the urge to second guess the syndicates. It is absolutely pointless to try to coldly calculate a comic strip or feature which will appeal to a syndicate (a strip on Yuppies?, a column written from a couch potato's point-of-view?). While such efforts might sell and even have limited success, they almost always flop face first into the concrete.

Be yourself. Write and draw about what interests *you* and see what happens. Channel your energy into creating a *better comic strip* — not in the calculation of characters which will look cute on coffee mugs, pajamas or suction-cupped to the rear window of a Toyota.

AMERICAN INTERNATIONAL SYNDICATE, 1324 ½ N. 3rd St., St. Joseph MO 64501. (816)279-9315. Considers comic strips, gag cartoons and spot drawings for syndication in newspapers and magazines. Reports back in 1 month. Will only return if accompanied by SASE. Payment is 50% of the gross sales. Buys all rights and second serial (reprint) rights.
Comic Strips/Panels: Buys 6 new comic strips or panels/year. Prefers syndicating cartoons strips/panels in which regular characters appear and which do not have continuing story lines; panels which do not incorporate regular, standard characters; strips which have continuing storylines or are serials. When buying a comic strip/panel, considers if it is truly unique in the marketplace; has merchandising/marketing potential; is very well drawn and is consistently funny or clever. Comic strip artists work between 6 to 12 weeks in advance. Submit 12-36 cartoons for proposed strip or panel to W.E. Clark, Director of Cartooning.
Humor Writing/Columns: Uses freelance writers for fiction — crime stories about famous American criminals; 500-1,000 words; magazine columns — 500-700 words. For first contact send query only to Linda Bennett, Editor/Director.
Clip Art: Works with approximately 2 freelance illustrators/year. When buying humorous clip art, considers if it reflects a broad style capable of effectively rendering a variety of subject matter and has generic appeal/versatility. For first contact send published tearsheets and copies to Linda Bennett.

ARTISTS AND WRITERS SYNDICATE, 1034 National Press Bldg., Washington DC 20045. (202)882-8882. Estab. 1974. Syndicates 1 comic strip/panel; 6 written columns ("Antiques," "Keys to Wheels"). Considers comic strips, editorial cartoons, caricatures and humorous columns/articles for syndication in newspapers. Reports back in 6 weeks. Will only return if accompanied by a SASE. Payment is 50% of the net sales. Buys first North American serial rights.
Comic Strips/Panels: Buys 1 new comic strip or panel/year. Prefers single panels which have overall quality and merit of feature. When buying a comic strip/panel, considers if it is truly unique in the marketplace; has merchandising/marketing potential; is very well drawn; is consistently funny or clever; is timely and relevant. Comic strip artists work between 6 and 10 weeks in advance. Submit 6-20 cartoons for proposed strip or panel to David Steitz, Vice President. Tip: "Always have a steady regular-paying job outside of cartooning! Markets are getting tighter and tighter."
Editorial Cartoons: Editorial cartoonist's political viewpoint does not matter. When hiring an editorial cartoonist considers: if cartoonist has a unique drawing style. For first contact send cover letter, resume, tearsheets, number of cartoons to David Steitz.
Humor Writing/Columns: Uses freelance writers for newspaper columns. For first contact send query with clips or tearsheets of published work to David Steitz.
Clip Art: Works with approximately 2 freelance illustrators/year. Needs antiques, collectibles, cars. When buying humorous clip art, considers work that is stylistic and unique to the market. For first contact send cover letter and copies to David Steitz.

CARTOON-CARICATURE-CONTOR, P.O. Box 400448, Munich, D-8000 Germany. 89/305356. FAX: 89/307064. Estab. 1975. Syndicates 250 editorial cartoons. Considers editorial cartoons, gag cartoons, humorous illustration and caricatures for syndication in newspapers, magazines, TV, books, advertising. Reports back in 2 months. Will return submissions if requested. Does not return unsolicited submissions. Payment is 40% of the gross sales. Prefers working with contributors who have fax capabilities.

Editorial Cartoons: When hiring an editorial cartoonist these abilities are considered: a unique drawing style; a proclivity for scathing, biting cartoons, humorous comment on the news of the day; an ability to draw like the top syndicated editorial cartoonists; lots of use of lettering, words and balloons, little use of dialogue; expresses a "middle-of-the-road" political viewpoint; drawn more on national rather than international politics/events. For first contact send cover letter, tearsheets and a number of cartoons.

CARTOON COLLEGE, P.O. Box 3008, Carlsbad CA 92009. (619)942-7487. FAX: (619)942-8575. Estab. 1990. Considers gag cartoons for purchase as a syndicated Sunday comic feature which buys one gag cartoon per week. Will only return if accompanied by a SASE. Payment is $25 for cartoon. "Cartoon College" is syndicated by United Features Syndicate of New York, New York. "Cartoon College reaches millions of households every week in USA and Canada."

Comic Strips/Panels: Buys 52 new panels/year. Editors and readers want strips/panels about general interest appropriate for Sunday newspaper/family readership.

COLLEGE PRESS SERVICE, Suite 7, 2505 W. Second St., Denver CO 80219. (303)936-9930. FAX: (303)936-0569. Considers comic strips and editorial cartoons.

Comic Strips/Panels: Buys 68 new comic strips or panels/year. Strips/panels should be submitted to Bill Sonn, Editor.

Editorial Cartoons: Editorial cartoons should be sent to Bill Sonn, Editor.

Humor Writing/Columns: Gags for comic strips/panels should appeal to college students. Humor writing should be submitted to Bill Sonn, Editor.

Clip Art: Works with approximately 12 freelance illustrators/year. When buying humorous clip art, considers work aimed at the college student. Clip art must stylistic and unique to the market. Clip art should be submitted to Bill Sonn, Editor.

CONTINENTAL FEATURES/CONTINENTAL NEWS SERVICE, Suite 400, 2020 Pennsylvania Ave., NW, Washington DC 20006. (202)452-7453. Estab. 1981. Syndicates: 1 comic strip/panel (Portfolio by William F. Pike); 9 written columns ("Assignment: Africa" and "David Pitts' Window on Britain"). Considers comic strips for syndication in newspapers and magazines. Reports back in 4 weeks. Will only return if accompanied by a SASE. Payment is 70% of gross sales. Contributor retains rights; we publicize, promote and distribute.

Comic Strip/Panels: Buys a variable number of new comic strips or panels/year. Prefers strips in which regular characters appear and strips which do not have continuing storylines. Editors and readers want strips/panels about contemporary life problems and situations. When buying a comic strip/panel, considers if it is truly unique in the marketplace; has merchandising/marketing potential; is very well drawn; is consistently funny or clever; is nonoffensive, harmless and noncontroversial; is timely and relevant. Submit 10-15 cartoons for proposed strip or panel to Gary P. Salamone, Director.

COPLEY NEWS SERVICE, 350 Camino de la Reina, San Diego CA 92108. (619)293-1818. Not accepting any material from freelancers at this time.

CREATORS SYNDICATE, Suite 700, 5777 W. Century Blvd., Los Angeles CA 90045. (213)337-7003. Considers comic strips, editorial cartoons, gag cartoons, humorous illustration, caricatures, spot drawings and humorous columns/articles. For contributor's guidelines send SASE.

Comic Strips/Panels: Buys 2-3 new comic strips or panels/year, "but growing fast." Strips/panels should be subnmitted to Editorial Review Board, "specify cartoon or column."

Editorial Cartoons: Editorial cartoonist's political viewpoint does not matter. Submit editorial cartoons to the Editorial Review Board.

Humor Writing/Columns: Uses freelance writers for fillers, jokes/one liners, newspaper columns and features, news items and promotions. Submit humorous material to the Editorial Review Board.

Clip Art: When buying humorous clip art, considers bold, graphic and dynamic material or work that is cute, pleasing to the eye and non-offensive. Clip art should be stylistic and unique to the market, reflect a broad style capable of effectively rendering a variety of subject matter and have a generic appeal/versatility. Submit clip art to the Editorial Review Board.

EDITOR'S CHOICE, P.O. Box 715, Liverpool NY 13088. (315)453-1010. FAX: (315)453-3950. Estab. 1985. Syndicates: comic strips/panels and written columns. Considers comic strips, editorial cartoons, gag cartoons, humorous illustration, caricatures and humorous columns/articles for syndication in weekly newspapers, newsletters. Reports back in 1 month. Will return if requested. Will negotiate payment.

Comic Strips/Panels: Prefers syndicating cartoon strips/panels which do not incorporate regular, standard characters and which do not have continuing storylines. When buying a comic strip/panel, looks for work which is truly unique in the marketplace and very well drawn. Submit 10-30 cartoons for proposed strip or panel to Peggy Ries, Editor.

Humor Writing/Columns: Uses freelance writers for jokes/one liners, newspaper columns and one-shot humorous material. "Would be interested in syndicating a humorous column on a weekly basis. We are not doing so right now, but are interested in finding someone who can provide weekly articles." For first contact send complete manuscript to Peggy Ries, Editor.

Clip Art: Works with approximately 8 freelance illustrators/month. Needs holidays, employee communication, people, daily life, financial, fundraising. When buying humorous clip art, considers work that is cute, pleasing to the eye and non-offensive and reflects a broad style capable of effectively rendering a variety of subject matter. For first contact send cover letter, copies of b&w work only to Peggy Ries, Editor. Tip: "Clip art styles should be easy to copy onto a computer and should come out clean."

EXTRA NEWSPAPER FEATURES, 18 First Avenue SE, Rochester MN 55904. (507)285-7671. FAX: (507)285-7666. Estab. 1985. Syndicates: 3 comic strips/panels ("Stampede" by J. Palen); 3 editorial cartoons (Fischer, Plante, Jorgensen); 7 written columns ("Rural Life" and "This & That"); 1 editorial service. Considers editorial cartoons, caricatures and humorous columns/articles for syndication in newspapers and magazines. Reports back in 3-4 months. Will only return if accompanied by a SASE. Payment and purchase of rights are negotiated.

Comic Strips/Panels: Buys 1 new panel/year. Prefers single panels in which regular characters appear and which do not have continuing storylines. Editors and readers want panels about rural life, farming, ranching and agriculture. When buying a panel, considers if it is truly unique in the marketplace; has merchandising/marketing potential; is very well drawn and if it is consistently funny or clever. Panel artists work between 1 and 2 weeks in advance. Submit 12-36 panels to Michele M. Thompson, Associate Director.

Editorial Cartoons: Editorial cartoonist's political viewpoint does not matter. When hiring an editorial cartoonist these abilities are considered: a unique drawing style; little use of dialogue. For first contact send cover letter, resume and 12 cartoons to Michele M. Thompson.

Humor Writing/Columns: Uses freelance writers for fillers — 500-750 words per column 1 per week; newspaper columns — 500-750 per column 1 per week; newspaper features — 500-750 words per column 1 per week. For first contact send query with clips or tearsheets of published work to Michele M. Thompson.

HARRIS AND ASSOCIATES, 12084 Caminito Campana, San Diego CA 92128. (619)487-1789. Estab. 1970. Syndicated features: "How to Take the Fun Out of Golf," "How to Take the Fun Out of Tennis," "How to Take the Fun Out of Jogging" and "How to Take the Fun Out of Skiing." Considers editorial cartoons, gag cartoons, humorous illustrations and caricatures for syndication in newspapers and magazines. Reports back in 2 weeks. Will only return if accompanied by a SASE. Pay is negotiated. Buys first North American serial rights.
Comic Strips/Panels: Buys 1 new comic strip or panel/year. Submit editorial cartoons to Dick Harris, Owner/Editor. Tip: "Trends in editorial cartooning include more sports, fitness and health."

JSA PUBLICATIONS, INC., Box 37175, Oak Park MI 48237. (313)546-9123. Estab. 1982. Syndicates 40 comic strips/panels ("Future Features," "The BobZone"); 3 editorial cartoons ("Lewis" by Frank Lewis); 10 written columns ("Rags to Riches," "Word Salad"); 10 miscellaneous humor, mazes, etc. ("A-Maze-In," "Medical Breakthrough," "Great Disasters in History"). Considers comic strips, editorial cartoons, humorous columns/articles, riddles, history, puzzles, trivia for syndication in primarily weekly newspapers and special interest magazines. Reports back in 3-4 weeks. Will only return submissions if accompanied by a SASE. Payment is 50-60% of net sales and by special contract too. Represents first North American serial rights.
Comic Strips/Panels: Buys 6-10 new comic strips/panels a year. Prefers syndicating cartoon strips in which regular characters appear, but which do not have continuing storylines. When buying a comic strip/panel, considers if it is truly unique in the market-place, has merchandising/marketing potential, is controversial or groundbreaking, is timely and relevant. Comic strip artists work between 4 and 6 weeks in advance. Submit 12-20 samples. Strip/panels should be submitted to Paul Ammar, Features Chief.
Editorial Cartoons: For first contact send cover letter, resume and tearsheets (12-20 cartoons) to Paul Ammar.
Humor Writing/Columns: Uses freelance writers for fiction occassionally (any length), newspaper columns, news items occassionally (over 400 words), and historical trivia and general interest. For first contact query only to Joseph S. Ajlouny, Director.

KING FEATURES SYNDICATE INC., 235 E. 45th St., New York NY 10017. (212)455-4000. FAX: (212)983-6259. Considers comic strips, editorial cartoons, gag cartoons and panels.
Comic Strips/Panels: Buys 3-10 new comic strips or panels/year. Strips/panels should be submitted to Jay Kennedy, Comic Editor.

LEOLEEN-DURK CREATIONS — LEANORD BRUCE DESIGNS, Box 2767 #226, Jackson TN 38302. (901)668-1205. Estab. 1981. Syndicates: 4 comic strips/panels ("The Mc-Nabs"). Considers comic strips, editorial cartoons and gag cartoons for syndication. Reports back in 3 weeks. Will only return if accompanied by a SASE. Payment is 30% of net sales. Buys all rights.
Comic Strips/Panels: Buys 3 new comic strips or panels/year. Prefers syndicating strips and single panels. Editors and readers want strips/panels about family and today's ideas. When buying a comic strip/panel, considers if it is truly unique in the marketplace; has merchandising/marketing potential; is very well drawn; is consistently funny or clever; is controversial or groundbreaking; is timely and relevant. Comic strip artists work between 8 and 12 weeks in advance. Submit 15-21 cartoons to Leonard Bruce, Cartoonist/

Syndicator. Tip: "Tough competition towards using well-known established cartoonists, so your comic strip must be almost perfect to break in."

Editorial Cartoons: Editorial cartoonist's political viewpoint does not matter. When hiring an editorial cartoonist these abilities are considered: a unique drawing style; humorous comment on the news of the day; little use of dialogue. For first contact send cover letter, resume, tearsheets and a number of cartoons to Leonard Bruce. Tip: "Trends are on topics more than people."

Humor Writing/Columns: Uses freelance writers for gag writers for comic strip/panels — off the wall humor and humor with respect to the elderly and single parents; one-shot humorous material. For first contact send query with clips or tearsheets of published work to Leonard Bruce. Tip: "Everyone should get the humor, not just a certain few."

LEW LITTLE ENTERPRISES, INC., Box 850, Borrego Springs CA 92004. (619)767-3148. Estab. 1986. Syndicates: 2 comic strips ("The Fusco Brothers" and "Sibling Revelry"). Considers comic strips, editorial cartoons, gag cartoons and humorous columns/articles for syndication in newspapers. We also develop and broker comics to the major syndicates. Reports back in 6 weeks. Will only return if accompanied by a SASE. Payment is negotiable. Buys all rights. For contributor guidelines send a SASE and two first-class stamps.

Comic Strips/Panels: Buys 1-2 new comic strips or panels/year. Prefers syndicating strips/panels in which regular characters appear. When buying a comic strip/panel, considers if it is truly unique in the marketplace; has merchandising/marketing potential; is very well drawn; is consistently funny or clever; is controversial or groundbreaking; is timely and relevant. Comic strip artists work between 6 and 12 weeks in advance. Submit 12 strip/panels to Lewis A. Little, Editor. Tip: "New children's comics are needed, but they must appeal to adults as well as children as 'Calvin & Hobbes' and 'Sibling Revelry.'"

Editorial Cartoons: Editorial cartoonist's political viewpoint does not matter. When hiring an editorial cartoonist these abilities are considered: a unique drawing style; a proclivity for scathing, biting cartoons; humorous comment on the news of the day; little use of dialogue; drawn more on national rather than international politics/events. For first contact send cover letter, resume, 12 cartoons and a brief description of feature proposed to Lewis A. Little.

Humor Writing/Columns: Uses freelance writers for newspaper features; gag writers for comic strips/panels. "We buy gags for some well-known syndicated cartoonists. We occasionally add new writers to a small group of regular contributors." For first contact send query with clips or tearsheets of published work to Mary Ellen Corbett, Managing Editor. Tip: "The market is very hard to crack; editors are looking for a truly fresh approach."

LOS ANGELES TIMES SYNDICATE, Times Mirror Square, Los Angeles CA 90053. (213)237-7987. Considers comic strips, editorial cartoons, gag cartoons, humorous illustration, caricatures, spot drawings, humorous columns/articles and politics. For contributor's guidelines send SASE.

Comic Strips/Panels: Buys 3-4 new comic strips or panels/year. Strips/panels should be submitted to Steven Christensen, Managing Editor.

Editorial Cartoons: It is essential that an editorial cartoonist be on staff at a daily newspaper. "We prefer that an editorial cartoonist have 'likeminded politics.'" Editorial cartoons should be sent to Steven Christensen, Managing Editor.

Humor Writing/Columns: Uses freelance writers for newspaper columns and one-shot humorous material. Humor writing should be submitted to Don Michel, Vice President/Editor.

MINORITY FEATURES SYNDICATE, Box 421, Farrell PA 16121. (412)342-5300. Estab. 1980. Syndicates: 20 comic strips/panels; 25 editorial cartoons; 20 written columns. Considers comic strips, editorial cartoons, gag cartoons and humorous columns/articles for syndication for newspapers, magazines and newsletters. Reports back in 1 month. Will return if requested and accompanied by a SASE. Payment is 20% of the gross sales or by contract. Buys all rights. For contributor guidelines send $2 and a SASE.

Comic Strips/Panels: Buys 100 new comic strips or panels/year. Prefers syndicating panels in which regular characters appear and which have continuing storylines or are serials. Editors and readers want strips/panels about family-oriented material. When buying a comic strip/panel, considers if it is truly unique in the marketplace; has merchandising/marketing potential; is consistently funny or clever; is nonoffensive, harmless and noncontroversial. Comic strip artists work between 2 and 6 weeks in advance. Submit 2-10 cartoons for proposed strip or panel to Merry Frable, Editor.

Editorial Cartoons: "We prefer that an editorial cartoonist have a conservative point of view." When hiring an editorial cartoonist these abilities are considered: a unique drawing style; humorous comment on the news of the day; little use of dialogue and draws more on national rather than international politics/events. For first contact send cover letter, resume, tearsheets and 2-10 cartoons to Merry L. Frable.

Humor Writing/Columns: Uses freelance writers for fiction—short story 500 words or less; fillers—50 words general interest; jokes/one liners—clean 10 minimum; magazine columns—200 words general interest; newspaper columns/features—150 words general interest pertaining to today's news; news items—200 words general interest nationally pertaining to today's news; promotion general interest; one-shot humorous material—clean 100 words general interest. For first contact send query with clips or tearsheets of published work to Merry L. Frable.

Clip Art: Works with approximately 50 freelance illustrators/year. Needs general interest. When buying humorous clip art, considers work that is bold, graphic and dynamic; stylistic and unique to the market; reflects a broad style capable of effectively rendering a variety of subject matter; has generic appeal/versatility. For first contact send cover letter, 5 copies, b&w work only and resume to Merry L. Frable.

THE NEW BREED, King Features Syndicate, 235 E. 45th St., New York NY 10017. Estab. 1915. Considers single panel cartoons for syndication in newspapers. Reports back in 3-5 weeks. Will only return submission if accompanied by a SASE. Payment is $50 flat fee. Buys first world-wide serial rights. For contributor's guidelines send a SASE.

Comic Strips/Panels: Buys 468 new panels/year. Prefers only single panels. Editors and readers want panels on the cutting edge of single panel cartooning—wacky, smart, clever and modern cartoons. When buying a panel, considers if it is very well drawn; is consistently funny or clever. "We also consider the cartoonist's overall talent when we consider buying a single New Breed. We look for controversial or groundbreaking cartoons that are timely and relevant." Submit 10-30 cartoons for proposed panel to The New Breed Editors.

SINGER MEDIA GROUP, 3164 Tyler Avenue, Anaheim CA 92801. (714)527-5650. FAX: (714)527-0268. Estab. 1940. Syndicates: comic strips/panels and written columns. Considers comic strips for newspapers, magazines, book publishers, ad agencies and greeting cards. Reports back in 3 weeks. Will only return if accompanied by a SASE. Payment is 50% for world-wide syndication. Tip: "We see a need for the following cartoon material in the 1990's: computers, medicine, spousal support, fax, credit cards, crazy hairstyles, corporate takeovers and Japanese investment."

TRIBUNE MEDIA SERVICES, INC., 64 E. Concord St., Orlando FL 32801. (407)839-5600. FAX: (407)839-5794. Estab. 1933. Syndicates 28 comic strips/panels ("Shoe," "Mother Goose and Grimm"); 10 editorial cartoons (MacNelly, Don Wright); 50+ written creators (Royko, Dave Barry, Andy Rooney, Bob Greene, Jumble). Considers comic strips, editorial cartoons, humorous columns for syndication in newspapers. Reports back in 6 weeks. Will only return submissions if accompanied by a SASE. Negotiated contract. Buys all rights. For contributor guidelines send SASE.

Comic Strips/Panels: Buys varying number of new comic strips or panels a year. Prefers syndicating strips/panels in which regular characters appear and which do not have continuing story lines. When buying a comic strip/panel, considers if it is truly unique in the marketplace; is consistently funny or clever; is timely and relevant. Comic strip artists work between 6 and 10 weeks in advance. Submit 18-30 cartoons. Strip/panels should be submitted to Evelyn Smith, Managing Editor.

Editorial Cartoons: It is essential that an editorial cartoonist be on staff at a daily newspaper. When hiring an editorial cartoonist these abilities are considered: a unique drawing style; a proclivity for scathing, biting cartoons; humorous comment on the news of the day; moderate use of dialogue. For first contact send cover letter, resume, tearsheets and 18 cartoons to Evelyn Smith.

Humor Writing/Columns: Uses freelance writers for newspaper columns. "We require writers with solid credentials, preferably with books, magazine articles or newspaper columns to writer's credit." For first contact send query with clips or tearsheets of published work to Evelyn Smith.

UNITED FEATURE SYNDICATE, Newspaper Enterprise Assoc., 200 Park Ave., New York NY 10166. (212)692-3700. Syndicates: comic strips/panels ("Peanuts," "Garfield," "Born Looser," "Frank & Ernest"); editorial cartoons (Mike Peters, Ed Stein); written columns (Jack Anderson, Miss Manners). Considers comic strips, editorial cartoons and humorous columns/articles for syndication in newspapers and reprint in magazines and books. Reports back in 8-10 weeks. Will only return if accompanied by a SASE. Payment is 50% of the net sales. Buys all rights.

Comic Strips/Panels: Buys 2-4 new comic strips or panels/year. Prefers syndicating cartoon strips/panels which do not have continuing storylines but like to see anything. When buying a comic strip/panel, considers if it is truly unique in the marketplace; has merchandising/marketing potential; is very well drawn; is consistently funny or clever; is timely and relevant. Comic strip artists work between 6 and 10 weeks in advance. Submit 18-40 cartoons for a proposed strip or panel to Sarah Gillespie, V.P., Director of Comic Art. Tip: "It's a tougher market than ever and rejection should not be taken as a sign that the work is particularly bad—we just can't use it."

Editorial Cartoons: It is essential that an editorial cartoonist be on staff at a daily newspaper. Editorial cartoonist's political viewpoint does not matter. When hiring an editorial cartoonist these abilities are considered: a unique drawing style and humorous comment on the news of the day. For first contact send cover letter and 12 cartoons to Gail Robinson, Managing Editor.

Humor Writing/Columns: Uses freelance writers for newspaper columns and newspaper features. For first contact send query with clips or tearsheets of published work and at least 6 samples to Robert Levy, Assistant Managing Editor.

UNIVERSAL PRESS SYNDICATE, 4900 Main St., Kansas City, MO 64112. (816)932-6600. FAX: (816)932-6648. Estab. 1970. Syndicates: 15 comic strips/panels ("Calvin & Hobbes," "Doonesbury," "The Far Side"); 6 editorial cartoons (Oliphant, Auth); 50 written columns ("Dear Abby," Erma Bombeck). Considers comic strips, editorial cartoons and gag cartoons for syndication in newspapers. Reports back in 1 month. Will only return if accompanied by a SASE. Payment is 50% of the net sales. Buys all rights.

Close-up

Sarah Gillespie
Vice President and Director of Comic Art
United Media

There is always a lot of cartoon traffic in the department of Sarah Gillespie, Vice President and Director of Comic Art at United Media. "Peanuts," "Garfield," "Francie" and about 25 others arrive each morning to be looked over and edited before being sent out to production. There are also the over 3,000 unsolicited submissions which arrive annually.

Gillespie's "traffic manager" makes sure all of these incoming submissions are recorded. They are then sent to one of Gillespie's assistant managers who pulls out those she thinks show promise. "However, I look at things she doesn't pull out, just in case," Gillespie says. "It's a very important part of my job to see the submissions."

She says these submissions have a number of different fates which range from immediate acceptance to rejection. She uses an example, Jimmy Johnson, creator of "Arlo and Janis," as one whose cartoons have run the gamut. "He informed me that I had actually rejected an earlier submission of his and I don't even remember. But he came up with a new idea. He persevered and 'Arlo and Janis' was just right for us. I thought he was a real talent and I called him and told him so."

She says "Arlo and Janis" is an example of the sort of strip she is looking for, one which communicates well through art and words in a humorous way, and sustains its characters through a long period of time. "I don't look for hot trends that are going to be here and gone in two years. I'm much more interested in genuinely funny writing about genuinely interesting characters. I'm not interested in themes, and I don't care about doing a yuppie strip. There are people that would call Arlo and Janis yuppies. But 'Arlo and Janis' will be around well beyond yuppies because 'Arlo and Janis' is really about people in the early part of their marriage, in their early thirties, facing the trials of adulthood, and that's always going to be of interest."

Gillespie says she does not find many of the submissions she receives professional or funny enough. "Sometimes," she says, "I don't read the cover letter because I don't want to hear this person's story." She says, "Just because their friends laugh, they think, 'I get the feeling I'm really funny.' Well of course—they're their friends. They're supposed to do that."

Other problems she finds with submitted comics are attempts "to overintellectualize comics and who their appeal will be to" and too great a concern with licensing potential. "We don't consider a comic strip in terms of whether we can license it or not. I think there are people who submit to us who are more to blame for this than we are, thinking 'if I stick in a cute cuddly worm everything's going to be okay and I'll make money.' "

Overall, Gillespie believes it's a tough time for comics. "It's harder and harder for a new cartoonist who is just a darn good cartoonist to get syndicated, because it's harder and harder for us to get him into the paper.

"There are fewer and fewer competitive papers out there. We just lost another one in Los Angeles. The market is smaller. Add to that the fact that newsprint is very expensive. So no newspapers are expanding their comics, even though it's known that comics sell papers.

"My greatest fear," she says, "is that the comic pages will tend to get homogenized, that readers aren't getting a chance to see all that's out there. " She says that now "rather than looking at something and saying 'this is funny, this makes me laugh. I'm going to take a chance on it,' editors now cautiously wait to see what cartoons prove successful in other papers, what cartoon books sell and what cartoons show up on TV.

"There's no longer another newspaper across the street that's going to grab a good cartoon if the editor doesn't grab it first. And so the editor can say, 'Well, we'll see what happens if you get published. I'll ask my competitors. If they like it, come back in a year.' "

Still it is not all bleak. United Media introduces two to four new strips each year and, says Sarah Gillespie, "I don't believe you should always take no for an answer. All of the great cartoonists were rejected before they got syndicated. So there's no shame in it." She says, "Cartoonists are wise to study the best and know that we all know who they are. Don't imitate them; learn from them. And always stick with what you know."

— Lauri Miller

Snoopy, Garfield and Rose adorn the cover of United Media's 1989-1990 catalog.

Comic Strip/Panels: Buys 2 new comic strips or panels/year. When buying a comic strip/panel, considers if it is truly unique in the marketplace; is consistently funny and clever; is controversial or groundbreaking. Comic strip artists work between 4 and 8 weeks in advance. Submit 24 cartoons for proposed strip or panel to Lee Salem, Editorial Director.

Editorial Cartoons: It is essential that an editorial cartoonist be on staff at a daily newspaper. Editorial cartoonist's political viewpoint does not matter. When hiring an editorial cartoonist these abilities are considered: a unique drawing style and a proclivity for scathing, biting cartoons. For first contact send cover letter and 24 cartoons to Lee Salem.

For Better or For Worse®   by Lynn Johnston

Maybe It's Out of Gas: Lynn Johnston not only has her own unique view of family life, she's paid to express it. Her comic strip, "For Better Or Worse", is seen in over 1,000 newspapers internationally. Distributed by Universal Press Syndicate, Johnston is paid 50% of the net profit generated from the sale of the feature to newspapers, greeting card publishers, television production companies or merchandising ventures. "The syndicate basically tells me to get the strip in on time," Johnston says, "and I generally work six weeks ahead for the daily strips and eight weeks for the Sunday panels."

WASHINGTON POST WRITERS GROUP, 1150 15th Street NW, Washington DC 20071. (202)334-6375. Estab. 1974. Syndicates: comic strips/panels (Outland); editorial cartoons (Dana Summers/Mike Lane); written columns (Stephanie Brush). Considers comic strips, editorial cartoons, humorous illustration and humorous columns/articles for syndication in daily, Sunday and college newspapers throughout the United States, Canada and abroad. Reports back in 2 weeks. Will return all submissions. Payment is not disclosed until contract agreement is made. Buys all rights.

Comic Strips/Panels: Syndicates 1-2 new comic strips or panels/year. Prefers syndicating cartoon strips/panels in which regular characters appear and which have continuing storylines or are serials. When buying a comic strip/panel, considers if it is truly unique in the marketplace; is very well drawn; is consistently funny or clever; is timely and relevant. Comic strip artists work between 3 and 5 weeks in advance. Submit 10-25 cartoons for proposed strip or panel to William Dickinson, General Manager. Tips: It's a very competitive market!

Editorial Cartoons: A cartoonist's political viewpoint does not matter to us. When hiring an editorial cartoonist these abilities are considered: a unique drawing style; humorous comment on the news of the day. For first contact send cover letter, tearsheets and 10-20 cartoons to William Dickinson.

Humor Writing/Columns: Uses freelance writers for newspaper columns (The Stephanie Brush column). For first contact send query with clips or tearsheets of published work to William Dickinson.

WHITEGATE FEATURES SYNDICATE, 71 Faunce Drive, Providence RI 02906. Estab. 1988. Syndicates: 3 comic strips/panels (Jane Adler, Dave Berg "Citizen Senior", Dick Rogers "Puzzleman"); 15 written columns (Indoor gardening, by Jane Adler, Gloria Linterman's "Beauty, Health & Fashion"). Considers comic strips, editorial cartoons, gag cartoons, humorous illustration, spot drawings and humorous columns/articles for syndication in newspapers and magazines. Reports back in 3 months. Will only return if accompanied by a SASE. "We like to keep material on file if we like it for future reviews (no promises)." Payment is 50% of the net sales. Buys all rights.
Comic Strips/Panels: "We will be buying a number of new comic strips or panels this year. We don't like to get material from cartoonists, etc. who say we've tried all the big syndicates so now we'll try you!!! *We're* looking for the same quality as the bigger syndicates." When buying a comic strip/panel, considers if it is truly unique in the marketplace; has merchandising/marketing potential; is very well drawn; is consistently funny or clever; is controversial or groundbreaking; is timely and relevant and good writing. Comic strip artists work between 4 and 8 weeks in advance. Submit 12 (minimum) cartoons for a proposed strip or panel to Eve Green, Talent Manager.
Editorial Cartoons: It is essential that an editorial cartoonist be on staff at a daily newspaper. Editorial cartoonist's political viewpoint does not matter. No rules for hiring an editorial cartoonist, just the "best". For first contact send cover letter, resume, tearsheets, a number of cartoons and "anything to tell us who he is and what he's done plus work. Do not ask us if we'd like to see work unless you include a SASE." Send editorial cartoons to Eve Green.
Humor Writing/Columns: Uses freelance writers for fiction (sometimes); fillers (very little); jokes/one liners/ magazine columns; newspaper columns; newspaper features (sometimes); promotion (looking for free lance workers to do occasional work); gag writers for comic strip/panels (looking for gag writers to pair with cartoonists); one-shot humorous material. For first contact send complete manuscript, query with clips or tearsheets of published work to Eve Green. Tips: Trends lean towards lots of humor. "We're actively looking for good material but try us before the big syndicates. We don't want the 'rejects' we're looking for the new stars!"

THE WORDTREE, 10876 Bradshaw W117, Overland Park KS 66210-1148. (913)469-1010. Estab. 1984. Publishes columns serialized in technical periodicals. Recently published the column New Times, New Verbs.
Humorous Illustration: Works with approximately 2 freelance humorous illustrators/ year. Needs cartoons or caricature. Uses freelance humorous illustrators primarily for illustrating the part of the New Times, New Verbs column that is called "A Needed Verb." "Submit one nonreturnable specimen of each of two cartoons illustrating the far ranges of your ability, whether or not they have already been published." When hiring a freelance humorous illustrator, considers skill, drawing style, ability to take art direction well, compatibility of drawing style with text, professionalism, businesslike attitude. Buys all rights. For first contact send portfolio of two items to Dr. Henry G. Burger, Editor. Reports back only if interested. Returns materials if accompanied by a SASE. Pays $15-100 b&w inside illustration. Tip: "We need ability to draw very precise lines in small space, to illustrate complex ideas."

Happily, looking and talking like Wink Martindale is not a prerequisite to working in television or radio. If it were, the industry would have few employees and the public, no doubt, would turn off their TVs and radios and take up reading again.

But the idea, while appealing, ain't all that practical. TV remains indisputably the most powerful communications medium on the face of the earth, and radio plays an equally important role in the dissemination of news, information, entertainment and the latest Paula Abdul tune.

To look at TV or to listen to radio, one is unable to fully appreciate the countless individuals behind the scenes (the "little people" who the stars thank when accepting awards). Indeed there are plenty of little people. Producers, directors, editors, sound engineers, lighting specialists, make-up artists, hair stylists, even trainers who coax collies to bark on cue.

And yes, writers, humorous illustrators and animators play a major role in television. Radio, however, is a different story. Writers are regularly hired, but we have yet to come across a humorous illustrator or animator who ever received a check from a radio station.

Listed here are independent television producers, film/video production companies and radio comedy services. Do they have a common thread? You bet. They'd all laugh if they saw a nun slip on a banana peel. Put another way, they all have a sense of humor and if you write, draw or animate funny, they want to see your stuff.

Radio

Most radio comedy services publish weekly, biweekly or monthly newsletters of jokes, one-liners, anecdotes and pithy, yet nonoffensive, patter. Disc jockeys, entertainers and even public speakers receive this material when they subscribe to the service. Then when they recite the material in public, they come across as possessing lightning-fast, improvisational talents sure to make David Letterman worry about job security.

Since you don't send portfolios or VHS demo tapes to radio comedy services, you'll be shipping samples of your writing for review. Photocopy some representative examples, include a brief cover letter, resume and client list and ship with a SASE.

But be forewarned: Most radio comedy services pay rates almost as funny as their jokes. For a service, $10 a joke would be considered terrific, but five bucks seems to be the most common per-joke rate. However, we *have* seen per joke rates as low as $1—and that ain't no typo.

Television

Yet television has a deep pocket. Like advertising, television lures freelancers with promises of Porsches, stucco condos and bottled water from subterranean springs near the Lichtenstein border.

With cable's advent, opportunities for the independent television production companies have increased dramatically. Once only able to sell their properties to the big three commercial networks, producers now have greatly expanded options. Subsequently, increased opportunities trickle down to writers.

However, production companies produce far more corporate or industrial films than they do commercials or theatrical programming. Company XYZ may have to explain their new solar-powered personal ionizer to a technically naive public—consequently, a corporate film may be produced to explain the product in friendly, layman's terms.

"We use humor all the time in our corporate films," says Scott Hadden, Producer/Director of Hadden Manganello & Associates. "People aren't stoic. When they turn on the TV, they want to be entertained while they're being informed. And humor is at least one of the tools which we run up the flagpole."

Hadden says that television production companies offer terrific opportunities for the freelance writer, especially those who can adapt from project to project and make technical information accessible.

If a writer wants to pique the interest of a producer like Hadden, they should "get my attention first with a printed self-promo piece. *Then* show me samples of your writing." Hadden's suggestion can be applied generally, as most producers are quite literally inundated with unsolicited material. Use any means possible to get their attention—before the *next* guy's letter does.

However, theatrical programming (movies and sit-coms) is a considerably tougher nut to crack. Production companies are involved in the creation of everything from game shows to sit-coms, variety shows to made-for-TV movies. They have their own specific agendas and it is almost impossible to generalize on the industry as a whole.

That's why this chapter is so terrific. You're able to easily determine the *individual* needs of these companies. One company may produce nothing but made-for-TV movies, the next may only create sit-coms. So by reading the listings, you'll be able to direct your material to those companies which seem the most receptive to it.

Not surprisingly, television production companies have a need, though not constant, for humorous illustration and animation. Since you (nor they) never know when such services will be needed, it's best to send them material which they can keep in their resource files.

An animator should send a demo tape (¾" is best), a cover letter, resume and maybe a business card. A humorous illustrator should assemble a color promotional page, perhaps some past storyboard work, a cover letter, resume, client list and business card. In your cover letter, ask the recipient if he would kindly keep your materials on file and to call "if an appropriate project comes up."

Take heart. Television and radio employ far more behind-the-scenes people than on-the air personalities. Happily, the industry needs more than pretty faces, more than satiny voices and less people named Wink.

ALL GOD'S CREATURES, Division of Mirimar Entertainment, P.O. Box 4621, N. Hollywood CA 91617. (818)784-4177. Estab. 1965. TV and film production company that provides print advertising, TV and film production and slide shows for ad agencies, TV production companies and film studios. Some top clients are Mirimar Entertainment, Margery Productions, PBS, independent production companies in LA and NYC and ad agencies (subcontracting). Needs storyboards, humorous copywriting, animation, animatics, slide shows and theatrical-based humor for industrial films, print ads, radio spots, promotions, TV commercials, slide shows and TV and film production. 30% of work done by freelance humorous illustrators is for print ads.
Humorous Illustration: Works with 1 freelance illustrator/year. When hiring freelance illustrators, looks for "someone who fits our limited needs." Uses freelance humorous illustrators on a one-time-only basis. For first contact send slides to Mirk Mirkin, CEO. Reports back within 1 month. Returns materials only if requested and accompanied by a SASE. Negotiates rights purchased. Pays by the project: $100-300. Considers complexity of project, skill of illustrator, ability of illustrator to work well under art direction, client's budget, usage, schedule of illustrator and originality of thought process when establishing payment.
Humor Writing: Works with 3 freelance writers/year. When hiring freelance writers, looks for professionally oriented (though a novice) in style and quality. Must be highly original. For first contact send cover letter, resume, tearsheets, photocopied writing samples, ½" demo tape, audio tape (film is OK, but prefer tape) to Mark Mirkin, CEO. Reports back within 1 month only if interested. Returns materials only if requested and accompanied by a SASE. Negotiates rights purchased. Pays by the project $100-1,000. Considers complexity of project, skill of writer, ability of writer to work well under direction of creative team, client's budget, possibility of long term agency/writer relationship, originality of thought process when establishing payment. Tips: "We are only interested in completely new and fresh ideas, not reworked formulae, especially for TV and other video-based media (but also for print)."

BEAR CREEK RECORDING AND MUSIC PRODUCTION, 6313 Maltby Rd., Woodinville WA 98072. (206)481-4100. FAX: (206)481-8179. Estab. 1974. Recording studio and music production house that is a 24-track studio (Dolby) providing recording and creative services to the commercial, film and production industry. Clients include Evans/Kraft Advertising, Borders Perrin Norrander and McCann/Erickson. Needs humor writing and lyrics (humorous). Humorous material is used for radio spots and TV commercials. Uses freelancers for 20% of humor writing.

Humorous Scriptwriting: Works with approximately 1-2 scriptwriters per month or 12-20 per year. Looking for comedy scripts or concepts on all subjects—"keep them commercial in nature." For first contact send cover letter, resume and audio cassette tape. Send scripts to Vickielee Wohlbach, Studio Manager. Reports back within 7 days only if interested. Keeps material on file. Negotiates rights purchased. Pays $100-500 for average commercial project.

LEE CAPLIN PRODUCTIONS, INC., 8274 Grand View Trail, Los Angeles CA 90046. (213)650-1882. FAX: (213)650-7969. Estab. 1980. TV and feature film production company and comic publishing (books/graphic novels) that provides development and production of feature films and TV programs. Recent productions/projects include the original "Pee Wee," "Nervous Rex" and "Crow of Bear Clan" (animation). Needs humorous scriptwriting and cartoon characters/stories. Humorous material is used for developmental projects, programming and comic books. Uses freelancers for 100% of illustrations, humor writing and animation.

Humor Writing: Uses freelance humor writers for developmental projects and screenplays. Needs reality-based, contemporary action/humor for live action feature films; reality-based, contemporary humor for TV sitcoms. For first contact send cover letter, resume, signed standard release form and completed screenplay for feature, treatment for TV *only*, to Sonia Mintz, Director of Development. Reports back within 2 months if interested. Keeps materials on file, does not return. Negotiates rights purchased.

Animation: Works on approximately 3 animation projects/year. Uses animation for programming. Looks for contemporary, traditional and stylish animation style. For first contact send cover letter, resume and demo tape (½″) to Sonia Mintz. Reports back in 2 months if interested. Does not return materials. Negotiates rights purchased.

CLASSIC ANIMATION, 2330 Byrd Dr., Kalamazoo MI 49002. (616)382-0352. Estab. 1986. Video production house that provides traditional and computer animation—2-D, 3-D—cartoon illustration services. Recent productions/projects: Amway video report (graphics), Upjohn employee communication videos and anti-drug abuse video for children (in progress). Clients include Amway, Upjohn and Allen Testproducts. Needs humorous illustration, humorous scriptwriting, cartoons, animatics, animations and storyboards. Humorous material is used for developmental projects, programming, promotion and TV commercials. Uses freelancers for 50% of all illustrations; 100% of all humor writing; 25% of all animation.

Humorous Illustration: Works with approximately 10 humorous illustrators/month. Needs corporate illustrations for newsletter articles. For first contact send cover letter, resume and video tape (job reel) to David B. Baker, President. Reports back within weeks only if interested. Returns materials if accompanied by a SASE. Keeps materials on file. Buys all rights. Pays $5-35 an hour; $50-200 a day; $100-5,000 per project.

Humorous Scriptwriting: Works with approximately 1 humor scriptwriter/month or 3/year. Looking for comedy scripts or concepts on school programs and corporate communications. Doesn't want to see comedy scripts on sex, drugs and rock 'n' roll. For first contact send cover letter, resume, demo tape (½″). Concept submissions should be submitted with query detailing premise of concept and outline. Send scripts to David Baker. Reports back within weeks only if interested. Returns materials if accompanied by SASE. Keeps materials on file. Buys all rights. Pays $100 minimum.

Humor Writing: Works with approximately 1 freelancer/month or 3/year. Uses freelance humor writers for advertising/promotion, writing for specific shows and developmental projects. Needs corporate communications and commercials. For first contact send cover letter, resume, and demo tape (½″) to David Baker. Reports back within

weeks only if interested. Returns materials if accompanied by a SASE. Keeps materials on file. Buys all rights. Pays by the hour: $20-35.
Animation: Works on approximately 3 animation projects/month or 30/year. Uses animation for programming, commercial advertising and promotional purposes. Looks for avant garde, contemporary, traditional, stylish ("and we're open to suggestions") animation style. For first contact send cover letter, resume, and demo tape (½″) to David Baker. Reports back within weeks only if interested. Returns materials if accompanied by a SASE. Keeps materials on file. Buys all rights. Pays by the frame $5-15; by the hour $5-20; by the project $200-5,000.

CONTEMPORARY COMEDY, P.O. Box 271043, 5804 Twineing, Dallas TX 75227-1043. (214)381-4779. Estab. 1974. "We are a comedy service that supplies topical and seasonal comedy material (jokes) on a subscription basis." Clients include CBS, NBC, BBC and 800 local radio stations in the U.S., Canada, Europe and Australia. Needs one-line jokes. Humorous material is used for programming by local disc jockeys. Uses freelancers for 50% of humor writing.
Humor Writing: Works with approximately 7-8 freelancers per month or 15/year. "Use regular contributors, but always looking for new ones." Uses freelance humor writers for topical and seasonal one-liners: weather, fads, fashions, sports, movie/television. "We purchase approximately 100 one-line jokes per month." For first contact send cover letter and writing samples to Joe Hickman, Editor. Reports back in 3 weeks. Returns materials if accompanied by SASE. Does not file materials. Buys all rights. Pays $3 per one-liner on acceptance; regular contributors may receive more.

DELTA MAX PRODUCTIONS, Paramount Pictures Corp., 5555 Melrose Ave., Hollywood CA 90038. (213)468-5000. FAX: (213)468-5555. Estab. 1983. Film production company that provides feature film productions and computer graphics. Recent productions/projects: Due Process, Klone, Father Figure. Needs humorous illustration, caricatures, "on scene" illustrations, animations and storyboards. Humorous material is used for developmental projects, posters, advertising and promotion. Uses freelancers for 100% of illustrations, humor writing and animation. Prefers working with freelancers with fax capabilities.
Humorous Illustration: Works with approximately 5 humorous illustrators/year. For first contact send cover letter, resume, client list and portfolio to Robert Swanson, President. Reports back only if interested. Returns materials if accompanied by a SASE. Keeps materials on file. Buys all rights or negotiates rights purchased. Pays by the project: $1000 minimum.
Humorous Scriptwriting: Works with approximately 7 humor scriptwriters per year. For first contact send cover letter, resume, client list and demo tape (½″). Concept submissions should be submitted with script to Robert Swanson. Reports back only if interested. Returns materials only if requested and accompanied by a SASE. Buys all rights. Pays $1000 minimum.
Humor Writing: Uses freelance humor writers for developmental projects. For first contact send cover letter, resume, client list and demo tape (½″) to Robert Swanson. Reports back only if interested. Returns materials if requested and accompanied by a SASE. Buys all rights. Pays by the project: $1,000 minimum.
Animation: Works on approximately 12 animation projects/year. Uses animation for films. Looks for avant garde animation style. For first contact send cover letter, resume, client list, demo tape (½″). Reports back only if interested. Returns materials if accompanied by a SASE. Buys all rights. Pays by the project: $1000 minimum.

THE ELECTRIC WEENIE, INC., P.O. Box 2715, Quincy MA 02269. (617)749-6900. FAX: (617)749-3691. Estab. 1970. Humor publication servicing radio industry that provides a monthly publication of 160 topical gags, one-liners and jokes. Currently working on humor publication for speakers. "We service 1,500 subscribers in U.S., Canada, New Zealand and England." Needs short humor writing (one or two lines), topical gags, jokes and observations. Humorous material is used for radio spots and by disc jockeys. Uses freelancers for 100% of humor writing.

Humor Writing: Works with approximately 20-30 freelancers/month or 60-70/year. Uses freelance humor writers for brochures, on-air announcements, writing for specific shows and brainstorming. Needs topical, witty, short (2-3 line) gags, jokes, observations—95% clean humor—we use 10 "off-color" jokes per issue. For first contact send cover letter, writing samples and other available samples to Jimbo Donohue, Managing Editor. Reports back within 3 weeks. Returns materials if accompanied by a SASE. Buys all rights and reprint rights. Pays by the project: $2-5 per joke/gag.

BERT ELLIOTT SOUND, INC., 2080 Peachtree Industrial Court, #115, Atlanta GA 30341. (404)452-1140. FAX: (404)455-3356. Estab. 1979. Video production house and 24-track audio production house/original music composers that provide sync to picture. Recent productions/projects: many Delta Airlines "in-flight" programs, radio and TV commercials. Clients include Delta, Research Institute of America and Peat Marwick. Needs humorous scriptwriting, cartoons, animations, storyboards. Humorous material is used for TV commercials, advertising, radio spots and children's programming.

Humorous Illustration: For first contact send cover letter to Bert Elliott, President. Reports back within 7 days only if interested. Returns materials if accompanied by SASE. Keeps materials on file.

Humorous Scriptwriting: Looking for comedy scripts or concepts on children. For first contact send cover letter and demo tape. For a concept for a comedy series or programming, submit script to Bert Elliott. Reports back in 7 days only if interested. Returns materials if accompanied SASE. Keeps materials on file.

Animation: Uses animation for programming, commercial advertising and promotional purposes. Looks for avant garde, contemporary, stylish animation style. For first contact send cover letter and demo tape to Bert Elliott. Reports back in 7 days only if interested. Returns materials if accompanied by SASE. "We are mostly doing soundtracks, sound effects, video sound, etc. for animators and other prjects. We can customize sound for many types of production. Children's programming has been a long time interest of mine."

ENTERTAINMENT PRODUCTIONS, INC., 2210 Wilshire Blvd. #744, Santa Monica CA 90403. (213)456-3143. Estab. 1971. TV production company and motion picture production company that provides feature film and television productions. Recent productions/projects: "The Inventor," "Here Comes Trouble," "Las Vegas Shows," "The Hawks & The Doves." Clients include various world-wide distributors, cable and syndicators. Needs humorous illustration and storyboards. Humorous material is used for developmental projects and posters. Uses freelancers for 5% of all illustrations.

Humorous Illustration: Works with approximately 5 humorous illustrators/year. "Needs illustrations that need no words of explanation." For first contact send best sample(s) of work to Edward Coe, Producer. Reports back within 1 month. Returns materials if accompanied by a SASE. Negotiates rights purchased. Pays by the project: $100 minimum.

G NINE PRODUCTIONS, 2030 Scott St., San Francisco CA 94115. (415)922-0531. FAX: (415)567-1701. Estab. 1987. TV production company and commercial production company that provides design, direct and produces on air promotions and commercials. Recent productions/projects: commercials for Apple Computer, Rainier Beer and broadcast promotions for Disney. Clients include Disney, Fox Broadcasting and advertising agencies throughout the US. Needs humorous writing, animations and storyboards. Humorous material is used for developmental projects, programming, advertising and TV commercials. Uses freelancers for 50% of all illustrations; 10% of all humor writing; 50% of all animation.

Humorous Illustration: Works with various amounts of humorous illustrators/year. For first contact send cover letter and resume to Kate Montgomery, Executive Producer. Returns materials if accompanied by a SASE. Keeps materials on file. Buys all rights.

HOWARD GLADSTONE & ASSOCIATES, 2144 W. Thomas, Chicago IL 60622. (312)276-8659. Film and video production house. Occasionally needs humorous scriptwriting, storyboards and humorous material for promotional projects. Uses freelancers.

Humorous Scriptwriting: For first contact send cover letter and resume to Howard Gladstone, Producer. Returns materials if accompanied by a SASE. Keeps materials on file.

HADDEN MANGANELLO & ASSOCIATES, 3500 Maple #1175 LB21, Dallas TX 75219. (214)528-5862. FAX: (214)520-6251. Estab. 1983. Video production house and business communication agency that provides design and produces corporate communications for marketing, training and employee information. Clients include Mary Kay Cosmetics, Club Corp of America and Whata Burger. Needs humor writing, humorous scriptwriting, cartoons, animations and storyboards. Humorous material is used for developmental projects, posters and programming. Most humor oriented material has been done in-house to this point. Prefers working with freelancers with fax capabilities.

Humorous Illustration: For first contact send cover letter, resume and tearsheets to Scott Hadden, Producer/Director. Reports back only if interested. Returns materials only if requested and accompanied by a SASE. Keeps materials on file. Negotiates rights purchased. Pays by the project: $150-2,500.

Humorous Scriptwriting: Works with approximately 3/year. Looking for comedy scripts or concepts on business. For first contact send cover letter, resume and photocopied writing sample to Scott Hadden. Reports back only if interested. Returns materials if requested and accompanied by a SASE. Keeps materials on file. Negotiates rights purchased. Pays $500-4,500.

Humor Writing: Uses freelance humor writers for brochures, direct mail, writing for specific shows, creative consulting, developmental projects and brainstorming. For first contact send cover letter, resume, tearsheets and writing samples to Scott Hadden. Reports back only if interested. Returns materials only if requested and accompanied by a SASE. Keeps materials on file. Negotiates rights purchased. Pays by the project: $250-2,500.

Animation: Works on approximately 2 animation projects/year. Uses animation for programming. Looks for styles that fit project needs. For first contact send cover letter, resume and demo tape to Scott Hadden. Reports back only if interested. Returns materials if requested and accompanied by a SASE. Keeps materials on file. Negotiates rights purchased. Pays by the project: $500-10,000.

HANDSOME BROTHERS MUSIC SERVICE, INC., 63 Melcher Street, Boston MA 02210. (617)423-0280. Estab. 1976. Music production company that provides creation and production of musical soundtracks. Clients include: ABC, Disney, Sheraton, Digital Equipment Corporation and Continental Cablevision. Needs humor writing and music soundtracks for animated productions. Humorous material is used for radio spots, advertising and TV commercials.

Humorous Scriptwriting: Works with approximately 1 humorous scriptwriter/month; 15/year. Looking for comedy concepts on selling. Doesn't want to see comedy scripts on Superman. For first contact send cover letter, client list, demo tape (½") and audio tape.

Animation: Works with approximately 1 animation project/month; 15/year. Uses animation for commercial advertising and promotional purposes. Looks for stylish animation style. For first contact send demo tape (½″) and audio tape to Douglas Stevens, Production Director. Does not return materials. Keeps materials on file.

HEDQUIST PRODUCTIONS INC., P.O. Box 1475, Fairfield IA 52550. (515)472-6708. FAX: (515)472-7400. Estab. 1984. Audio production company that provides radio spots, original music, audio for TV, film and video, audiovisual animation and audio cassette programs. Recent productions/projects: national radio commercials for Hardee's, Lennox and Konica. Regional commercials for clients in 23 states. Clients include: AETna, Farmer's State Bank and Regional Oldsmobile Dealers in 6 states. Needs humor writing and humorous scriptwriting for radio spots. Uses freelancers for 10% of all humor writing. Prefers working with freelancers with fax capabilities.
Humorous Scriptwriting: Works with approximately 1 humorous scriptwriter/month; 10/year. For first contact send cover letter, resume, audio tape and photocopied writing sample to Jeffrey P. Hedquist, President. Returns materials if accompanied by SASE. Negotiates rights purchased. Pays $50-300.
Humor Writing: Works with approximately 1 freelancer/month; 10/year. Uses freelance humor writers for creative consulting, developmental projects, brainstorming and radio spots. Needs freelance humor writers with the ability to "integrate the humorous, entertainment value of a commercial with marketing and selling value." For first contact send cover letter, resume, client list, audio tape and writing samples to Jeffrey P. Hedquist. Returns materials if accompanied by a SASE. Negotiates rights purchased. Pays $50-300/project.

KDOC-TV, 1730 S. Clementine, Anaheim CA 92802. (714)999-5000. FAX: (719)999-1218. Estab. 1982. Television company. Needs humorous illustration, humor writing, humorous scriptwriting, caricatures, cartoons, animations, animatics and storyboards. Humorous material is used for radio spots, programming, advertising, promotion and TV commercials. Prefers working with freelancers with fax capabilities.
Humorous Illustration: Would like to start using humorous illustrations. For first contact send cover letter, resume and portfolio to Tricia Krause, Promotions Coordinator. Reports back within weeks only if interested. Returns materials if accompanied by a SASE. Keeps materials on file.
Humorous Scriptwriting: Looking for comedy scripts or concepts on anything new. Doesn't want to see comedy scripts on old humor. For first contact send cover letter, resume and demo tape (¾″). Concept submissions should be submitted with synopsis of concept/programming. Send scripts to Dill Dailey, Program Director. Reports back within weeks only if interested. Returns materials if accompanied by a SASE. Keeps materials on file.
Humor Writing: Uses freelance humor writers for advertising/promotion, brochures, on-air announcements, creative consulting and brainstorming. For first contact send demo tape (¾″) to Tricia Krause. Reports back within weeks only if interested. Returns materials if accompanied by a SASE. Keeps materials on file.
Animation: Uses animation for programming, commercial advertising and promotional purposes. Looks for contemporary, traditional and stylish animation style. For first contact send cover letter, resume, and demo tape (¾″) to Tricia Krause. Reports back within weeks only if interested. Returns materials if accompanied by a SASE. Keeps materials on file.

JIM KEESHEN PRODUCTIONS, Suite 265, 1950 Sawtelle B1, Los Angeles CA 90025. (213)478-7230. FAX: (213)478-5142. Estab. 1982. Video storyboard presentation producer that provides animation for commercials and shorts. Recent productions/projects: PSA spots for airlines. Clients include major ad agencies. Needs humorous illustration,

Close-up

Steve O'Donnell
Head Writer
"Late Night"

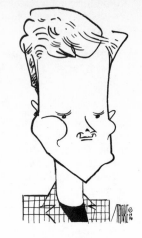

Until 1982, Steve O'Donnell's only television experience had been using the remote control to change the channels on his set at home.

Then as a staffer in NBC's video tape library, O'Donnell heard that the network was developing a new, late night talk show hosted by a sarcastic, quick-witted comedian named David Letterman. Better yet, the show was looking for writers, so the Harvard educated O'Donnell wrote some material expressly for Letterman and submitted it to then "Late Night" Head Writer, Merrill Markoe.

Markoe liked what she read and hired O'Donnell. Just like that.

O'Donnell was stunned. Up until then, his writing experience was limited to greeting card blips for American Greetings, funny copy for industrial films and freelance journalism. But suddenly, O'Donnell was an official, card-carrying TV writer—and today, he's Head Writer of the show that is effectively redefining television comedy.

"It's completely amazing," says O'Donnell, "but of the 11 writers here on the show, only one has had a job in television prior to "Late Night." I think the producers didn't worry about hiring such a young, inexperienced staff because "Late Night" was placed into such a marginal time period."

Indeed, "Late Night" debuted on February 2, 1982 to validate NBC's hypothesis that people would stay up after Carson to watch dogs chase their tails, see cans of beer flattened by a steamroller and witness a human oddity named Larry Bud Melman who dressed as a Navy officer because the uniform made him "look good—damn good."

However, "Late Night" was anything but an overnight success. "For the first two years," recalls O'Donnell, "it really was a little cult TV program." Now the show has almost become mainstream. Guests whom the producers couldn't book in the early days are lining up to be harassed by Dave. Years ago, "Late Night" needed celebs—today, it is the celebs who need "Late Night" as the hip, hour long show has become the nightly staple of the 18-34 market. In spite of its success, "Late Night" maintains its comic edge and "pierces the TV screen" as Letterman himself has said.

"We couldn't do the show we do now an hour earlier, let alone at 8:00 p.m.," O'Donnell points out. "I don't think people would want to watch us and I don't think we'd want to do it. I find it a blessing that we're on very late at night where it doesn't really matter. That way, the show can be looser and stupider."

O'Donnell and staff aren't given free reign to wantonly wreak havoc within their allotted time slot each night. "Objections to the writing come from all directions," O'Donnell explains. "Not just puritanical objections, but often they are liberal, well-meaning objections like 'You can't portray all old people as dowdy or stereotype all florists as gay.' We don't run into hassles over profanities because we really don't write that kind of stuff. Although occasionally, you'll hear Dave murmur 'bite me.'

"The kind of writing we do," says O'Donnell, "ranges from the most simple one sentence premise that Dave improvises on to detailed scripts with lines, dialogue and stage directions. An ordinary, representative day consists of the writers gathering mid-morning at maybe 10:30 or 11:30 and taking a look at what's going on—but I don't call one of those meetings every day.

"There are a dozen writers, including Dave who contributes ideas and writing and everything else. We'll work in different combinations for a couple of hours; we'll rehearse from 2:00 to 4:00 and then we'll tape the show at 5:30.

"The one time we generally do all get together," O'Donnell says, "is to write the Top Ten List which we do right before the taping to keep as fresh as possible. Writing the list is pretty fun—we'll sit down and come up with maybe 20 to 30 items and go through them with Dave—the ones he likes best we'll slap down. But we're literally typing that stuff into the character-generating machine as Dave is coming out onto stage."

Letterman himself is a discriminating editor and has ultimate control over the show's content. "Dave is very selective about material," O'Donnell explains. "He certainly doesn't use everything we write—in fact, his turndown rate is really high—like 80%. But if something doesn't work on the air, Dave doesn't storm off the set yelling 'Who wrote this shit?,' because if he didn't care for the material, he wouldn't have used it."

O'Donnell has great respect for Letterman's ability as a writer. "He's a great writer," says O'Donnell. "Be it specific lines ('from New York—freeway close to Hell') to whole ideas like dropping stuff off of a five-story tower just to see what happens. I mean, Dave's contribution is both large and small and each day he sits around talking with me and the other writers."

Assuming the miracles are all used up, assuming they were already used on O'Donnell and his fellow 11 "Late Night" writers, those who aspire to write for the tube should take the road most traveled—and don't count on a tail wind.

"Bizarre happenstances do seem to occur," O'Donnell suggests, "but I think the logical, sensible suggestion is that you write whatever you can—magazine stuff, TV commercial stuff, while you work on TV scripts. Then if some particular show really suits your sensibilities, send them a spec script (although you really need an agent for that). I guess I'd be the first to say start small and get big.

"And of course," O'Donnell recommends, "use a lot of words with hard 'K' sounds like 'pickle' or 'hockey puck.' "

—*Bob Staake*

humorous scriptwriting, "on scene" illustrations, cartoons, animatics, humor writing, animations and storyboards. Humorous material is used for developmental projects, TV commercials and animated shorts. Uses freelancers for 90% of all illustrations, 90% humor writing, 50% animation.

Humorous Illustration: Works with approximately 5 humorous illustrators/year. Needs good drawing ability in exaggeration. For first contact send cover letter and call Jim Keeshen, Director. Reports back only if interested. Returns material only if requested and if accompanied by SASE. Negotiates rights purchased. Pays $5-20/hour; also per day or per project.

Humorous Scriptwriting: Works with approximately 2 humor scriptwriters/year. Looking for comedy scripts on family, children and sex. For first contact, phone. For a concept for a comedy series or programming, submit outline to Jim Keeshen. Reports back only if interested. Returns materials only if interested and if accompanied by SASE. Negotiates rights purchased. Pays $100.

Humor Writing: Works with approximately 1 freelancer/year. Uses freelance humor writers for advertising/promotion and brainstorming. "We need good writers who understand character." For first contact, send cover letter and writing samples to Jim Keeshen. Reports back only if interested. Returns materials only if interested and if accompanied by SASE. Negotiates rights purchased. Pays $5/hour.

Animation: Works on approximately 2 animation projects/year. Uses animation for commercial advertising and shorts. Looks for avant garde, contemporary, traditional and stylish animation. For first contact send cover letter and demo tape to Jim Keeshen. Reports back only if interested. Returns materials only if interested and if accompanied by SASE. Negotiates rights purchased. Pays $10-150/frame.

NEAL MARSHAD PRODUCTIONS, 76 Laight St., New York NY 10013. (212)925-5285. FAX: 212-925-5634. Estab. 1983. TV production company and video production house providing creative production of TV programming. Recent productions/projects: Johnnie Walker Comedy Search, short films for NBC Saturday Night Live and segments for HBO comedy channel. Clients include NBC. Needs humorous scriptwriting, humor writing, storyboards. Humorous material is used for developmental projects, programming, promotion. Uses freelancers for 50% of all humor writing. Prefers working with freelancers with fax capabilities.

Humorous Illustration: For first contact send cover letter to Neal Marshad, Producer. Reports back in days only if interested. Returns materials only if requested and if accompanied by SASE. Keeps materials on file. Buys all rights. Pays $150-250/day.

Humorous Scriptwriting: Works with approximately 1 humor scriptwriter/month; 10/year. Looking for comedy scripts or concepts on adult humor. No comedy scripts on 14-year-olds and sex. For first contact send cover letter, resume, client list, tearsheets and demo tape. For a concept for a comedy series or programming, submit query detailing premise of concept, script, and synopsis of concept/programming. Send scripts to Neal Marshad. Reports back in 2 weeks. Buys all rights. Pays $500/project/property.

Animation: Works on approximately 2 animation projects/year. Uses animation for programming. Looks for avant garde, contemporary, stylish animation. For first contact send cover letter and demo tape to Neal Marshad, Producer. Reports in 2 weeks. Returns materials if accompanied by SASE. Buys first time rights. Pays $250/project.

PDK PICTURES, INC., Suite C-203, 3712 Barham Blvd, Los Angeles CA 90068. (213)851-0572. FAX: (818)506-6276. Estab. 1976. Film production company. Clients include Universal, MGM, Warner Brothers, ABC, CBS and NBC. Needs humor writing and humorous scriptwriting. Humorous material is used for developmental projects and programming. Uses freelancers for 100% of all humor writing.

Humorous Illustration: For first contact send cover letter and resume to Wilbur Stark, President. Reports in weeks if interested. Returns materials if accompanied by a SASE. Buys all rights or negotiates rights purchased. Pays by project: $500-5,000.

Humorous Scriptwriting: Works with approximately 6 humor scriptwriters/year. For first contact send cover letter, resume and photocopied writing sample. Concept submissions should be submitted with script and outline. Send scripts to Wilbur Stark. Reports back within 2 months. Buys all rights or negotiates rights purchased. Pays $500-5,000.

Humor Writing: Works with approximately 10 freelancers/year. Uses freelance humor writers for writing for specific shows and developmental projects. For first contact send cover letter and resume to Wilbur Stark. Reports back within 2 months only if interested. Returns materials only if accompanied by a SASE. Buys all rights or negotiates rights purchased. Pays by the project: $500-5,000.

VERNE PERSHING PRODUCTIONS, 1800 N. Argyle #100A, Hollywood CA 90028. (213)463-1511. FAX: (213)463-3548. Estab. 1980. TV production company that provides corporate and industrial film and video production. Recent productions/projects: Cheryl Tiegs for Light & Lively Yogurt, Vidwitz, the Brainwave to the Games-Nintendo of American. Needs humorous scriptwriting. Humorous material is used for programming. Uses freelancers for 25% of all humor writing.

Humorous Scriptwriting: Works with approximately 3 humor scriptwriters/year. Looking for comedy scripts or concepts on anything. For first contact send cover letter, resume, client list, demo tape (½″ and ¾″) and photocopied writing sample. Concept submissions should be submitted with script and synopsis of concept/programming to Verne Pershing, owner. Reports only if interested. Returns materials if accompanied by a SASE. Keeps materials on file. Negotiates rights purchased. Pays $1000 minimum.

PROIMAGE, 6311 N. O'Connor Rd. LB #85, Irving TX 75039. (214)869-7639. Estab. 1980. TV production company, video and film production house that provides production and creative services to clients. Recent productions/project: "Tom Landry—A Legend?" PBS special. Clients include: Hertz, ABC and NBC. Needs humor writing and humorous scriptwriting for radio spots, programming, advertising and TV commercials. Uses freelancers for 10% of all humor writing. Prefers to work with freelancers who have fax capabilities.

Humorous Scriptwriting: Works with 2-3 humorous scriptwriters/year. Looking for comedy scripts on relationships and sex farces. For first contact send cover letter and resume. For a concept for a comedy series or programming, submit query detailing premise of concept to F.A. Hutchison, CEO. Reports back in 1 month. Negotiates rights purchased. Pays $100.

Humor Writing: Works with approximately 2-3 freelance humor writers/year. Uses freelance humor writers for advertising/promotion, on-air announcements, developmental projects and movies. Needs Dallas/Ft. Worth-based writers. For first contact send cover letter and resume to F.A. Hutchison. Reports back in 1 month. Negotiates rights purchased. Pays by the hour: $15-75; by the project: $100.

Animation: Uses animation for commercial advertising. Looks for styles which are avant garde. For first contact send cover letter and resume to F.A. Hutchinson. Reports back in 1 month. Returns materials only if interested. Negotiates rights purchased.

SINNOTT AND ASSOCIATES, INC., 676 N. LaSalle, Chicago IL 60610. (312)440-1875. Estab. 1975. TV commercial production company that does animation and special effects. Recent productions/products: Cap'n Crunch, McDonald's, Amaco, Spots & Long Animated Projects. Clients include Hallmark, McDonald's, Quaker Oats, Amaco and major advertising agencies. Needs humorous illustration, animation and storyboards. Humorous material used for development projects and TV commercials. Uses freelancers for 75% of illustrations and 25% of animation. Prefers freelancers with fax.

Animation: Works on approximately 20 animation projects/year. Uses animation for commercial advertising and promotional purposes. Looks for avant garde, contemporary and traditional animation style. For first contact send cover letter and (½" or ¾") demo tape to Steven A. Jones, Director. Reports if interested. Keeps materials on file.

EDGAR S. SPIZEL PRODUCTIONS, 1782 Pacific Avenue, San Francisco CA 94109. (415)474-5735. Estab. 1950. TV/video production company that provides TV, video, audio-creative work with celebrities from sports, entertainment, TV and motion pictures. Recent productions/projects: Bay Area Rapid Transit, Henny Youngman, San Francisco Office of Economic Development, City of Oakland, Oakland A's Jose Canseco.
Humorous Illustration: Send cover letter, resume, client list and tearsheets to Edgar S. Spizel, President. Reports if interested. Returns materials if SASE. Keeps materials on file.
Humorous Scriptwriting: For first contact send cover letter, resume, client list and audio tape. Reports if interested. Returns materials if accompanied by a SASE.

TALCO PRODUCTIONS, 279 E. 44th St., New York NY 10014. (212)697-4015. Estab. 1968. TV/video/radio production company providing TV documentaries, industrials, PR and radio series. Recent productions/projects: "Can you Name the Year?", "A Funny Thing Happened. . . . " Needs humor writing and humorous scriptwriting. Humorous material used for radio spots/programming. Uses freelancers for 60% of all humor writing.
Humorous Illustration: For first contact send cover letter and resume. Reports back in weeks. Returns materials if a SASE. Buys all rights. Pays by project: $200-5,000.
Humorous Scriptwriting: Works with approximately 1 humor scriptwriter/month. Will not read unsolicited scripts. For first contact send cover letter and resume to Alan Lawrence, President. Reports back within 2 weeks. Returns materials if accompanied by a SASE. Buys all rights. Pays by the project: $100-10,000.
Humor Writing: Works with approximately 1 freelancer/month. Uses freelance humor writers for on-air announcements and writing for specific shows. For first contact send cover letter and resume to Alan Lawrence. Reports back within weeks. Returns materials if accompanied by a SASE. Buys all rights. Pays by the project: $100-10,000.

RICK TOWER CREATIONS, Box 4858, St. Louis MO 63103. (314)825-0206. Estab. 1985. "We write 400-500 gags/month for radio personalities on over 800 stations coast to coast." Clients include: KIIS/LA, WHTZ/NYC, WYTZ-Chicago, Armed Forces Radio. Needs humor writing and topical one-liners. Humorous material is used for programming and broadcast. Uses freelancers for 10% of gags.
Humor Writing: Works with approximately 15 freelancers/month, 100/year. Uses freelance writers to write for radio broadcasters. Needs topical one-liners about people, places and topics in today's news. For first contact send writing samples to Steve Mitchell, Asst. Editor. Reports in 5 days. Returns materials if accompanied by a SASE. Does not file materials. Buys all rights. Pays by the project: $2-10/min per gag.

U.S. TELEVISION CO., INC., 175 E. 62nd St., New York NY 10021. (212)758-9828. FAX: (212)421-3386. Estab. 1976. TV production company/video production house. Commercials and industrials. Needs humor writing, humorous scriptwriting and storyboards for radio spots, advertising, TV commercials and industrials. Uses freelancers for 25% of all humor writing. Prefers working with freelancers with fax capabilities.
Humorous Scriptwriting: Works with 1 humor scriptwriter/month or 10/year. Looking for comedy scripts or concepts on advertising and sales training. No comedy scripts on bad salesmen. For first contact send cover letter, resume, client list, demo tape (½").

At last, a bunch of contests where if you win, you aren't tortured with a visit by Ed McMahon!

We sat down and calculated that if you entered each and every one of these contests, you'd spend a total of 8 days, 17 hours and 36 minutes filling out entry forms. And out of that time, exactly 24 minutes and 16 seconds would be devoted to sharpening your pencil.

Hey, *you* may have that kind of time, but I've got a life to live, a pond to drain and leaves to rake. Besides, unless you're a Renaissance man to the sixth power, it would be tough to have something to enter in *every* one of these contests. But happily, if you *write* humor, we got contests. If you *draw* humor, we got contests. In fact, we got slightly more contests than there are species of baboon.

Prizes range from cash to a handshake, publication of your winning entry to a formica dinette set with matching vinyl-covered chairs. Oops, sorry—I mistakenly listed a prize from "Wheel Of Fortune."

Seriously, there are some pretty nifty contests here—more than I thought *existed*. Listed are the basic facts (type of contest, amateur/professional, deadline, etc.), but we would highly recommend that you request the *complete* entry information from the contest directors themselves.

After all, many have extensive requirements which we could not possibly list, and we did our best translating the information provided by foreign contest officials. For example, we think we've listed an Italian cartooning contest, but then again it may be a competition for the best veal parmigiana in the whole world.

On your mark. Get set. Fill out forms!

ANN ARBOR FILM FESTIVAL, P.O. Box 8232, Ann Arbor MI 48107. (313)995-5356. Estab. 1963. Contest is for a 16mm independent and experimental film and animation festival. Contest is open to all. Deadline: March. Deadline is the same every year.
How to Enter: Write or call for details. Entries are returned. Receives 250 entries/ year. Fees: $25/film entry. Judged by 3 filmmakers; award is $6,000 cash distributed according to judges. Winners notified by mail. For contest rules and forms, send SASE.

BAY GUARDIAN CARTOON CONTEST, 2700 19th St., San Francisco CA 94110. (415)824-7660. Contest for cartooning—single panel, single strip, ongoing strip, silent cartoon, political cartoon, comic strip parody, single cartoon with San Francisco Bay area focus, computer generated cartoon and cartoon drawn by children 14 years and under. Open to all. Deadline is July 11, 1990.
How to Enter: "Must enclose SASE. Available in May, 1990."

BIG MUDDY FILM FESTIVAL, Dept. of Cinema and Photography, Southern Illinois University, Carbondale IL 62901. (618)453-2365. Estab. 1977. Contest showcases achievement in independently produced film and video for all types of film, video and animation. Contest is open to all. Past recipients: "Tin Toy," animation category. Deadline: January 17,1990. "Entry deadline has been pushed closer to festival."
How to Enter: Entry format is limited to 16mm film and ¾" videotape. Film judged separately from video. Must have been completed after December, 1988. Entries will be judged on style, originality and artistic merit. Entries are returned. Receives 135-150 entries/year. Fees: $20 film/video under 20 min.; $25 film/video from 20-50 min.; $30 film/video 50 min. Judged by guest juror/filmmakers; award is $1,500 total. Winners notified by mail or phone. Entrant can agree to have work aired on local public television station.

CA "90", P.O. Box 10330, Palo Alto CA 94303. (415)326-6040. Contest is for all areas of humorous writing and illustration. Contest open to all. Must be a published piece. Deadline: July 1.
How to Enter: Send entry to Jean Coyne.

CREATIVITY "90", 6th Floor, 10 E. 39th St., New York NY 10016. (212)889-6500. Contest for cartooning, humorous nonfiction and fiction writing, humorous illustration and advertising. Deadline: May 4, 1990.
How to Enter: Call or write. Send SASE. Send entry to Claris Barron or Mae Wills.

DEJA VU (The Psychic's Journal), P.O. Box 371371, El Paso TX 79937. (915)595-2625. Contact: Rio Grande Press. Estab. 1989. Contest is to give new and experienced artists/ cartoonists a place to show their work and to be published for cartooning, humorous illustration and specialized cover designs. Contest is open to all. Quarterly deadlines: May 31, August 31, November 30 and February 28.
How to Enter: Send humorous cartoons, illustrations and cover designs concerning psychics, psychic phenomena, etc. Entries will be judged on originality, art qualities, professionalism and appropriateness for publication intended. Entries are not returned. Receives 10-12 cartoons/year; 5-6 cover designs/year. Judged by Managing Editor; award is publication plus copy of issue in which work appears. Winner notified by mail. Winning entries are published in *Deja Vu.* Buys first North American serial rights. After publication, all rights return to artist. For contest rules and forms, send SASE. Upon being selected to be published in *Deja Vu,* winning artists are given the opportunity to be published in Rio Grande Press' other two publications, *Editor's Digest* and *Se La Vie Writer's Journal.*

DELACORTE PRESS PRIZE FOR A FIRST YOUNG ADULT NOVEL, 666 Fifth Ave., New York NY 10103. (212)765-6500. FAX: (212)492-9698. Contact: Delacorte Press, Dept. BFYR, ATTN: L. Oldenburg. Estab. 1983. Contest is to encourage the writing of contemporary young adult fiction. Contest is open to all, providing that the entrant has not previously published a young adult novel. Deadline: Entries must be *postmarked* after Labor Day and before the first day of the next year.

How to Enter: Send a book length manuscript of 100-224 pages. Entries will be judged on merit. Entries are returned if accompanied by SASE. Receives 230 entries/year. Judged by editors; award is $1,500 cash prize, $6,000 advance against royalties and publication of novel. "Honorable Mentions may also be published, terms to be negotiated, if we find such a manuscript." Winning entries are published as soon as possible, depending on how much work they need. 7th Contest winner will be published 4/90. Write and request for contest rules and forms. "We do like entrants to comply with the rules. Approximately 10% of entrants are rejected every year for, say, sending us a historical novel. Our contest is not exclusively for humorous fiction, but humor goes a long way with us."

THE DELAWARE VALLEY COMEDY COMPETITION, % The Comedy Cabaret, 33 Harmony Dr., Richboro PA 18954. (215)322-6642. FAX: (215)322-5693. Contest is for standup comedy; open to all. Deadline: September 1990.

How to Enter: Contest rules and entry forms available; send SASE.

D'JUSTIN, Centre Européen Humour Communication, 100, rue de Lille, 59200 Tourcoing France. (33)202-67238. Estab. 1984. Contest is about actuality and news during the past year for cartooning and humorous illustration. Contest is open to all, but the cartoons must have been published. Deadline: March/April annually.

How to Enter: Send 2 originals of humorous illustration. Entries will be judged on whether they are able to make people laugh about actuality and news. Entries are returned. Receives 100-200 entries/year. No fees. Judged by professors and cultural critics; award is cash and trophy. Winners notified by mail or telegram. Winning entries are published in local and national press and agencies. Deadline: between 1st of February and 31st of March."

DOG WRITERS' ASSOCIATION OF AMERICA, 1828 Shady Lane, Louisville KY 40205. (502)454-7018. Contact: Susan J. Jeffries, Contest Chair. Estab. 1959. Contest is to recognize excellence in cartooning and writing about dogs (humorous nonfiction writing, humorous illustration and humorous fiction writing). Contest is open to all. Deadline: October 1.

How to Enter: Send 3 copies of each entry with entry form and fee. Entries will be judged on originality and quality. Entries are not returned. Fee: $10. Judged by Members of DWAA. Awards are plaques, certificates and some cash. Winners are notified by mail. Winning entries are published in a compilation called "Best of the Best." Buys only for compilation for "Best of the Best." For contest rules and forms, send a SASE. "Talk about going to the dogs! This contest has seven classes (newspaper, magazines, club publications, books, graphic arts, poetry, audio/visual) and 29 contests within those classes. We're particularly curious about *The Sulfodene/Scratchex Journalistic excellence in Dog Grooming Award*, but there are plenty others if you're inclined to 'put on the dog.' " Prizes vary—from $200 to $500. Send SASE for complete rules.

EDITOR'S DIGEST, Box 371371, El Paso TX 79937. (915)595-2625. Contact: Rio Grande Press. Estab. 1989. Contest is to give artists and/or editor/artists/cartoonists a chance to publish their work in publications other than their own for cartooning, humorous nonfiction writing, humorous illustration and cover designs. Contest is open to all, specifically editors. Quarterly deadlines: March 31, June 30, September 30 and December 31.

How to Enter: Send humorous cartoons, illustrations and cover designs relating to small press editors and publishers. Entries will be judged on originality, humor, appropriateness for intended publication and professionalism. Entries are not returned. Receives 10-12 cartoons/year; 7-8 cover designs/year. Judged by Managing Editor. Award is publication plus one copy of issue in which work appears. Winner(s) are notified by mail. Winning entries are published in *Editor's Digest.* Buys First North American serial rights; after publication all rights return to artist. For contest rules and forms, send a SASE. Upon being selected to be published in *Editor's Digest,* winning artist(s) are given the opportunity to be published in Rio Grande Press' two other publications, *Se La Vie Writer's Journal* and *Deja Vu.*

EUROPEAN CARTOON CONTEST, 9970 Kruishoutem, Belgium. (091)83-66-96. Contact: Waregemsesteenweg 113. Contest is to promote the cartoon as a form of art—offer people the possibility to see the real thing (and not just as a publication in a magazine) by organizing exhibitions of selected cartoons. Contest is open to all. Deadline: November 15, 1991. Contest is organized every two years.
How to Enter: Send unpublished cartoons on a given theme (for 1991: Circus). Entries will be judged on originality of the idea, artistic merit and style. Entries are not returned, they become property of the organization. Receives 2267 entries every two years. Judged by art professors, artists, officials, ministry of culture and journalists; awards are 1st, 20,000 BF & Trophy (golden egg); 2nd, 15,000 BF and silver egg; 3rd, 10,000 BF and bronze egg and free stay in the village hotel. Winners are notified by mail or telegram. Winning entries are published in cartoon book edited by the organization and newspapers and become the property of the organization. For contest rules and forms, send a letter. Contest is organized every two years. Selected cartoons are published in free catalogue that is sent to each participant. Selected cartoons are shown during Easter exhibition in Kruishoutem. Afterwards, at exhibitions all over Belgium. The "Eurokkartouenal is an organization of a Flemmish cultural association called Willemsfonds."

JOHN FISCHETTI EDITORIAL CARTOON COMPETITION, 600 South Michigan Avenue, Chicago IL 60605. (312)663-1600. Contact: Columbia College Chicago. Estab. 1982. Contest is to help raise funds for journalism scholarship endowment for cartooning. Contest is open to professionals. Past recipients: Lee Judge, Bill DeOre, Tom Toles, Scott Willis, Doug Marlette, Dich Locher and Arthur "Chip" Bok, Lambert Der. Deadline: September 1.
How to Enter: Submit 1-3 published editorial cartoons. All entries must include letter of nomination or endorsement from editor, publisher or employer. Entries will be judged on style, humor and political and social relevance. Entries are not returned. Receives 125-150 entries/year. Judged by editors, professors, news people. Awards are 1st, $2,500; 2nd, $500; plaques to other winners, including 8 Honorable Mentions. Winners are notified by mail. Winning entries are displayed at annual dinner.

GLOBAL MEDIA AWARDS FOR EXCELLENCE IN POPULATION REPORTING, The Population Institute, Suite 207, 110 Maryland Ave NE, Washington DC 20002. (202)544-3300. FAX: (202)544-0068. Contact: The Population Institute. Estab. 1980. Contest includes cartooning in 15 categories and is open to professionals. Past recipients: Dik Browne, Bill Mauldin, Paul Fell, David Horsey. Deadline: September 15.
How to Enter: Send one copy of cartoons published between September 15, 1989-September 15, 1990 and a statement on why they merit this award. Entries will be judged on relevancy to issues of global population and environment. Judged by journalists, editors and international population and development experts. Award is plaque, free transportation to awards presentation, usually held in a developing country. Winner(s) are notified by telegram. Send material directly to the Global Media Awards with cover sheet or may be nominated.

THE GREEN EYESHADE: EXCELLENCE IN JOURNALISM AWARDS, SPJ Chapter, WXIA-TV, 1611 W. Peachtree St., Atlanta GA 30309. ATTN: Nancy Ellard. (404)351-5219. New contest. An all format journalism award competition for editorial cartooning and humorous commentary. Open to professionals. Deadline: January 10, 1991.
How to Enter: Send editorial cartooning and humorous commentary. Include no more than 5 cartoon tearsheets mounted on matboard; no more than 3 examples of humorous commentary. Judged on "overall excellence, service to community, contribution to public's understanding of issues and events." Entries not returned. Entry fee: $25/entry. Judged by journalism professionals. Award is Green Eyeshade Plaque and $1,000. Winner notified by mail. Rules and entry forms are available. Eligibility limited to fulltime journalists working in states of AL, AR, FL, GA, KY, LA, MS, NC, SC, TN, WV.

HARVEY AWARDS, % Lone Star Comics, 511 E. Abram St., Arlington TX 76010. Contact: Buddy Saunders. (817)265-0491. Contest for work done in comic book market. Open to professionals. Nominating is done in March and April. Selection is by ballot.

ILLUSTRATORS 33, 128 East 63rd Street, New York NY 10021. (212)838-2560. Contact: Society of Illustrators. Contest is to recognize illustrators, cartoonists, artists and graphics professionals for communication arts achievement. Contest is open to professionals. Deadline: October 6.
How to Enter: Request complete rules from the Society. Entries are not returned. Fee: $17 per 1 entry. Judged by professionals from the graphics industry; award is gold medal, silver medal, award certificate, certificate of merit. Winners are notified by mail. Winning entries are published in *Illustrators 33.* Request contest rules and forms.

INTERNATIONAL 3-DAY NOVEL CONTEST, 100-1062 Homer St., Vancouver, British Columbia V6B 2W9 Canada. (604)687-4233. Contact: Pulp Press. Estab. 1978. Contest to write the best novel in 3 days, held during Labor Day weekend. "Location and method are not important, just good writing." Contest is open to all. Past Recipient: bp nichol, Marc Diamond, James Dunn. Deadline: Friday before Labor Day weekend, annually.
How to Enter: Send name, address and entry fee of $7 prior to Labor Day weekend. Entrants should send finished entries along with a statement signed by a witness confirming the novel's completion in 3 days. Entries will be judged on best writing. Entries are returned if requested and accompanied by SASE or IRC's from outside Canada. Receives 500 entries/year. Fee: $7 per entry. Judged by editors; award is publication. Winner is notified by phone. Winning entries are published in book form. For contest rules and forms send SASE or IRC's (from outside Canada).

LOS ANGELES INTERNATIONAL ANIMATION CELEBRATION, 2222 S. Barrinton Ave., Los Angeles CA 90064. (213)473-6701. FAX: (213)444-9850. Contest for any animation. Open to all, including an award for first work by student. Deadline: June 15, 1990.
How to Enter: Send all entries to Kathy Edrich, General Manager.

NATIONAL 10-MINUTE PLAY CONTEST, Actors Theatre of Louisville, 316 W. Main St., Louisville KY 40202-2916. (502)584-1265. Estab. 1989. Contest is to discover the best new ten-minute play by an unknown or established playwright. Contest is open to all U.S. residents. Deadline: December 1.
How to Enter: Send typed, secured manuscript with manuscript sized SASE. Limit 10 pages per script, 2 scripts per author. Unsolicited full-lengths and one-acts will be returned unread. Entries will be judged on literary and dramatic merit. Entries are returned if accompanied by SASE. Receives 2,000 entries/year. Judged by theater staff; award is $1,000 with possible production. Winner(s) are notified by mail. For contest rules and forms, send SASE.

OVERSEAS PRESS CLUB AWARD, Suite 2116, 301 Madison Avenue, New York NY (212)983-4655. Estab. 1940. Contest is to find the best editorial cartoon in foreign affairs. Contest is open to professionals. Past recipients: Herblock, Paul Conrad, Tony Auth. Deadline: January 30.
How to Enter: Send 4-10 different cartoons per entry. Entries are returned if accompanied by SASE. Fee: $40 per 1 entry. Judged by journalism professionals; award is $500. For contest rules and forms, send SASE.

PREMIO SATIRA POLITICA, Premio Satira Politica % Comune di Forte dei Marmi, 55042 Forte dei Marmi, Lucca Italy. (584)82966. FAX: (584)83843. Estab. 1973. Contest for cartooning, humorous nonfiction writing, humorous illustration, humorous fiction writing, movies, cabaret, radio and TV. Contest open to all. Past recipients: David Levine (1987), Jules Feiffer (1989), "Punch" (Great Britain), Claude Serre (France). Deadline: April, annually.
How to Enter: "Cartoonists should send copies of their work. Then cartoonists are invited to have an exhibition here in Forte dei Marmi. Another possibility is to make a show with all the different cartoons which arrive from the States." Entries will be judged on wit and artistic merit. Entries not returned. Judged by editors, professors and journalists; award is plaque and sculpture. Winning entries are published in catalogue.

QUILL & SCROLL NATIONAL WRITING, PHOTO CONTEST, University of Iowa, School of Journaliam, Iowa City IA 52242. (319)335-5795. Contest for cartooning (editorial — single or strip), feature writing and newspaper editorial. Open to students only. Deadline: February.
How to Enter: "Each entry must have been published in a high school or college paper. Contact: Richard John. Winners are eligible to enter scholarship contest.

SALON DEL COMIC "CINDAD DE OVIEDO", Av. Galicia, 31, 33005 Oviedo Spain. (85)235311. FAX: (85)25105. Contact: Fundecion Municipal de Cultura. Estab. 1983. Contest organized to exhibit comics, cartoons and humorous illustrations of amateurs. Contest is open to students and amateurs. Deadline: November 10.
How to Enter: Send tearsheet of actual printed piece. Entries will be judged on artistic merit. Entries are returned if requested. Receives 500 entries/year. Judged by editors, professors and illustrators; award is "cash." Winner(s) are notified by mail. Winning entries are published in *The Wendigo* comic magazine. Write to obtain complete rules.

SALON INT'L DU DESSIN DE PRESSE ET D'HUMOUR, Saint Just Culture et Loisirs, 31 Rue Du III Novembre 1918, 87590 Saint Just Le Martel. Phone: 55-09-26-70. Contact: Mr. Vandenbrouke. Estab. 1982. An international cartoon exhibition. Contest for cartooning open to professional press cartoonists or humorous illustrators.
How to Enter: Cartoonists interested in participation must send introduction letter and 8-10 original cartoons. Entries returned. 350 cartoonists participated in 1989. The Salon involves cartoonists from England, Ireland, France, Spain, Italy, Germany, Switzerland, Phillipines, Turkey, United States and Japan. "There is a competition of sorts. All cartoonists present at the St. Just Salon are asked to draw a special satirical cartoon and the public votes for their favorite, the winner receives, you guessed it, a *COW*."

THE CHARLES M. SCHULZ FOR COLLEGE CARTOONIST, The Charles M. Schulz Award, 200 Park Ave., New York, NY 10166-0079. Contact: c/o United Media. Estab. 1980. Contest is to honor outstanding college cartoonists and to encourage them to launch past graduate professional careers for cartooning and editorial cartoons. Contest is open to students. Past recipients: 1988, Chris Kalb, Yale University; 1987 Michael

Thompson, University of Wisconsin/Milwaukee. Deadline: January 5 (approximately the same time each year).
How to Enter: Send portfolio of no fewer than five or more than 15 representative samples of cartoon work published in a college newspaper or college magazine. Do not submit original artwork. Entry blank must accompany entry. Entries not returned. Receives 200 entries/year. Judged by editor, professor and illustrator; award is $2,000 and bronze plaque. Winner(s) notified by mail. Send request for fact sheet and entry blank to Scripps Howard Foundation, 1100 Central Trust Tower, Cincinnati OH 45202.

SCRIPPS HOWARD FOUNDATION, NATIONAL JOURNALISM AWARD, COLLEGE CARTOONIST/CHARLES M. SCHULZ AWARD, 1100 Central Trust Tower, Cincinnati, OH 45202. (513)977-3035. Contest for humorous and editorial cartooning; open to college students. "Work must be published during calendar year." Deadline: January, 1990. Contest rules and entry rules available. Contact: Mary Lou Marusin, Executive Director.

SE LA VIE WRITER'S JOURNAL, P.O. Box 371371, El Paso TX 79937. (915)595-2625. Contact: Rio Grande Press. Estab. 1987. Contest is to give new or experienced artists/ cartoonists a place to show their work and be published. Contest is open to all. Deadline: quarterly March 31, June 30, Sept. 30 and Dec. 31.
How to Enter: Send humorous cartoons, illustrations about poets, writers, etc. For cover designs, send post card query for subject. Entries will be judged on originality, humor, appropriateness for publication in which entered and professionalism. Entries are not returned. Receives 15 cartoons/year; 8-10 designs/year. Judged by managing editor; award is publication plus copy of issue in which work appears. Winner(s) are notified by mail. Winning entries are published in *Se La Vie Writer's Journal.* Purchases first North American serial rights; after publication, all rights return to artist. For contest rules and forms, send SASE. Upon being selected to be published in *Se Le Vie,* winning artist(s) are given the opportunity to be published in Rio Grande Press' other two publications, *Editor's Digest* and *Deja Vu.* The contest organizers want material that reflects "life" theme (La Vie), be it poem, essay, story, cartoon, column or article.

SNICKER'S ENVELOPE CONTEST, Snicker Magazine, 1248 Oak Bark Dr., St. Louis MO 63146. (314)993-1633. Estab. since "the beginning of the pony express." Contest is to "drive the post office crazy and for us to show our readers and neighbors that we get the wildest mail in the country!" Contest for cartooning, humorous illustration and oragami. Contest open to all "and to U.S. Post Master General." First year of contest.
How to Enter: "Send us a decorated, painted, airbrushed, cartooned, homespun or otherwise artful envelope (any size) that you've created especially for lil' ol' us. It can even be empty inside (but we hope it isn't!). Entries will be judged on imagination, invention, color, design, humor, cleverness and the fact that the post-office could actually figure out where to send it!" Entries not returned. Judged by editors; award is publication of "coolest" envelopes and letters; "we'll mail you back a free Snicker poster (while they last) or some other hip item." Winners notified by mail. Winning entries are published in Snicker Magazine. Buys no rights. Contest rules and forms not available.

UC3D-ART-1990, Apartment 3-D, 1009 S. Berry Rd., St. Louis MO 63122. (314)961-2303. FAX: (314)961-6771. Estab. 1987. Contest is to "foster and promote the art of 3D and to prove just how cool you look in a pair of 3-D glasses." Contest for cartooning and humorous illustration. Open to professionals. Past recipients: 2-D work of these artists converted into 3-D: Elwood Smith, Dave Calver, Steven Guarnaccia, Mark Marek, Jeff Faria, Jack Dickason, Gary Hallgren, Bob Staake, Bill Plympton. Deadline: October 31 annually.

Let's Drive the Postmaster General into Early Retirement! *Oh sure, St. Louis has an arch, a muddy river and Bob Costas, but it also has a pretty nifty humor magazine called* Snicker *(they seriously considered Zagnut). In any event,* Snicker *is a receptive forum for the sophisticated and/or sophomoric cartoonist and they have this cool little contest going on. All you need is a creative thought, a pen or pencil, an envelope and two bits for a stamp.*

How to Enter: Entrants should send two stats of black and white line art — suggested size of stats 9 × 12 (horizontal or vertical). Stats no larger than 10 × 16. Entries will be judged on 3-D potential, foreground to background effects and psychotic originality. Entries not returned. Fees: $8/entry (payable to: Apartment 3-D). Judged by professional panel of 3-D artists and illustrators; award is your work transformed into 250 3-D posters. Winner also receives 100 3-D glasses and national promotion of his or her 3-D art. Winners notified by mail. Apartment 3-D reserves the (2) rights of winning 3-D art. Winner reserves 2-D rights. Contest rules and forms for SASE. "3-D is a wild and wacky art form. Things that work well in 2-D, don't always fly in 3-D. Therefore, we suggest you send for complete contest rules which include an order form for 3-D glasses and 3-D poster samples. Please understand that you need draw your art only once. If your art wins, we transform it into 3-dimensional imagery."

YOMIURI INTERNATIONAL CARTOON CONTEST, 1-7-1 Otemachi, Chiyoda-Ku, Tokoyo 100-55 Japan. (03)24-2-1111. Contact: Yomiuri Shimbun. Estab.1979. Contest is to offer cartoonists worldwide opportunity to compete for the most thought-provoking cartoons. Contest is open to all. Deadline: Adult Division - October 31; Junior Division (18 or under) October 14.
How to Enter: There are 3 phases of contest: 1) Theme Section; 2) Free Section: any topic; 3) Junior Division: any topic. Color or b&w art may be submitted, but it must be a piece previously unpublished and no longer than 297 mm × 420 mm, single panel, multi panel, with words or without. Entries are not returned. Received 14,296 entries in 1988 from 62 countries. Winning entries are published in *Yomiuri Shimbun Magazine* newspapers, exhibition, posters, museum showing. The Yomiuri Shimbun reserves the right to publish and reproduce cartoon entries as listed above.

Resources

Agents/ Representatives

Besides lunch, what exactly do agents *do*?

Well, the good ones do much more than schmooze with potential clients over a plate of chicken salad. Presenting your portfolio or manuscript, negotiating fees, distributing promotional materials, handling the billing, these are the responsibilities of an agent or representative. At least that's the theory.

Yet the jury is still out on agents. Some humorous illustrators consider a rep a lifesaver, others would rather administer to the business themselves. Some writers swear *by* their agents, others swear *at* them.

The animosity is not unfounded. Agents and representatives seem to have little interest in handling an up and coming "talent." Rather, they prefer to represent illustrators and writers who have firmly established themselves. In fact, it is not uncommon that an agent declines to represent a developing talent, only agreeing to represent that talent years later—once he has "made" it.

However, agents do fulfill valuable functions. Illustrators and writers have notorious reputations of being poor business people and this reputation is not entirely off base. Therefore, the agent protects his talent by insuring that clients conduct business directly and professionally through him. An agent also helps to "legitimize" the talent. For this, the agent is paid a percentage of the fee negotiated for the job. Most illustrator representatives take 25% to 30% commissions, while literary agents receive 10% to 20%.

Agents *do* take a chance when they agree to represent individual talent. They are gambling that the market *will* be receptive to your particular brand of illustration or writing. If you're an illustrator, your representative will probably test the market's receptiveness by sending out printed promotional samples of your work. Both illustrator and agent share in the cost of this promotion. If printing of the promotional material costs $800 and postage costs $1,200, an agent with whom you have a 25% commission agreement would pay $500 of that total promotional bill.

However, agent and illustrator can mutually agree to *anything*. For example, an arrangement can be made where the illustrator pays for the printing of promotional materials and the agent is responsible for the cost of mailing them.

The relationship has immediate benefit to the talent. The illustrator or writer essentially doubles his sales force with no out-of-pocket expense. (No agent or representative should ask you for "up front" money before agreeing

to represent you.) It is then up to the agent to effectively sell your talents to various buyers.

If you're a writer interested in representation, put together a package which includes a cover letter explaining your desire to be represented, a few samples of your writing (or sample chapter of proposed manuscript), a resume, client list and, of course, a SASE. If you do not hear any word or receive your materials within a month, call to touch base. Most literary agents keep meticulous records of what and when things are sent in.

An illustrator will want to assemble the same package he would to send to any prospective client. You're essentially selling yourself to an agent, so paint the best picture possible. You'll find, however, that most agents have little interest in representing humorous illustrators who do extensive "editorial" work in magazines, newspapers and other publications. They prefer representing humorous illustrators who do advertising work for the simple reason that that's where the money (and the big commission) is.

Particularly with illustration agents, representation can be exclusive (one agent covering the entire country) or a series of regional representatives (an agent covering the West Coast, one for the Southeast, one for New York City, etc.). Do your homework. Talk with other humorous illustrators who have exclusive representatives, regional representatives or no representative to get a better sense of the delights and dilemmas.

But with agents and representatives, the pros far outweigh the cons. If the opportunity of representation presents itself, it would be foolish to ignore it. As long as the illustrator or writer incurs no out-of-pocket expense, signing a representation agreement with an agent opens up doors that you need not personally knock on.

JOSEPH S. AJLOUNY, ESQ., LITERARY AGENT, 8400 Kenwood St., Oak Park MI 48237. (313)546-9123. Contact: Joseph S. Ajlouny, Director. Estab. 1986. Represents humorous illustrators, cartoonists, humor writers and comedy writers. Current clients include

Franklin Folger, Phil Ryder, Bill Kitchen. Prefers representing experienced talents who have complete projects to offer.
Terms: Takes a 15% agency commission from talent and nothing more unless specifically negotiated. Talent works for syndicates, book publishers, illustration projects.
How to Contact: For first contact send cover letter, tearsheets and synopsis of project. Reports back in 1 month. Returns materials only if requested and if accompanied by SASE. Send flats to P.O. Box 37175, Oak Park MI 48237.

THE AUTHORS AND ARTISTS RESOURCE CENTER, P.O. Box 64785, Tucson AZ 85740-1785. (602)325-4733. Contact: Diane C. Gore, Associate. Estab. 1984. Represents humorous illustrators, cartoonists and humor writers. "We will begin representing artists January, 1990." Prefers representing talent that can illustrate books, magazines and has some professional training.
Terms: Takes a 15% agency commission from our talent. Talent works for book and magazine publishers.
How to Contact: For first contact send cover letter, resume, tearsheets and photocopies of samples. Reports back in 3 months. Returns materials if accompanied by SASE. Keeps materials on file.

CAROL BANCROFT & FRIENDS, 185 Goodhill Road, Weston CT 06883. (203)226-7674. FAX: (203)226-1468. Contact: Carol Bancroft, Owner. Estab. 1972. Represents humorous illustrators. Current clients include publishing houses. Prefers representing talent that is marketable and new, but shows promise. Prefers working with talent who is marketable, new but shows promise and has fax capabilities.
Terms: Takes a 30% agency commission from talent. Talent works for book publishers and ad agencies.
How to Contact: For first contact send cover letter and tearsheets. Reports back within 2 months. Returns materials if accompanied by a SASE.

MEREDITH BERNSTEIN LITERARY AGENCY, Suite 503A, 2112 Broadway, New York NY 10023. Contact: Meredith Bernstein, President. Estab. 1981. Represents humorous illustrators, cartoonists, humor writers and comedy writers. Current clients include Leigh Rubin. Prefers representing talent that has some track record.
Terms: Takes a 15% agency commission from talent. Talent works for book publishers.
How to Contact: For first contact send cover letter and resume. Reports back within 2 weeks. Returns materials if accompanied by a SASE.

CREATIF LICENSING, 31 Old Town Crossing, Mt. Kisco NY 10549. (914)241-6211. FAX: 914-666-4794. Estab. 1970. Licensing agents. "We represent artists for the purpose of creating a licensing program in all potential product areas including clothing, giftware and publishing paper products. Stylistic needs range from fine art to cartooning."

DYNA-SEARCH, INC., Suite 202 Westwood Blvd., Los Angeles CA 90064. (213)470-2993. FAX: (213)470-1341. Contact: Hitomi Yamomoto, Program Director or Shinobu Ishizuka, President. Represents comic book artists/writers. Current clients include Kodansha, Comic Morning Department.
Terms: Pays per page, depending on artist. Talent works for Kodansha, a weekly Japanese comic magazine.
How to Contact: For first contact send copies of his/her works in complete comics form. Reports back within 1-2 months. Returns materials only if requested. Keeps material on file.

HK PORTFOLIO, INC., 458 Newtown Turnpike, Weston CT 06883. (203)454-4687. FAX: (203)227-1366. Contact: Harriet Kasak, President. Estab. 1986. Represents humorous illustrators, as well as other illustrators such as Eldon Doty, Stephanie O'Shaughnessy, Benton Mahan and Randy Chewning. Current clients include Oglivy & Mather, Wells Rich Green, Saatchi & Saatchi, Muller Jordan Weiss, Ross Roy, Time-Life, Reader's Digest, Bantam Doubleday Dell, D.C. Heath, HBJ, Simon & Schuster, Macmillan and Viking Penguin. Prefers representing talent that has an individual look, is not super realistic, but most important is committed to his or her success. Prefers working with talent who has fax capabilities.

Terms: Takes a 25% agency commission. Talent primarily works for book publishers and ad agencies.

How to Contact: For first contact send cover letter, client list, tearsheets, promo pieces and slides. Reports back within 3-4 weeks. Returns materials only if requested and accompanied by SASE. Keeps material on file if interested.

L. HARRY LEE LITERARY AGENCY, P.O. Box 203, Rocky Point NY 11778. (516)744-1188. Contact: L. Harry Lee, President. Estab. 1979. Represents humor writers, comedy writers, TV sketch writers, sit com and motion picture screenplay comedy writers. Current clients include J.G. Kingston, Ed Van Bomel, Frankie Pace, Joey Kohler, Katie Polk, Fil Marchese, Jane Broege, Dan & Kathy White, Ralph Schiano, Mark Cooper, Anastassia Everueaux and Tom Sierchio. Prefers representing talent that writes sit coms or feature film comedies, but will read a new writer's query letter with a resume attached.

Terms: Takes a 15% agency commission from talent. Talent works for sit coms, writes TV sketches and feature comedy films.

How to Contact: For first contact send cover letter and resume. Reports back within 3-4 weeks. Returns materials only if requested and accompanied by SASE.

KANE & BUCK, 566 7th Ave., New York NY 10018. (212)221-8090. FAX: (212)221-8092. Contact: Sid Buck, President. Estab. 1960. Represents humorous illustrators and cartoonists. Prefers representing talent that has a proven success record.

Terms: Takes a 25% agency commission from talent. Talent works for book publishers and ad agencies.

How to Contact: For first contact send cover letter, tearsheets and promo pieces.

SCOTT MEREDITH LITERARY AGENCY, INC., 845 Third Ave., New York NY 10022. (212)245-5500. FAX: 212-755-2972. Contact: Jack Scovil, Vice-President and Editorial Director. Estab. 1946. Represents humorous illustrators, cartoonists (book collections only), humor writers, comedy writers (for publication only), comedians (for publication only), comedy entertainers (for publication only). Current clients in humor field include Roseanne Barr and Steve Allen (their books and other writings for publication); cartoonists such as Syd Hoff and Patrick McDonnell (collections of their cartoons, book and magazine art, etc.); and humor writers such as P.G. Wodehouse (Estate) and James Howard Kunstler. "We're interested in established authors and promising new writers."

Terms: Takes a 10% agency commission from talent on domestic deals, 20% on foreign deals. "We charge a fee for considering material by unproven writers." Talent works for book publishers, magazines and ad agencies.

How to Contact: For first contact send cover letter and material you've written (potential clients may either write first or send material). "We guarantee response on submitted material within two weeks." Returns materials if accompanied by SASE (We ask for an SASE).

THE NORMA-LEWIS AGENCY, 521 Fifth Ave., New York NY 10175. (212)751-4955. Contact: Norma Liebert, Partner. Estab. 1980. Represents humor writers. Prefers representing talent that is marketable.
Terms: Takes a 15% agency commission from talent. Talent works for book publishers.
How to Contact: For first contact send cover letter. Reports back within 1 month. Returns materials if accompanied by SASE.

THE PENNY & STERMER GROUP, 48 West 21 Street, New York NY 10010. (212)243-4412. FAX: (212)627-0832. Contact: Carol Lee Stermer, Vice President. Estab. 1971. Represents humorous illustrators and cartoonists. Current clients include ad agencies, publishers, magazines, newspapers and corporations for annual reports. Prefers representing talent that works a lot. Prefers working with talent who has fax capabilities.
Terms: "Depends on complexity of project."
How to Contact: For first contact send promo pieces. Reports back only if interested. Keeps materials on file.

PUBLISHERS' GRAPHICS, INC., 251 Greenwood Ave., Bethel CT 06801. (203)797-8188. FAX: (203)798-8848. Contact: Carole J. Costello, Director of Sales. Estab. 1969. Represents humorous illustrators. Current clients include trade book and text book publishers, encyclopedia publishers, magazines and toy companies. Prefers representing talent that is marketable.
Terms: Takes 25% agency commission from talent. Talent works for book publishers.
How to Contact: For first contact send cover letter, client list, tearsheets and photocopies. Reports back within 1-2 months. Keeps material on file.

S. J. INTERNATIONAL, 43 E. 19th St., New York NY 10003. (212)254-4996. FAX: (212)995-0911. Contact: Dr. H. Spiers, Director. Estab. 1960. Represents humorous illustrators and cartoonists. Current clients include people involved in advertising and editorial. Prefers representing talent that is marketable and established. Prefers working with talent who has fax capabilities.
Terms: Takes a 25-30% agency commission from talent. Talent works for book publishers, ad agencies and magazines.
How to Contact: For first contact send cover letter, tearsheets and promo pieces. Reports back within 2 weeks. Returns materials if accompanied by SASE.

A TOTAL ACTING EXPERIENCE, Suite 100, 14621 Titus St., Panorama City, CA 91402. (818)901-1044. Contact: Julianna Fresca, Humor Director. Estab. 1984. Represents humorous illustrators, cartoonists, humor writers, comedy writers, comedians, comedy entertainers and screenplays. Current clients are confidential. Prefers representing talent that can create an original idea/concept; can orchestrate and execute clearly on paper; has patience and persistence to fruition.
Terms: Takes a 10% agency commission from talent. Talent works for book publishers, ad agencies, sitcoms, comedians, how-to audio and video tapes and music videos.
How to Contact: For first contact send cover letter, resume, client list, tearsheets, promo pieces, cassette, audio tape or demo on VHS video. Include SASE. Reports back within 6-12 weeks only if interested. Keeps material on file.
Tips: "We will accept your submission by fulfilling *one* of our Agency requirements: (1) You have studied professionally and have taken courses from a State Accredited University for at least 2 years and can supply verification with your submission. (2) You are now, or have been, a working professional who desires to explore/expand your market. (3) Your work accompanies a recommendation by a working professional in your specific area/skill. We seek what Hollywood lacks most of all: talent that can unfold from within, a long-term commitment and loyalty. What you write is secondary. Your true character and substance is most important to us."

AUSTIN WAHL AGENCY, 53 W. Jackson Blvd., Chicago IL 60604. (312)922-3331. Contact: Mr. Ernest Santucci, Vice President. Estab. 1935. Represents stage and screenplays. Clients include international clients. Also, "hard to place" writings and drawings.
Terms: Takes a 10-20% agency commission from talent. Talent works for book, film and TV. Clients responsible for expense dispersements.
How to Contact: For first contact send cover letter, resume and synopsis. Reports back within 3 weeks. Returns materials if accompanied by a SASE.

WRITER'S READERS LITERARY AGENCY, Box 14863, Austin TX 78761. (512)928-0000. Contact: Bob Burrill, Owner/director. Estab. 1982. Represents humor writers, novelists and nonfiction. Prefers representing talent that has literary background, college degrees; mature writers.
Terms: Takes a 10% agency commission from talent; set-up $30, 40¢/page (returnable on publication). Talent works for books publishers and individual authors.
How to Contact: For first contact send cover letter, resume and summary or outline. Reports back within 3 weeks. Returns materials if requested and accompanied by a SASE.
Tips: "Our lack of interest is keyed by our lack of success with cartoon and humor books. As I get older, less and less gets funny, including getting older!"

Organizations

Now that you're an official, card-carrying humorist, you'll want to find professional organizations which offer you the opportunity to schmooze within the species. We couldn't find an address for the Teamsters, so these groups will have to do:

THE ADVERTISING COUNCIL, 825 Third Ave., New York NY 10022.

AMERICAN ASSOCIATION OF ADVERTISING AGENCIES, 13th Floor, 666 Third Ave., New York NY 10017.

AMERICAN SOCIETY OF JOURNALISTS AND AUTHORS (ASJA), Suite 1907, 1501 Broadway, New York NY 10036.

THE ART DIRECTORS CLUB, INC., 250 Park Ave. S., New York NY 10003.

ASIFA-EAST (ANIMATION), % The Optical House, 25 W. 45th St., New York NY 10036.

ASSOCIATION OF AMERICAN EDITORIAL CARTOONISTS (AAEC), 1100 Raleigh Bldg., 5 W. Hargett, Raleigh NC 27601.

ASSOCIATION OF COMEDY ARTISTS, 2 Bond St., New York NY 10012.

THE AUTHOR'S LEAGUE OF AMERICA, INC., 234 W. 44th St., New York NY 10036.

CARTOONISTS ASSOCIATION, Box 4203, Grand Central Station, New York NY 10017.

COMEDY WRITERS/PERFORMERS ASSOCIATION, P.O. Box 023304, Brooklyn NY 11202-0066.

COMIC ART PROFESSIONAL SOCIETY (CAPS), 139 S. Carr Dr. #7, Glendale CA 91205.

EDITORIAL FREELANCERS ASSOCIATION, 1001 Connecticut Ave. NW, Washington DC 20036.

FREELANCE EDITORIAL ASSOCIATION, Box 835, Cambridge MA 02238.

GRAPHIC ARTIST'S GUILD, 11 W. 20th St., New York NY 10011.

MEDIA ALLIANCE, 2nd Floor, Fort Mason Bldg. D, San Francisco CA 94123.

NATIONAL CARTOONIST SOCIETY (NCS), Suite 904, 157 W. 57th St., New York NY 10019.

NATIONAL SOCIETY OF NEWSPAPER COLUMNISTS (NSNC), Box 8318, Fremont CA 94537.

NATIONAL WRITERS UNION, 13 Astor Place, New York NY 10003.

PROFESSIONAL COMEDIANS ASSOCIATION, 3rd Floor, 410 W. 42nd St., New York NY 10036.

SOCIETY OF ILLUSTRATORS, 128 E. 83rd St., New York NY 10021.

TELEVISION INFORMATION OFFICE, 746 Fifth Ave., New York NY 10151.

WRITER'S ALLIANCE, Box 2014, Seatucket NY 11733.

WRITER'S GUILD OF AMERICA (WGA), East: 555 W. 57th St., New York NY 10019; West: 8955 Beverly Blvd., W. Hollywood CA 90048.

Glossary

Acceptance (payment on). Payment is made as soon as the buyer decides to use your work.
All rights. If a buyer or publisher purchases all rights to material, they have the exclusive ownership of the material and can publish, republish or sell rights at any time without further compensation to the creator.
Animatics. Simple, low-cost animation showing limited motion or none at all.
Balloon. A floating orb in which comic strip character dialogue or thoughts are placed.
Camera-ready. Art that is completely prepared for copy camera platemaking.
Cel animation. Hand-drawn animation inked and painted on a clear acetate "cel."
Collateral. Any printed material distributed to promote or market one's services (e.g., a printed, self-promotional flyer is a piece of collateral).
Comprehensive (comps). Rough, yet fairly detailed drawing which shows client what proposed, finished art will look like.
Copyright. The exclusive legal right to reproduce, publish and sell the matter and form of a literary or artistic work.
Direct mail package. Sales or promotional material that is distributed by mail. Usually consists of an outside envelope, a cover letter, brochure or flyer, SASE or reply postcard, or an order form and business reply envelope.
First North American serial rights. The right to publish material in a periodical for the first time in North America.
First rights. The right to publish material for the first time, one time. The artist or writer agrees not to publish the material anywhere else for a limited amount of time.
Gagline. The words printed, usually directly beneath a cartoon; also called a caption.
Halftone. Reproduction of a continuous tone illustration with the image formed by dots produced by a camera lens screen.
Inbetweening. If a second of animation requires 12 drawings, the animation studio may draw the first, sixth and twelfth frames. An "inbetweener" draws all the cels inbetween those done by the studio.
IRC. International Reply Coupon. A coupon purchased at the post office which can be turned in for stamps in any country. IRCs should be sent instead of stamps when you want a foreign buyer to return mail.
Keyline. Identification, through signs and symbols, of the positions of illustrations and copy for the printer.
Kill fee. Portion of the agreed-upon price received for the job that was assigned and started, but then canceled.
Layout. Arrangement of photographs, illustrations, text and headlines for printed material.
License. An arrangement wherein the owner of the copyright grants permission allowing another person (or company) to exercise one or more of the owner's exclusive rights.
Mechanicals. Paste-up or preparation of work for printing.
Monologue. A routine, skit, series of jokes or act performed by a solitary comedian (e.g., Johnny Carson performs a "monologue" at the beginning of "The Tonight Show").
Ms,mss. Abbreviation for manuscript, manuscripts.
One-time rights. The right to publish material for one time only.
Overlay. Transparent cover over copy, where instruction, corrections or color location directions are given.
Panel. In cartooning, a boxed-in illustration; can be single panel, double panel or multiple panel.
Paste-up. Procedure involving coating of the backside of art, type, photostats, etc., with rubber cement or wax and adhering them in their proper positions to the mechanical board. The boards are then used as finished art by the printer.
Pencil test. A rough test (video or film) used to make sure that pencilled, animated scenes move correctly before they are inked.
Photostat. Black-and-white copies produced by an inexpensive photographic process using paper negatives; only line values are held with accuracy. Also called stats.
PMT. Photomechanical transfer; photostat produced without a negative, somewhat like the Polaroid process.
P.O.P. Point-of-purchase; display device, signage or structure located at retail outlets to attract attention to a product.
Portfolio. A group of samples assembled to demonstrate an artist's or writer's talent and abilities, often presented to buyers.
Publication (payment on). Payment for work made when it is published.

Query. Letter of inquiry to an editor or buyer eliciting interest in a work you want to illustrate or write.

Reprint rights. The right to publish material that has been previously published.

Roughs. Preliminary sketches of drawings.

Royalty. An agreed percentage paid by the publisher to the writer or artist for each copy of work sold.

SASE. A self-addressed, stamped envelope. Sent for the postage-paid return of materials or reply to a letter or inquiry.

Signage. Posters, banners—any graphic essentially designed to be viewed from a distance.

Simultaneous submission. Submission of the same material at the same time to more than one publisher, agent or potential buyer.

Speculation. Creating material with no assurance that the buyer will purchase it or reimburse expenses in any way, as opposed to creating work on assignment. Sometimes called creating work "on spec."

Spot illustration. Often just called spots. A small drawing used to break up an otherwise gray, boring, solid block of copy.

Storyboards. Comprehensive color marker drawings plotting the various scenes of animation, film or video production.

Tearsheets. Published prints of your work as they appeared in a publication.

Thumbnail. A rough layout done in smaller than actual size.

Transparency. A photographic positive film such as a color slide.

Velox. Photoprint of a continuous tone subject that has been transformed into line art by means of a halftone screen.

Wash. Thin application of transparent color or watercolor black for a pastel or gray tonal effect.

Work-for-hire. An agreement which essentially transfers all rights of one's creative product to the buyer. Often involves transfer of the copyright to the buyer.

General Index

Y

Z

Other Books of Interest

Humor Writing/Art Books
    Comedy Writing Secrets, by Melvin Helitzer $18.95
    How To Draw & Sell Cartoons, by Ross Thomson & Bill Hewison $18.95
    How To Draw & Sell Comic Strips, by Alan McKenzie $18.95
    The Art & Craft of Greeting Cards, by Susan Evarts (paper) $15.95
    The Complete Guide to Greeting Card Design & Illustration, by Eva Szela $27.95

Annual Market Books
    Artist's Market, edited by Susan Conner $19.95
    Children's Writer's & Illustrator's Market, edited by Connie Eidenier (paper) $15.95
    Novel & Short Story Writer's Market, edited by Robin Gee (paper) $18.95
    Photographer's Market, edited by Sam Marshall $19.95
    Poet's Market, by Judson Jerome $18.95
    Songwriter's Market, edited by Mark Garvey $18.95
    Writer's Market, edited by Glenda Neff $23.95

General Writing Books
    Annable's Treasury of Literary Teasers, by H.D. Annable (paper) $10.95
    Beginning Writer's Answer Book, edited by Kirk Polking (paper) $13.95
    Beyond Style: Mastering the Finer Points of Writing, by Gary Provost $15.95
    Discovering the Writer Within, by Bruce Ballenger & Barry Lane $16.95
    How to Write a Book Proposal, by Michael Larsen $10.95
    On Being a Writer, edited by Bill Strickland $19.95
    The Story Behind the Word, by Morton S. Freeman (paper) $9.95
    The 29 Most Common Writing Mistakes & How to Avoid Them, by Judy Delton $9.95
    Word Processing Secrets for Writers, by Michael A. Banks & Ansen Dibell (paper) $14.95
    The Writer's Digest Guide to Manuscript Formats, by Buchman & Groves $16.95

Fiction Writing
    The Art & Craft of Novel Writing, by Oakley Hall $16.95
    Best Stories from New Writers, edited by Linda Sanders $16.95
    Characters & Viewpoint, by Orson Scott Card $13.95
    The Complete Guide to Writing Fiction, by Barnaby Conrad $17.95
    Dare to Be a Great Writer: 329 Keys to Powerful Fiction, by Leonard Bishop $15.95
    Dialogue, by Lewis Turco $12.95
    Handbook of Short Story Writing: Vol 1, by Dickson and Smythe (paper) $9.95
    Handbook of Short Story Writing: Vol. II, edited by Jean M. Fredette $15.95
    Manuscript Submission, by Scott Edelstein $13.95
    Plot, by Ansen Dibell $13.95
    Revision, by Kit Reed $13.95
    Theme & Strategy, by Ronald B. Tobias $13.95
    Writing the Novel: From Plot to Print, by Lawrence Block (paper) $10.95

Special Interest Writing Books
    The Complete Book of Scriptwriting, by J. Michael Straczynski (paper) $11.95
    How to Write Mysteries, by Shannon OCork $13.95
    How to Write Romances, by Phyllis Taylor Pianka $13.95
    How to Write Tales of Horror, Fantasy & Science Fiction, edited by J.N. Williamson $15.95
    How to Write the Story of Your Life, by Frank P. Thomas (paper) $11.95
    How to Write & Sell Your Personal Experiences, by Lois Duncan (paper) $10.95
    Successful Scriptwriting, by Jurgen Wolff & Kerry Cox $18.95

The Writing Business
    The Complete Guide to Self-Publishing, by Tom & Marilyn Ross (paper) $16.95
    Is There a Speech Inside You?, by Don Aslett (paper) $9.95
    The Writer's Friendly Legal Guide, edited by Kirk Polking $16.95
    A Writer's Guide to Contract Negotiations, by Richard Balkin (paper) $11.95

To order directly from the publisher, include $3.00 postage and handling for 1 book and 50¢ for each additional book. Allow 30 days for delivery.

Writer's Digest Books, 1507 Dana Avenue, Cincinnati, Ohio 45207
Credit card orders call TOLL-FREE
1-800-289-0963
Prices subject to change without notice.

Write to this same address for information on *Writer's Digest* magazine, Writer's Digest Book Club, Writer's Digest School, and Writer's Digest Criticism Service.